D1234336

The West and Reconstruction

EUGENE H. BERWANGER

THE WEST
AND
RECONSTRUCTION

UNIVERSITY OF ILLINOIS PRESS
Urbana   Chicago   London

Publication of this work has been supported by a grant from the Oliver M. Dickerson Fund. The Fund was established by Mr. Dickerson (Ph.D. Illinois, 1906) to enable the University of Illinois Press to publish selected works in American history, designated by the executive committee of the Department of History.

Library of Congress Cataloging in Publication Data

Berwanger, Eugene H
The West and Reconstruction.

Bibliography: p.
Includes index.
1. Reconstruction—The West. 2. The West—
History—1848–1950. I. Title
F594.B47   978'.02   80-26357
ISBN 0-252-00868-5

For Betsy

Contents

Acknowledgments

This book developed from a pilot research effort into post–Civil War Colorado sources. There I found intense feeling exhibited over Johnson's quarrel with his radical Congress and over black suffrage, to mention two topics, and I was encouraged to check further. Research in Nebraska and Minnesota archives revealed a similar intensity and convinced me of the potential—and the need—for a study encompassing Reconstruction and the West as a whole. Once undertaken, the project called for extended visits to historical libraries throughout the West and to repositories in the East. In financial support, the American Philosophical Society very generously provided two grants-in-aid from the Penrose Fund. I wish to express my sincere appreciation to the society for its help. The faculty research council at Colorado State University awarded two grants for the purchase of microfilmed sources not readily available in the Rocky Mountain region. Norris Hundley, Jr., editor of the *Pacific Historical Review*, offered encouragement in my initial writings on Colorado. Additionally, he has granted permission to incorporate portions of my article which appeared in the August, 1975, issue into the chapter dealing with equal suffrage in the territories.

For aid in my research, I wish to thank the staffs of the many historical society and university libraries I visited. Several persons from these repositories deserve special mention. Joan Hoffman of the Beinecke Library at Yale University brought to my attention items I might otherwise have overlooked; Susan Suddeth of the Oregon Historical Society answered my queries and verified points on Oregon's history well after I had finished my work at the society library; Joseph G. Gambone, then of the Kansas State Historical Society, clarified aspects of Kansas's post–Civil War years, especially regarding the woman suffrage movement of the 1860s; and Marian Howey of the University of Kansas Library permitted me to borrow the rare *Senate Executive Proceedings* through interlibrary loan so that I might comb those volumes at leisure. Merle W. Wells of the Idaho State Historical Society and Joseph Snell of the Kansas State Historical Society allowed me the rare treat of browsing in their archives, where I chanced upon items relevant to my study. I appreciate the willingness of Loretta Saracino, Julie Wessling, and Joel Rutstein of the Colorado State University Library to process my numerous interlibrary loan requests. Quotations from manuscripts held by the Houghton and Beinecke libraries are published with the permission of those institutions.

Colleagues and friends in the historical profession have been generous with information particular to their own research and interests. Robert W. Larson of the University of Northern Colorado explained peonage in New Mexico Territory and helped to clarify in my mind that complicated bondage system. Liston Leyendecker of Colorado State University, Gerald Stanley of California State College at Bakersfield, and Robert Chandler in the history department of Wells Fargo Bank, San Francisco, shared their research findings in Colorado and California history respectively. Likewise, Mark Plummer, professor of history at Illinois State University, freely offered suggestions on Edmund G. Ross's role in Andrew Johnson's impeachment trial. From his own work in patronage problems between Stephen A. Douglas and James Buchanan in the 1850s, David E. Meerse of the State University College in Fredonia, New York, provided insight for my study of Andrew Johnson and western patronage. At the University of Montana, Don Spencer verified several important facts and corrected my thinking about Montana's postwar history. Through the long months of research and writing Arthur J. Worrall of Colorado State University, William Gillette of Rutgers University, and Jason Silverman of Yale University offered steady encouragement: they bolstered my spirits when the project appeared never-ending. Portions of the manuscript were read by Charles J. Bayard, Colorado State University's western historian, and by Robert W. Johannsen at the University of Illinois, Urbana. Their criticism strengthened my interpretations and improved the text in its final form. Mrs. Bonnie Depp of the University Press meticulously edited the manuscript and made valuable suggestions to improve footnote and bibliographical citations. Of course, I accept the responsibility for any errors that appear in the published edition. My wife encouraged me at every step of the project and offered suggestions for style in the completed manuscript. To Betsy I express my deepest appreciation and dedicate this book. And finally a note of thanks to Abbie and Tad, whose child's play lightened the heavy moments sustained concentration can bring.

Fort Collins, Colorado
April, 1980

Abbreviations Used in the Notes

AHR   *American Historical Review*
AHS   Arizona Historical Society, Tucson
AW   *Arizona and the West*
BL   Bancroft Library, University of California, Berkeley
CM   *Colorado Magazine, Quarterly of the State Historical Society of Colorado*
CSHS   Colorado State Historical Society, Denver
CSL   California State Library, Sacramento
CSUC   California State University at Chico
CUWC   Western Collection, University of Colorado, Boulder
DWC   Western Collection, Denver Public Library
F   *Forum*
GRTD   U.S. Department of the Treasury, General Records of the Treasury Department (MSS)
HEH   Henry E. Huntington Library, San Marino, Calif.
HL   Houghton Library, Harvard University, Cambridge, Mass.
ISHS   Idaho State Historical Society, Boise
ITER   Executive Records of Idaho Territory, 1863–1874 (MSS)
JAH   *Journal of American History*
JNH   *Journal of Negro History*
KHQ   *Kansas Historical Quarterly*
KSHS   Kansas State Historical Society, Topeka
KU   University of Kansas, Lawrence
LAR   U.S. Department of State, Letters of Application and Recommendation during the Administrations of Abraham Lincoln and Andrew Johnson, 1861–1869 (MSS)
LC   Manuscript Division, Library of Congress, Washington, D.C.
MnHS   Minnesota Historical Society, St. Paul
MtHS   Montana Historical Society, Helena
MtHSC   *Historical Society of Montana Contributions*
MtM   *Montana, the Magazine of Western History*
MVHR   *Mississippi Valley Historical Review*
NARG   National Archives, Record Group

NH   *Nebraska History*
NMHR   *New Mexico Historical Review*
NMRC   New Mexico Records Center and Archives, Santa Fe
NSHS   Nebraska State Historical Society, Lincoln
NSHSP   *Publications of the Nebraska State Historical Society*
NvSHS   Nevada State Historical Society, Reno
OHQ   *Oregon Historical Quarterly*
OHS   Oregon Historical Society, Portland
PHR   *Pacific Historical Review*
PNQ   *Pacific Northwest Quarterly*
RBM   U.S. Department of the Treasury, Office of the Director of the Mint, Records of the Bureau of the Mint (MSS)
SDDL   U.S. Department of State, State Department Domestic Letters (MSS)
SM   *Scribner's Magazine*
SNF   U.S. Congress, Senate, Records of the U.S. Senate: Nomination Files (MSS)
SQ   *Southwestern Social Science Quarterly*
SSJ   *Social Science Journal*
SU   Stanford University, Palo Alto, Calif.
TP   U.S. Department of State, State Department Territorial Papers (MSS)
TPS   U.S. Congress, Senate, Territorial Papers of the U.S. Senate (MSS)
UCLA   University of California at Los Angeles
UNvR   University of Nevada, Reno
UWa   University of Washington, Seattle
WaHQ   *Washington Historical Quarterly*
WHR   *Western Humanities Review*
YWA   Western Americana Collection, Beinecke Rare Book and Manuscript Library, Yale University, New Haven, Conn.

The West and Reconstruction

Why the West?

The Reconstruction era remains one of the more complex periods in the history of the United States. While Americans of the day sought to resolve the numerous problems arising out of the Civil War, the working relationship between the legislative and executive branches of the federal government was coming to a virtual standstill. Andrew Johnson and Congress were unable to cooperate, and the Reconstruction process degenerated into a series of congressional acts passed over presidential vetoes, implemented by a recalcitrant president. The issues themselves were both recent in origin and rooted more deeply in the American past. These included not only the restoration of the seceded states but also the assurance that the people living in those states would remain loyal to the government which had lately subdued them. Included too was some modification of the states' rights philosophy, the concept that the states and the central government were coequals and, from the southern viewpoint, that final authority lay with the states in matters of difference. While Republicans in Congress were by no means ready to subvert the states in all respects, they were indeed more inclined than any other political group since the Federalist party of the 1790s to advocate national supremacy. This new mood was to have its impact in certain western territories as well as in the South.

Reconstruction inevitably brought focus to the black man's political role in American society. The war had liberated the slave, but it became clear during Reconstruction that emancipation in itself provided no guarantee of humane treatment. As congressmen became convinced of the need, they passed a series of laws designed to secure the new-found freedom of southern blacks. Among these were the extension of the Freedmen's Bureau, the Civil Rights Act, and the Fourteenth Amendment in 1866, and finally in 1867 the equal voting provision of the first Reconstruction Act. More important, Congress was to go a step further and extend equal suffrage to the North and

West as well. Whether lawmakers who advocated giving blacks in the South the right to vote did so for humanitarian or practical reasons, they soon began to see the inconsistency of forcing black suffrage on one section of the nation while permitting its denial elsewhere. As a result Congress stipulated equal suffrage in the District of Columbia and in all territories at about the same time that it imposed the reform on the South. Then, by means of the Fifteenth Amendment in 1870, it decreed black suffrage in all states where still expressly denied. Thus measures taken to reconstruct the South evolved into policy felt throughout the North and the West as well as in the former Confederacy.

Yet if certain aspects of Reconstruction became national in character, American historians were to ignore the role of the West and its reaction and relationship to the changes which occurred; they were to overlook as well the role played by westerners in shaping the events that followed the Civil War. This oversight is evident from the earliest writings to the present. Hubert Howe Bancroft, for example, in his classic nineteenth-century studies of the western states and territories, showed no interest in Reconstruction. Writing in the late 1870s and 1880s, at a time when Americans were looking back upon Reconstruction as unworthy and an age of corruption, Bancroft conscientiously avoided the subject. He stressed instead local western politics, failing to reveal, for the Reconstruction era at least, the impact of national issues at the state or territorial level. Recent, more general histories of the greater frontier follow the same trend. Their authors fleetingly recount Civil War activities in the West and then hasten to the coming of the transcontinentals and the cattlemen. Certain state histories do offer perspective, but these studies, by their very limitation, fail to relate local attitudes to the national or regional picture. After a careful reading of early western history, therefore, one may conclude that the approximately two million residents scattered from the Great Plains to the Pacific slope in the years 1865–70 had little concern for the political chaos in Washington and in the South. Despite the fact that many of them had recently migrated from the North and South, one must presume from the literature that they were just as oblivious to the various moves to grant blacks public equality—that is, civil and political parity with whites.

Such an impression is erroneous. Even the most cursory reading of western newspaper editorials from 1865 to 1868, whether written in urban San Francisco or rural Kansas, even a glance at letters to editors in Democratic and Republican journals, or perusal of campaign speeches by westerners who sought state or national office indicates clearly that the restoration of the South and its peripheral issues were a major political concern in the West at the time. Local politics did sometimes overshadow Reconstruction, and certain western editors began to reduce coverage of national affairs once the military Reconstruction acts were passed in 1867; they believed the reunification issue settled. Still, until 1868 Americans in the West were as eager as their compatriots in the East to learn the outcome of President Johnson's quarrel with Congress; they were just as anxious about the extension of suffrage to blacks and the necessity of ensuring the loyalty of the subdued South.

When interest began to falter, politicians played upon the issue, worked it into campaign oratory. Reconstruction, after all, was the one issue upon which western Republicans and Democrats substantially differed. On local questions members of both parties in the newly established territories as well as in the more settled regions were often in frank agreement. Frequently local politicians found themselves at odds over nothing more exciting than the exact moment at which the territory should request admission into the Union. The argument was inconsequential, for Democrats and Republicans in all territories favored statehood and were in opposition only when they feared the other party might control the new state. When one party came up with an innovative idea, the other often adopted it as a political ploy. During the 1867 gubernatorial campaign in California, for example, Democrats pressed their demand for the eight-hour working day. Just as readily Republicans took up the campaign, thus eliminating the one statewide issue upon which Democrats had hoped to ride to power. As a result the California campaign turned, as did others, to national issues—federal enactment of black suffrage in the South and the territories and the constitutionality of the recent military Reconstruction acts. Tension mounted and the lines were drawn as Republicans began to label Democrats as traitors; Democrats in turn accused Republicans of seeking a biracial society. Over and over this echo was heard throughout the West—hardly an indication of lack of interest in national politics.

Just as people in the trans-Mississippi West have been regarded as insular, so have they been seen as "conservative" from the beginning of their political development. While there is some justification for this concept, unfortunately it is based on western ideals since the mid-1870s, not before that time. The protest movement of western farmers in the late nineteenth century was a valiant effort to secure needed economic reform; still, it revealed some conservative proclivities in its anti-urban and anti-immigrant outlook. A similar bias was later evident in the western Ku Klux Klan movement during the 1920s. Throughout their political history, in fact, the rural western states, with occasional exception, have cast their electoral votes for the more conservative presidential candidates. In their attitude toward world affairs westerners have been deservedly characterized as isolationist. Yet conservatism and introversion are not necessarily western norms. Between 1865 and 1868 there was a difference: westerners overwhelmingly supported the Republican party and congressional Reconstruction—a political party and program which was considered liberal, even radical by some, in its outlook. Western political interest in this time focused on events outside, not within, the region. During these years western Republican leaders and numerous Republican editors openly approved the more advanced racial viewpoint engendered in radical Republican thought. Even more significantly, liberal ideas in the West toward southern blacks were expressed in urban centers and hamlets alike. They emanated not from San Francisco or Minneapolis alone but from Marysville, California, and Hastings, Minnesota, as well. The twentieth-century American's belief that the more rural the area, the more conservative its stand holds no validity for the West and the early years of Reconstuction.

Reform thought in the Reconstruction West did have its limitations, however. While liberal westerners demanded equal suffrage for southern freedmen, considerable among their numbers were less ready to extend public equality to blacks in their own area. These same westerners, moreover, gave no support to extending into the West reforms being agitated by eastern Republicans. Unlike Republicans in Massachusetts, Pennsylvania, and Illinois, western Republicans seemed unconcerned about initiating prohibition, eradicating prostitution, and expanding trade unionism. Except for the eight-hour workday in California and a brief woman suffrage campaign in Kansas during 1867, Reconstruction reform thought in the West focused on the restoration of the South and the extension of legal equality to blacks. By failing to encourage reform generally in their states and territories, western Republican leaders stood in sharp contrast to most party spokesmen in the northeastern quadrant of the nation. Still, narrow reform ideals were not confined to the West alone. Republicans in Ohio showed the same reluctance to engage in a broad-based reform effort: in Ohio, as in the West, Republicans were avoiding issues which might give political advantage to the Democrats.[1] Where Republicans controlled the governmental process, they preferred to retain the status quo. There was an additional factor peculiar to the West: reform would have been premature in many newly developed areas. Budding societies in the rough, they were not yet ready to refine themselves in eastern terms.

Lack of study of the interaction between the West and the rest of the nation during Reconstruction has created the impression that postwar western politics operated in a vacuum, that political development in the bulk of the trans-Mississippi was not linked to national issues. The idea itself, were it true, would be an enigma and require volumes to explain. In truth, no outlying political unit in America—whether a distant state or a territory—has been at any time during its existence totally divorced from national problems and politics. Historians have admirably explained the relationship between local and national issues in pre–Civil War Oregon, California, and Kansas. Yet the response to Reconstruction in the very same region, the variation in thought, has never been examined systematically. It is time that the western response to Reconstruction be brought into national perspective.

Just as the West has been accorded so little importance in Reconstruction politics, so have westerners themselves been subject to summary perusal. Americans tend to think of the early West as a vast land inhabited solely, if spectacularly, by cowboys and Indians. An only slightly more enlightened overview pictures them as physically strong but intellectually colorless individualists, lacking capacity for deep and sustained thought. In popular myth the heroes of the

---

1. See James C. Mohr (ed.), *Radical Republicans in the North: State Politics during Reconstruction* (Baltimore, 1976). More detailed studies of northern states include Felice A. Bonadio, *North of Reconstruction: Ohio Politics, 1865–1870* (New York, 1970); James C. Mohr, *The Radical Republicans and Reform in New York during Reconstruction* (Ithaca, N. Y., 1973); and David Montgomery, *Beyond Equality: Labor and Radical Republicans, 1862–1872* (New York, 1967). For recent interpretations of the border states, see Richard O. Curry (ed.), *Radicalism, Racism, and Party Realignment: The Border States during Reconstruction* (Baltimore, 1969).

West during the late 1860s and early 1870s are not those leaders who offered new ideas or shaped the region's growth but, rather, a collection of somewhat degenerate gamblers, thieves, and prostitutes. Forgotten is the fact that for every outlaw with a smoking six-shooter, there were dozens of families and businessmen who led orderly lives and contributed in a meaningful way to the development of the society around them.[2] Admittedly, it is the novelist and the script writer rather than the historian who have popularized western history and elevated to hero status such personalities as Jesse James, Wild Bill Hickok, and Calamity Jane—all of whom lived in the West during Reconstruction. But perhaps they have focused on these figures for lack of substantial information on others. Wild Bill Hickok might take second place to U.S. Senator William Stewart, a Nevadan who played a key role in shaping the Fifteenth Amendment at the national level. Instead of Calamity Jane, whose alcoholism drove her to virtual prostitution, one might offer Clarina Nichols. Her efforts on behalf of woman suffrage in Kansas in 1867 rivaled at the state level the activities of Susan B. Anthony in the national arena. Or there is Edmund G. Ross, U.S. senator from Kansas, who offered a key vote to acquit Andrew Johnson of the impeachment charges. Because of his action, Ross has been glorified by some as the "man whose vote saved the President." At the very least, the politicians, editors, suffrage advocates, and essayists whose opinions frame this study are more truly representative than are the Wyatt Earps, Buffalo Bills, Matt Dillons, and Miss Kittys whom Americans have come to regard as typical late nineteenth-century westerners.

The popular notion of blacks in the West during Reconstruction is even less valid than that of whites. Their very existence was practically ignored for a century. Then in the early 1960s, as the civil rights movement began to take hold, several western novelists made prominent a number of western blacks through fictional biographies. While appealing as pulp literature, these "biographies" create myth which is historically untenable. In Colorado, for example, novels written to explain the life and thought of "Aunt" Clara Brown of Central City and Barney L. Ford of Denver have gained local popularity. Based on the authors' imagination, with little reliance on historical fact, the books make claims which cannot be substan-

---

2. My interpretation is derived from Peter Lyon, "The Wild, Wild West," *American Heritage*, XI (Aug., 1960), 33–48.

tiated. Nevertheless, the ideas have taken hold and have been re-printed as fact.[3] Recently there have been several more valid historical studies recognizing the contributions of blacks as soldiers in the West or as cowboys. Yet very few of the 25,000 blacks in the West lived such romantic lives. Most of them were to be found in urban centers, where their living pattern and economic standing corresponded to that of blacks in eastern cities. With their numbers and the leadership that emerged among them, their presence had important political effect. It was from these urban centers of the West that black liberal thought and demands for equal rights emerged in the post–Civil War years. Instead of pointing to Isom Dart, the cattle rustler, or to Deadwood Dick, the cattle trail driver, as examples of western blacks, should not one instead refer to William J. Hardin of Denver? In the immediate postwar years Hardin led a drive for equal suffrage in Colorado Territory, a movement which to some extent served as catalyst for the Territorial Suffrage Act of 1867. At the same time Charles Langston of Leavenworth was leading a similar campaign on the plains of Kansas. Other blacks of note in the quest for equal rights include Philip Bell, editor of the San Francisco *Elevator*, who eloquently described the meaning and limitations of equality, and Thomas Detter, a Nevadan who critically assessed Republican racial ideology in the postwar era. The activities and thinking of these men indicate that blacks in the West were being influenced by the more liberal ideals of the era and that they were just as avid in their desire to achieve public equality as were blacks in the East or the South.

There is, then, good reason to strive for an understanding of western thought in regard to Reconstruction and to be aware of the roles played by individual westerners. Not only does such knowledge modify present-day, popular concepts about the early West and its people, but it reveals the impact of national Reconstruction policy on the West itself. Historians have long been aware that the Civil War and Reconstruction period is not just "southern" history but an era which affected the entire nation. But not until 1959, with the publication of Professor Stanley Coben's essay examining the reaction

3. Forbes Parkhill, *Mister Barney Ford: A Portrait in Bistre* (Denver, 1963); Kathleen Bruyn, *"Aunt" Clara Brown: Story of a Black Pioneer* (Boulder, Colo., 1970). One example indicating the uncritical acceptance of Parkhill's portrayal of Ford appears in "Colorado's Negro 'President Maker,' " Empire Magazine Section, *Denver Post*, Sept. 14, 1963, 4.

of business in the Northeast to radical Reconstruction, did they seriously begin to broaden their investigation of the era and to look at the impact of the period on the Northeast and the Midwest as well as the South.[4] It is important that the trans-Mississippi West be included in such historical analyses. The region remained loyal to the Union during the war and reflected, although to a lesser extent, the same influences that touched the states east of the Mississippi River. In addition, the trans-Mississippi region expressed the postwar attitudes of a politically immature frontier.

The traditional historian might argue, with persuasion, that since the military Reconstruction acts applied strictly to the South, the West therefore could not have felt the impact of Reconstruction. That argument, however, confines Reconstruction to its narrowest sense. When the term is broadened, more realistically, to include the reforms of the era and the changing Republican concept of federal-state and territorial relations, it becomes apparent that Republican Reconstruction ideals had implication for the whole nation, not just the South alone. With regard to suffrage it is often forgotten (indeed, it is almost never mentioned) that Congress gave blacks in the territories the right to vote a full two months before it decreed equal suffrage in the former Confederacy. Other actions of Congress in the postbellum years indicate that Republicans no longer accepted without qualification the doctrine of popular sovereignty, or "home rule" for the territories. Radical Republicans in Washington proceeded to nullify the acts of the Montana territorial legislature in 1867 and worked, unsuccessfully, at eradicating polygamy in Utah. This imposition of black suffrage and the other acts would cause many westerners, Republicans and Democrats alike, to declare that there was little difference in Congress's treatment of the rebel South and the loyal West. But the action indicates that Congress desired to have some input into local affairs throughout the nation, not just in the South. And that knowledge is vital: federal interference in the South was not merely a form of punishment for rebellion but reflected a changing concept about the power of the central government itself.

As I have envisioned the West in the late 1860s, it consisted of those trans-Mississippi states and territories which were newly settled and in which slavery had taken no firm hold: Minnesota, Dakota,

4. Stanley Coben, "Northeastern Business and Radical Reconstruction: A Reexamination," MVHR, XLVI (June, 1959), 67–90.

Nebraska, Kansas, Colorado, New Mexico, Arizona, Utah, Wyoming, Montana, Idaho, Nevada, California, Oregon, and Washington. Because of their pro-southern orientation, I chose not to include the pre–Civil War slave states which lay west of the Mississippi River. Likewise, I omitted Iowa, which in the 1860s retained its closest economic and emotional ties with the Old Northwest. My decision has been strengthened by the work of Iowa historian Robert Dykstra. He claims that conditions in Reconstruction Iowa were so dissimilar from those in the trans-Missouri West that comparison between the two regions is not a feasible undertaking.[5]

It has been my intention to give all points of view on the western reaction to Reconstruction and to reveal their depth and intensity. My choice in this particular approach, which precludes emphasis on any one political or social group, is arbitrary and may be questioned by some. But I regard this as an initial study, and I have sought therefore to compile an overview vital in itself and a necessary preview for more concentrated studies on western Democrats, Republicans, and blacks and their response to Reconstruction. In addition, I have made every attempt to incorporate the views of lesser-known westerners as well as prominent individuals. To me, statements made by Serena Wright, housewife in Minnesota, or Franklin Kirkaldie, farmer in Montana, bear as much importance as those made by contemporary politicians and editors, however much more influence the latter may have had. For their candor Mrs. Wright and Mr. Kirkaldie have significant appeal; they expressed themselves in private correspondence, with no thought to gain votes or influence public opinion. Not only did their ideas show less bias, but often they were more lucid in their assessment than those in the thick of the political foray.

In sum, this study focuses on racial thought in the post–Civil War West and western response to Reconstruction. Under examination both issues reflect the finely honed differences in western thought and point out glaring inconsistencies in western ideals. For while the majority of western Republicans could see the need for black participation in the governance of the South, many were unable to justify giving blacks a voice in western politics. From early on western Republicans revealed a contradictory stand on the race question: they

5. Robert R. Dykstra, "Iowa: Bright Radical Star," in Mohr (ed.), *Radical Republicans in the North*, 169.

were willing to impose on the South what most were reluctant to grant at home. In regard to Reconstruction itself, westerners showed less accord. Attracting whites and blacks from the South as well as the North, and in states like Minnesota appealing to a substantial foreign-born population, the West varied in political outlook from one area to the next according primarily to demographic factors. From 1865 to 1867 more liberal Republican ideals tended to dominate the West, with radical strength becoming less influential following the passage of the first Reconstruction Act in 1867. The result was a revitalization of the Democratic party along the Pacific slope and a growing conservatism elsewhere. This development in part caused an early decline of interest in Reconstruction. By the time Andrew Johnson retired from the presidency, the West had turned its attention inward and had become somewhat more preoccupied with strictly local concerns. But the shift in focus was distinct, and a dramatic change from the more liberal tone set in the immediate postwar years.

CHAPTER ONE

The Advent of Reconstruction

"Reconstruction is the principal topic now."
—Serena Wright, Minnesota

With Abraham Lincoln's assassination Reconstruction became a viable and immediate concern in the West. From that fateful April 14, 1865, until the election of President Grant in 1868, Reconstruction dominated political life throughout the trans-Mississippi. Its intensity varied among the states and territories, for differing reasons. Local factors having influence included physical isolation and availability of news, political leanings and composition of population. Democratic states with a substantial number of southern-born inhabitants, such as California and Oregon, expressed conservative views. In Kansas and Minnesota, where Republicans from the Northeast and Midwest dominated politics, radical ideas found greater favor. The era was thrust so quickly and intensely upon westerners that many were confused about the nature and scope of Reconstruction, but respond they did. The focus finally centered on the return of the seceded states to the Union and the extension of civil rights to freedmen; these limits were both acceptable and politically expedient. A newly liberal attitude emerged and, in showing more sympathy toward blacks than it had before the war, the West followed a trend that was evident in states north of the Ohio and east of the Mississippi rivers. Yet as in many areas of the North this enlightened attitude was qualified, for it did not include "freedom" in all respects. In its economic awareness the West differed markedly from the northeastern quadrant of the nation: it shared little concern for national monetary problems, the greenback issue, and declining prices. George Pendleton's 1868 "Ohio Idea"—to pay off federal bonds in greenbacks instead of coin—went almost unnoticed in the West. And New Mexico, for one, had its own very peculiar circumstance. Wealthy

13

Mexican-Americans there contravened the intent if not the exact meaning of the Thirteenth Amendment by continuing peonage, their particular system of servitude. Such distinctions set the West apart while the region was at the same time being drawn into the national scene. Each is integral to the understanding of the role of the West in the traumatic and absorbing Reconstruction era.

A prime factor conditioning the western response to Reconstruction was the region's distance from Washington, D.C., and from the former Confederacy. Western citizens cherished the news, eagerly awaiting word from the East whether relayed via telegraph or traveler. But getting the news at all was a real achievement at times, and westerners' widespread interest in the politics of postwar restoration was all the more stunning in the face of haphazard and imperfect communications. It is true that portions of the West received their news with relative ease. Cities in eastern Kansas and Nebraska, settled areas in Minnesota along the Mississippi River, and those served by the transcontinental telegraph, which spanned the West from St. Louis to San Francisco, usually learned of happenings in the East within a day. Populated areas off the main line of travel were less fortunate; news of an event might not arrive for months after its occurrence. Whether word came quickly or not, poor communication and lack of efficient transportation reinforced a feeling of separation from the East. Until the coming of the transcontinental railroad in 1869, much of the West was like an island apart from the mainland. According to historian Rodman Paul, westerners of the era were also reflecting their sense of geographical isolation when they termed the more eastern states as "America," or "the other side." They begrudged lawmakers in Washington who, in their belief, gave all their time to Reconstruction and correspondingly little to local problems in the West. Growing rancor was evident among Democrats and Republicans alike. Alluding to Congress's lack of interest in the Far Southwest, John Howard, a conservative, referred to Arizona as a "benighted territory," a phrase others might deem applicable to their own territories as well. Likewise, in the early days of Montana Wilbur Fisk Sanders, a staunch Republican with radical leanings, was to observe, "It appeared to many of us [in the territory] as if we were forgotten."[1]

1. Rodman Wilson Paul, *Mining Frontiers of the Far West, 1848–1880* (New York, 1963), 7; J. W. F. to editor, Junction House, Colo., Aug. 10, 1865, in Atchison

The vast distances of the West hindered mail delivery from the East, which was erratic even at its best. Despite the 275 postal facilities in Kansas in 1865, settlers in outlying areas still complained of being sixty miles and more from the nearest postal outlet. Citing inadequate service, Jonathan Hunt, temporary editor of the *Emporia News*, charged that the federal government was treating Kansas more like a rebel than a loyal state. John A. Clark, a federal officeholder in New Mexico, noted his declining interest in the outcome of the 1866 congressional elections because of the sporadic news coverage he received. Clark had avidly followed several close contests in the Midwest, but the longer his newspapers from the East were delayed, the less interest he had in the outcome.[2]

Statements by three editors indicate the effect of slow mail delivery on their reporting of eastern news. Robert Meacham, editor of the *Arizona Miner*, acknowledged in January, 1867, his failure to comment on national affairs over a span of months; even though now he had details on events in the East, he saw little point in giving them extended coverage. His only source of information was month-old San Francisco newspapers, to which most of his readers had belated access just as he did. Like most mail addressed to Arizona, the newspapers had been sent the southerly route, from San Francisco around the Baja peninsula and then north again up the Colorado River. Mail delivery in the northern regions was even less efficient. To reach the mining towns of Idaho or Montana, a letter postmarked in the East normally took three months or longer, and editors felt the delay keenly. James O'Meara of the *Idaho World* could withhold bitter comment no longer when, in the winter of 1867, the weeks without mail seemed to stretch interminably: "For the past four or five months this portion of the country has been almost totally deprived of mail communication with the vast country east of the Rocky Mountains." James Reynolds, editor of the *Idaho Statesman*, said that he could appreciate the difficulties involved in transporting mail across the continent, but in his estimation Wells Fargo could work toward more efficient service. In September, 1868, he routinely re-

---

(Kans.) *Daily Free Press*, Aug. 18, 1865; John Howard to Andrew Johnson, Prescott, Ariz., Jan. 20, 1866, Andrew Johnson Papers, LC; Robert G. Athearn, "The Civil War and Montana Gold," MtM, XII (Apr., 1962), 63–64.

2. Albert Castel, *A Frontier State at War: Kansas, 1861–1865* (Ithaca, N.Y., 1958), 7; *Emporia* (Kans.) *News*, May 13, 1865; John Clark to Elihu Washburne, Santa Fe, Oct. ?, 1866, Elihu Washburne Papers, LC.

ceived a letter from Washington, D.C., dated some thirteen months earlier—in August, 1867![3]

The bulk of the news concerning Reconstruction was transmitted westward by telegraph. The fastest and most effective means of communication, the telegraph was but a frail link between East and West. The lines were often blown down by high winds or, not so accidentally, cut by Indians. With the vast distances and sparse settlement, breaks were difficult to locate. From Minnesota to California editors who purchased telegraphic dispatches complained always of irregular receipt. Typically, the lines followed the overland stage route, but in 1865 when the mail route between Denver and Salt Lake City was moved south, the telegraph lines were left unprotected and service to the West coast became seriously interrupted. As the *Oregonian* explained the situation to its readers, Indians were numerous in the area and the lines could not be guarded at all points at once.

Useful as they may have been at times, telegraphic dispatches were not widely utilized by smaller newspapers. Costs ran high, and editors disliked having to pay for dispatches whether they received them or not. As a result, they usually copied telegraphic reports, mistakes included, from other newspapers. D. W. Tilton, editor of the *Montana Post*, explained the situation rather aptly. Following the completion of the initial telegraph line between Salt Lake City and Virginia City, Montana, Tilton duly purchased telegraphic dispatches, hoping that their publication might enhance his circulation. In short order he was admonishing other editors in the territory for reprinting these reports at will. It is easy to understand Tilton's indignation: reportedly his costs were running one dollar per word between New York and Virginia City. Whether or not the editor overstated his claim, one observer found the money wasted in any event, for the lines were usually down.[4]

Frequently telegraphic messages themselves were not properly

3. *Daily Arizona Miner* (Prescott), Jan. 26, 1867; Larry Barsness, *Gold Camp: Alder Gulch and Virginia City, Montana* (New York, 1962), 21; *Idaho* (City) *World*, Jan. 12, 1867; *Idaho Tri-Weekly Statesman* (Boise), Sept. 19, 1868.

4. W. A. Elinson to John Bidwell, Santa Rosa, Calif., Jan. 26, 1866, John Bidwell Papers, CSUC; *Winona* (Minn.) *Daily Republican*, June 2, 1865; *Morning Oregonian* (Portland), July 3, 1865; *Daily Alta California* (San Francisco), July 15, 1865; *Walla Walla* (Wash.) *Statesman*, Dec. 29, 1865; San Francisco *Evening Bulletin*, Feb. 2, 1866; *Montana Post* (Virginia City), Mar. 2, Oct. 12, 19, 1867; Barsness, *Gold Camp*, 195–96.

coded, and it is difficult for the historian using western newspapers to place events in the East into their proper context. Two examples suffice. In February, 1866, newspapers from Denver to San Francisco made conflicting statements about Johnson's veto of the Freedmen's Bureau bill. As editors later explained, they had trouble understanding the president's reasons for vetoing, because of the garbled telegraphic summary of his message. Even as late as 1868 the Sacramento *Bee* apologized for its sporadic coverage of Johnson's impeachment trial. Inept telegraphers were relaying unclear reports which could not be deciphered. The telegraph may have served as a vital communication line with the East, but in providing news coverage of the events of Reconstruction it was neither accurate nor wholly dependable.[5]

The birthplace and political background of people living in the West had the most profound influence upon their reaction to Reconstruction. In 1870 the West contained 1,931,789 people, of whom 72 percent were not native to the region. They had migrated into the West from foreign countries and from the eastern United States— the former Confederacy, the border slave states, the Northeast, and the Midwest. Although most of those born in the East had come

5. Petaluma (Calif.) *Journal & Argus*, Mar. 1, 1866; *Daily Rocky Mountain News* (Denver) Apr. 26, 1866; Sacramento *Daily Bee*, Apr. 16, 1868. Western newspapers are a good source for public opinion on national problems, but they have their limitations. Basically political sheets, they usually presented only one viewpoint. Editorships, moreover, changed hands frequently; while these transfers rarely altered editorial policy, subtle differences did become apparent. Even when the editor remained constant, shifts in policy took place. For example, Republican newspapers in Colorado favored Johnson's Reconstruction plan until he vetoed the Colorado statehood bill in 1866; thereafter, they supported the radicals. Sometimes inexplicable changes occurred. J. W. Avard, editor of the *Esmeralda Union*, did a political somersault within a two-week period. On May 16, 1868, he published both his defection from the Republican party and an anti-Johnson tirade. On May 23 Avard came out in support of Johnson's presidential candidacy for 1868, only to announce, one week later, his return to Republicanism and his endorsement of Grant's nomination. *Esmeralda Union* (Aurora, Nev.), May 16, 23, 30, 1868. Occasionally newspapers were even purchased by their political opposition. Democrats bought the Republican *Idaho Statesman* in 1869 and reversed its editorial policy. When the Democratic *St. Paul Pioneer* attacked his monopoly of the shipping trade on the upper Mississippi, John Davidson responded by purchasing the paper and converting it into a Union sheet. This left Democrats in St. Paul with no editorial outlet from Nov., 1865, until July, 1866, when they repurchased the *Pioneer*. *Idaho Statesman*, Feb. 2, 1869; *St. Paul* (Minn.) *Daily Pioneer*, Nov. 5, 1865, July 31, 1866.

to the West prior to the war, approximately 100,000 Americans immigrated westward between the years 1860 and 1870. Some came to seek their fortune in the newly opened gold fields of Montana and Idaho, others to avoid military service. The flight to the West was of such proportion by 1864 that Governor William Stone of Iowa issued a proclamation forbidding Iowans of military age to cross the state's western boundary. In the same year Captain Eugene Ware, on temporary assignment in Julesburg, Colorado, described the men of that region as "bounty jumpers, secesh, deserters, [and] people fleeing from the draft." As Cornelius Hedges of Montana observed, "There are a great many . . . that came out to get away from the draft or that deserted from the army." In the main, these wartime immigrants supported the Democratic party and, although not necessarily secessionist, they sympathized with the southern cause.[6]

The postwar years, 1865 to 1870, witnessed a second wave of migration to the West. This new group consisted principally of Union army veterans, Republican in politics and generally supportive of radical Reconstruction. Veterans, too, from the Confederate army found their way westward to avoid anticipated punishment or to make a new life for themselves outside the devastated South. Thus did the people in the West represent diverse political allegiance and sectional bias. Despite the motives which had lured them westward, the new immigrants could not, in the end, divorce themselves from old feelings and issues.

The census of 1870 revealed northerners to be in the majority throughout the western states and territories. Of the 1,835,401 Caucasians living in the West, 742,059 had been born in the more eastern states—586,210 in the free states and 155,849 in the former slave states. The remaining 1,093,342 whites were western by birth or had immigrated from abroad. Although New York by 1870 had contributed more whites than any other state—118,814—most of the people from the eastern portion of the country gave as their birthplace

6. U.S. Bureau of the Census, *Eighth Census of the United States: 1860, Population* (Washington, D.C., 1864), 23–35, 158–61, 250–53, 400–401, 546–47, 550–51, 554–57, 566–67, 574–75, 580–81; *Ninth Census of the United States: 1870, Population* (Washington, D.C., 1872), 328–35; Dan E. Clarke, "The Movement to the Far West during the Decade of the Sixties," WaHQ, XVII (Apr., 1926), 107; Stanley R. Davison and Dale Tash, "Confederate Backwash in Montana Territory," MtM, XVII (Oct., 1967), 50–51; Cornelius Hedges to his parents, Helena, July 22, 1865, Hedges Family Papers, MtHS.

an Ohio Valley state or Missouri, regions harboring both strong Democratic and pro-southern feeling before and during the war. From Illinois, Indiana, Ohio, and Iowa had come some 252,214 persons, while 86,099 were listed as native to Missouri or Kentucky.[7]

Those states which had seceded from the Union contributed only 62,518 white people to the total western population in 1870, an increase of 20,000 over 1860.[8] However, contemporary accounts indicate that actual numbers from the former Confederacy were far greater between 1865 and 1868, years in which the West reacted most strongly to Reconstruction. Republican Frederick Low complained, for example, of the difficulty he faced as governor of California from 1864 to 1867 in dealing with the "large secession element" that had migrated to the state. The *Sacramento Union,* one of the leading Republican newspapers in the state, warned Californians at the close of the war that rumors of a massive westward migration by Confederates foreshadowed "a kind of immigration [which] will cause more anxiety than satisfaction." Yet a comparison of 1860 and 1870 census figures reveals that the population from the Confederate states in California had increased by less than 700 people during the decade.[9]

In other states as well the presence of former Confederates seemed greater than the census indicates. One commentator pointed to "Unionville" as a misnomer for the Nevada town of that name. Southern sentiment was so pervasive in the community, said he, that many of its homes displayed pictures of Confederate generals instead of northern heroes. In Oregon Jesse Applegate, the state's leading Republican, had to concede that a Democratic victory was possible in 1866, so large was the influx of new residents from the South. Finally, in Montana and Idaho southerners were said to be present in overwhelming numbers. Official and private papers leave the impression that southerners comprised the actual majority of the population from 1865 to 1868. But such statements conflict with 1870 census figures. Oregon and Nevada each contained less than

7. *1870 Census, Population,* 328–35.

8. *Ibid.; 1860 Census, Population,* 23–35, 158–61, 250–53, 400–401, 546–47, 550–51, 554–57, 562–63, 566–67, 574–75, 580–81.

9. Frederick F. Low, *Some Reflections of an Early California Governor Contained in a Short Dictated Memoir between Governor Low and Hubert Howe Bancroft in 1883* (Sacramento, 1883), 12; *Sacramento Daily Union,* Apr. 29, 1865; *1870 Census, Population,* 328–35; *1860 Census, Population,* 23–35.

5,000 people born in the Confederate states, while fewer than 900 such persons were counted in Montana and Idaho, reported hotbeds of secession sentiment.[10]

What, then, accounts for this obvious discrepancy between con-temporary statement and the 1870 census figures? One explanation lies in the fact that Republicans exaggerated potential or actual mi-gration from the Confederate South. Moreover, they overestimated the number of individuals with pro-Confederate leanings. For Re-publicans tended to label everyone who disagreed with them as "Rebel" or "Copperhead," and this included many people from In-diana, Ohio, Illinois, and Missouri who, while mildly pro-southern and Democratic, opposed both secession and radical Reconstruction. Too, many Confederates fleeing war and internal chaos in the mid-1860s chose to return to the South after 1868, once relative calm had been restored to the region. This movement, peaking as it did between decennial censuses, would not have been reflected in the 1870 population statistics. David Ballard, Republican governor of Idaho Territory, explained the outward movement of southerners candidly. In 1866, he recalled, Republicans in Idaho "lived in per-petual danger" from the rebel element. It controlled all local political offices and the territorial legislature. Pro-southern sympathizers lev-eled such numerous threats that Ballard remained in constant touch with the commandant at Fort Boise, should he need the protection of the army units stationed there. Then suddenly in the fall of 1868 the southerners "started to flee the country. They fled in the night

10. By state or territory, the number of white inhabitants born in the Confederate states were: California, 21,045; Oregon, 4,457; Nevada, 1,531; Washington, 848; Montana, 851; and Idaho, 484. William W. Bailey to William M. Bailey, Humboldt, Nev., Sept. 20, 1867, HEH Miscellaneous Collection; Jesse Applegate to James W. Nesmith, Yoncalla, Ore., Jan. 4, 1866, James Willis Nesmith Papers, OHS; Thomas Francis Meagher to William Seward, Virginia City, Mont., Dec. 11, 1865, in TP: Montana, 1864–1872, NARG 59; Robert Fisk to Lizzie Fisk, Helena, Dec. 6, 1866, Fisk Family Papers, MtHS; N. P. Langford to Alexander Ramsey, Virginia City, Mont., Feb. 27, 1866, Alexander Ramsey Papers, MnHS; George B. Wright to John Sherman, Fort Benton, Mont., Oct. 6, 1866, John Sherman Papers, LC; Cornelius Hedges to his parents, Helena, Sept. 13, 1865, Hedges Family Papers; Caleb Lyon to William Seward, n.p., n.d., in TP: Idaho, 1863–1872, NARG 59; *1870 Census, Population,* 328–35. See also Robert G. Athearn, *Thomas Francis Meagher: An Irish Revolutionary in America* (Boulder, Colo., 1949), 147; Davison and Tash, "Confederate Backwash," 50–53; Barsness, *Gold Camp,* 20; Hubert Howe Bancroft, *History of Washington, Idaho, and Montana, 1845–1889,* vol. XXXI, *The Works of Hubert Howe Bancroft* (San Francisco, 1890), 268, 448

on stages, in wagons, or on horseback, and some, I fear on foot. . . . A stranger coming here now, in 1870, and seeing how peaceful this country is, can form but little idea of the exciting times we had from 1866 to 1868."[11]

Evidence, though scattered and sparse, indicates that on the Pacific coast, where the southern population was relatively large, southerners were well received and conservative Reconstruction principles found greater acceptance. In California approximately one-third of the eastern-born white population had come from the slave states. Here Claggertt D. FitzHugh, a Confederate veteran, found life very congenial in Gilroy, a town located just east of Monterey Bay. Never quite satisfied with the jobs he held, FitzHugh could report nonetheless that his southern background was not a deterrent to finding employment. Further, he encountered little discrimination among nonsoutherners despite his Confederate service and pro-secession leanings. "All of them know who I am," he stressed, "and treat me with the respect due a Southern gentleman." In Los Angeles, where pro-southern sympathy had been prevalent during the war, strong Unionists welcomed back those who had fought for the Confederacy. One Union advocate, John M. Griffin, even offered $300 outright to a former Confederate officer that he might re-establish himself. In Oregon and Washington Territory citizens reportedly held little resentment against newly arriving southerners who had fought for their independence.[12]

As attested by Ballard, southerners and Democrats did not fare so well in Montana and Idaho. However, it should be noted that most of the extant criticisms against them were voiced by Republican officials or political hopefuls who found compromise with Democrats or election to office difficult. Wilbur Fisk Sanders, unsuccessful candidate for delegate to Congress from Montana in 1864 and again in 1867, regarded southerners and Democrats alike as clannish and without honor. "I have," he wrote in reference to the Democrats

11. Thomas Donaldson, *Idaho of Yesterday* (Caldwell, 1941), 243–45; Clark C. Spence, *Territorial Politics and Government in Montana, 1864–89* (Urbana, Ill., 1975), 22.

12. Claggertt D. FitzHugh to George M. Shearer, Gilroy, Calif., Dec. 19, 1865, May 10, 1866, George M. Shearer Papers, ISHS; Albert Lucian Lewis, "Los Angeles in the Civil War Decades, 1850–1868" (Ph.D. dissertation, University of Southern California, 1970), 281–82; John S. Cocke to William W. Miller, Jefferson City, Tenn., Nov. 15, 1867, William Winlock Miller Papers, YWA.

who controlled the 1866 territorial legislature, "no hope for this generation of Machiavellis, and rely on a long strong effort of the missionary society (ours) and the school masters to reconstruct us and make a whole nation of whole men." Henry W. Moulton, a Republican and U.S. marshal in Idaho, shared Sanders's view. Moulton aspired to the territorial governorship and solicited help directly from Charles Sumner. At the same time Moulton took it upon himself to inform the Massachusetts senator that the presence of large numbers of southerners in Idaho, and in Boise in particular, was preventing orderly growth. "The 'Barbarism of Slavery,' " he complained, "flares upon you from every street in the city, although a *slave* never trod this soil." For southerners in the territory refused to support schools and churches and more readily patronized the gambling houses. Claiming the territory in need of some purging, Moulton was eager for the challenge and believed himself more able than the incumbent, Republican David Ballard, to change the prevailing atmosphere.[13]

A strong disregard for southerners was expressed as well in Minnesota, a state inclined toward radicalism. The southern-born actually comprised less than 2 percent of the white population, 7,069 out of 439,706 people. Writing from Minneapolis, George L. Baker informed his friend and former Union comrade, William Hale, that the war had left him undecided about his future. Baker wanted to begin anew in another section of the country but, after his wartime experience, would not go south, "for the south I do not like, nor its people." Another Minnesotan did head for Alabama immediately following the war but soon lamented the move as a great mistake. "I don't like this southern country so far," he complained. "I don't like the people. I think I will try old Minnesota again if I can get through this year all right." It was William Windom, congressman from Winona, who expressed most poignantly local disdain for southerners. Criticizing President Johnson's willingness to pardon southerners who had supported the Confederacy, Windom declared, "I have no confidence in the 'good faith' of these constitutional oathbreakers. Treason had debauched their entire moral nature. . . . I want some better guarantee for future loyalty than is to be found in

13. Barsness, *Gold Camp*, 20; Caleb Lyon to William Seward, n.p., n.d., in TP: Idaho; Wilbur Fisk Sanders to W. S. Fergus, Virginia City, Mont., Feb. 14, 1866, Wilbur Fisk Sanders Papers, MtHS; Henry Moulton to Charles Sumner, Boise, Nov. 15, 27, 1869, Charles Sumner Papers, HL.

the oath of a thrice-perjured traitor."[14] Strong in itself, Windom's response was also the most caustic anti-southern statement recorded by a western member of Congress during the postwar years.

Among minorities in the West—Indians, Asians, and Afro-Americans—only blacks expressed concern for Reconstruction and its impact on their race. Unlike Indians, who resided in tribal organizations, and Asians, who existed as a subculture along the Pacific coast, blacks lived in every western state and territory.[15] Surprisingly, they retained a strong interest in the political process even though they were not allowed to participate.

During the 1860s the number of blacks in the West increased several times over, from 5,430 in 1860 to 25,031 in 1870. Whereas most Caucasians in the trans-Mississippi had immigrated from the North, the majority of blacks had come from the upper South. Over half, 13,864, claimed as their birthplace Missouri, Kentucky, Virginia, or Tennessee.[16] In terms of percentage growth, the largest

14. *1870 Census, Population*, 328–35; George L. Baker to William Hale, Minneapolis, Nov. 11, 1866, William D. Hale and Family Papers, MnHS; Royall Lovell to Ignatius Donnelly, Drummond, Ala., Dec. 25, 1865, Ignatius Donnelly Papers, MnHS; *Congressional Globe*, 39 Cong., 1 Sess., 3168.

15. The Asian population numbered 63,000 in 1870. The table below indicates the western black, white, and Chinese population by state and territory in 1870 (from *1870 Census, Population*, 606–9):

State or Territory	White	Black	Chinese
Arizona	9,581	26	20
California	449,424	4,272	49,310
Colorado	39,221	456	7
Dakota	12,887	94	-
Idaho	10,618	60	4,274
Kansas	346,377	17,108	-
Minnesota	438,257	759	-
Montana	18,306	183	1,949
Nebraska	122,117	789	-
Nevada	38,959	358	3,152
New Mexico	90,840	72	-
Oregon	86,558	346	3,330
Utah	86,044	118	445
Washington	22,195	207	234
Wyoming	8,726	183	143

16. *1860 Census, Population*, 23–35, 158–61, 250–53, 400–401, 546–47, 550–51, 554–57, 562–63, 566–67, 574–75, 580–81; *1870 Census, Population*, 328–35.

increase occurred in Kansas, the smallest in California. From 625 in 1860, the Kansas black population swelled to 12,527 at war's end. This phenomenal growth was caused almost exclusively by slaves fleeing from Missouri and Arkansas. A continued influx brought the number of blacks in Kansas to 17,108 by 1870. More remote California in the same decade realized an increase of only 186 blacks, from 4,086 to 4,272. Although it is not clear why the California black population remained at a near constant, an actual decline in the male population by 300 suggests that the search for wealth in other western mining areas may have been as appealing to blacks as to whites.[17]

Recent historical scholarship has emphasized the romantic aspect of the western Afro-American experience by focusing on blacks as miners, cowboys, or soldiers who remained in the army after the war and were deployed in the West against the Indians.[18] The number of blacks engaged in such endeavors was actually small. The majority of the black population in every western state and territory was concentrated in established communities. Their numbers in individual towns ranged from a low of two in Yuma, Arizona, to over 1,000 each in San Francisco and Lawrence, Atchison, Leavenworth, and Wyandotte, Kansas. Of course their percentage in the total population and their visibility were sometimes in contradiction. The 1,300 blacks in San Francisco made up less than 1 percent of the population, and their presence was substantially overshadowed by 12,000 Chinese. In Leavenworth, on the other hand, the 4,284 blacks comprised nearly one-fourth of the citizenry. Of the remaining western cities only Sacramento, Omaha, Nebraska City, and Denver contained a black population in excess of 200. Certain other urban centers, like Minneapolis and St. Paul, approached that number, but most did not.[19]

17. *1870 Census, Population,* 606–9; *1860 Census, Population,* 23–35, 158–61; D. W. Wilder, *The Annals of Kansas, 1541–1885* (Topeka, 1886), 419; Castel, *Frontier State,* 208–10.

18. Kenneth Wiggins Porter, *The Negro on the American Frontier* (New York, 1971); Philip Durham and Everett L. Jones, *The Negro Cowboys* (New York, 1965); Richard Henry Pratt, *Battlefield and Classroom: Four Decades with the American Indian, 1867–1904,* ed. Robert M. Utley (New Haven, Conn., 1964), 7, *passim;* John M. Carroll, *Black Military Experience in the American West* (New York, 1971). See also William Loren Katz, *The Black West* (Garden City, N.Y., 1971).

19. *1870 Census, Population,* 12, 15–17, 23, 29–30, 40–41, 46–48, 50, 67, 71, 74, 606–9.

Not only did most western blacks live in cities, but they held the more menial jobs or worked in those professions relegated to minorities. The manuscript 1870 census schedule for Denver points out this fact very clearly. There were, for example, 230 blacks in the city, including 105 males over eighteen years of age. Of the 104 who designated their employment, forty-nine indicated "laborer." Of the remaining fifty-five, most worked as domestic servants or porters, cooks or waiters, even painters. Some fourteen blacks were engaged in barbering—a typical black trade in nineteenth-century America—although it is unclear how many of them were self-employed. There were among black males one school teacher, one minsister, and a single restaurant owner. Women specifying employment usually listed laundry work, a task they could carry on in their homes. Of Denver's sixty-one black women over eighteen years of age, eighteen of the twenty-seven working for wages did so as "laundress." Aside from one dressmaker and one music teacher, the remainder served white families in a domestic capacity.[20] Thus while the unemployment rate among blacks in Denver appears low, they were winning primarily the unskilled positions.

While the most singular development in western black-white race relations during the Civil War and Reconstruction years was the more liberal attitude displayed by whites, the outlook was anything but liberal in 1860. In the prewar West blacks were denied suffrage and service in the militia, they were excluded from public schools and jury duty, and they could neither intermarry with whites nor offer testimony in cases where whites were litigants. Oregon prohibited their immigration in its 1857 constitution, and exclusion clauses were considered, but not adopted, in Kansas, California, New Mexico, and Nebraska as well.[21] Even after 1860, legislatures in the new territories were enacting discriminatory legislation; some lawmakers in Idaho and Dakota territories sought to ban the immigration of blacks altogether but without success.[22]

20. U.S. Bureau of the Census, "Population Schedules of the Ninth Census of the United States, 1870: Colorado" (Ms), NARG 29.

21. For detail see Eugene H. Berwanger, *The Frontier against Slavery: Western Anti-Negro Prejudice and the Slavery Extension Controversy* (Urbana, Ill., 1967), chs. 3, 4, 5. I might add, parenthetically, that Chinese in the Far West faced similar restrictions.

22. Harmon Mothershead, "Negro Rights in Colorado Territory, 1859–1867," CM, XL (July, 1963), 212–23; Russell R. Elliott, *History of Nevada* (Lincoln, Nebr.,

There were, of course, westerners who had opposed this early anti-Negro legislation. Those outside politics could not stem the tide, while many politicians acquiesced to popular feeling in order to retain public support. After 1864, however, liberals began to speak out on behalf of blacks; notable among them were Republican officeholders. For instance, Sidney Edgerton, governor of Montana Territory in 1865, vetoed an act which forbade blacks from testifying against white persons. Two years later Governor Alexander Cummings of Colorado Territory vetoed similar legislation, characterizing it a "surprising" attempt to thwart the national will. Nebraska's Governor Alvin Saunders sought aid for blacks even though his suggestion was sure to find disfavor with Democrats. Delivering his annual address in 1865, Saunders expressed strong sympathy for the freedmen who had fled to Nebraska. "It is not the fault of these people that they were held in bondage," he commiserated, "and it certainly is no fault of their's[sic] that they are now or that they come to us without money, without property, without education." Saunders then asked the legislature to devise a plan to aid the former bondsmen. Wary nonetheless of the political consequences, he gave careful instructions not to allocate tax money for this philanthropy.[23]

1973), 387; Davison and Tash, "Confederate Backwash," 52; "House Bill No. 27," in TP: Montana; Jay J. Wagoner, *Arizona Territory, 1863–1912: A Political History* (Tucson, 1970), 65; Howard R. Lamar, *Dakota Territory, 1861–1889: A Study in Frontier Politics* (New Haven, Conn., 1956), 86–87; *Idaho World*, Jan. 7, 1865; Tom LeRoy McLaughlin, "Popular Reactions to the Idea of Negro Equality in Twelve Nonslaveholding States, 1846–1869: A Quantitative Analysis" (Ph.D. dissertation, Washington State University, 1969), 58.

23. Mary Edgerton to Martha Carter, Bannack, Mont., Mar. 6, 1865, Edgerton Family Papers, MtHS; Territory of Colorado, *House Journal*, 1866–1867 (Central City, 1867), 144–45; *General Laws of the Sixth Session of the Colorado Territorial Legislature* (Central City, 1867), 69. Saunders's speech is found in TP: Nebraska, 1854–1867, NARG 59. California in 1863 was the first western state to abolish its restrictive testimony law. The repeal came in response to black protests of the measure, but whites were in favor as well since the law in itself inhibited justice: a white man accused of murder had recently been acquitted in California because of the court's refusal to admit the pivotal testimony of a certain black witness. As a result, blacks in 1862 organized a "Franchise League" for the purpose of securing the repeal of the discriminatory act. The league achieved its aim, but its members must have been saddened during the debate in the state legislature to hear a number of lawmakers in turn vent their prejudices and call for the expulsion and exclusion of all blacks from California. Delilah L. Beasley, *The Negro Trail Blazers of California* (Los Angeles, 1919), 54–59; William Penn Moody, "The Civil War and Reconstruction in California Politics" (Ph.D. dissertation, University of California at Los Angeles, 1950), 255–57; Berwanger, *Frontier against Slavery*, 75–76.

Liberal individuals from the private sector as well began to advocate a more charitable attitude. Jesse Applegate of Oregon, writing to federal Judge Matthew P. Deady in 1865, declared stridently, ". . . it is not right to indulge prejudices of creed or race. It is necessary to God's justice that all races of men should be endowed with facilities sufficient to secure their happiness here and hereafter. . . ." Applegate apparently had a motive: Oregon's constitution adopted in 1857 did indeed contain a provision excluding blacks, and it was Deady who had chaired the constitutional convention. Even though there is no record of an immediate reply, Applegate's argument may not have been lost on Deady. For later, as Applegate was to note with satisfaction, Deady had become a "wiser and better man" regarding blacks.[24]

Western Republican editors in the postwar period took their cue and expressed themselves with less constraint on prejudicial actions and attitudes. Charles DeYoung, editor of the *Chronicle*, openly censured white civic groups who, once blacks had been given permission to join in, refused to participate in the July 4, 1865, parade in San Francisco. Their attitude, in DeYoung's opinion, revealed a prejudice in some respects stronger in the North than in the South. When Democrats campaigned actively against black suffrage, even the *Alta California*, only moderate in its Reconstruction outlook, took offense. To Frederick MacCrellish, the editor, the Democratic policy was clearly defamatory with its emphasis on crimes committed by blacks. Supporting MacCrellish, DeYoung asked why Democrats insisted on a greater degree of morality for black people than for the rest of society. More radical Republicans took an uncompromising stand against accusations of black inferiority. Said John Martin of the *Atchison Champion* in Kansas, "Give the negro a chance to make a man of himself. This is all that is necessary to make a man of him. Treat him as a human being and he will quickly assert by his own capacities and exertions his right to be regarded as one."[25]

Such expressions indicate a declining anti-Negro prejudice, but they should not be construed to imply that resentment against blacks had become insignificant. Some western Republicans simply could

24. Jesse Applegate to Matthew P. Deady, Yoncalla, Ore., Apr. 23, 1865, Dec. 17, 1868, Matthew Paul Deady Papers, OHS.

25. San Francisco *Daily Dramatic Chronicle*, July 6, 1865, May 17, 1867; D. Smith to William W. Miller, San Francisco, July 7, 1865, Miller Papers; *Alta California*, May 4, 1867; Atchison (Kans.) *Daily Champion*, Jan. 11, 1865.

not divest themselves of ingrained prejudice, and Democrats openly opposed most efforts to ameliorate civil restrictions against blacks. Thus, when the "Negro Question," as it was called by contemporaries, arose, controversy usually erupted. Moreover, the "Question" was compounded by the fact that it came to involve two separate and distinct issues. One centered on the protection and rights of freedmen in the South, the other concerned civil rights for blacks in the West. While the first, viewed from afar, elicited sympathy from all Republicans and even some Democrats, the second raised conflicting sensitivities and would be subject to heated and prolonged debate.

The easing of racial attitudes, along with moral repugnance and the belief that slavery had caused the war, produced a favorable response toward the Thirteenth Amendment in the West. Even in Arizona, where pro-Confederate sympathy had been strong and where citizens had elected a territorial delegate to the Confederate Congress, Robert Meacham could observe, "All men in Arizona, whatever their sympathies in the rebellion were, rejoice at the passage of the 13th Amendment."[26] Within one year after Congress had submitted the amendment, it was ratified by the legislatures in the five western states of Kansas, Minnesota, Nevada, Oregon, and California. In more conservative Oregon and California, twenty Democratic legislators voted against ratification. According to contemporary sources, their opposition did not stem from a desire to retain slavery. For some it was a protest against federal encroachment on states' rights, for others a refusal to support any Republican-sponsored measure.[27]

Despite overwhelming support for the Thirteenth Amendment in the West, the practice of servitude, under the name of peonage, continued in New Mexico well into the late nineteenth century. The holders of peons preferred to believe that the amendment had no bearing on their situation even when they were informed otherwise. Perhaps they reached this conclusion because peonage did

26. *Arizona Miner*, Feb. 14, 1866.
27. *Kansas Weekly Patriot* (Burlington), Feb. 11, 1865; William Seward to Addison C. Gibbs, Washington, D.C., Sept. 23, 1865, in SDDL, NARG 59; State of California, *Senate Journal, 1865–1866* (Sacramento, 1866), 75; *House Journal, 1865–1866* (Sacramento, 1866), 34–35; *Oregonian*, May 4, Dec. 9, 1865; *Oregon Statesman*, Dec. 11, 1865; *Monterey* (Calif.) *Gazette*, Dec. 29, 1865; Moody, "Civil War," 353–55; Thomas E. Malone, "The Democratic Party in California, 1865–1868" (M.A. thesis, Stanford University, 1949), 43–44.

not, of course, involve blacks nor were all peons forced into the system against their will. As practiced in New Mexico, peonage developed from two separate types of servitude. Under the more traditional, inherited from Spain and Mexico, peons and their families knowingly entered servitude to discharge debts or obligations; they and their descendants remained in service until there was no further responsibility toward the master. In a distinctly less lawful approach to getting household and field help, New Mexican residents had taken to raiding Indian villages and enslaving their captives. The majority of these Indian slaves were women and children.

No matter how peonage evolved or how "voluntary" its appearance, many western Republicans were rankled by its continued practice in New Mexico after 1865. They saw almost no difference between peonage and black slavery. Pointing out that there were 400 peons in Santa Fe alone, many of whom were held by officers of the U.S. army, the *Alta California* in 1867 vigorously decried the practice: carried on with the knowledge and sanction of territorial officials, raids to obtain Indian slaves were no less scrupulous, wrote the *Alta*, than the African slave trade. W. F. M. Arny, as territorial secretary, had brought with him from Kansas a strong antipathy against servitude; he took a firm stand urging the territorial legislature to eliminate both systems. As acting governor in 1862, Arny first suggested a general abolition for Indian slaves and proposed that peons pay their debts in money and not by indentured labor. The legislature took no action. By 1865 Arny was seeking aid from Washington, and as a result Andrew Johnson issued a special proclamation ordering an end to Indian slavery in the territory. New Mexicans ignored the proclamation even though Arny warned them in 1866 that raids on Indian villages could no longer be tolerated.[28]

Servitude continued because the leading Mexican-American families opposed emancipation, and territorial officials, including Governor Henry Connelly, dared not go against them. Connelly even defended the slavery system as a viable means of punishing Indian marauders and insisted that peons seek their freedom as individuals

28. *Alta California*, Feb. 13, 1867; Lawrence R. Murphy, "Reconstruction in New Mexico," NMHR, XLIII (Apr., 1968), 100–101; "Annual Message of Acting Governor Arny, 1866," and "Johnson's Proclamation, June 8, 1865," both in TP: New Mexico, 1851–1872, NARG 59; George H. Kelley (comp.), *Legislative History of Arizona, 1864–1912* (Phoenix, 1926), 4–6.

through the courts. The governor's stand brought a sharp retort from Theodore S. Greiner, a Republican member of the territorial legislature, who relayed its irony to William Seward: "For three years it has been our shame to see daily, often hourly, issuing from the Government House (the 'Palacio') the family of Governor Connelly wending their way to the Plaza . . . escorted by three or four Navajos . . . stolen in raids . . . and held as property."[29]

It took both a territorial court decision and action from Congress to bring about the final disintegration of the peonage system. When local authorities returned Thomas Heredia, an escaped peon, to his owner, Heredia appealed for his freedom to the territorial supreme court. Citing peonage as "involuntary servitude," Justice John Slough decided in Heredia's favor in January, 1867. Slough then appointed two commissioners to travel throughout the territory and inform peons of their right to freedom. At almost the same time Charles Sumner was proposing a bill in the U.S. Senate which would outlaw peonage; it stipulated fines and prison terms for persons who disobeyed or refused to enforce the law. With the bill's enactment in March, 1867, Robert Mitchell, the new territorial governor, issued a proclamation calling attention to the federal legislation and declaring invalid all territorial laws to the contrary. Because enforcement was lax, holders of peons showed no readiness to comply with the law. Acknowledging a year later that peonage still flourished in the territory, Congress turned in desperation to General William T. Sherman, now commander of the Division of the Missouri, and by joint resolution in July, 1868, ordered him to devise a means to end servitude in New Mexico. He responded by sending Major George W. Getty to the territory to inform peons and slaves of their freedom. By law servitude had been disallowed, but it would linger; many Indians, now assimilated into white society, chose to stay on with their masters.[30]

For national economic issues which plagued the East during the immediate postwar years the West revealed almost no concern. These

29. Theodore S. Greiner to William Seward, Santa Fe, Sept. 11, 1865, in TP: New Mexico; Murphy, "New Mexico," 101.

30. Murphy, "New Mexico," 102–6; *Congressional Globe*, 39 Cong., 1 Sess., 1571; William A. Keleher, *Turmoil in New Mexico* (Santa Fe, 1952), 470–73; *Santa Fe* (N.Mex.) *Weekly Gazette*, Jan. 25, 1868; *New Mexican* (Santa Fe), Mar. 3, Aug. 6, 1868.

problems included the inequality between gold coin and greenbacks—paper money without bullion backing which had been printed during the war—rampant inflation, and a postwar recession. Seeking to ease these pressures and to gain political prestige at the same time, Democrat George Pendleton in 1868 detailed his "Ohio Idea," calling for the payment of federal bonds in greenbacks instead of hard money. The scheme was designed to end the disparity between paper and coin and equalize their value to the benefit of the debtor class. It would also deprive individuals who had purchased government bonds in cheaper greenbacks from amassing the hard money by which the government redeemed its debts. For beleaguered farmers in the Midwest, whose prices fell dramatically once the wartime market had dissolved, the "Ohio Idea" offered real hope. Unfortunately for those most hard pressed, Republicanism prevailed with the election of Grant, and Pendleton's plan fell by the way.

In his study of Reconstruction entitled *The Critical Year*, Howard K. Beale fully explained this impact of the faltering economy on the "western" farmer. Unfortunately Beale's use of the word "western" (without defining the term) has misled historians into believing that the entire West faced economic hard times in the immediate postwar years. The Midwest did, but not so the trans-Mississippi West—and Beale failed to make the distinction. His sources lay principally in the Ohio Valley, in fact, and as a result he gave almost no attention to the trans-Mississippi. Several historians have attempted to modify Beale's interpretation, but their comments on western postwar economy have gone unnoticed.[31]

The trans-Mississippi evinced little interest in eastern economic problems because, quite frankly, it did not feel their impact. Wartime industrial expansion was an eastern phonomenon alone. With limited means to produce finished goods, most industrial expansion in the trans-Mississippi between 1860 and 1865 was not based on wartime

31. Howard K. Beale, *The Critical Year: A Study of Andrew Johnson and Reconstruction* (New York, 1958), 237, *passim*; Eric L. McKitrick, *Andrew Johnson and Reconstruction* (Chicago, 1960), 369–73; Robert P. Sharkey, *Money, Class, and Party: An Economic Study of Civil War and Reconstruction* (Baltimore, 1959), 284–85; Gilbert C. Fite, *The Farmers' Frontier, 1865–1900* (New York, 1966), 70–75. For a detailed explanation of California's unique situation in the species versus paper money question, see Walter T. K. Nugent, *Money and American Society, 1865–1880* (New York, 1968), 59–60, and Samuel Bowles, *Across the Continent: A Summer's Journey to the Rocky Mountains, the Mormons, and the Pacific States* (Springfield, Mass., 1865), 342–47.

economy. Thus there were few layoffs and no significant unemployment at war's end. Instead, the West witnessed expansion—the building of the transcontinental railroad and an influx of settlers, some to seek their fortune in the gold mines, others to establish farms or businesses.

Individuals who came west as miners were to be disappointed, for gold mining was in the doldrums in the late 1860s. The earlier Colorado gold rush of 1859–60 had ended by 1861, and mining was not to become profitable again in Colorado until a means was devised to extract the region's large silver deposits. The Comstock lode in Nevada gave out in 1864 and would remain unworked until techniques were found to mine the gold below the surface. These declines were somewhat offset by booms in Idaho and Montana during the war, but these bonanzas were also destined to be short-lived, reaching their height in 1867. Thereafter, miners pushed on to eastern Oregon, Arizona, or other regions where rumor offered the possibility of riches.[32] For miners who tired of the transient life—and most did not—there was always farming, a lucrative occupation in the late 1860s. Comparing mining to farming, Henry Pittock, editor of the *Oregonian* in Portland, described the latter as more profitable despite the inflated prices for farm equipment and supplies in the West.[33]

Agriculturally, the West was still underdeveloped between 1865 and 1870. True, large tracts of land had been opened to farming during the war, but that expansion was limited to southwestern Minnesota, northwestern Iowa, and eastern Kansas and Nebraska. Further to the west, intensive agriculture was practiced only in California, Oregon, and Utah. Demands for foodstuffs in the mining areas of Colorado and Montana had encouraged the establishment of farms on the eastern slope of the Rockies and around Fort Benton, Montana.[34] But the Great Plains remained untilled and the cattle

32. Augustus Wildman to his mother, Denver, July 24, 1865, Augustus Wildman Papers, YWA; Paul, *Mining Frontiers*, 50, 80, 143–44; Ray Allen Billington, *Westward Expansion: A History of the American Frontier* (New York, 1960), 626–28; Donaldson, *Idaho*, 120–27, 243–45.

33. *Oregonian*, July 15, 1865. Samuel Bowles concluded that "nowhere in the whole Nation is agriculture so profitable" as in the trans-Mississippi West. Comparing the profit potential between farming and mining, he advised easterners who planned to emigrate westward that farming offered greater monetary reward. Bowles, *Across the Continent*, 91.

34. Fite, *Farmer's Frontier*, 9–10; Ovando J. Hollister, *The Mines of Colorado* (Springfield, Mass., 1867), 423.

industry lay in the future, for this growth had to await the 1870s and the arrival of the railroad.

On goods offered for exchange, farmers experienced a favorable cash flow during the immediate postwar years. A ready market, plus the fact that western farming had not yet been drawn into the commercial complex which determines price structure, prevented the rapid price decline witnessed in the East. A brief survey of farm prices shows an upward, not a downward, trend during the Reconstruction years. Winter wheat, for example, in 1863 brought 90¢ a bushel in Kansas; at the same time the price in California ranged from $1.45 to $1.50 depending upon quality. By the end of the war prices had stabilized and a bushel of wheat was selling for $1.70 in both states. The spiral inclined and early in 1868 reached a high of $2.00 a bushel; thereafter, a gradual decline lowered the price to $1.30 in 1870. The exception was Minnesota, where the price of a bushel of wheat plummeted from $2.00 to $1.00 between February and December, 1868, and was only bringing 57¢ by 1870.[35] Farmers in Minnesota became concerned with declining prices, as might be expected, but elsewhere discontent with farming was tied to adverse weather conditions and destruction of crops by grasshoppers.[36]

Western politicians and editors did predict that regional economic prosperity could not last. Lacking a really compelling economic issue, however, politicians seeking office focused on heavy and unequal taxation and on federal spending, not the general economy. Democrats in California especially made an issue out of taxation, charging that tax schedules were designed to benefit the corporations and the

35. All prices quoted are for winter wheat in Kansas, number one wheat in Minnesota, and "good" wheat in California. Spring wheat, number two wheat, and "common" wheat brought 10 to 40¢ less per bushel. The price quotations are taken from *St. Paul* (Minn.) *Dispatch*, June 1, July 3, Sept. 5, Oct. 12, Nov. 2, 12, 1868; *St. Charles* (Minn.) *Herald*, Feb. 19, 1869, Mar. 25, 1870; *Shakopee* (Minn.) *Spy*, Jan. 14, 1869; *Emporia News*, Mar. 14, 1863, Feb. 21, 1868, Apr. 22, 1870; Atchison *Free Press*, May 8, 1865; *Sonoma County Democrat* (Santa Rosa, Calif.), Dec. 16, 1865; *Petaluma Journal & Argus*, Apr. 25, 1867; San Francisco *Daily Morning Call*, Dec. 10, 1863. Corn prices followed the same trend. For a price index of the period see Allan G. Bogue, *From Prairie to Corn Belt: Farming on the Illinois and Iowa Prairies in the Nineteenth Century* (Chicago, 1963), 285.

36. Augustus Wildman to his mother, Denver, July 24, 1865, Wildman to his father, Denver, Dec. 24, 1865, both in Wildman Papers; *Winona Republican*, Nov. 24, 1865, Sept. 14, 1866; *St. Charles Herald*, Dec. 23, 1868, Jan. 29, 1869; *Idaho World*, June 28, 1867, Oct. 10, 1868; *Idaho Statesman*, Aug. 17, 1867; Atchison *Free Press*, July 31, 1867.

wealthy at the expense of the poor. In California and elsewhere they fretted publicly about the cost of Reconstruction in the South. Expenditures for the Freedmen's Bureau, in particular, and for the high salaries paid officials who administered the programs were declared excessive and a drain on the federal treasury. Although Republicans seldom agreed with their opponents, in this case some saw validity in the Democratic argument.[37] The more complicated issues involving the national monetary system—contraction of the currency and redemption of bonds in greenbacks instead of gold—attracted attention in San Francisco, a financial center, but little notice in other portions of the West. J. W. Wyman, editor of the *Humboldt Times*, surveyed the general attitude toward national fiscal problems during the presidential campaign of 1868, the point at which Pendleton introduced his "Ohio Idea." Finding all aspects of the financial situation worthy of review, Wyman determined nonetheless that "it is so little understood by the masses, that its discussion will inevitably be tedious and uninteresting. On the contrary, reconstruction, with or without negro suffrage, is a live issue which the people fully comprehend, and in which they feel a deep interest."[38] Still a developing region and not yet drawn into the complex eastern economic system, the West in the immediate postwar years remained largely unconcerned about the complexities of the money question and focused instead on Reconstruction itself.

It was the assassination of Abraham Lincoln, coming at war's end, that stimulated western thinking about postwar problems. Until then westerners expressed only occasional interest in Reconstruction. Lincoln's wartime Reconstruction Proclamation in late 1863 did receive widespread notice among western newspapers, but during subsequent months Grant's and Sherman's military campaigns and the coming presidential election overshadowed the Reconstruction topic. Western Republican editors were eager to underplay differences between Lincoln and the radicals over Reconstruction in this election year;

37. *Wathena* (Kans.) *Reporter*, Jan. 2, 1868; *Kansas Daily Tribune* (Lawrence), Jan. 22, 1868; *Leavenworth* (Kans.) *Daily Conservative*, Aug. 9, 1867; Governor Henry Haight, "Inaugural Address," in State of California, *House Journal, 1867–1868* (Sacramento, 1868), 15–16; *Yreka* (Calif.) *Union*, Dec. 9, 1865, Nov. 3, 1866; San Francisco *Call*, July 19, 1867, Jan. 18, 1868; Moody, "Civil War," 347.

38. *Humboldt Times* (Eureka, Calif.), July 26, 1868.

accordingly they gave little attention to the Wade-Davis bill, even though most congressmen from the West voted for the measure, and to the succeeding Wade-Davis Manifesto. Democrats, because they did not favor the Wade-Davis bill, showed no readiness to publicize it. Once the Republican (Union) party had nominated Lincoln for a second term in June, 1864, western Republicans suppressed conflicting views and united to secure his re-election. Jacob Stotler, editor of the *Emporia News*, who previously had censured the president, for example, now hastened to gloss over his critical remarks and offer praise instead for the incumbent.[39]

The assassination itself unleashed an emotional shock wave and pent-up resentment against the South. "What deep hellish spirit of hell could prompt men to commit so damnable a deed. . . . —Oh, how the cusses [curses?] of an outraged people go up to high heaven asking for revenge & blood. . . . [Southerners] aimed the blow at every one of us . . .," cried G. L. Bilby of Kansas, " . . . tis not enough for them that rivers of blood have already been shed. They ask for more, more to glut their hellish appetite." In stunned reaction to news of the assassination arriving in Washington Territory, Republican Joseph Cushman could only utter, "Good God! What are we coming to?" The impact of the assassination was widely apparent: many of those who kept diaries, which in ordinary times were little more than personal account ledgers, now allowed themselves brief or extended reference to Lincoln's death.[40] In the Gallatin Valley

39. *Emporia News*, July 2, 1864. The conclusions in this paragraph are based on the following newspapers, Dec., 1863, to Apr., 1865: *Emporia News*; *Weekly Osage Chronicle* (Burlingame, Kans.); *Kansas Patriot*; *Rocky Mountain News*; *Daily Miner's Register* (Central City, Colo.); *Petaluma Journal & Argus*; *Placerville* (Calif.) *Mountain Democrat*; San Francisco *Call*; *Alta California*; *Sonoma Democrat*; and *Oregon Statesman* (Salem).

40. G. L. Bilby to his mother, ?, Kans., Apr. 19, 1865, in Samuel Crawford Correspondence, Governor's Papers, KSHS; Joseph Cushman to William W. Miller, Olympia, Wash., Apr. 16, 1865, Miller Papers. The diaries referred to are the Doten Diary, Apr. 15, 1865, Alfred Doten Papers, UNvR; Nye Diary, Apr. 14, 1865, James Warren Nye Papers, NvSHS; John Rudd Brown Diary, Apr. 15, 1865, CSL; Henry Mills Moore Journals, Apr. 15, 16, 1865, YWA; William Berry Cross Diary, Apr. 16, 1865, CSL. For additional reaction to Lincoln's assassination, see W. A. Goulder, *Reminiscences: Incidents in the Life of a Pioneer in Oregon and Idaho* (Boise, 1909), 375–76; Samuel Pomeroy to Samuel Newitt Wood, New York, Apr. 17, 1865, Samuel Newitt Wood Papers, KSHS; John Maltby to his wife, New Orleans, Apr. 25, 1865, John Rogers Maltby Papers, NSHS; B. Strong to Sara T. D. Robinson, Prairie Ford, Kans., Apr. 15, 1865, Charles and Sara T. D. Robinson Papers,

of Montana, where word of the slaying did not arrive until June, Franklin Kirkaldie, a farmer, eloquently recorded his feelings toward the martyred president: "Never in the history of this country, I think, was the loss of any public man so keenly felt by the whole nation, never any, whose loss was mourned so sincerely & extensively as that of Abraham Lincoln. We did not know until he was taken from us *how much* we loved and respected him—or how we leaned upon him as a pillar of strength in these troublous times. And felt that whatever others might do or say that *He* could be relied upon in every emergency[,] that he would go calmly & steadily forward."[41]

Kirkaldie also predicted that the assassination would produce a cry for vengeance, a need for retaliation. Indeed Robert Ashley, a Republican from Minnesota, was already raging publicly that mere death itself was not enough punishment for southern leaders in their ignominy: they should *"be hung in chains till their rattling bones glisten through the bars of their narrow prisons!"* For all those who served in the Confederate army, Ashley called for total disfranchisement for ten years. With similar vehemence Sol Miller, a Kansas Republican, suggested massive deportation or extermination of southern whites in order that freedmen be assured their personal safety. Still another urged a long delay in Reconstruction until loyalty of the South were fully restored.[42]

Seeking retribution, Republicans in certain areas directed their anger against Democrats. The afternoon of April 15, 1865, saw a mob descend upon the offices of a number of Democratic newspapers in San Francisco and destroy their presses. So alarmed were citizens that the state militia had to patrol the city for the next three days to reinstate calm. In Sacramento Republicans and Democrats mingled threateningly on the streets and many fights broke out among the crowds. Disturbed by the news from California, Republican Governor

---

KSHS; Frank Goodnow to Isaac T. Goodnow, Birksville, Va., Apr. 19, 1865, Isaac T. Goodnow Papers, KSHS.

41. Franklin Kirkaldie to his wife, Gallatin Valley, Mont., June 19, 1865, Franklin Kirkaldie Papers, MtHS.

42. Robert Ashley to editor, Winona, Minn., Apr. 21, 1865, in *Winona Republican*, Apr. 25, 1865; *White Cloud Kansas Chief*, June 15, 1865; Lewis H. P. [?] to editor, Winona, Minn., July 20, 1865, in *Winona Republican*, July 24, 1865. Less vituperative comment appeared in the *Nebraska Advertiser* (Brownville), May 4, 1865, and H. H. Butts to Ignatius Donnelly, Plainview, Minn., Apr. 18, 1865, Donnelly Papers.

Henry Blasdel in neighboring Nevada kept a watchful eye and determined to remain in Carson City to quell any violence should it occur. People were so deeply distressed about the assassination, said he, that it was impossible to predict what form their grief might take.[43]

Democrats who were so injudicious as to speak disparagingly against Lincoln found themselves quickly dealt with. When one Democrat in Omaha, for instance, had the audacity to say that Lincoln "should have been killed two years ago," Lieutenant Thomas Griffin in command at headquarters post promptly had the man imprisoned. The accused was soon released, but Griffin did not relent: sincerely he believed his deed appropriate in squelching disloyalty.[44] A similar case came up in California. General Irvin McDowell, commander of the Department of the Pacific, ordered the arrest of John McCall for rejoicing publicly over the assassination. Jailed in Alcatraz, McCall subsequently brought suit against McDowell and in 1867 was awarded $600 in damages by the U.S. Circuit Court of Northern California. In the opinion of the court, McDowell lacked the necessary sanction from his superior to make the arrest in the first place; he therefore had preferred the charges unlawfully. Even at the late date of the decision, Republicans took offense and found their scapegoat in the presiding justice, Matthew P. Deady. Clearly, in their view, Deady's known prewar Democratic and proslavery sympathies were at work when he handed down a decision in McCall's favor. Republicans intimated, moreover, by the tone of their criticism that Deady shared McCall's unkindly opinion of Lincoln. The implication had no basis in fact. Accepting an invitation to serve as a public mourner at the time of the president's death, Deady made clear his sentiment. "Although at first, I regarded Mr. Lincoln as a man borne to the pinnacle by the waves of political revolution and estimated him accordingly," he wrote, "I have come to look upon him and trust him, as a man of Providence as well as of the people."[45]

43. Winfield Davis, *History of Political Conventions in California, 1849–1892* (Sacramento, 1893), 213; San Francisco *Call,* Apr. 16, 1865; *Alta California,* Apr. 16, 18, 1865; Henry Blasdel to Capt. J. B. Thomas, Carson City, Apr. 17, 1865, Henry Goode Blasdel Papers, NvSHS.

44. Thomas Griffin to Robert R. Livingston, Omaha, Apr. 20, 1865, Robert R. Livingston Papers, NSHS.

45. Matthew P. Deady to John McCraken and others, Portland, Ore., Apr. 22, 1865, Deady Papers; San Francisco *Call,* May 2, 1867; Sacramento *Bee,* Apr. 27,

Deady is merely one example of the many Democrats who sincerely grieved at Lincoln's death. J. Sterling Morton is another. Upon hearing of Lincoln's assassination, the prominent Nebraska Democrat expressed only regrets. The deed itself he described in his diary as a "rash & bloody act. . . . All good citizens of all creeds lament this portentous crime."[46] Daniel Gelwicks, editor of the *Placerville Democrat* in California, also strongly disapproved Lincoln's murder. Although he had disagreed with the president politically, Gelwicks harbored no personal enmity and could only conclude, "Our prayers to God are that the guilty may be punished, and that none who were in any way implicated in this dastardly transaction may escape." Indeed, Democratic good will became apparent enough for one California Republican to write: "There is scarcely a Copperhead journal in the State but that has come clothed in mourning, and filled with lamentations over the untimely fall of Abraham Lincoln."[47]

Western Democrats mourned Lincoln not only for the circumstances of his death. They had also come to appreciate his political acumen; they sensed in his Reconstruction ideas a leniency that was lacking in Andrew Johnson's public statements on restoration. Whereas Lincoln spoke of binding the nation's wounds, Johnson hinted at impoverishing its traitors. "Johnson will hang the leading rebels . . . in my opinion," wrote Illinois Democrat William A. Richardson to Morton. "If Lincoln could have lived," continued Richardson, "he would have pursued a more pacific course. Lincoln's death was a great national calamity and it made a disgrace of our age and our country. If the Rebel leaders were parties to it they were great fools as well as demons."[48] Despite political differences, most western Democrats had come to trust Lincoln. They regarded his "simplicity, honesty, and kindness of heart" as personal qualities

1867; San Francisco *Bulletin*, May 1, 1867; *Alta California*, Apr. 26, 1867; Hubert Howe Bancroft, "The Life of Matthew Paul Deady," in *Chronicles of the Builders of the Commonwealth*, 2 vols. (San Francisco, 1892), II, 486–88.

46. Morton Diary, Apr. 15, 1865, J. Sterling Morton Papers, NSHS.

47. *Placerville Democrat*, Apr. 22, 1865; *Petaluma Journal & Argus*, May 4, 1865. For other expressions by Democrats see *Mankato* (Minn.) *Weekly Record*, Aug. 19, 1865; *Idaho Statesman*, May 1, 1865.

48. Roy P. Basler (ed.), *The Collected Works of Abraham Lincoln*, 9 vols. (New Brunswick, N.J., 1953), VIII, 333; George W. Julian, *Political Recollections, 1840–1872* (Chicago, 1884), 257; William A. Richardson to J. Sterling Morton, Quincy, Ill., May 16, 1865, Morton Papers.

which enhanced the presidency, inspiring respect in followers and opponents alike. James Bassett of California perhaps reflected the general Democratic assessment of Lincoln: through his death the North had lost a president, "an almost irreparable loss, [but] the South [had] lost a friend who would have done more to bury the bitter enmity than any man with whom they will have to deal with in future."[49]

If western Democrats worried about the direction which Reconstruction might take under Andrew Johnson, their fears could hardly have been assuaged by the tone being taken by western radicals. Pressing for more stringent policy, some radicals began to regard Lincoln's death as a sign of the rightful vengeance to come. His death may even have been foreordained, said they, in order that justice prevail and Andrew Johnson have the opportunity to inflict harsher punishment. Indeed, this theme echoed from the pulpit throughout California and Nevada on the Sunday following the assassination. California's radical *Marysville Appeal* elaborated on the thesis. "Treason [was] too great a crime to be compromised. It must be punished," reasoned the editor, and this Lincoln would not have done. In making Johnson the president, "Providence seems to have willed that the wicked instigators and persecutors of the rebellion should not escape." Sol Miller, a Kansas radical, presupposed the explanation which later generations might use to explain Lincoln's murder: "God saw it would never do for Abraham Lincoln to follow Divine precepts in restoring peace, therefore, He . . . directed the hand of the assassin, named Booth, to slay the President. . . ." Calling for swift, harsh action to punish southern leaders and to subdue the South, radical Orville Brown of Minnesota likewise expressed his confidence in Johnson, for he alone would have "the nerve" to carry out a policy of total and binding reformation in the South.[50]

The ending of the war, Lincoln's demise, and Andrew Johnson's coming to the presidency mark the point at which Reconstruction

49. *Mankato Record*, Apr. 22, 1865; *Yreka Union*, Apr. 22, 1865.
50. Moody, "Civil War," 321–22; *Gold Hill* (Nev.) *Daily News*, Apr. 17, 1865; *Marysville* (Calif.) *Daily Appeal*, May 30, 1865—see also Apr. 26, 27, 30, June 10, July 21, 1865; *Kansas Chief*, May 18, 1865; Faribault (Minn.) *Central Republican*, Apr. 26, May 10, 1865.

became the pervasive topic in the West. From Johnson's Reconstruction Proclamation in May, 1865, right on through the passage of the first Reconstruction Act in March, 1867, westerners revealed an active concern for affairs in the South and in Washington, D.C. In this period most local matters paled before the force of the imbroglio between President Johnson and Congress. Interest was reinforced during the impeachment trial, but, now on the downturn, it did not quite reach the same intensity. In Oregon especially a state legislative election easily overshadowed impeachment. Yet in certain cases where more local problems appeared to obscure Reconstruction matters, closer scrutiny reveals the relationship of the local question to such national issues as reunification or equal rights. For example, in contemplating the 1867 legislative election in Kansas, F. B. Anderson acknowledged Reconstruction to be a "great [issue] before the American people." Still, local problems would prevail, he insisted, and would sway the electorate in determining the outcome of the election. Careful reading of Anderson's statement, however, indicates that the local issue of paramount concern was the granting of black suffrage, one among several referenda on the Kansas ballot. Political equality for blacks had been too long and intensively discussed throughout the nation to be considered merely a local question. Again, Californians mulled the significance of the Democratic victory in the state election of 1867. Democrats had waged an aggressive campaign against Reconstruction policies, black suffrage in particular, and perhaps struck a note of response among the electorate. Their gain, on the other hand, may have been more simply a result of the current split in the California Republican party. Whatever the reasons behind the vote, its example points out that issues were at once local and national, and often irreducible.[51]

From April, 1865, to 1868 Reconstruction dominated the editorial columns of western newspapers and the speeches of politicians, and it was reflected in private correspondence as well. Indeed, some westerners showed a preoccupation with the topic in their personal letters. In Oregon Matthew P. Deady carried on extended correspondence with friends and politicians alike about the impact and purposes of Reconstruction. Writing to her husband in June, 1865,

51. F. B. Anderson to editor, n.p., n.d., in *Wyandotte* (Kans.) *Commercial Gazette*, July 27, 1867; Gerald Stanley, "The Republican Party in California, 1856–1868" (Ph.D. dissertation, University of Arizona, 1973), 116–78.

Serena Wright of Minneapolis concluded that "Reconstruction is the principal topic now." Thereafter, the Wrights would make continued reference to national problems. Letters written by Augustus Wildman in Colorado and Thomas Adams of Montana at about the same time declared that "re-construction is the order of the day." As late as 1867 a Colorado editor wrote, "No question, just now, is so vital to the interests of the country as that of Reconstruction." Stephen Hewson, traveling throughout Minnesota in 1867, noted an "intense feeling" still being manifested over national affairs among the people he met. To Hewson, this was proof that their interest in Reconstruction had remained steady.[52]

The West not only revealed an ongoing concern over Reconstruction, but differences led to hard feelings, even violence at times. Although unclear about the exact details, Peter Bryant reported a fight in Holton, Kansas, between a returning Union army veteran and a "Copperhead," in which the latter stabbed the soldier. In Bryant's account, the "Copperhead" was placed under arrest but a mob rushed to lynch him before he could be brought to trial. With less tragic results, John T. Knox, a Democrat in Washington Territory, freely sparred over Reconstruction with his Republican neighbor, Joseph Cushman. Their quarrel was real and pride was at stake, for as Knox wrote after one such encounter, "I said to Cush that he was an old man, if it was not the case, I would nock [sic] him clear through [the] door, that I would not allow any body else to talk to me in that way, he grunted and fumed around, and left the house and I have not seen him since."[53]

As westerners expressed their concern over Reconstruction, they wondered too at its outcome. Absorbed between 1861 and 1865 with securing military victory over the Confederacy, most westerners had

52. Deady Papers, *passim*, especially his correspondence with Jesse Applegate and James Willis Nesmith; Serena Wright to George B. Wright, Minneapolis, July 13, 1865, George Burdick Wright and Family Papers, MnHS; Augustus Wildman to his mother, Denver, May 25, 1865, Wildman Papers; Thomas Adams to Granville Stuart, Washington, D.C., June 10, 1865, James and Granville Stuart Papers, YWA—Thomas Adams, a Montana resident, was in the national capital on personal business when he wrote the letter; *Denver Daily*, Mar. 8, 1867; Stephen Hewson to Ignatius Donnelly, Oxford, Minn., Jan. 21, 1867, Donnelly Papers.

53. Donald M. Murray and Robert M. Rodney, "The Letters of Peter Bryant, Jackson County Pioneer: First Installment, 1862–1902," KHQ, XXVII (Winter, 1961), 486; John T. Knox to William W. Miller, Olympia, Wash., Dec. 21, 1867, Miller Papers.

given little thought to what would follow the war. "*How strange* to think of looking *back* to Anti-Slavery times!" mused Serena Wright in June, 1865. "It seems as if it must have been a hundred years between the time when Mrs. Stowe could have written 'Uncle Tom,' and now, when all tragedy and pathos seem trifling to these realities [of war] so strange and terrible." Reconstruction and black suffrage had replaced "slavery expansion" as the "absorbing and vehement" topics, and Mrs. Wright wondered if they would create the same excitement. In California Charles DeYoung looked at the nation emerging from a war which had threatened dissolution, and he found it "on the verge of a new transition state." DeYoung acknowledged that "our institutions must undergo some modifications," but cautioned at the same time that these changes should be considered carefully and at length and conceived without regard to party prejudice or political strife.[54] Most westerners would live to see the changes of which DeYoung talked, but they were not to be devised within an atmosphere of political calm.

54. Serena Wright to George B. Wright, Minneapolis, June 13, 1865, Wright Family Papers; San Francisco *Chronicle*, Aug. 23, 1865.

CHAPTER TWO

Johnsonian Reconstruction

"We don't care much for Andy's southern policy."
—Ovando Hollister, Colorado

If Lincoln's assassination kindled the western response to Reconstruction, it was Andrew Johnson who intensified that response,
for the actions of this uncompromising, tactless southerner shaped
the final course of Reconstruction. The Republican party had reunited
the nation; party loyals in Congress expected to play a key role in
making the peace. Yet the president seemed bent on returning to
the rebel South an autonomy which most people in the North and
West were unwilling to grant. In their disappointment Republicans
rallied behind their congressmen; watchful Democrats in the West
grasped fleetingly at Johnson's disfavor among Republicans as their
chance for political gain. Undeniably Johnson's Reconstruction policy
and his personal foibles were cause for growing concern, and sparked
the intense resentment most westerners would come to feel against
their president.

No president in the nineteenth-century West received as much
praise or as much criticism as did Andrew Johnson. When he assumed
the executive office in April, 1865, western radical and moderate
Republicans alike were fully confident. ". . . the *country* and our
cause have nothing to fear," announced radical Senator Samuel C.
Pomeroy of Kansas. "God lives and Andrew Johnson is a plucky loyal
man. . . . The country is safe." William N. Byers, a moderate
Republican in Colorado, could agree that "frank, noble, . . . and
justice loving, [Johnson] stands today as the true representative of
popular feeling." Throughout the West Republicans lauded their new
president as "the man to rule in revolutionary times," and one "fully
equal to the duties . . . of his . . . position."[1]

1. Samuel Pomeroy to Samuel N. Wood, New York, Apr. 17, 1865, Wood

Within a year, however, Pomeroy would be circulating rumors that Johnson was a drunk and a lecher, and Byers would be referring to the president as "the original traitor." Nor were these instances of condemnation isolated. By mid-1866 sharp criticism against Johnson was being voiced from California to Minnesota. Included among the critics were Republican and Democratic editors and politicians such as John Martin of Kansas and George Miller of Nebraska, Indian agent Samuel R. Curtis of Montana, and John F. Miller, collector of customs at San Francisco. Widespread antagonism developed even among private citizens. Franklin Kirkaldie of Montana considered him "coarse . . . & egotistical" and declared that by his actions Johnson was ensuring the Republicans of victory in the 1866 congressional elections. In Minnesota Serena Wright was no less troubled. "But what a *mess* we are in politically!" she wrote disparagingly. "Did ever Christian Country witness so disgusting a spectacle as our precious President. . . . We have lived through a four year war, but can the nation survive four years of Johnson? Oh, to think of the disgrace and dishonor he has brought to us."[2]

The reasons for Johnson's decline in esteem throughout the West were varied. They stemmed from his failure to deal successfully with national problems, his somewhat paranoid style of politics, and his inability to understand that political favors at the local level might encourage "provincials" in the West to support Johnsonian Reconstruction. Finally, the president was unable to reverse or modify an opinion once made, and that may have been his ultimate undoing. Evidence indicates that had Johnson been more flexible, he could

Papers; *Rocky Mountain News*, May 5, 1866. See also Leavenworth (Kans.) *Daily Times*, May 28, 1865; *New Mexican*, May 5, 1865; "Truth" to editor, n.p., n.d., in *Seattle Weekly Gazette*, May 25, 1865. My interpretation of Pomeroy as a radical is derived from Michael Les Benedict, *A Compromise of Principle: Congressional Republicans and Reconstruction, 1863–1869* (New York, 1974), 351–52, 356–57, 360–62, 368–69. Benedict has concluded that, among western senators, only Pomeroy remained consistently radical during the Reconstruction era.

2. Samuel Pomeroy to the Reverend Mr. Joseph Dennison, Washington, D.C., Mar. 3, 1866, Goodnow Papers; *Rocky Mountain News*, May 16, 1866; Samuel R. Curtis to his wife, Washington, D.C., Sept. 18, 1866, Samuel R. Curtis Papers, YWA; Franklin Kirkaldie to his wife, Confederate Gulch, Mont., Oct. 5, 1866, Kirkaldie Papers; George Miller to J. Sterling Morton, Omaha, Oct. 20, 1866, Morton Papers; Serena Wright to George B. Wright, Minneapolis, Sept. 30, 1866, Wright Family Papers. See also James H. Holmes to Charles Sumner, Lawrence, Kans., Feb. 27, 1866, Sumner Papers.

have retained a substantial western following. Western Republicans repudiated Andrew Johnson, but for many it was a step reluctantly taken. They feared the political disruption their action would bring, but in respect to Reconstruction, many Republicans in the West concluded that party ideals should take precedence over political harmony.

Notwithstanding Johnson's own mistakes and miscalculations, a number of western Republicans harbored a basic distrust of the president because of his background and inappropriate behavior during his vice-presidential inaugural. A former Democrat and southerner, Johnson had been Lincoln's choice for a running mate in 1864 merely to attract votes from the war Democrats, those Democrats who supported military action against the South but who did not accept other principles of the Republican party. Despite Johnson's refusal to resign from the Senate when Tennessee seceded in 1861 and his efforts on behalf of the Union during the war, western Republicans of northern Whig or abolition antecedence were never able to accept him as a leader. "I distrust Johnson," wrote Edward W. McGraw in April, 1865; "I feel he is not the man to deal with the embarrassing facts and questions which the war will leave in his hands." At the same time Edwin B. Crocker, a Californian who had played a prominent role in organizing the state Republican party, echoed similar reservations but concluded that should Johnson prove unfit or unwilling to follow Republican aims, he would be "deposed."

During his inauguration as vice-president, Johnson, recovering from illness, drank three glasses of brandy to bolster himself for the ceremony. Unfortunately he became inebriated. Democrats played up the incident to portray Johnson as a "rum-sucker" and his inaugural ceremony as "drunk and disorderly," despite a concerted Republican effort to explain away the circumstances. Still, more temperate Republicans found Johnson's behavior difficult to excuse. The more charitable termed his lack of propriety as "unpardonable," but the less forgiving—the Reverend Mr. Stebbins of San Francisco is one example—simply called Andrew Johnson a "drunk."[3]

Western Republicans cast aside their early doubts during Johnson's

3. E. W. McGraw to Matthew P. Deady, San Francisco, Apr. 18, 1865, Deady Papers; San Francisco *Chronicle*, Apr. 20, 1865; *Sacramento Union*, Apr. 18, 1865.

first two months in office. Their initial reaction to the president's Amnesty Proclamation of May 29, 1865, was positive and gave the impression of general satisfction. Republican editors described the terms of the document as "magnanimous," and one which "tempered justice with mercy." Although in most respects Johnson's policy was similar to the one Lincoln laid down in 1863, Johnson did stipulate that southern landholders with taxable property in excess of $20,000 would have to seek pardon directly from the president. Western observers took the provision to mean that the politically elite and moneyed aristocrats of the South were to be deprived of their influence, a stand with which they heartily agreed. "We sympathize with the masses of subdued Southerners," concluded Marshall Murdock of Kansas, "but for their ambitious leaders, we have little love. . . ." Fellow Kansan John Martin agreed: "We cannot afford to give the slaveholding aristocracy another lease of power." Western Republicans saw the $20,000 stipulation as a way to give members of the lower white class in the South a voice in their political future.[4] This early, broad interpretation of Johnson's program confused some Democrats. They saw nothing in Johnson's proclamation which substantiated the Republican view or merited the unqualified praise most Republicans were lavishing on the document. Indeed, one Democrat in Nebraska questioned Johnson's very motive: might it be his intention to restore peace on the basis of Democratic states' rights principles rather than to reform the South at all?[5]

Among Republicans, radicals were the first to voice doubt about Johnson's policy. As the summer of 1865 advanced and as Johnson created provisional governments in the southern states through additional proclamations, western radicals found the president too lenient toward whites and oblivious to the needs of freedmen. "The President's 'Amnesty' *'excepts'* most all Rebels," declared Serena Wright suspiciously. "It is a bad thing to be beaten in a bad cause," she reflected, "but in the long run it might be worse to be successful."

4. James D. Richardson (ed.), *A Compilation of the Messages and Papers of the Presidents, 1789–1897*, 10 vols. (Washington, D.C., 1896–99), VI, 310ff.; *Osage Chronicle*, July 22, 1865; *Atchison Champion*, May 11, 1865; *Sacramento Bee*, June 10, July 15, 1865; *Sacramento Union*, July 10, 13, 1865; *Carson (City, Nev.) Daily Appeal*, June 11, 1865; *Miner's Register*, Sept. 28, 1865.

5. T. W. Bedford to J. Sterling Morton, Brownville, Nebr., Sept. 17, 1865, Morton Papers. For a description of Johnson as the "last Jacksonian," see Kenneth M. Stampp, *The Era of Reconstruction, 1865–1877* (New York, 1965), 50–82.

Musing over the president's $20,000 provision, Sol Miller of Kansas complained that only one-third of southern white males fell into the category of having to seek presidential pardon. This percentage he thought too small. Unmindful of the time and paperwork involved, Miller would have all persons who served in the Confederate forces seek pardon directly from the president. Orville Brown, a Minnesota radical, attacked Johnson's program for its indifference toward blacks. Brown lauded the past achievements of radicalism and declared that Republicans should now be primarily concerned with the moral and political elevation of former slaves—"and the work is bound to be carried forward to completion with or without Andy Johnson." Senator Samuel Pomeroy had been lavish in his praise of the president; now he, too, took stock and wondered openly about Johnson's failure to provide for the welfare of former slaves. Pomeroy suggested that pardon of Confederates be slowed and that greater economic security be provided for freedmen. To that end, he wanted the president to deed unconditionally ten acres of land to every adult male held in slavery after January 1, 1863. Steps should then be taken to give these men, as landholders, voting privileges. Enfranchising these freedmen, concluded Pomeroy, would lay the groundwork for black suffrage in the South.[6]

Moderate Republicans were not long in joining their radical cohorts in opposition. Rather than argue at this point that Johnson's plan was too lenient or lacked specific proposals to uplift freedmen, moderates noted its inconsistency: between his proposal for the punishment of treason and the leniency of actual implementation there was marked disparity. True, Johnson had been vague about a policy toward the South prior to the issuance of his Amnesty Proclamation, but his words bespoke a stern attitude: "Sir, treason must be punished; its enormity and the extent and depth of the offense must be made known!" and "I say the traitor has ceased to be a citizen and in joining the rebellion has become a public enemy." Yet by December, 1865, the president had pardoned thousands of rebels, had in some states permitted the organization of local militia units, and had re-

6. Serena Wright to George B. Wright, Minneapolis, May 30, 1865, Wright Family Papers; *Kansas Chief*, June 1, 1865; Faribault *Central Republican*, June 7, 18, 1865; *Atchison Champion*, June 22, 1865; *Miner's Register*, July 19, 1865; *Oregonian*, June 14, 1865; Salt Lake City (Utah) *Daily Union Vedette*, June 12, 1865; Samuel Pomeroy to James Harlan, New York, Sept. 16, 1865, Johnson Papers.

turned the control of nearly every seceded state to local politicians, many of whom were former Confederates. While he demanded compliance when certain states hesitated or refused to repudiate their war debt or nullify their secession ordinances, Johnson chose to ignore laws which stringently regulated freedmen and elections which were returning leading Confederates to state and national office. Watching this progress of events, moderate western Republicans conceded that the South had acquired too much local autonomy "just for giving up slavery."[7]

Reviewing the president's policy after it had been in effect for six months, Henry Pittock, editor of the *Oregonian*, offered a mild rebuke: "On his ascension to the Presidency, Mr. Johnson told the country that treason was a crime and must be punished with severity . . . he does not appear to have adhered to that opinion." More biting criticism came from a Kansan: ". . . we find President Johnson in the highest seat of the gift of the people, dealing out *Pardons* by the wholesale, and treating former enemies as old bosom friends who have merely gone astray from the path of virtue." Senator-elect Cornelius Cole of California wanted to think that the president might again reverse himself and "harmonize his [present] action with his own past record." Realignment of Johnson's actions with his stated goals should simplify the Reconstruction process but would not eliminate a general Republican feeling of betrayal, for, wrote Cole, "we must never trust Johnson . . . in any future contest."[8]

The force of the moderate Republican argument weakened quickly, and moderates soon found themselves echoing the major points of the radical opposition: Johnson's plan was too lenient on southern whites and guaranteed nothing to blacks. Ironically it was events in the South as well as the president's actions which produced this change of thought. Indeed, southerners did much to undermine the president's position with his western constituency. They voiced their approval of the president's program and their resentment against radical demands for a firmer policy. Writing to his family in Min-

7. W. E. B. DuBois, *Black Reconstruction in America, 1860–1880* (New York, 1935), 243; Stampp, *Era of Reconstruction*, 51; *Sacramento Union*, Sept. 23, 1865; *Alta California*, Sept. 25, 1865.

8. *Oregonian*, Nov. 7, 1865; Saxon to editor, n.p., n.d., in Atchison *Free Press*, Oct. 31, 1865; Cornelius Cole to George Gorham, San Francisco, Apr. 13, 1866, Cornelius Cole Papers, UCLA.

nesota, Thomas Montogomery, captain of a black infantry unit stationed in Louisiana, chronicled the shift in southern attitude from expectation of punishment to outright resistance against Reconstruction. In California reports of southern obstinacy caused another to remark, "The people in some parts of the South appear to be perfectly blind to the lessons of the war, and remain as sulky and defiant as if they still had an organized rebel army and government to rely on."[9]

The height of white southern defiance became apparent as elections were held to choose representatives to the national legislature. Voters in the South elected to Congress four Confederate generals, five colonels, six former members of Jefferson Davis's cabinet, fifty-eight Confederate congressmen, and the Confederate vice-president himself, Alexander H. Stephens. In the West, as in other areas of the nation, loyalists were taken sharply aback. They interpreted the election results to mean continued rebellion against the Union. The western press reported Johnson, too, as dismayed at the outcome of the elections. Yet paradoxically he made no move to reverse the decisions. In this evasive attitude on Johnson's part, westerners could see only justification, rather than condemnation, of the South. Angrily they rebuked the president for being "too espousing of traitors." Previously strong in defense of Johnson, the Sacramento *Bee* now charged that the election results in the South clearly indicated the fallacy of being lenient and the need for more stringent measures.[10]

So incensed were some western Republicans that they began demanding, as a countermeasure, denial of seats in Congress to the designated southern representatives. After all, these were "old rebel politicians . . . who should have been inexorably excluded from office." To permit them now to participate in government would be "virtually saying to them that they have done no wrong." In a letter to Charles Sumner urging that he do all possible to exclude the southern representatives, E. Clough of Kansas warned that Union

9. Thomas Montogomery to James Montogomery, Port Hudson, La., June 5, 1865, Montogomery to his father, Baton Rouge, Oct. 18, 1865, Apr. 14, 1866, all in Thomas Montogomery Papers, MnHS; R. T. Montogomery in *Napa* (City, Calif.) *Register*, Nov. 8, 1865; *Miner's Register*, Dec. 12, 1865; *Oregon State Journal* (Eugene), Dec. 16, 1865.

10. Fawn M. Brodie, *Thaddeus Stevens: Scourge of the South* (New York, 1959), 229–30; *Marysville Appeal*, Sept. 18, 1865; *Sacramento Bee*, Nov. 18, 1865; William R. Keithly to Elihu Washburne, Boise, Jan. 16, 1866, Washburne Papers. See Beale, *Critical Year*, 41–42, for Johnson's reaction to Stephens's election.

soldiers would rise in revolt rather than permit their former adversaries to legislate for the loyal people. Leander Holmes, antislavery spokesman in prewar Oregon, had even more bitter thoughts about reinstating rebels to high representative office. He wrote derisively, "They . . . slew our brothers and [would now] insult us by giving back the rag that did drain the blood . . . and bid us wipe our eyes with all."[11]

Thus did Republicans in the West applaud Congress's refusal to seat the southerners in December, 1865. Robert Fisk of Montana recognized that the strongly Democratic, pro-southern population in the territory would likely object to the move. But as he pointed out, there was a less attractive alternative: better that the former traitors be excluded from Congress than given the hanging they really deserved. Contrary to the implication of the president's policy, Fisk argued that southerners "are not masters of the situation" and would be far wiser to accept denial of their congressional seats in silence than to complain. Summarizing the achievements of Johnson's policy during his first months in office, one editor grasped the general tenor of the western Republican attitude. The loyal North had expected southern leaders to be punished and only "a foreigner was hung"; they expected that rebels would lose citizenship privileges for a time, yet "traitors are permitted to take office and estates are restored. Let the President stop sprinkling rose water, recall and respect the pledges he made when he assumed the Executive office, [and] take such a decided stand as will show that he is in full sympathy with . . . a victorious people."[12]

If moderate western Republicans came to regard Andrew Johnson as too forbearing toward southern whites, they soon considered as reprehensible his failure to protect former slaves from ill-treatment. During Johnson's first months in office western Republicans accepted certain presidential statements as a reasonable solution to the southern racial question. Johnson hoped the southern states would, through legislation, shield freedmen from abuse, but the extension of suffrage should remain a state matter. The president had no objection should

11. E. N. O. Clough to Charles Sumner, Leavenworth, Kans., Oct. 14, 1865, Sumner Papers; Leander Holmes to editor, n.p., n.d., in *Vancouver* (Wash.) *Register*, May 26, 1866; *Sacramento Union*, Sept. 20, 1865; *Nebraska Herald* (Plattsmouth), Aug. 8, 1866.

12. *Helena* (Mont.) *Herald*, Dec. 6, 1866; *Sacramento Union*, Dec. 30, 1865.

any state wish to enfranchise its own black population, but he felt the Constitution did not in any way empower the federal government to impose equal suffrage. Few westerners challenged this policy. In fact, they feared that former slaves, in their ignorance about political issues, might easily become pawns in the hands of scheming whites. Whether or not they saw merit in suffrage for ex-slaves, these westerners in 1865 agreed with John Colhapp, editor of the *Nebraska Advertiser:* "Negro suffrage . . . should be left to the action of the States, no matter, whether the States have been in rebellion or not."[13]

So firmly committed were moderate Republicans to a limited policy toward blacks that they challenged the more liberal position of the radicals. When Orville Brown, a Minnesota radical, criticized the president's reluctance to demand the ballot for freedmen and labeled Johnson's stand "an outrage upon justice," moderates took offense. To Brown's call for suffrage as a vital reform, for instance, one fellow Minnesotan may have seen its merit but pleaded for delay. Said John Wise, " . . . a majority of the Republicans consider that removing the chains of slavery and emancipating the negro in four years' time is doing a great work and ought to be considered sufficient for one generation." When western radicals, along with Brown, went on to demand black suffrage as a reward for military service during the war, moderates countered that whites had suffered greater losses on the battlefield than had blacks. Besides, said one, blacks from the South had joined the army to secure their freedom, not suffrage. Finally, radicals contended that the ballot was the only means by which freedmen could protect themselves, and it was this argument, over all others, which was to prove the most viable.[14] For equal suffrage, when it came in the South, was born of a pressing demand for laws to secure freedmen in their rights. The agitation arose in response to southerners' ill-treatment of their former slaves and Johnson's unwillingness to do anything about it.

13. *Nebraska Advertiser,* July 13, 1865. See also *Atchison Champion,* June 7, 1865; *Mantorville* (Minn.) *Express,* June 30, 1865; *Winona Republican,* June 19, 1865; *Oregonian,* Aug. 8, 1865; Sacramento *Bee,* Aug. 14, 1865; *Oregon State Journal,* Sept. 23, 1865; *Nebraska Republican* (Omaha), Oct. 16, 1865.
14. Faribault *Central Republican,* May 24, June 7, 1865; *Mankato Record,* July 1, 1865; Congressman James Henderson of Oregon to Addison Gibbs, Washington, D.C., Dec. 16, 1865, Addison Crandall Gibbs Papers, OHS.

The war had scarcely ended when reports about mistreatment of southern blacks began filtering into the West. In the opinion of one Nevada resident, southerners "cannot brook the thought of their former bondmen having freedom [and] will try any means to keep [them] under foot." Thomas Montogomery disclosed in letters to his family that freedmen were suffering daily abuse. They were still beaten in the fields and driven off without wages once their work was completed. In an indignant first-hand report A. P. French elaborated on the picture. For committing a minor offense while living in Demopolis, Alabama, the former Union officer alleged that local law officials had imprisoned him together with fifteen blacks. They were confined to a cage so small that none could lie down, a cage reeking of human filth and crawling with vermin. In retrospect, French wondered at "the hatred that the people of this country hold toward Yankees and the poor negroes. They hate the negroes just simply because we have made them free. . . . I have lived here ever since the surrender [but] I never knew of the tyranny & injustice practiced on the ignorant and defenceless negro until I was placed in jail." By the fall of 1865 J. W. Wyman of California took note of the fact that "every Eastern mail brings evidence of the extreme cruelty to which the freedmen are subjected by their late masters. . . ." In fairness, Wyman and fellow Republican editors had to admit to the possibility of exaggeration in reports they were receiving. But "one thing is certain," they agreed; "the whipped rebels of the South will do all they can do to make the negroes uncomfortable and wretched."[15]

In the midst of these reports came news of the passage of black codes by newly elected southern state legislatures. These laws, designed to re-establish social order, gave to former masters certain benefits of slavery without any of the responsibilities, and placed blacks into a labor system which lacked even the basic protections found in the peculiar institution. Looking over Tennessee's revised constitution, the editor of the *St. Paul Press* could perceive little difference between its provisions compelling vagrant blacks to labor for white men and securing a work force through the old slavery

15. *Gold Hill News*, June 13, July 15, 18, 1865; Thomas Montogomery to James Montogomery, Baton Rouge, July 21, 1866, Montogomery Papers; A. P. French to Ignatius Donnelly, Demopolis, Ala., Dec. 20, 1865, Donnelly Papers; *Humboldt Times*, Oct. 7, 1865; *Mantorville Express*, May 18, 1865; *Border Sentinel* (Mound City, Kans.), July 7, 1865; *St. Paul* (Minn.) *Press*, June 17, 1865.

system. In fact, he wrote, the provisions were a "palpable attempt to replace chattel slavery with . . . serfdom."[16]

The passage of black codes in Mississippi and South Carolina brought the wrath of western criticism upon the South. Western Republicans had actually been following closely events in the Palmetto State; they regarded South Carolinians as the most traitorous and recalcitrant of southerners. The ordinances themselves, aimed as they were at forcing blacks into a kind of servitude once again, were described as "monstrous [and] diabolic in spirit." Western editors saw those codes as designed to "outlaw the negro population [and] place them outside the pale of legal protection for any crimes committed against them, and leave them the helpless objects of the oppression and vengeances and passions of the white masters." As Sol Miller of Kansas assessed the situation, the blacks in the South may have been emancipated but were still "at the mercy of their former oppressors." Considering all aspects of their situation, Miller saw blacks doomed to "be worse off free, than they were as slaves." In the nation's capital Congressman William Windom of Minnesota expressed the western Republican view when, after summarizing the provisions of a number of black codes, he declared, "Sir, if this be liberty, may none ever know what slavery is."[17]

As they became more aware of the plight of freedmen in the South, greater numbers of moderates began to take stock in the radical Republican argument that suffrage was one means by which blacks might protect themselves. In that way they could at least attempt to vote out of office those lawmakers and officials who sought to proscribe them. From widely separated localities, the *St. Paul Press,* the *Kansas Chief,* and the *Marysville Appeal* alike began to advocate equal suffrage in the South during the fall of 1865. Even Henry L. Pittock of Oregon—a state in which black uplift was never a popular topic—reached the same conclusion in early 1866. In no other way, he declared, could southern blacks secure their rights.[18]

Not all moderates, of course, were willing to grant suffrage to

16. *St. Paul Press,* June 17, 1865.

17. *Leavenworth Times,* Nov. 19, 1865; *St. Paul Press,* Oct. 13, 1865; *Kansas Chief,* Sept. 7, 1865; *Congressional Globe,* 39 Cong., 1 Sess., 1160. See also *Atchison Champion,* Dec. 12, 1865; *Marysville Appeal,* Nov. 18, 1865; *San Francisco Chronicle,* Sept. 27, 1865.

18. *St. Paul Press,* Oct. 13, 1865; *Kansas Chief,* Sept. 7, 1865; *Marysville Appeal,* Nov. 28, 1865; *Oregonian,* Sept. 6, 1865, to Jan. 15, 1866, *passim.*

former slaves. "It is not the question of negro suffrage that at present most vitally concerns the nation," wrote Charles DeYoung of San Francisco in emphasizing the distinction; "it is the question of negro protection." DeYoung pointed out that the idea of elevating the freedmen to political equality was a divisive issue among Republicans but on one thing they all agreed: freedmen must be protected from "the vengeance of their late masters." If the president would not guarantee that protection, then Congress must do so, for the national legislature had become the guardian of southern blacks. Senator James Nye of Nevada, who was more free-thinking than most westerners on equal rights, was an early advocate of black suffrage as a solution to southern race problems. While he found opposition to the concept of giving blacks the right to vote, Nye discovered that most Republicans agreed with his statement: "It is the bounden duty of the Government to afford protection to emancipated negroes."[19]

Allied in their recognition of the need to secure freedmen in their basic human rights, moderate Republicans were stunned at the turn of events in Washington in early 1866. Congress forwarded to the president two bills, both of which were in part designed to protect former slaves from mistreatment—the Freedmen's Bureau bill and the Civil Rights Act. Johnson vetoed both. Even before the president's refusal to sign the freedmen's bill in mid-February, 1866, Johnson's Reconstruction program had been declining in popularity. But now, with that veto and the president's subsequent actions, moderate support dwindled sharply. There was also a significant shift in loyalties: as they learned of racial outbursts in the South, moderate Republicans in the West would henceforth tend to place the blame for them on Johnson.[20]

19. San Francisco *Chronicle*, Sept. 17, 1865; *Gold Hill News*, Sept. 15, 1865.

20. John Miller to Hugh McCulloch, San Francisco, Mar. 6, 1866, William Van Voorhies to Andrew Johnson, San Francisco, Mar. 3, 1866, John B. Fish to Johnson, St. Paul, Mar. 6, 1866, all in Johnson Papers; Enos Stutesman to Andrew J. Faulk, Pembina, Dakota, Oct. 1, 1866, Andrew Jackson Faulk Papers, YWA. Johnson's vetoes were considered the impetus behind racial unrest in Memphis and New Orleans in the spring and summer of 1866. In the minds of many westerners, the riots would never have occurred had the president demanded assurance of black rights. For comments see T. C. Miller to William M. Miller, Nashville, Tenn., Aug. 6, 1866, Miller Papers; *St. Paul Pioneer*, May 5, 12, 1866; Faribault *Central Republican*, Aug. 8, 15, 1866; *Nebraska Republican*, Aug. 11, 1866; *Border Sentinel*, Dec. 14, 1866; *Olathe* (Kans.) *Mirror*, Sept. 27, 1866; *Daily Mining Journal* (Black Hawk, Colo.), Aug. 4, 1866; *Idaho Statesman*, Aug. 14, 1866; *Oregonian*, Aug. 20, 1866; *Marysville Appeal*, May 8, 1866; *Oakland* (Calif.) *Daily News*, Aug. 9, 1866.

Johnson's popularity declined in the West, according to contemporary sources, because his veto of the Freedmen's Bureau bill confirmed Republicans' worst fears: he stood in awe of the southern aristocracy and he deprecated southern blacks. Not only was the president, by his veto, returning freedmen to the mercy of their old masters; he was saying in effect that former slaves should have no protection at all. The veto left former slaveholders free to "visit their vengeance upon the unhappy race." Blacks, faced as they were with a prejudice too strong to combat by peaceful means, would likely "have to resort to arms to protect themselves." In the veto message the president had insisted that southerners be permitted seats in Congress so they could help draft laws which would affect their section. Such an allowance was untenable, charged I. S. Kalloch, an editor in Kansas. It only revealed one certainty—that Johnson was primarily concerned for "the darling white race." To Kalloch, it was inconceivable that Johnson forsake loyal blacks for the very southern whites who had done "all in their power to destroy this government." In the Pacific Northwest "Vindex" summarized the western Republican attitude toward the nation's president: Andrew Johnson had prated on about protecting blacks and done nothing; now freedmen were helpless and it was the president's fault. Johnson had vetoed the freedmen's bill, said Vindex in reviewing the details, for the reason that southerners had had no voice in devising it. "Why should they! . . . Ye Gods! Ye Gods!" screamed Vindex, "must the American people endure all this."[21]

Veto of the Freedmen Bureau bill encouraged western Republican politicians, who heretofore had remained silent, to speak out. John Bidwell, congressman from California, began one letter with the quiet appraisal, "The President, I fear, is not in harmony with Congress." Bidwell had strong feelings on the subject, however, and before long was harshly criticizing Johnson's southern policy: the chief executive had blatantly ignored Congress and on his own had returned control

21. *Marysville Appeal*, Feb. 23, 1866; *Western Home Journal* (Ottawa, Kans.), Mar. 8, 1866; Faribault *Central Republican*, Mar. 7, 1866; "Vindex" to editor, Olympia, Mar. 8, 1866, in *Washington Standard* (Olympia), Mar. 10, 1866. For other adverse comments see "Lake" to editor, n.p., n.d., in *Humboldt Times*, Sept. 29, 1866; "Flag" to editor, n.p., n.d., in San Francisco *Elevator*, Mar. 2, 1866; *Leavenworth Conservative*, Feb. 22, 1866; *Rochester* (Minn.) *Post*, Mar. 3, 1866; *St. Paul Press*, Feb. 22, Mar. 1, 1866; *Winona Republican*, Feb. 23, 1866; *Carson Appeal*, Feb. 24, 1866; *Nebraska Herald*, Feb. 28, 1866; *Atchison Champion*, June 3, 1866.

to "former enemies." In effect, the policy rendered freedmen to a condition worse than bondage. "I feel," asserted Bidwell in conclusion, "it is the duty of Congress to insist on adequate protection to the freedmen and the right to instruct and elevate them."

Minnesota's Congressman Donnelly held a like opinion. He was aware of opposition in the North to securing rights for blacks because of their "inferiority." But, confided Donnelly, if black people were truly inferior, then that was all the more reason to protect them by law. Still, few western Republican politicians dared go so far as to advocate suffrage outright. In Minnesota, the most liberal of the western states, Cushman Davis recognized, "We have a burden to the African population we cannot defray." Still, Davis pointed out that the rectifying of past wrongs need not include, for the present at least, the granting of suffrage. Protection in rights by law and the right to vote were two quite separate issues. C. Stebbins, a fellow Minnesotan, shared Davis's viewpoint but at the same time sensed the growth of a more liberalized attitude toward black people—this, he decided, was the result of all the discussion about securing freedmen's rights. To be sure, the quarrel between Congress and the president had worked to Congress's advantage, wrote Stebbins, and "except upon the Universal Suffrage question, I believe it is judicious to move right forward."[22]

One year had elapsed between the issuance of Johnson's Amnesty Proclamation and Stebbin's conjecture on Republican readiness to move forward on black rights. In those twelve months western Republicans had shifted their view dramatically. Previously they had revealed little interest in Reconstruction and freedmen's rights; now these topics had become a vital concern. By early 1866 many westerners, perhaps to their own surprise, were expressing open sympathy toward the plight of former slaves. As yet, few Republicans in the West were willing to advocate suffrage for southern blacks, but proponents found less opposition to the reform than earlier. While they

22. John Bidwell to George A. Gillespie, n.p., n.d., quoted in Rockwell D. Hunt, *John Bidwell, Prince of California Pioneers* (Caldwell, Idaho, 1942), 192; Cushman K. Davis, "Criticism of Johnson's Reconstruction policy," undated Ms speech in Cushman Kellogg Davis and Family Papers, MnHS; Donnelly Diary, Jan. 14, 1866, and D. Stebbins to Ignatius Donnelly, Hastings, Minn., May 4, 1866, both in Donnelly Papers.

could not agree on equal suffrage, western Republicans did acknowledge that blacks in the South needed protection in their rights. Moreover, were the president not to provide such security, Congress might justifiably assume the responsibility. In implementing his policy, Andrew Johnson had not met western Republican expectations. But that is not the complete story. Many westerners were wondering, in fact, about the president's personal integrity.

Audiences everywhere were taken aback by Johnson's approach to public oratory. Over the years in campaigning on the frontier Johnson had used the "stump-speaking" approach to good effect; he never abandoned the technique. Delivered extemporaneously, this type of address tended toward the emotional and highly voluble. Typically the speaker enlivened audience interest by verbally attacking the opposition. For Johnson, during his term as president, delivery also included constant reminders of his advance from poverty—from town alderman to the chief magistracy of the land. At face value "stumping" did indeed arouse interest, but presidents were expected to have acquired more polish. Unfortunately, Johnson showed no restraint. Speaking before a crowd on Washington's birthday, three days after he had vetoed the freedmen's bill, the president replied to radicals critical of his action. Warming to his topic, Johnson insisted that some of his congressional adversaries were being as treasonous as Confederate leaders had been; when goaded by the crowd, he identified them outright—Thaddeus Stevens, Charles Sumner, and Wendell Phillips. As historian Eric L. McKitrick has explained, it was this incident which gave the American public its fullest glimpse of Johnson as a man since his inauguration as vice-president in 1865. Comments by westerners support this assertion. To Matthew P. Deady, for instance, the speech "smelt of bourbon." D. Bassett of Minneapolis wrote, "After reading Johnson's speech . . . I hardly know what to make of him." Republican editors from Kansas to California denounced the president for "lowering the dignity of his office." Individual criticism, of course, varied but the *Central Republican* of Faribault, Minnesota, echoed the general tone: "It should cause the face of every American," wrote editor Orville Brown, "to crimson with shame in reflecting that it was the utterances of the official head of our Government. . . . The president must have been in a state of disgraceful and maudlin intoxication. In no other condition would he have so descended below the dignity appertaining to his position."[23]

Johnson only reinforced this image during his "swing around the circle" in late summer. Ostensibly a trip to dedicate Stephen A. Douglas's tomb in Chicago, his tour was actually an attempt to gain support in the face of growing criticism. Westerners, although not given the opportunity to hear the president themselves, reacted negatively to reports of Johnson's tirades. Republicans called his speeches "a national disgrace," "out of place," "infamous," "drunken harangues," and "shameful." Even to Democrats such as August Harvey of Nebraska it was apparent that "Mr. Johnson lacks a certain degree of dignity." J. Selwyn Brittain of California, who claimed to be politically independent, perhaps reflected the thought of many westerners when he wrote, "Johnson talks too much. He should be restrained. He will do more harm than good to the cause he is endeavoring to support."[24]

Johnson was no more politic in his relations with members of the national legislature. On several occasions the president gave the impression of basic accord on certain congressional measures, only to reverse himself and send resounding veto messages to Congress. His inconsistency created a void and led to the belief that the president could not be trusted. Within his first year in office, as a result, Johnson lost the support of virtually every Republican senator from the West. Among Republicans he was able to retain only the backing of Daniel Norton of Minnesota and James Nesmith of Oregon, both former Democrats turned Unionist. Extant sources do not explain Norton's approval, but they do expand on Nesmith's position. The Oregon senator offered continued support for the president not out of personal loyalty but because their positions on Reconstruction were

23. McKitrick, *Andrew Johnson and Reconstruction*, 292; Matthew P. Deady to James Nesmith, Portland, Ore., Mar. 20, 1866, Nesmith Papers; D. Bassett to Ignatius Donnelly, Minneapolis, Feb. 26, 1866, Donnelly Papers; Faribault *Central Republican*, Feb. 28, 1866; *Manhattan* (Kans.) *Independent*, Mar. 3, 1866; *Marysville Appeal*, Feb. 25, 1866; *Olathe Mirror*, Mar. 1, 1866.

24. *Nebraska Herald*, Sept. 19, 1866; *Oakland News*, Oct. 15, 1866; *Miner's Register*, Sept. 6, 1866; *Rocky Mountain News*, Sept. 4, 1866; *Border Sentinel*, Sept. 21, 1866; *Monterey Gazette*, Sept. 14, 1866; *St. Paul Press*, Sept. 13, 1866; *Nebraska Statesman*, Sept. 21, 1866; *Atchison Champion*, Mar. 13, 1866; John Miller to Hugh McCulloch, San Francisco, Mar. 6, 1866, Johnson Papers.

similar. Like Johnson, Nesmith insisted that the southern states had not left the Union, that Reconstruction should be an executive function, and that black suffrage should not be imposed by federal law.[25] Norton and Nesmith paid a price for sustaining the president, however. Nesmith lost his bid for re-election in 1866; the Republican Minnesota legislature requested Norton's resignation in 1867, a request he ignored but which made him anathema to every Republican in the state.

Johnson's most serious loss in the West was that of Senator William Stewart of Nevada. A lawyer in California before taking up residence in Nevada, Stewart had strong political influence in both states. A moderate, he approved Johnson's policy on the ground that, despite its drawbacks, the plan was more definite than ideas then being formulated in Congress. But Stewart came to the conclusion that Johnson had betrayed his trust, and the senator could summon little personal sympathy for the president thereafter. Opposed to the 1866 Freedmen's Bureau bill because he felt it created too many federal jobs, Stewart had defended Johnson's veto. When it looked as if the Senate were going to override the president's objections, Johnson asked Stewart to sustain him. The senator agreed, but only after receiving assurance that the president would sign the Civil Rights Act. Accordingly the senator cast his vote to uphold the veto of the freedmen's bill, and only ten minutes later, by Stewart's account, Johnson's message vetoing the Civil Rights Act arrived in the Senate. Stewart never again supported Johnson. Even though the senator was later to disagree with portions of the Fourteenth Amendment, he voted for the measure in order to show greater unity in face of Johnson's defiant opposition to Congress.[26]

It may well have been the strained relations between himself and Stewart that caused the president to lose the support of Cornelius Cole, whose friendship Johnson wished heartily to cultivate. Cole had been elected senator from California in late 1865, and he arrived in Washington at the height of the controversy over Johnson's vetoes. He replaced James McDougall, a Democrat and a Johnson backer, and appeared a likely ally because he had read law with William

25. *Congressional Globe*, 39 Cong., 1 Sess., 289–93.

26. *Ibid.*, 1079–82, 2795–2803; William M. Stewart, *Reminiscences of Senator William M. Stewart of Nevada*, ed. George Rothwell Brown (New York, 1908), 198–201, 226; *Gold Hill News*, Apr. 3, 1866.

Seward; he was also reputed to be a "true friend" of the administration. Johnson was destined to disappointment, however. By his own
account, Cole worked closely with the Nevada senators and undoubtedly became aware of Stewart's bitterness. Thus, when Johnson
personally invited him to the White House and, according to one
report, offered the western patronage, Cole declined the offer. Unknown to the president, Cole himself had a strong aversion to Johnson. While still in California he had written, "My dislike of [Johnson]
is intense. . . . He is stopping the car of progress & trampling upon
humanity. . . . He is a devil and ought to be in H—l—if there is
any. . . . He is only fit to patch the old clothes of the dirtiest
niggers. . . . Booth spoiled a good tailor when he made him President." As late as the impeachment trial, the president hoped Cole
might vote to acquit him. But he was mistaken, for in Cole Johnson
had no friend.[27]

James H. Lane of Kansas was another western senator who became
disillusioned in his relationship with the president. Lane had supported congressional radicals in 1865; suddenly in 1866 he found
himself amenable to certain aspects of Johnson's plan. This reverse
on Reconstruction was prompted by Lane's desire to retain a strong
hold on federal patronage in Kansas and portions of the West. Actually Lane had had much influence over Lincoln's western appointments, and he sought similar input with Johnson. To his chagrin
Lane found that Johnson ignored his initial suggestions regarding
appointments. Lane came to fear, realistically, that his senatorial
colleague, Samuel Pomeroy, a closer friend to Johnson, would likely
have the larger voice in Kansas patronage decisions. Then, as it
became evident that Pomeroy was siding with the radicals, Lane
moved quickly. Although in October, 1865, he had criticized Johnson's leniency in issuing pardons, now in January, 1866, he publicly
defended the president.[28]

27. Cornelius Cole to Olive Cole, San Francisco and Washington, D.C., Mar.
6, Apr. 29, May 2, 1866, Cole Papers; Asa Hatch to Charles Sumner, San Francisco,
Feb. 16, 1866, Sumner Papers; R. C. Gaskill to John Bidwell, San Francisco, Jan.
21, 1866, Bidwell Papers, CSUC; John Miller to Andrew Johnson, San Francisco,
Jan. 18, 1866, Johnson Papers; *Sacramento Union*, Dec. 17, 1865; Sacramento *Bee*,
July 16, 1866; Cornelius Cole, *Memoirs of Cornelius Cole, Ex-Senator of the United
States from California* (New York, 1908), 277.
28. Lane implored Johnson to appoint Charles W. Adams of Kansas as governor
of Colorado Territory, but in the end the post fell to Alexander Cummings of
Pennsylvania. James H. Lane to Andrew Johnson, Washington, D.C., Apr. 17,

Anxious not to narrow his political options, Lane at the same time introduced into the Senate a series of resolutions which had radical support. But the senator was forced to make his stand known once Johnson vetoed the Civil Rights Act. Still equivocal, Lane assured his fellow senators he would vote to override; instead, he attempted to filibuster and finally sustained the veto. Even so, Johnson was no more responsive to Lane on patronage matters than before. Thus without much backing from the president, Lane now had to defend his new conservatism to a Kansas electorate which was siding with the Congress. The effort brought a physical and mental breakdown and Lane committed suicide in July, 1866.[29]

If Lane had supported Johnson in order to have a dominant role in Kansas patronage, he soon found his faith ill-placed. Johnson, in actuality, had few appointments to make in Kansas. Still, he named only two of Lane's men to postmasterships in Kansas at a time when the senator's political influence was being threatened.[30] Perhaps the

---

1865, and Lawrence, Kans., July 15, 1865, both in LAR, Charles W. Adams File; *Congressional Globe*, 39 Cong., 1 Sess., 1803–4; Atchison *Free Press*, Oct. 30, 1865; *Leavenworth Times*, Jan. 7, 1866; *Kansas Chief*, Jan. 18, 25, 1866; *Leavenworth Conservative*, Jan. 7, 1866; *Border Sentinel*, Jan. 19, 1866; Martha Belle Caldwell, "The Attitude of Kansas toward Reconstruction, before 1875" (Ph. D. dissertation, University of Kansas, 1933), 20–22; William Frank Zornow, *Kansas: A History of the Jayhawk State* (Norman, Okla., 1957), 123–24; Wendell Holmes Stephenson, *The Political Career of General James H. Lane*, vol. III of *Publications of the Kansas State Historical Society* (Topeka, 1930), 151–55; Samuel J. Crawford, *Kansas in the Sixties* (Chicago, 1911), 235.

29. There is little disagreement among Lane's contemporaries that emotional instability led to his suicide. John Speer, editor of the *Kansas Tribune* and later Lane's biographer, claimed that Lane had suicidal tendencies. John Speer, *The Life of General James H. Lane* (Garden City, Kans., 1896), 315–16. Publishing several newspaper articles on Lane's last days, R. B. Taylor, editor of the *Wyandotte Gazette*, maintained that Lane regretted his efforts to gain the president's favor. Lane thought himself on the verge of insanity, induced partly by his loss of political prestige. "Lane lived on the smiles of the people of Kansas," wrote Taylor, "and when he came to the conclusion . . . that he had lost their confidence[,] his mind gave way and with his own hand he did what thousands of border ruffians and rebels would gladly have done if they could, slew Jim Lane." *Wyandotte Gazette*, July 7, 14, 1866. Lane's wife, however, denied Taylor's conclusions. Mary Lane to "Dear Sir," Lawrence, Kans., July 25, 1866, James H. Lane Papers, KU. George Chapman to Charles Sumner, Atchison, Kans., May 5, 1866, Sumner Papers; Atchison *Free Press*, Apr. 17, 1866; Stephenson, *Lane*, 156–57; Crawford, *Kansas in the Sixties*, 235; Joseph B. James, *The Framing of the Fourteenth Amendment* (Urbana, Ill., 1956), 92–93; *Manhattan Independent*, May 19, 1866; *Western Home Journal*, Apr. 19, 1866; *Council Grove* (Kans.) *Democrat*, Apr. 27, 1866.

30. Johnson replaced radical D. R. Anthony with James L. McDonald in Leav-

president's lack of generosity stemmed from his mistrust of Lane's own reliability. Throughout his political career Lane was somewhat of a maverick, changing endorsement and allies whenever it appeared to his advantage to do so. But the death of Lane brought Edmund G. Ross to the Senate, and until the impeachment trial he was an ardent supporter of congressional Reconstruction.

Despite the seeming inconsistency between Johnson's words and actions and his questionable posture before the public, the president retained a modicum of western Republican support into the late summer of 1866. Because of their distance from the national capital, some Republicans tended to doubt the intensity of Johnson's quarrel with Congress as reported in the newspapers. More important, western Republicans preferred to temper their differences with the president for fear that open strife would lead to a breakup of the Republican and a resurgence of the Democratic party. Reactions in individual states and territories varied, but had Johnson been willing to modify his steadfast position during the spring of 1866, evidence indicates that he might have retained a voice in Reconstruction.

Among the western states California suffered the most disagreement over the executive. But there the Union party, a coalition of Republicans and war Democrats, had begun to split as early as 1865, and there deep divisions among Unionists on local as well as national issues had become quickly apparent. On the one hand, Republicans in the legislature were successfully adopting resolutions condemning Johnsonian Reconstruction, and Republican-conducted mass meetings were taking a similar stand. The press, on the other hand, was more restrained; while certain California papers were criticizing the president, many of the major Republican newspapers, especially in San Francisco, preferred to back him. The *Chronicle*, for example, found presidential Reconstruction "wise and more just than the distrustful and harshly repressive system favored by the Congressional majority." Even after the civil rights veto a number of far western newspapers remained with Johnson.[31]

enworth and appointed John Martin, editor of the *Champion*, as postmaster in Atchison. U.S. Congress, Senate, *Journal of the Executive Proceedings of the Senate* (Washington, D.C., 1887), XIV, p. 1, cclxxviii, p. 2, 1533; Caldwell, "Kansas," 86; *Carson Appeal*, Sept. 13, 1866; Mark A. Plummer, *Frontier Governor: Samuel J. Crawford of Kansas* (Lawrence, 1971), 56–57.

31. San Francisco *Chronicle*, Mar. 27, 1866; San Francisco *Bulletin*, Apr. 13,

In Nevada, Kansas, and Minnesota the response was cautious; clearly party leaders wished to avoid political disruption. In Nevada Republicans for the most part supported the vetoes of both the freedmen's bill and the Civil Rights Act. In fact the Republican Nevada legislature, by a vote of twenty-five to four, gave hearty approval to Johnson's first veto. Nevada editors were probably just as happy to see Johnson's veto of the subsequent Civil Rights Act. While they sympathized with the plight of freedmen, they were uneasy about its implications for the local Asian population. They feared, simply, the act's potential for broadening the civil status of the Chinese.[32] In Kansas the legislature took a more ambivalent stand. As one Kansan reported, the majority of the legislators were unwilling to "either condemn or endorse" the president. As Republicans they did not know what to make of Johnson's deeds and were waiting to see what might happen. Even when confronted with the civil rights veto, Governor Samuel Crawford did not overreact: Johnson "looks honest and talks very fair. . . . I don't think the loyal people of the country should be too hasty in condemning him. . . . If he goes over to the democracy, let him go of his own free will. . . ."[33] Showing less restraint, the Minnesota legislature passed resolutions favoring Congress, but it was Johnson's February 22 tirade against the radicals, not his veto of the freedmen's bill, that brought about their move. Republicans there agreed that a break with the president should be avoided unless, of course, continued support for Johnson meant an abandonment of principles. Congressman Donnelly's mail indicated that while Minnesota Republicans were leaning toward Congress, "all parties are keeping remarkably quiet [hoping] for a settlement of the differences between Congress & the President."[34]

Certain radical Republican editors in Kansas decided to publish

1866; *Alta California*, Feb. 22, 1866; *Humboldt Times*, Mar. 3, 1866; *Idaho Statesman*, Mar. 3, 1866; Chico (Calif.) *Weekly Courant*, Mar. 17, 1866.

32. State of Nevada, *House Journal, 1866* (Carson City, 1866), 319; *Gold Hill News*, Apr. 5, 9, 1866; *Nevada State Journal* (Carson City), May 16, 1866.

33. G. W. Glick to Samuel Wood, Atchison, Kans., Mar. 22, 1866, Wood Papers; Thomas Carney to James H. Lane, Topeka, Feb. 27, 1866, Johnson Papers; Samuel Crawford to J. B. McAfee, Washington, D.C., Apr. 25, 1866, Crawford Papers.

34. *St. Paul Press*, Mar. 8, 1866; S. I. R. McMillan to Alexander Ramsey, St. Paul, Mar. 8, 1866, Ramsey Papers; D. Bassett to Ignatius Donnelly, Minneapolis, Mar. 6, 1866, J. B. Mills to Donnelly, St. Cloud, Minn., Apr. 3, 1866, A. G. Foster to Donnelly, Wabasha, Minn., Apr. 11, 1866, all in Donnelly Papers.

lists of newspapers which disapproved Johnson's vetoes. Thus might they give the impression that great numbers of Republican papers had dropped the president. Their supposition was faulty, however, for there were editors who objected to Johnson's stand and still were not ready to withdraw all support. Three editors made it quite plain that while they disliked the vetoes, they were in no way considering a break with Johnson. R. B. Taylor of the *Wyandotte Gazette* saw nothing to be gained by denouncing the president, and George Martin of the *Junction Union* pointed out that Johnson had done nothing revolutionary by vetoing acts of Congress. Marshall Murdock, editor of the *Osage Chronicle*, offered the most protracted comment. Proud to affirm his own Republicanism, Murdock admonished the radicals for their inflammatory behavior. In the end their outspoken stand would only pose a threat to party unity. "We shall not denounce Johnson while there is hope . . . ," concluded Murdock firmly, "until he clearly deserts our party and repudiates [its] principles. . . ."[35]

In the territories Republicans showed a greater reluctance to break with Johnson. This situation developed, in part, because the president and Congress shared final governing authority in territories, and an action which irritated either could be politically damaging. The president nominated most federal appointees and directed their activities through his cabinet; the Senate confirmed these nominees and the Congress as a whole appropriated the federal portion of each territorial budget. Thus territories found it advisable not to side firmly with either the president or Congress. Randall Hewitt, editor of the *Pacific Tribune*, reflected the awkwardness of the territories' position when in the spring of 1866 he refused to publish an anti-Johnson letter. "I did receive your communication but did not publish it," said Hewitt in acknowledging the correspondence, "for the reason that it condemned the President much too strongly. . . . I do not think we should condemn him very strongly yet, as we are awkwardly situated in this Territory, as indeed, all Territories, and I do not wish to compromise the Federal officers, as I fear publishing anything very strong would. I trust you will take the same view of the subject as I do."[36]

35. *Leavenworth Conservative*, Apr. 20, 1866; Atchison *Free Press*, Mar. 8, 1866; *Wyandotte Gazette*, Mar. 3, 1866; *Junction City* (Kans.) *Union*, Mar. 17, 1866; *Osage Chronicle*, Apr. 14, 1866.

36. Randall Hewitt to Daniel Bagley, Olympia, Wash., Mar. 31, 1866, Daniel Bagley Papers, UWa.

Slowly political support for one side or the other—for Johnson or Congress—emerged in the territories during 1866. Because of their moderate views or perhaps fearing the president's power to remove them, territorial governors of New Mexico, Colorado, Dakota, and Idaho openly voiced their approval of Johnson's course. More radically inclined officials like the governor of Washington Territory and the territorial secretary in New Mexico sided with the radicals. The legislatures of Idaho and Montana, almost totally Democratic, sustained the president, while Democrats in Washington Territory attacked radicalism but mustered only lukewarm support for Johnson.[37] In Utah Brigham Young favored the president's policy, and Young's esteem for Johnson continued during the whole of his administration. Johnson espoused a states' rights philosophy of which Young approved. He sensed in Johnson's attitude toward southern whites a "desire to be fair and straight-forward" with unpopular groups, even Mormons. Through their petitions requesting religious freedom and their correspondence about the president, it was clear that Mormon leaders regarded Johnson as a bulwark against the radical attempt to eliminate polygamy in Utah.[38]

In Nebraska Republicans chose deliberately to remain silent once the tension between Johnson and Congress became apparent. Officials there were determined above all to attain statehood, an accomplishment that needed sanction from both the national legislature and the executive, and they considered it unwise to take a firm stand for either side. Two weeks before Johnson's denial of the freedmen's bill the territorial legislature had, in fact, expressed confidence in the president's policy.[39] Then came the veto, and for three months Nebraska Republicans dared say little about national affairs. There was nonetheless an undercurrent of displeasure. "Things are not working

37. Robert Mitchell and others to Andrew Johnson, Santa Fe, Sept. 27, 1866, in TP: New Mexico; *Santa Fe Gazette*, Dec. 2, 1865, May 19, 1866; Robert W. Larson, *New Mexico's Quest for Statehood, 1846–1912* (Albuquerque, 1968), 92–93; Murphy, "New Mexico," 102; *Idaho World*, Mar. 19, 1866; Caleb Lyon to William Seward, Boise, Mar. 10, 1866, Seward to Lyon, Washington, D. C., Mar. 22, 1866, both in SDDL; S. D. Durgin to ———, Olympia, Wash., Sept. 22, 1866, in LAR, William Pickering File, NARG 59; Spence, *Montana*, 22.

38. Brigham Young to William Hooper, Salt Lake City, Feb. 13, June 3, 16, 1866, Brigham Young Papers, YWA; John M. Bernhesil and others to Hooper, Salt Lake City, Mar. 11, 1866, Johnson Papers.

39. "Joint Resolution of the Nebraska Territorial Legislature, February 10, 1866," and Algernon S. Paddock to William Seward, Omaha, Feb. 13, 1866, both in TP: Nebraska; Seward to Paddock, Washington, D.C., Mar. 7, 1866, in SDDL.

as they ought to have by any means," mused John W. Williams. "There is not that out and out proclamation, 'I am for the Administration policy of reconstruction.' " Williams and his friends discerned strong leanings toward Congress among Nebraska Republicans, but only a "thorough Radical paper," they thought, would bring them out. The lack of direction about national affairs caused enough concern for one Republican to warn the territorial party leaders that the "people . . . expect some unequivocal stand to be taken . . . and will not look with favor upon the one that is afraid to speak out."[40]

In part Nebraska Republicans took their cue from opposition which the Colorado statehood bill was encountering from both Congress and Johnson. Introduced in January, 1866, the measure met resistance from congressmen on two counts: the territory had as yet a very limited population, and the state constitution restricted voting to whites only. Congress finally endorsed the bill in May, only to have the president promptly veto it. While the statehood measure was before Congress, pro-statehood Coloradans were careful to approve Johnson's every action on Reconstruction. They learned sadly and abruptly, as had so many others, that President Johnson did not always remember his friends.[41]

Johnson did have a firm rationale, however, behind his denial of the Colorado bill. Unfortunately for proponents of statehood, a number of western Republicans agreed with him and Congress was unable to override his veto. The president's primary objections focused on the lack of support for statehood from within the territory itself and, again, on its small population. Coloradans had rejected a state constitution in 1864; a second document, written in 1865, passed by a margin of only 155 votes. Even that majority was secured fraudulently, claimed the anti-statehood faction, and because of these charges the territorial legislature later asked the president to submit the statehood question to yet another referendum.[42] Pro-statehood

40. John W. Williams to ———, Omaha, Apr. 28, 1866, in TP: Nebraska; R. S. Knox to Samuel Maxwell, Omaha, Apr. 9, 1866, Samuel Maxwell Papers, NSHS; *Nebraska* (City) *Statesman*, Apr. 14, 1866.

41. Frank Hall, *History of the State of Colorado*, 4 vols. (Chicago, 1889), I, 376–86; *Congressional Globe*, 39 Cong., 1 Sess., 1353, 2373.

42. *Oregonian*, June 6, 1866; *Winona Republican*, May 19, 1866; *St. Paul Pioneer*, May 16, 1866; U.S. Congress, Senate, *Senate Executive Documents*, 39 Cong., 1 Sess., Doc. 45 (ser. 1238); Alexander Cummings to Andrew Johnson, Denver, Jan. 10, 1867, Johnson Papers; *Congressional Globe*, 39 Cong., 1 Sess., 1327–30, 1352–53. Augustus Wildman noted that political victories in Colorado went to men

Coloradans were in the meantime claiming sufficient population for statehood, but Alexander C. Hunt, an anti-statehood federal marshal in the territory, reminded the administration that a census had not been taken since 1861; at that time the population came to 25,000 and had diminished with each succeeding year. Indeed, the number of voters in the territory had been declining. Whereas 9,354 individuals had voted in the first election held in 1861, only 5,769 votes were cast in the 1865 constitutional referendum.[43] These figures had their impact on Johnson; he reasoned that inasmuch as the average congressional district elsewhere contained 127,000 people, Colorado with its less than 25,000 inhabitants was scarcely entitled to voting representation in Congress.

Pro-statehood Coloradans were drawn into the Reconstruction debacle despite themselves. One month before Johnson's denial of Colorado statehood the Senate had overridden the civil rights veto by the narrow margin of thirty-three to fifteen. Had Johnson been able to secure only two more votes, his veto would have been sustained. To that end the president tried unsuccessfully to bargain at the time with John Evans and Jerome Chaffee, Colorado's senators-elect. He was willing to approve the statehood bill, he said, if they in turn would endorse Johnsonian Reconstruction. Evans and Chaffee refused to commit themselves to Johnson's program and for that reason, according to the Colorado pro-statehood interpretation, Johnson determined to withhold consent from their bill.[44]

---

who could purchase the most votes. Wildman to his father, Denver, Dec. 24, 1865, Wildman Papers. Harry E. Kelsey, Jr., *Frontier Capitalist: The Life of John Evans* (Denver, 1969), 166–67 *passim,* describes questionable practices employed in the statehood referendum of 1865.

43. A[lexander] Cameron Hunt to James Grimes, Denver, Apr. 19, 1866, Johnson Papers. A census taken during the latter part of 1866 showed Colorado's population to be 27,981, but even its accuracy was questioned: in some counties the population was simply estimated rather than enumerated. Anti-statehood people claimed the estimates too high, while pro-statehood individuals found them too low. Alexander Cummings to Orville Browning, Denver, Jan. 4, 1867, Johnson Papers; U.S. Congress, Senate, *Senate Executive Documents,* 39 Cong., 2 Sess., Doc. 7 (ser. 1277); *Miner's Register,* Dec. 16, 1866. For comments from leading politicians in the East, see Gideon Welles, *The Diary of Gideon Welles,* 3 vols. (Boston, 1911), III, 22–23; James G. Blaine, *Twenty Years of Congress: From Lincoln to Garfield,* 2 vols. (Norwich, Conn., 1893), II, 280.

44. *Rocky Mountain News,* Aug. 24, Dec. 26, 1866; Hall, *Colorado,* I, 377; Howard R. Lamar, *The Far Southwest, 1846–1912: A Territorial History* (New York, 1966), 260; Kelsey, *Frontier Capitalist,* 166–67; Jerome C. Smiley, *History of Denver* (Denver, 1901), 494–98.

Prior to Johnson's veto the three leading Republican editors in Colorado—William Byers, Ovando Hollister, and D. C. Collier—had voiced common good will toward the president.[45] At the news of the veto, however, they reacted strongly and with indignation. ". . . to have the president, whom we have honored and defended, both in good and evil report, veto the measure of our prosperity, is entirely too much," declared Byers of the *Rocky Mountain News.* Thereafter, Byers termed Johnson's veto message a "miserable subterfuge" to hide an underlying reason: he did not want Evans and Chaffee's presence adding to radical strength in the Senate. When word of Johnson's statehood veto arrived in the mining town of Black Hawk, Hollister of the *Mining Journal* wrote, "Lincoln was a nigger Moses but he was true to his friends. We don't care much for Andy's southern policy. The restoration policy is no business of ours." Frank Hall, territorial secretary, and Collier, co-owners of the *Miner's Register,* expressed their disappointment thus: "Our State has been refused admission by one Andrew Johnson . . . we who have struggled so hard for this change from Territorial to State government do not appreciate it fully. It would appear to be the President's policy to annihilate all regular and implied opposition which may come in the way of his plan of reconstruction." Dissatisfied with the veto and unhappy over other difficulties with the president in his capacity as secretary, Hall moved to the radical position. Shortly the editors of the *Register* announced that the newspaper's editorial policy would conform to the "principle of the Union party and to the principle that freedom is for all men."[46] Although only a small part of the entire Reconstruction story, Johnson's veto nonetheless revealed, for pro-statehood Coloradans, the danger of placing too much confidence in the president. It served as yet another example of Johnson's inability to retain or secure an element of support at little cost to himself. For despite their profession of radicalism and their endorsement of congressional Reconstruction, Colorado Republicans re-

45. See, for example, *Rocky Mountain News,* Sept. 20, 1865, Feb. 24, Mar. 2, 8, 30, 1866; *Miner's Register,* Feb. 25, 27, Apr. 11, 1866; *Mining Journal,* Apr. 7, 1866; Eugene H. Berwanger, "Three against Johnson: Colorado Republican Editors React to Reconstruction," SSJ, XIII (Jan., 1976), 149–58.

46. *Rocky Mountain News,* May 16, 1866; *Mining Journal,* May 19, 1866; Frank Hall to his mother, n.p., May 15, 1866, Frank Hall Papers, DWC; *Miner's Register,* Oct. 4, 1866.

mained conservative about national affairs. Although Republicans in Colorado were to voice their return to conservatism earlier than other sections of the West, their reaction seldom included a defense of the president.

As Republicans abandoned the president, a number of Democrats came over to his side. Some were attracted in the early months of Johnson's presidency by his lenient policy toward the South. One Democratic editor in Minnesota admitted to "unspeakable relief" upon reading the president's remarks to delegations visiting the White House. *"The States are to be preserved in all their integrity . . . ,"* he decided happily. "We guess, after all, Andy is sound." Democratic conventions or legislatures meeting in Colorado, Nebraska, and Idaho in late 1865 or early 1866 adopted resolutions approving Johnsonian Reconstruction. Following the veto of the Freedmen's Bureau bill, Democrats in Montana, Washington, Kansas, and Nevada offered similar votes of confidence. During the critical months from February to August, 1866, Democrats as groups or as individuals came forth to express their allegiance to the president they had once considered a renegade.[47]

Politically astute Republicans wondered at the motive behind this Democratic shift to Johnson and believed it insincere. Matthew P. Deady, a former Democrat himself, wrote, "The Democracy are willing to use [Johnson], but will adopt him never." John Miller also doubted the good faith of the Democrats, and he regarded their

47. Caleb Lyon to Andrew Johnson, Boise, Jan. 16, 1866, Joseph McCorkle to Johnson, Virginia City, Nev., Apr. 21, 1866, Oscar Stephenson to Johnson, St. Paul, Feb. 24, 1866, George Miller to Johnson, Omaha, Feb. 24, 1866, James Cavanaugh to Johnson, Virginia City, Mont., Oct. 2, 1866, Helena Montana Bar Association to Johnson, Oct. 2, 1866, all in Johnson Papers; "Concurrent Resolutions Unanimously adopted by the Idaho Legislature, January 12, 1866," in TP: Idaho; *St. Paul Pioneer,* Apr. 28, 1865; *Rocky Mountain News,* Oct. 21, 1865; *Nebraska Republican,* Oct. 30, 1865; *Nebraska Advertiser,* Sept. 28, 1865; J. Sterling Morton and Albert Watkins, *Illustrated History of Nebraska,* 3 vols. (Lincoln, 1905–13), I, 499–500; *Idaho World,* Feb. 3, Apr. 14, 1866; Spence, *Montana,* 38–39; Davis, *Political Conventions,* 234–35; San Francisco *Bulletin,* Feb. 27, 1866; "A Looker On" to editor, n.p., n.d., in *Pacific Tribune* (Olympia, Wash.), Sept. 22, 1866; "Mass Meeting of the Friends of President Johnson" (broadside, YWA); *Montana Democrat* (Helena), Aug. 30, 1866; Wilder, *Annals of Kansas,* 431; Omaha (Nebr.) *Weekly Herald,* Mar. 2, 1866; *Montana Radiator* (Helena), Mar. 31, 1866; *Nebraska City News,* May 26, 1866; *Council Grove Democrat,* Apr. 6, 1866; *Santa Fe Gazette,* Mar. 24, 1866; *Oregon Herald* (Portland), Mar. 17, 1866.

alliance with the president as the "unkindest cut of all," for it was their move which arrayed "Union men pretty generally on the side of Congress."[48]

Miller was correct. The mutual flirtation between Johnson and Democrats, culminating in the National Union Movement and its convention in Philadelphia in August, 1866, brought about complete severance of ties between Johnson and the Republican party, nationally as well as in the West. During July and August, 1866, even many of the more conservative western Republicans dropped the president. D. C. Collier of Colorado stated the issue clearly: the National Union Movement had effectively refocused the quarrel between Congress and Johnson. Rather than an issue between radical and conservative wings within a single party, the struggle now waged between the Republicans on one side and the combined efforts of Democrats, Johnson, and rebels on the other. "It is evident now that there can be no peace," wrote Cornelius Cole. "The President & the Democrats have joined hands & sealed the Union by a call for a convention." A Norwegian immigrant in Minnesota evidently agreed. Just a month later he made the observation: "I now consider Johnson a big _____, though I defended him when I was in Christiania [Norway]. He has completely surrendered to the 'copperheads' and the rebels of the South allied with them." As a result, many moderate and conservative Republicans in the larger cities as well as hamlets of the West were now to abandon the president, and they emphasized that it was Johnson's support of the National Union Movement that had brought about their disillusion. Robert Montgomery, editor of the *Napa Register,* reflected the attitude of many who could no longer accept Andrew Johnson: "It pains us to abandon one whom we have regarded so highly. . . . Although we have voted for Andy Johnson, advocated his election, vindicated his character and endurance, the time has come when we can no longer approve his course, or apologize for it."[49]

48. *Esmeralda Union,* Dec. 14, 1867; Matthew P. Deady to James Nesmith, Portland, Ore., Apr. 7, 1866, Nesmith Papers; John Miller to Hugh McCulloch, San Francisco, Mar. 6, 1866, Johnson Papers.

49. *Miner's Register,* July 2, 4, 1866; Cornelius Cole to E. Burke, Washington, D.C., July 4, 1866, Cole Papers; "Letter from a resident of Faribault, Minnesota to Friends, September 28, 1866," in Theodore C. Blegen (ed.), *Land of Their Choice: The Immigrants Write Home* (Minneapolis, 1955), 434; *Napa Register,* Aug. 4, 1866.

The National Union convention in and of itself failed to cause much political excitement in the West because it seemed such a fleeting affair. Formal organization did not begin until July, 1866, and most western delegates were selected on the eve of the convention. The short notice given by the organizers and the time necessary to reach Philadelphia hindered rather than encouraged participation of westerners. As a result, delegations from the Far West consisted primarily of individuals who were already in the East. Half of those representing California did not even live in that state.[50] The delegates from the less remote portions of the West, while indeed bona fide residents, hardly inspired confidence. From Minnesota came Henry Rice, who had suffered recent defeat in his race for the governorship, and Daniel Norton, who would be asked shortly to resign from the Senate. Nebraska Unionists sent William Lockwood and George Francis Train, the latter an eccentric whom few took seriously. Democrats in Nebraska were represented by J. Sterling Morton and George Miller, men of stature who were more truly representative of their party than were the Unionist delegates. But Nebraska Unionists successfully shoved Morton and Miller into the background because of their advocacy of peace during the war. The Kansas delegation was also divided between Unionists and Democrats; neither group included men of political importance. Looking over the names of those attending from throughout the West, Selwyn Brittain of California found the membership as undistinguished as it was inept. "The National Convention might have been made an instrument of great good, but we are afraid for it now," he said with concern. "It will be a hodge podge, and we fear a failure."[51]

Western Democrats and Unionists did not play an important role at the convention. Delegates from the western states and territories were appointed to various committees but, except for the resolutions committee, these assignments were merely perfunctory. Consequently there was little direct news to report from the western viewpoint.

50. The broadside announcing the convention was issued July 10, 1866. A copy can be found in LAR, Herman Heath File. *Idaho World*, Sept. 15, 1866; *Alta California*, Aug. 14, 1866; Davis, *Political Conventions*, 239; Walter C. Woodward, *The Rise and Early History of Political Parties in Oregon, 1843–1868* (Portland, 1913), 251.

51. *Nebraska Statesman*, July 21, 1866; Henry Gere to Maril Clapham, Omaha, July 27, 1866, Charles Henry Gere Family Papers, NSHS; Wilder, *Annals of Kansas*, 435; *Monterey Gazette*, Aug. 10, 1866.

Republicans contented themselves by poking fun at the convention, and western Democrats failed to support the affair wholeheartedly. In fact, a number of them warned that any cooperation with Johnson would be detrimental in the long run to their party. While they found acceptable the president's ideas on Reconstruction, they doubted his sincerity because of his previous defection to the Republican cause.[52] As the fall elections of 1866 turned against the president, it became apparent to his Democratic allies that there was little political advantage to be gained by sticking with Johnson.

Why did some Democrats ally with the president if they generally mistrusted him? Contemporary suggestions differ, but in the Republican view Democrats expected Johnson to reward them with federal positions.[53] He had said he would replace federal officeholders who opposed him; the Democratic assumption was therefore logical. But Johnson was not always true to his word. He spoke of harsh punishment for rebels and granted pardons readily. He said freedmen's rights should be protected and he did nothing to secure that protection. To Senator Stewart he gave a promise to sign the Civil Rights Act and then he vetoed it. He may have dealt backhandedly with James H. Lane as well. Democrats also were destined to disappointment. The president had spoken of rewarding his supporters with political jobs, but when the time came, Andrew Johnson was both unwilling and unable to deliver the patronage.

52. *New York Times*, Aug. 14, 1866; *New York Tribune*, Aug. 13, 1866; *Chicago Tribune*, Aug. 15, 16, 1866; *St. Paul Press*, Aug. 23, 1866; *Daily Territorial Enterprise* (Virginia City, Nev.), Aug. 21, 1866; *Marysville Appeal*, Oct. 4, 1866; *Los Angeles Semi-Weekly News*, Aug. 8, Sept. 11, 1866.

53. John Miller to Hugh McCulloch, San Francisco, Mar. 6, 1866, Johnson Papers; *Western Home Journal*, Feb. 8, 1866.

CHAPTER THREE

Johnson and the Western Patronage

"The gate is closing. . . ."
—James Nesmith, Oregon

Western Democrats were confident that their support of presidential Reconstruction would endear them to Andrew Johnson, and that he in turn would reward them with federal patronage. Their hope emerged when radicals in 1865 openly began criticizing the president's policy; it was not finally dulled until 1867, when Congress passed the Tenure of Office Act and thus placed limits on the president's power to remove officeholders. Only months after Johnson's succession to office James M. Woolworth of Nebraska, with something other than selfless interest, wondered if the president would "turn the government over to our party" should a break develop among Republicans. Such a possibility continued to excite Woolworth's political colleagues, and some eighteen months later Democrats in the West were requesting Johnson to name to federal posts within their respective states or territories only those individuals who met their approval. So open were some western Democrats about their patronage designs that Republicans accused them of putting their political ambition before the interests of national reunification.[1]

To a degree the charge was unfair, but Democrats in the West did seem obsessed with the idea of displacing Republicans from federal posts. Former presidents had manipulated the patronage to achieve their purpose; why should Johnson not use his appointment power to force acceptance of his Reconstruction policy, Democrats queried. To encourage him, F. L. Hatch, a California Democrat, informed

1. James M. Woolworth to J. Sterling Morton, Omaha, Sept. 19, 1865, Morton Papers; Morton and others to Andrew Johnson, Brownville, Nebr., Feb. 16, 1867, Johnson Papers; H. G. Wait to Ignatius Donnelly, Minneapolis, Apr. 4, 1866, Donnelly Papers.

the administration: "Every federal officer, perhaps, is bitterly opposed to the President. Of course, [he] knows what to with them. . . . With the federal patronage of this coast in the hands of the friends of the administration, the President will unquestionably sustain himself and come out of the conflict sustained by the people."[2]

Democratic hopes were reinforced by Johnson himself. Soon after his break with Congress he had threatened to remove all officeholders opposed to his policy. Later during the "swing around the circle" he spoke with more conviction. "I believe that one set of men have enjoyed the emoluments of office long enough . . . ," said Johnson to a St. Louis audience, "and God being willing, I will kick them out. I will kick them out just as fast as I can."[3] As a result, leading western Democrats felt sure that Johnson was determined to remove every radical. So optimistic were they, in fact, that on the advice of their eastern friends, Democrats in several western states and territories prepared dossiers on possible appointees for federal positions in the West. Others traveled east to appeal directly to the president. In 1866 Cornelius Cole reported Washington, D.C., so crowded with Democratic office seekers that one could almost imagine there had been a change of administration. "The Copperheads seem to think that they have fallen heir to all the patronage . . . and the city is full of them," he wrote. "I almost feel like an interloper among them."[4]

2. F. L. Hatch to James McDougall, Marysville, Calif., Mar. 11, 1866, Johnson Papers. See also E. R. Chase to Andrew Johnson, Austin, Nev., Mar. 22, 1866, Paul Hubbs to David T. Patterson, Port Townsend, Wash. Terr., Oct. 12, 1866, both in Johnson Papers; Jared C. Brown to William Seward, Port Angeles, Wash. Terr., May 10, 1866, in LAR, Jared C. Brown File; *St. Paul Pioneer*, Sept. 28, 1865, Oct. 24, 1866; *Sonoma Democrat*, Sept. 1, 1866; *Humboldt Times*, Apr. 7, 1866; Albany (Ore.), *States Rights Democrat*, Sept. 5, 1866; *Mankato Record*, Aug. 11, 1866; San Francisco *Chronicle*, Aug. 30, 1866.

3. Quoted in Brodie, *Thaddeus Stevens*, 290.

4. William A. Richardson to J. Sterling Morton, Washington, D.C., June 13, 1866, Morton Papers; Cornelius Cole to Olive Cole, Washington, D.C., Aug. ?, 1866, Cole Papers. Democrats unable to travel to the national capital gave assurance of personal loyalty and requested office through correspondence. Space limitations preclude listing all the letters, but the more interesting in LAR include: H. Garbanati to Andrew Johnson, Central City, Colo., Aug. ?, 1868, Garbanati File; A. H. Jackson of Nebraska to Johnson, Washington, D.C., Nov. 25, 1865, Jackson File; William Conklin to William Seward, Port Angeles, Wash. Terr., Feb. 19, 1866, Jared C. Brown File; Joshua H. Gest to Johnson, Denver, Mar. 14, 1866, Gest File; Anson Potter to Johnson, Virginia City, Mont., Aug. ?, 1866, John T. Bruce File; John Titus to Johnson, Salt Lake City, Sept. 5, 1866, Amos Reed File; from the

Yet in terms of actual positions gained, many Democrats saw the rewards as too few. The president did replace certain radical office-holders in the West and Democrats did receive a share of these positions, but the number fell far short of their expectations. Those who wished to fault Johnson could, like Republicans, claim that he had disappointed them. This argument would become a major complaint of Democrats in their disillusion with the president. More astute Democrats, however, realized the limitations of manipulating the patronage system. Some of them—A. J. King of California, for example—regarded Johnson's threats as sheer bluster.[5] Because King doubted the advisability of seeking political rapport with the president, he remembered what other Democrats were forgetting in their excitement: the president did not have total control over patronage; there existed legal as well as popular restraints which limited his appointing power.

Popular opinion served as one restriction upon the executive. Arbitrary removals on a large scale would likely have an adverse effect, and the infusion of too many Democrats would irritate Republicans regardless of their stand on Reconstruction. Johnson might conceivably appoint a war Democrat with some hope of receiving senatorial confirmation, but his chances of placing a peace Democrat into public office were extremely slim. As the Bigler-Avery case in California proves, Republicans were always prepared to challenge the nomination of staunch Democrats. Johnson was to learn that such attempts posed a very real threat to his own credibility.

John M. Avery served as the assessor of internal revenue for the Fourth District of California. Among fellow Republicans he was recognized for his competence in office, but to the national administration Avery was deemed unacceptable for his radical views. As a consequence, Johnson nominated to the office John Bigler, former Democratic governor of California and reputed southern sympathizer. Armed with a commission signed by Johnson and Secretary of the

Johnson Papers: Thomas Tutt to Johnson, ?, Mont., Dec. 24, 1866; and in GRTD: California, NARG 56: John Bigler to Hugh McCulloch, Sacramento, Nov. 23, 1866; Bigler to Johnson, Sacramento, Oct. 26, 1867.

5. *Los Angeles News*, Sept. 4, Oct. 5, 1866. The best discussion of restrictions on Johnson's patronage power is found in McKitrick, *Andrew Johnson and Reconstruction*, 377–94.

Treasury Hugh McCulloch, Bigler arrived in Sacramento on October 20, 1866, demanding that Avery vacate the assessor's office and surrender all records. Avery refused, insisting that without Senate approval Bigler's appointment was not valid. Undaunted, Bigler established a second office in the same building and requested an opinion from Delos Lake, U.S. attorney for the district. Lake determined in Bigler's favor, but still Avery balked. Bigler thereupon brought suit in federal court to force Avery's removal.[6]

The Bigler-Avery case reached the U.S. Circuit Court for the Northern District of California in April, 1867, with Judge Matthew P. Deady presiding. The justice accepted Avery's reasoning that by law the president had no authority to remove him. The first Congress, however, had conceded the right of removal, determined the judge, and every president since George Washington had dismissed office-holders without seeking Senate approval. In appointing Bigler, Johnson had merely followed established precedent which now could be changed only by law. Thus Deady upheld Avery's removal and fined him court costs. For Bigler it was a technical victory and nothing more: the Senate in the meantime had rejected his nomination, even before the case was brought to court. Avery did vacate the assessor's office, but instead of Bigler it was Thomas Blankeney who assumed the duties with senatorial approval in March, 1867.[7]

Throughout the affair California Republicans, from radical to conservative, sided with Avery. Several appealed his dismissal to Lucian Curtis, revenue inspector in Washington, D.C. Congressman John Bidwell pleaded directly with the president to withdraw Bigler's nomination. Moderate Republicans were at odds over Johnson's authority

6. John Bigler to Andrew Johnson, Sacramento, Oct. 22, 1866, in GRTD: California; Delos Lake to Bigler, San Francisco, Oct. 31, 1866, in *Alta California*, Nov. 3, 1866.

7. United States *ex rel.* Bigler v. Avery (1 Deady, 204), in *Federal Cases Comprising Cases Argued and Determined in the Circuit and District Courts of the United States* (St. Paul, 1896), XXIV, 902–6; *Senate Executive Proceedings*, XV, p. 1, xxx; *Oregonian*, Apr. 5, 1867; *Oregon Herald*, Mar. 27, 1867. Deady's personal sympathy in the case lay with Avery. Several months earlier he had come out in favor of restricting the president's removal power. In his reminiscences Deady would later maintain that it was his decision in the Bigler-Avery case which hastened the enactment of the Tenure of Office Act. But since his decision was rendered on Apr. 10, 1867, a full month after the act's passage, and since Deady referred to the act itself in his argument, there can be no substance to his assertion. James Nesmith to Deady, Washington, D.C., July 14, Oct. 2, 1866, Deady Papers; Bancroft, "Life of Deady," 488–89, 513.

to remove officials, but all could agree that the replacement of Avery with Bigler was ill-advised because of his Democratic proclivities. Republicans censured Johnson for his choice, with the conservative *Chico Courant* publishing the most biting criticism: "Andrew Johnson, when you ask us to swallow John Bigler, and the bummers who will hang on his skirts and eat pap with him . . . our stomach revolts, and we can't." Editor A. W. Bishop did go on to reaffirm his support of Johnson's Reconstruction policy. But should the plan include a proliferation of Democratic officeholders in federal positions throughout the state, then Bishop would readily back the anti-Johnson Republicans.[8]

The president's ability to manipulate patronage was to some extent handicapped by the limited number of federal positions actually at his disposal. Out of 53,000 federal posts in 1866, approximately 1,700 were presidential, that is, nominated directly by the president himself and confirmed by the Senate. To cabinet officers and division directors in Washington and to heads of local offices throughout the country fell the responsibility for filling the greater majority of federal posts. While the executive certainly influenced his subordinates in their decision-making, they themselves were not immune from local pressure.[9] In the West as of September, 1867, presidential positions—

8. Aiken and Luce to Lucian Curtis, Sacramento, Nov. 25, 1866, Fred Charlton to Curtis, Sacramento, Nov. 27, 1866, John Bidwell to Andrew Johnson, Washington, D.C., Dec. 31, 1866, all in GRTD: California; *Chico Courant*, Oct. 27, 1866. See also *Marysville Appeal*, Oct. 31, 1866; and Sacramento *Bee*, Sacramento *Union*, San Francisco *Bulletin*, *Alta California*, and San Francisco *Chronicle*, Oct. 22–30, 1866 passim.

9. James Lewis Baumgardner, "Andrew Johnson and the Patronage" (Ph.D. dissertation, University of Tennessee, 1968), 9–10; Ari Hoogenboom, *Outlawing the Spoils: A History of the Civil Service Reform Movement, 1865–1883* (Urbana, Ill., 1961), 1–10. For example, Jacob Schirrver, assayer of the branch mint at Denver, made all appointments and removals locally, pending approval of the director of the mint at Washington. To please certain Republicans, Schirrver in one instance appointed William Hardin, a black Denver political figure, as weigher. Presently Hardin was accused of bigamy and Schirrver requested authorization for his release. But when Hardin in addition confessed to draft evasion during the war, public sentiment against the man grew so strong that Schirrver dismissed Hardin summarily, and without counsel from Washington. Jacob Schirrver to H. R. Linderman (director of the mint), July 21, 1873, and Linderman to Schirrver, June 30, July 29, 1873, in RBM: Appointments and Removals, Apr. 1, 1873–Feb. 17, 1879 (Ms Letterbooks, Legislative, Judicial and Fiscal Branch), NARG 104; Eugene H. Berwanger, "William J. Hardin: Colorado Spokesman for Racial Justice, 1863–1873," CM, LII (Winter, 1975), 52–65.

excluding presidential postmasterships and militarily related presidential posts—were limited to some 247 offices. These included eight territorial governors, eight territorial secretaries, twenty-four territorial judges, thirty federal marshals and attorneys, seven federal judges, thirty-eight assessors and collectors of internal revenue, three customs collectors (one each at San Francisco and Astoria, Oregon, and one for Montana and Idaho), sixty-four registers and collectors of public moneys at land offices, six surveyors general, and fifty-nine heads or superintendents of Indian agencies. In the West, then, Johnson had primarily land offices and Indian agencies at his disposal. There were only four Indian agencies east of the Mississippi River, and over half of the nation's land offices were located in the West. The president had greater exercise over appointments in the East because of the larger number of internal revenue and customs positions in that section of the country.[10]

In regard to the Post Office Department, which contained the largest number of federal employees, the direct participation of both the president and the Senate was minimal. The majority of the postmasterships in the West were nonpresidential appointments. For example, the 1867 *Register* listed 505 post offices and postmasters in Minnesota. A cross check between the 1865 and 1867 *Registers* indicates a change in 208 postmasterships during the two-year period. Up to November, 1867, according to the *Senate Executive Proceedings*, Johnson submitted only nine of these for senatorial confirmation. Thus few of the postmasterships in the state were actually at the president's disposal. Similarly in Kansas, out of the 108 changes among the 237 postmasters between 1865 and 1867, Johnson submitted only seven to the Senate. In California, fourteen of the seventy-seven changes (out of 410 post offices) went to the Senate.[11]

10. U.S. Department of Interior, *Register of Officers and Agents, Civil, Military and Naval in the Service of the United States, on the Thirtieth of September, 1867*, (Washington, D.C., 1868).

11. U.S. Department of Interior, *Register . . . 1865* (Washington, D.C., 1866), 26–32, 111–15, 170–77; *Register . . . 1867*, 343–49, 426–30, 488–95; *Senate Executive Proceedings*, XIV and XV, indices, *passim*. In Minnesota the postmasterships submitted by Johnson included St. Paul, Stillwater, Red Wing, St. Cloud, Mankato, Minneapolis, Rochester, Faribault, and Winona; in Kansas those of Leavenworth, Fort Leavenworth, Topeka, Atchison, Fort Scott, Junction City, and Lawrence; and in California, Petaluma, Columbia, Placerville, Marysville, Yreka, Sacramento, San Jose, Stockton, San Francisco, Los Angeles, Napa, Grass Valley, Chico, and Downieville. James Ford Rhodes, John and LaWanda Cox, Michael Les Benedict, and

For the dismissal of nonpresidential postmasterships, Johnson had to depend upon the postmaster general and his subordinates. As the figures indicate, their percentages of removal dropped from 40 percent or above in Minnesota and Kansas to less than 17 percent in California.

From the beginning of the patronage struggles that were to plague the postwar administration, it was the Senate which served as chief deterrent to Johnson's maneuvers. Because he had to seek Senate approval for his nominees, be they partisan or not, Johnson had no choice but to maintain a somewhat cordial relationship with the upper house or at least show a willingness to compromise difficult appointments. But even superficial cooperation and support vanished with his civil rights veto in March, 1866, and in the face of Johnson's threats Republicans in the Senate stood ready to scrutinize every nominee. Indeed, almost as soon as Johnson threatened to manipulate the patronage, the Senate began to retaliate. James Nesmith, senator from Oregon, recognized as early as May, 1866, that massive rejections would be the Senate's tactic. Responding to an office seeker among his constituency, Nesmith offered little hope for approval of his nomination. "The gate is closing," he wrote, "and the Radicals manifest a determination that no conservative man shall be confirmed no matter what his past services have been to the party or the

---

Hans Trefousse variously have made the claim that Johnson replaced between 1,283 and 1,664 postmasters in 1866 and 1867 for political reasons. The figures, taken from a House of Representatives impeachment investigation report, may be accurate, but it was the Post Office Department which made the actual removals. The figures as cited were the approximate total of all presidential appointments for the period. James Ford Rhodes, *History of the United States, from the Compromise of 1850, to the Restoration of Home Rule, 1877*, 7 vols. (New York, 1893–1906), V, 621; LaWanda and John H. Cox *Politics, Principle & Prejudice, 1865–1866: Dilemma of Reconstruction America* (New York, 1963), 107–8; Michael Les Benedict, *The Impeachment and Trial of Andrew Johnson* (New York, 1973), 47–49; Hans L. Trefousse, *Impeachment of a President: Andrew Johnson, the Blacks, and Reconstruction* (Knoxville, Tenn., 1975), 43–44. Moreover, as the case of William Byers attests, it is not always possible to determine why removals were made or resignations submitted. Byers, postmaster at Denver from Nov., 1864, to Feb., 1866, was charged with mismanagement. Postmaster General William Dennison accepted his resignation and agreed not to investigate the charges; hence post office records imply that Byers was in the wrong. Byers insisted that the department forced his resignation for political reasons; he favored statehood for Colorado while the administration opposed it. William Byers to William Dennison, Denver, Oct. 11, Nov. 16, 1865, Byers to A. N. Graveley, Denver, Oct. 11, 1865, Jan. 2, 1866, all in William Newton Byers Letterbooks, CUWC.

country." Throughout the West Republicans were assured that "the Senate has come to the rescue . . . and is refusing to confirm obnoxious appointments.[12]

The Senate's vigilance had several effects in the West: not only did it keep in office some individuals who were totally unacceptable to the administration, but it also encouraged radical Republican officeholders to hold on to their posts. Secondarily it led to increasing pettiness among Republicans. In the latter instance the Senate could not be aware of every nominee, and should western Republicans strongly oppose a given appointee, they protested to congressmen even outside their own district.[13] Often well-intentioned, these protests occasionally took the form of libel: an ambitious politican would accuse his rival, unjustly, of party disloyalty or unprincipled behavior. The *Mankato Record* reported with disbelief the Senate's rejection of Daniel Cameron as collector of internal revenue in Minnesota's First District. Since Cameron was "an out and out Republican, not a Johnson man," he should easily have received confirmation. Cameron's failure to secure the appointment was due, claimed the editor, to slander leveled by Republican enemies at home. In view of this kind of threat, lest any statement be construed against him, the aspiring officeholder might well decide to say as little as possible while awaiting confirmation. Andrew Faulk, nominated for governor of Dakota Territory, made remarks praising Johnson in his opening address to the territorial legislature. Surprised, a personal friend urged Faulk to withhold, pending confirmation, further comment on national affairs. He understood the Faulk inclined toward conservatism

12. James Nesmith to L. D. Campbell, Washington, D.C., May 20, 1866, Nesmith Papers; *St. Paul Pioneer*, May 6, 1866; *Humboldt Times*, Apr. 7, 12, 1866; San Francisco *Chronicle*, May 19, 1866; *Idaho World*, May 19, 1866; *Mankato Record*, Aug. 11, 1866.

13. For example, see W. S. Gross to Alexander Ramsey, Red Wing, Minn., Dec. 1, 1866, in SNF, 39 Cong., W. W. DeKay File, NARG 46; C. C. Webster to Ignatius Donnelly, Red Wing, Dec. 5, 1866, Donnelly Papers; Alexander Johnson to Alexander Cummings, Washington, D.C., Nov. 20, 1866, in LAR, J. R. Hood File; Cornelius Cole to Elihu Washburne, San Francisco, Feb. 14, 1866, John A. Clark to Washburne, Santa Fe, Oct. ?, Dec. 8, 1866, Willard Teller to Washburne, Central City, Colo., Nov. 2, 1867, all in Washburne Papers; Robert Graham to Benjamin Wade, Atchison, Kans., Mar. 14, 1867, Benjamin Franklin Wade Papers, LC; S. Weldy to Wade, Boise, Dec. 21, 1867, in SNF, 40 Cong., R. H. Lindsay File, NARG 46.

but cautioned that too many expressions favoring the president might "injure your prospects before a radical senate."[14]

On the other hand, a known anti-Johnson or pro-radical viewpoint could be an asset in obtaining support in the upper house. Frank Hall of Colorado and David Ballard of Idaho retained their posts, but only by dint of the Senate's refusal to confirm their more conservative replacements. Hall had been appointed secretary of Colorado Territory in February, 1866, at the urging of Governor Alexander Cummings. Shortly it became apparent that the governor and his secretary were not politically compatible. Hall favored statehood, Cummings opposed it. The governor supported Johnsonian Reconstruction, Hall became a radical after Johnson's veto of the Colorado statehood bill in 1866. Cummings had come directly from Pennsylvania to assume his gubernatorial duties, and most Coloradans considered him an outsider still. Hall had lived in Colorado prior to his appointment and acquired many personal and political friends in the territory. With the territorial election for delegate to Congress in late summer of 1866, open conflict erupted between the two officials. Immediately following the voting and while Cummings was away from the capital, Hall convened the board of canvassers, which declared the pro-statehood candidate elected. The governor in his turn rejected the decision and awarded a certificate of election to the conservative candidate. Further, Cummings began a campaign with Secretary Seward to have Hall removed. In response Hall's supporters collaborated with friends in the Senate to keep their secretary in office. Between September, 1866, and April, 1867, the administration attempted to displace Hall by submitting four different nominations for secretary to Colorado Territory; each was rejected. From the nation's capital Assistant Secretary of the Treasury E. W. Chandler encouraged Hall to remain true "to the principle of your party in the Territory & I will take care of your interest in Washington." Hall was to retain his position throughout the entire Johnson administration, but with no further concessions. While it was usual for federal officers in the West to be granted leaves of absence, none was ever awarded to Hall. Rejecting his every request, Seward advised that Hall consider resigning if other matters were so pressing as to necessitate his absence from

14. *Mankato Record*, Mar. 2, 1867; Henry Johnson to Andrew J. Faulk, Muncy, Pa., Dec. 20, 1866, Faulk Papers.

Colorado. But the secretary's tenacity served him well. Hall retained his position until 1874 and thereafter dedicated his efforts primarily to the preparation of a multivolume history of Colorado, an achievement highly respected for its time.[15]

David Ballard was governor of Idaho Territory. A Republican from Oregon, Ballard adopted a moderate approach to Reconstruction; at least he spoke out strongly neither for Johnson nor for the radicals. Even so his presence in the governor's chair was an irritation to Edward Holbrook, avid Democrat and southern sympathizer, who served as Idaho's delegate to Congress. Holbrook accordingly undertook a campaign to oust Ballard and to replace the Republican governor with someone more politically compatible. To the State Department Holbrook fired repeated charges of Ballard's inefficiency in office; to the Interior Department he protested Ballard's mishandling of Indian affairs. On account of both, the delegate demanded the governor's removal. Johnson responded by sending Ballard a notice of dismissal in January, 1867. But Ballard gamely remained in office, watching as the Senate denied confirmation to one replacement and then another. With the passage of the Tenure of Office Act in March, 1867, the Senate also adopted a policy of filling only existing vacancies and confirming no changes for others. Because Ballard continued to carry out his gubernatorial duties, his office was not considered vacant.

Holbrook redoubled his efforts. He obtained a statement from the Bureau of Claims verifying that the governorship of Idaho was indeed vacant: Ballard had been removed in January and thus was not covered by the Tenure Act. Encouraged by this opinion, Johnson decided to try once again, and he submitted the name of a third nominee. Oregon's Republican senators retaliated with a determined campaign to keep Ballard in office. Armed with an opinion from the attorney general's office, they persuaded the Senate that the Idaho governorship was not "vacant" merely because Johnson had dismissed Ballard,

15. Frank Hall to his father, Golden, Colo., Nov. 17, 1866, Hall to his mother, Central City, Colo., Sept. 9, 1867, both in Frank Hall Papers, CSHS; John Evans to Benjamin Wade, Denver, July 2, 1867, Wade Papers; Jerome Chaffee to Zachariah Chandler, Central City, Sept. 24, 1866, Zachariah Chandler Papers, LC; Alexander Cummings to William Seward, Denver, Jan. 25, 29, Sept. 28, 1866, in LAR, Frank Hall and H. P. Bennett Files; Atchison *Free Press*, Oct. 3, 1866; *Senate Executive Proceedings*, XV, p. 2, 491, 633; Earl S. Pomeroy, *The Territories and the United States, 1861–1890: Studies in Colonial Administration* (Seattle, 1969), 125.

and they disproved all of Holbrook's charges against the governor. Faced with irrefutable evidence of Ballard's integrity, Johnson reinstated him and authorized compensation once again; Ballard had received no salary for eight months.[16]

In both Hall's and Ballard's cases Johnson failed in his efforts to secure a new appointee because friends in the Senate or in other governmental agencies rose to the incumbents' defense and successfully frustrated the administrative ploy. Hall's position was strengthened by his known radical stand, Ballard's by suspicion of Holbrook's motives to secure his removal. In neither case do extant sources imply that Hall and Ballard actively challenged their dismissal or refused to turn over their offices to their Johnson-appointed successors. Rather, they merely continued to perform their official duties while the Senate steadfastly worked to impede efforts aimed at their removal. In bowing to the Senate's refusal to confirm the replacements for Hall and Ballard, Johnson was in the end forced to acknowledge the legal restraint which the upper house held on him.

Bolstered by the fact that the Senate would not sanction staunch Democrats, other western Republicans dared resist their own dismissal outright. In each case they insisted that a successor could not assume office without actual senatorial confirmation. This was a new tactic; prior to Johnson's administration, it had been the usual practice for officeholders to relinquish their posts once the president specified a new appointee. The resisters did not, for the most part, dispute Johnson's authority to remove them; they simply remained on the scene to keep Democrats from assuming federal positions until such time as the Senate saw fit to make a change. The court decision in the Bigler-Avery controversy, of course, rejected the contention of these Republican officeholders. But the passage of the Tenure of Office Act did offer protection: now they could not be dismissed without Senate approval. Besides Avery, other Republicans refusing to yield included Charles Dorsey, register at the land office at Brown-

16. Edward Holbrook to William Seward, Washington, D.C., June 17, 1867, Bureau of Claims statement dated Apr. 30, 1867, both in TP: Idaho; Holbrook to Andrew Johnson, Washington, D.C., Nov. 26, 1866, in LAR, John Murphy File; "Resolutions of the Idaho Legislature, December 29, 1866," in SNF, 40 Cong., John Cummings File, NARG 46; *Idaho Statesman*, Aug. 17, 1867; *Idaho World*, Sept. 21, 1867; Merle W. Wells, "David W. Ballard, Governor of Idaho, 1866–1870," OHQ, LIV (Mar., 1953), 16–22. Donaldson, *Idaho*, 245–47, gives an inaccurate account of the Holbrook-Ballard controversy.

ville, Nebraska; William L. Adams, collector of customs at Astoria, Oregon; and William Pickering, governor of Washington Territory.[17] Of the three, it was Pickering whose case became the most celebrated, for his political adversaries publicly slandered his name and accused him of graft as they campaigned for his removal.

Pickering had been named to the executive chair in Washington Territory by Lincoln in 1862, and Johnson routinely renewed the appointment in 1865. With the break between Johnson and Congress in 1866, Pickering's radical leanings became evident and his politics less tolerable to the central administration. Had he kept silent, the governor might have retained his office. But he chose to criticize Johnson openly and thus provide Democrats with substantive reason to demand his removal. Through James Nesmith they informed the federal administration that Pickering had denounced the president as a "dictator," a "Copperhead," a "traitor," and "no better than Jefferson Davis." In addition, Pickering had committed an indiscretion in recommending that a contract for the publication of federal laws be granted to the *Pacific Tribune*: it so happened that he was owner of the *Tribune*. For his veto of a bill giving the territorial government more control over local shipping on Puget Sound, Democrats charged that Pickering had accepted bribes from shipowners. To these accusations Nesmith added "incompetence" and "alcoholism." Pickering was "a man of intemperate habits," wrote Nesmith, as well as "an incompetent old creature" and a "drunken old imbecile." Hesitating no further, the senator recommended that Pickering be replaced by Democrat George E. Cole—"a gentleman of capacity and integrity, and one of our best *friends.*" Johnson acceded to Nesmith's wishes, but when Cole attempted to assume the governorship, Pickering balked: he refused to relinquish his office on the pretext that Cole had not yet been confirmed. Pickering's friends in the Senate went on expressly to deny Cole's approval and, later, even a second Johnson appointee. Ultimately, however, a moderate Republican was confirmed for the post, in April, 1867, when it became apparent that Pickering lacked broad Republican support in the territory.[18]

17. See Morton and Watkins, *Nebraska,* I, 538; William L. Adams to David W. Craig, Astoria, Ore., Jan. 6, 1867, David Watson Craig Papers, OHS; W. W. Parker to Elwood Evans, Astoria, Mar. 2, 1867, Elwood Evans Papers, YWA.

18. James Nesmith to Andrew Johnson, to William Seward, to Alexander Ran-

Just as individual Republicans in the West resisted their displacement from office, the Senate in Washington held firm, steadily impeding Johnson's efforts to manipulate the patronage. Overall, its record was impressive. From December, 1865, to July, 1866, the Senate approved 95 percent, 146 of 154, of the nominees for positions in the West. This number compares with an 86 percent approval for the rest of the nation during the same period. Relations between the chief executive and the legislature were fairly smooth during these early months of the Johnson presidency, and the upper house was amenable to most of the president's appointments. With the next session of Congress, once Johnson had threatened to remove Republicans disagreeing with his policy, the Senate clearly began to cast a more watchful eye on nominations brought for consideration. The change was dramatic. Between December, 1866, and November, 1867, Johnson was able to secure confirmations for only 57 percent of his western nominees, or 120 of 209 put forward. Still, this was above the 45 percent confirmed for eastern appointees. Johnson's poorest record in the West came after February, 1868, to the close of his term in 1869; in that year the Senate confirmed 62 of 133 nominations, or 47 percent. At this point senators were unwilling to act on many patronage appointments. Of the seventy-one names that went unconfirmed, they declined action on forty-five rather than reject so many appointees outright.[19]

Determined and successful as the Senate was in its course, the averages show that the national legislators mustered somewhat less force in blocking Johnson's nominees in the West than in the East.

---

dall, all College Hill, Ohio, Aug. 21, 1866, George L. Curry and others to Johnson, New York, Sept. 2, 1866, all in LAR, George Cole File; S. D. Durgin to ———, Olympia, Wash. Terr., Sept. 22, 1866, Thornton F. McElroy to Nesmith, Olympia, Sept. 9, 23, 1866, and summary of charges against Pickering, n.d., all in LAR, William Pickering File; Durgin to William Miller, Olympia, Jan. 14, 1867, McElroy to Miller, Olympia, Jan. 13, 1867, both in Miller Papers; *Vancouver Register,* Jan. 19, 1867; *Senate Executive Proceedings,* XIV, p. 1, iccclxxxviii, XV, p. 2, 761; Mercedes S. Gleason, "The Territorial Governors of the State of Washington, 1853–1889" (M.A. thesis, University of Washington, 1955), 42–43.

19. These figures are compiled from the indices of the *Senate Executive Proceedings,* XIV, XV, XVI. Lists of rejections can also be found in SNF, 39 and 40 Cong. For the non-West the number of nominations and confirmations were, Dec., 1865, to July, 1866—888 nominations, 764 confirmations; Dec., 1866, to Nov. 1867—1,828 nominations, 834 confirmations; Feb., 1868, to Mar., 1869—422 nominations, 180 confirmations (44 percent).

As indicated, the upper house was unable to retain his office for every western Republican, and in a number of instances senators even confirmed Johnson's first nominee, a move implying that they had no argument with his choice. Several factors contributed to Johnson's relative success in the West. For one, many eastern Republicans who might otherwise have sought nomination were reluctant to serve under President Johnson and thereby give the impression of endorsing his policy. As a result, there was less than the usual competition among easterners for federal positions in the West, and these jobs went to western residents.[20] In the main, those selected were Union veterans, moderate or conservative Republicans, and Unionists—groups less "suspect" than Democrats. While both Johnson and the Senate were likely to have firsthand information on potential officeholders from the East, they had less acquaintance with nominees from the West. Here, both had to rely on outside advice, and Johnson had the clear advantage. His informants on western patronage matters were, for the most part, knowledgeable and judicious in their recommendations and able to suggest appointees who met the approval of both the executive and the Senate.

Johnson's advisers on patronage in the West fell into two groups—Democrats and Republican-Unionists. For Idaho and California he relied on Democrats, and here he ran into trouble. The Senate scrutinized nominees for these two areas very closely, often requiring that the president offer two or even three names for a single position before finally granting approval. For the postmastership at Boise, presidential only as of 1867, the Senate blithely rejected the first five nominees. The upper house also denied three successive nominees for the Idaho territorial governorship in one year, with the result that the incumbent was able to carry out his duties during the entire Johnson administration. In California rejection occurred most repeatedly in land office posts. Five men nominated as register at Marysville and three at Visalia failed to secure confirmation. Johnson had to submit a second nomination for the receiverships of public moneys at Marysville, Stockton, and Sacramento, and even a third for the Humboldt office.[21]

The president's lack of success in Idaho was most likely due to the

20. Pomeroy, *Territories*, 76.
21. *Senate Executive Proceedings*, XV and XVI, indices.

partisan attitude of Edward Holbrook. Having been highly recommended to Johnson as *"the only man left in Congress, from our coast, who is your friend,"* Holbrook was given a dominant voice in the selection of nominees for federal positions in the territory. Nonetheless, Holbrook was a dismal failure as an adviser on patronage matters. The Senate confirmed only seven of his twenty-eight recommended changes for Idaho between December, 1866, and November, 1867. Holbrook was so strongly Democratic that any appointee for Idaho was immediately suspect. Nor was Holbrook's position as adviser enhanced by a rumor that he had taken an oath "to do all that lay in his power to have every Union son of a b—h in the territory removed from office."[22]

In California Johnson was unable to find any one person upon whom he could rely for advice, and the rate of confirmations was only slightly more favorable. Although James McDougall, a Democrat fully loyal to the president, held his Senate seat until March, 1867, he appears to have had little influence in patronage decisions. Johnson did offer Cornelius Cole a major voice in the selection of federal appointees on the West coast, but Cole rejected the overture. As a result, Johnson accepted counsel from numerous Californians, among them well-known Democrats. The confirmation rate for California held at 50 percent between December, 1866, and November, 1867, still somewhat below the rate for most western states and territories.[23]

Where Johnson solicited advice from Republican-Unionists, response from the Senate was more positive: between two-thirds and three-fourths of these nominees received senatorial confirmation. Here there are no instances of repeated rejections for the same position as in Idaho and California.[24] Making appointments in Kansas,

22. James Nesmith to Andrew Johnson, Washington, D.C., Mar. 4, 1867, in LAR, Edward Holbrook File; *Idaho World*, Jan. 8, 1867; *Senate Executive Proceedings*, XV, index.

23. John Bigler to Andrew Johnson, Sacramento, Oct. 26, 1867, in GRTD: California; M. L. Whiting to Johnson, San Francisco, Aug. 9, 1866, J. McCormick to Johnson, San Francisco, Apr. 21, 1866, A. D. Rock to Johnson, San Francisco, Sept. 10, 1866, S. B. Axtell and others to Johnson, San Francisco, Oct. 18, 1866, all in Johnson Papers; *Senate Executive Proceedings*, XIV, index.

24. This analysis is based on a study of the *Senate Executive Proceedings* indices, which list in alphabetical order the nominee, the position for which he was designated, and the action taken. The reason for each nomination, i.e. reappointment, death, or removal of incumbent, etc. is found in the body of the *Proceedings*.

for example, Johnson sought counsel from Thomas Ewing, Jr. Formerly chief justice of the Kansas Supreme Court, Ewing moved to Washington in 1865 to seek his livelihood as lawyer and lobbyist. Because of his conservative stand on Reconstruction and his access to official Washington through his father, Thomas Ewing, Sr., former U.S. senator and cabinet officer, the younger Ewing soon found himself unofficial confidant to President Johnson. Ewing, Jr., received his information about western politics through H. B. Denman, a nephew living in Omaha, and Edmund G. Ross, Lane's replacement in the Senate. The president was undoubtedly happy to have a Kansas ally in Ewing, Jr., for Johnson placed little trust in Senator Pomeroy, and Ross was a reputed radical. It may have suited Ross, too, inasmuch as it allowed him a voice in Kansas patronage matters without his appearing too close to the president.[25] Between December, 1866, and November, 1867, Johnson was relatively successful with his Kansas nominees: the Senate confirmed fourteen of twenty-one, or two-thirds. Ross was in part responsible. For his recommendations, confided Ross to Ewing, Jr., he had chosen only individuals to whom Senator Pomeroy was indebted for past service or in whom Pomeroy could find no objection.[26]

In Minnesota control of the patronage lay with Senator Daniel Norton, in Oregon with Senator James W. Nesmith. Both men were Democrats but had been elected by Union-Republican and war Democrat coalitions in their respective legislatures. Both sustained Johnson's Reconstruction policy from its inception, a stand for which they faced criticism at home. Aside from their conservative stand on Reconstruction, both men were regarded as exemplary senators in advancing the interest of their states.[27] Of the two, less is known

25. H. B. Denman to Thomas Ewing, Jr., Omaha, Dec. 7, 1866, Edmund G. Ross to Ewing, Jr., Lawrence, Kans., May 31, 1867, both in Thomas E. Ewing Family Papers, LC; Ewing, Jr., to Andrew Johnson, Philadelphia, May 3, 1867, in LAR, Thomas Ewing, Jr., File. See also Denman to John Sherman, Omaha, Dec. 7, 1866, Sherman Papers.

26. *Senate Executive Proceedings*, XV, index; Edmund G. Ross to Thomas Ewing, Jr., Lawrence, Kans., May 31, 1867, Ewing Family Papers.

27. James Nesmith to Matthew P. Deady, College Hill, Ohio, Oct. 16, 1865, Deady to C. H. Crane, Portland, Ore., Apr. 14, 1866, both in Deady Papers; Daniel Norton to William King, Washington, D.C., Mar. 7, 1866, William Smith King Papers, MnHS; John Sonier to Alexander Ramsey, St. Paul, Jan. 10, 1865, Ramsey Papers; David Ballard to George Drew, Boise, June 30, 1866, David W. Ballard Papers, YWA; Martin Ridge, *Ignatius Donnelly: The Portrait of a Politician* (Chicago, 1962), 103.

of Norton's patronage activities because few of his personal papers have come to light. The papers of Ignatius Donnelly and Alexander Ramsey, however, do reflect something of Norton's side. Numerous Republicans wrote to complain to Donnelly about their dismissal from office; almost without exception they blamed their fate on Daniel Norton.[28] The bulk of these letters indicate that Norton was active and fairly successful in replacing nonpresidential appointees—if he were, indeed, the one responsible for all changes. Considering that Congressmen Donnelly and William Windom and Senator Ramsey of Minnesota were all working to defeat Norton's nominees, his accomplishments through Johnson are all the more noteworthy. At least during the 1866–67 session the Senate confirmed fifteen of the twenty-two individuals slated for presidential appointments in Minnesota.[29]

As for Oregon, Nesmith's contemporaries recognized the senator's dominance in patronage appointments for the whole of the Pacific Northwest. So powerful was he that he remained influential even after his retirement from the Senate in 1867. For example, in 1866 Idaho Democrats seeking to replace their territorial secretary assured Johnson that their candidate would "meet with approval of Nesmith." William Wallace, first governor of Idaho Territory, unsuccessful at securing a second term in 1866, could only write, "Defeated again, I am satisfied I am indebted to Nesmith for this result." In 1868 William L. Adams asked the president to delay an appointment decision until he had heard from Nesmith.[30] In recommending nominees to the president, Nesmith typically suggested men who favored Johnson's program and who were more moderate than extremist. During the summer of 1866 he requested from Matthew P. Deady

28. See especially Donnelly Papers, Mar., 1866–Feb., 1867 *passim*.

29. *Senate Executive Proceedings*, XV, index. William James Ryland, "Alexander Ramsey: A Study of a Frontier Politician and the Transition of Minnesota from a Territory to a State" (Ph.D. dissertation, Yale University, 1930), 356–57, asserts that Senator Ramsey controlled the patronage in Minnesota and that the Senate rejected every Norton appointee. Ryland's assumption is undocumented and contrary to all evidence I have been able to assemble.

30. G. Collier Robbins and others to Andrew Johnson, Owyhee County, Idaho, June 26, 1866, in LAR, Gilmore Hays File; William H. Wallace to his son, Washington, D.C., Dec. 5, 1866, William Henson Wallace Papers, ISHS; W. L. Adams to Johnson, Washington, D.C., July 9, 1868, in LAR, Adams File. For additional evidence see James Nesmith to Thornton McElroy, Rickreall, Ore., Aug. 25, 1867, Thornton F. McElroy Family Papers, UWa; Nesmith to Johnson, Salem, Ore., Aug. 18, 1867, and Rickreall, Oct. 13, 1868, both in Johnson Papers.

possibilities for federal marshal for Oregon. "I will have any man appointed whom you may recommend," Nesmith assured Deady, "*provided* always that he is a supporter of the President's policy, and is not in sympathy with what is known as the Radicals. I have had the last appointment of that kind made that I intend to. Neither will I recommend any man who was opposed to the prosecution of the war. If you can recommend a man who comes between these extremes, I will take his case into consideration." Once they had Nesmith's backing, nominees from the Pacific Northwest still faced stiff opposition from George Williams, Nesmith's more radically inclined colleague from Oregon, but the conservative senator's self-imposed qualifications for candidates guaranteed at least moderate success. Between December, 1866, and November, 1867, the Senate confirmed fifteen of the twenty-four appointments submitted for Oregon and Washington Territory.[31]

For the West the president realized the greatest percentage of confirmations in the Southwest and in Dakota Territory. During the months in which rejections ran high, December, 1866, to November, 1867, the Senate approved every nomination for Dakota and all but one of the thirteen submitted for New Mexico and Arizona territories.[32] In part the president could thank J. Francisco Chaves in New Mexico's case and Walter Burleigh for Dakota; the two men were Republican delegates from their respective territories to Congress. Chaves had voiced approval of Johnsonian Reconstruction and in return received patronage favors. So influential was he that even Allen Bradford, Colorado Territory's delegate, enlisted Chaves's aid in seeking the governorship of Colorado for himself. Similarly, it was to Chaves that Congressman J. Newton Pettis of Pennsylvania turned when he was about to retire from the House of Representatives in 1869; he wished Chaves to intercede with Johnson in his bid for a territorial judgeship in New Mexico.[33]

While Burleigh was both personal friend to Johnson and advocate of his policy, he was careful at the same time to maintain a personal

31. James Nesmith to Matthew P. Deady, Washington, D.C., July 6, 1866, and Rickreall, Ore., June 22, 1868, both in Deady Papers; *Senate Executive Proceedings*, XV, index.

32. *Senate Executive Proceedings*, XV, index.

33. J. Francisco Chaves to Andrew Johnson, Washington, D.C., Dec. 29, 1866, in TP: New Mexico; Chaves to Johnson, Washington, D.C., Mar. 25, 1867, in LAR, Allen Bradford File; Pomeroy, *Territories*, 84–85.

rapport with radicals in Congress. From this vantage point he could easily render any opposition from Dakota ineffective. In a key move Burleigh was able to persuade Johnson to dismiss Governor Newton Edmunds in 1866 and replace him with his own father-in-law, Andrew J. Faulk. With Faulk directing appointments in the territory and Burleigh prevailing in the nation's capital, the Edmunds faction soon found itself squeezed out and turning to Congress for help. One Edmunds partisan, Jacob Branch, made a direct appeal to Benjamin Wade, chairman of the Senate Committee on Territories. Seeking to interject the issue of Reconstruction into his attempt to break Burleigh's control, Branch argued that Burleigh had misrepresented Dakotans by labeling them "conservative." There was indeed a large radical faction in the territory, and in order that it might have a chance to surface, Branch pleaded with Wade to reject Burleigh's nominees and demand the appointment of radicals. Branch's suggestion evidently came to naught, for Burleigh and Faulk were able to keep a tight rein on Dakota politics throughout the Johnson administration.[34]

What effect did Johnson's western appointments have on federal administration of the West? Both contemporaries and later historians of the period have looked carefully at the impact of Johnson's patronage policy. With bitterness Democrats and Republicans alike charged in the late 1860s that the struggle had produced a wave of corruption. Many Republicans came to believe that all who accepted appointments from Johnson were disloyal to the party. In their view, new appointees were therefore often unqualified and assumed office only for personal gain. Democrats in turn blamed the Tenure of Office Act; under its provisions dishonest officeholders had open license to "rape the public till." Unfortunately there was enough graft to give credence to such ideas. Still, considering the total number of federal employees, corrupt officials were in the minority in the later 1860s.[35]

In his book on territorial administration, historian Earl Pomeroy attests to a general decline in governmental efficiency during the

34. Walter Burleigh to Andrew Johnson, Washington, D.C., Apr. 16, 1866, in LAR, Andrew J. Faulk File; Jacob Branch to Benjamin Wade, Yankton, Dakota, Nov. 15, 1866, Wade Papers; Lamar, *Dakota Territory*, 110–12; George W. Kingsbury, *History of Dakota Territory*, 5 vols. (Chicago, 1915), I, 435.

35. *Oregonian*, Dec. 30, 1867; *Boise* (Idaho) *Democrat*, Mar. 27, 1869.

Johnson administration. The responsibility, he believes, lay with territorial policies espoused by radicals in Washington, D.C. But cases that come readily to mind do not bear out his supposition. Because Coloradans disliked Alexander Cummings for his opposition to statehoood and leveled every charge imaginable against him does not prove that he was an inefficient governor. Indeed, on the statehood question Cummings had a firmer grasp of the situation than did his pro-statehood enemies. Unfortunately, the major source for Cummings's thought and actions is Frank Hall's *History of Colorado*, a work certainly not free from bias. David Ballard in Idaho, while disliked by more vocal Democrats, was well regarded by Democrats generally. During Holbrook's attempts to remove Ballard, it was James O'Meara of the *Idaho World*, one of the most anti-Republican editors in the West, who spoke out in Ballard's defense. To Idaho Democrats, Ballard was not totally acceptable as a Republican in the governorship, but they had to admit that he handled the responsibilities of his office more adeptly than had either of his two predecessors. W. F. M. Arny of New Mexico provides yet another example. Dismissed as territorial secretary in December, 1865, Arny patiently and without malice carried out the duties of office until the arrival of his successor in July, 1867.[36] Similar cases of good will and selfless devotion may be cited throughout the West. Given the lack of firm direction from the nation's capital during the turbulent months from 1866 to 1868 and the constant threat to job security for those inclined to radicalism, territorial officials in fact gave an extremely creditable performance.

In one sense the territories derived benefit from Johnson. Despite the antagonism surrounding removals from office, Johnson chose to appoint more inhabitants from within the territories themselves than had any previous president.[37] Such deference pleased westerners, for they had long disliked eastern politicians being imposed as their leadership from Washington, D.C. In part the change in policy was due to recommendations by Johnson's western advisers, who were cognizant of the electorate's feelings and whose own purposes it served to appoint local residents. Of course, westerners had better access

36. Pomeroy, *Territories*, 111; *Idaho World*, Sept. 21, 1867; W. F. M. Arny to Andrew Johnson, Santa Fe, July 18, 1867, in TP: New Mexico.
37. Pomeroy, *Territories*, 76.

to appointment because fewer eastern Republicans were willing to serve under the president.

The patronage situation in Nebraska was particularly delicate and revealed in microcosm the forces involved in the national picture— Democratic pressure upon the president, Democratic–conservative Republican rivalry for jobs, and the public and legal restraints placed on Johnson. On the one hand, it is easy to conclude that Johnson handled the Nebraska situation ineptly by failing to remove radical officeholders on the eve of an important election when he might have done so. On the other, his failure to act may have been the only feasible choice. Unlike other western areas where Johnson had limited input on patronage affairs, he appeared willing to listen to all sides in Nebraska. As a result, he received advice from different and not necessarily compatible groups. These included Democrats within and outside of the territory, conservative Republicans in Ne-braska, and H. B. Denman, who kept Ewing Jr. informed about the radical proclivities of certain Republicans in the territory. Further complicating the picture was Nebraska's appeal for statehood, achieved over executive opposition in 1867, with each different political fac-tion seeking to control the new state. Democrats, with few territorial offices to their credit, hoped to realize their ambition through whole-sale replacement of Republican officeholders. They seemed not to comprehend that Johnson's object was to preserve presidential Re-construction rather than to revitalize the Democratic party.[38]

In 1864 Congress had passed enabling acts for Nevada, Colorado, and Nebraska. Nevada achieved statehood almost immediately, while Coloradans did not approve a state constitution until 1865. At the urging of Republicans, Nebraskans held a constitutional convention in 1864, but the convention adjourned without drafting a constitution when a majority of delegates were found to be against statehood at that time. Republicans were unwilling to accept the setback. When the territorial legislature met in early 1866, Republican governor Alvin Saunders chose a different ploy: he persuaded lawmakers that a constitutional convention was unnecessary. The legislators them-

38. Hugh McCulloch to Samuel J. Tilden, Oct. 22, 1866, in John Bigelow (ed.), *The Letters and Literary Memorials of Samuel J. Tilden*, 2 vols. (New York, 1908), I, 205–6.

selves could write a constitution, he said, and submit it for popular approval. The solution met ready acceptance; upon the document's completion the legislature ordered a referendum on the constitution and the election of the proposed state's executive department, both to be held on June 2, 1866.[39] Democrats previously disinclined toward statehood now decided against further opposition. The close division between the two major parties in the territory stimulated Democratic hopes that they might gain control of the inchoate state.[40] At any rate, both parties began preparing for the election in June, a contest whose outcome would determine Nebraska's executive officers and the fate of the proposed constitution as well.

The Johnson administration was apparently perplexed that Republicans in Nebraska had taken no public stand in the quarrel between Congress and the president; accordingly Johnson sought to learn more about Republican attitudes in the territory. He turned to Herman H. Heath—Democrat before the war, recently discharged Union general, and sometime editor of the *Nebraska Republican.* Through available newspaper clippings, correspondence with other Nebraskans, and by his own statement, Heath informed the administration that every major officeholder in Nebraska, with the notable exception of territorial secretary Algernon S. Paddock, was active in support of the radical cause. As proof Heath cited a pro-Johnson meeting called in Omaha which not a single territorial official bothered to attend. Perhaps it mattered not that Heath himself, without consulting the officeholders, had dreamed up the event and that the principal speaker was George Francis Train, a well-to-do Washington eccentric who let it be known that he had journeyed to Nebraska Territory to further Johnson's policy and thereby receive an appointment for himself. In addition, leading territorial Republicans spurned Heath's request that they pass a pro-Johnson resolution at their April, 1866, convention at Plattsmouth. Instead, they ignored the sugges-

39. Albert Watkins, "How Nebraska Was Brought into the Union," NSHSP, XVIII (1917), 390–97; Wallace Brown, "George L. Miller and the Struggle over Nebraska Statehood," NH, XLI (Dec. 1960), 301–4.

40. George Miller to J. Sterling Morton, Omaha, Sept. 30, 1865, Morton Papers; H. D. Hathaway to Samuel Maxwell, Omaha, Jan. 22, 1866, J. W. Marshall to Maxwell, Plattsmouth, Nebr., Jan. 26, 1866, both in Maxwell Papers; J. D. Brown to Samuel M. Chapman, Plattsmouth, Feb. 5, 1866, Samuel M. Chapman Papers, NSHS.

tion and, to Heath's further dismay, chose for the election in June a slate which was undeniably hostile to the president. "Silence proved their [radical] convictions," surmised Heath knowingly, "and their nominations established their opposition." The chief offenders, in his view, were Governor Saunders and E. B. Taylor, northern superintendent of Indian affairs. Remove these two and their followers, encouraged Heath, and Nebraska would be made a loyal state.[41]

If Republicans showed no desire to cater to the administration, Democrats seized opportunity where they saw it. They used their convention, called to nominate a slate for the June election, as a means of enticing presidential favor. Meeting in Nebraska City on April 19, they passed resolutions endorsing Johnsonian Reconstruction and condemning Nebraska Republicans for their radicalism. Quickly J. Sterling Morton and George Miller, leading Democrats, sent copies of the platform, along with assurances of personal loyalty, both to the president directly and to his intermediaries. On the surface this action seemed innocent enough, but Morton had a motive; he wished to secure control of federal patronage in Nebraska. As he confided to his diary, "We propose to carry on war against officials."[42]

Election results in June confirmed the even split between Democrats and Republicans in the territory. The electorate approved the constitution by a majority of 100 votes and chose David Butler, Republican candidate for governor, over Morton, Democratic candidate, by a mere 109 votes. Angry Democrats contested the results, charging that Republicans had obtained their victory by fraud. According to Democratic calculations, the results should have more accurately shown a defeat for the constitution and Morton's election to the governorship. Republicans paid no heed. Instead they pushed for a dual election for October 9, 1866, at which time the people would choose a delegate to Congress and select a territorial legislature

41. Herman H. Heath to Edmund Cooper, Washington, D.C., May 12, 1866, J. Patrick to Heath, Omaha, May 5, 1866, Exhibits A through E attached to Heath's letter, all in TP: Nebraska.

42. J. Sterling Morton Diary, Apr. 15, 16, 19, 1866, Morton Papers; Morton to Andrew Johnson, and Morton to "Acona" for forwarding to the president, both Omaha, Apr. 26, 1866, both in Johnson Papers; *Nebraska Advertiser*, Apr. 26, 1866; Morton and Watkins, *Nebraska*, I, 520.

should Nebraska fail to be admitted, and a congressman and a state legislature in case statehood were granted. The state legislature in turn would elect two U.S. senators.[43]

Deploring the results of the June election and afraid of another radical victory, Democrats and conservative Republicans turned to each other resignedly. Heath made the initial overture when he confessed his Democratic leanings to Morton and proposed unification of the groups in order to "divest the patronage . . . from the opponents to the friends of Mr. Johnson." A meeting in July achieved little, and as a result conservative Republicans and Democrats each sent their own delegations to the National Union convention—Heath and Train for the conservatives, Morton and Miller for the Democrats. It was not until the next month that the two groups arrived at a semblance of unity. Conservatives and Democrats both convened in Plattsmouth on September 11, 1866, in the same building but on different floors. Committees from each group met to approve a platform and a common slate for the October election. The offices were parceled out equitably. Conservatives agreed that Morton should be the candidate for delegate to Congress and Democrats accepted Algernon Paddock as candidate for congressman.[44]

In their effort to ensure victory at the polls, conservatives and Democrats failed to make an agreement about distribution of the patronage; each group labored instead in its own behalf. For the Democrats, Morton worked out a plan to present Johnson with a list of nominees and urge their appointment after Congress's adjournment in July. Morton and Miller also stopped in Washington on their way to the Philadelphia convention. There they were introduced to Johnson and exhorted the president to remove Nebraska radicals from

43. Thomas Kennard to Andrew Johnson, Omaha, July 1, 1866, Thomas Perkins Kennard Papers, NSHS; James R. Porter to J. Sterling Morton, Plattsmouth, Nebr., June 11, 28, 1866, Morton Papers; Alvin Saunders to Johnson, Omaha, July 3, 1866, James M. Woolworth to Johnson, Omaha, July 30, 1866, both in TP: Nebraska; *This Pamphlet is True!! It is a History of the Manner in which Nebraska became a State, Elected its State Officers and its First U.S. Senators, and Entered the American Union* (Omaha, 1866), 13; *Nebraska City News*, July 21, 1866; Addison Erwin Sheldon, *Nebraska: The Land and the People*, 3 vols. (Chicago, 1931), I, 344–45.

44. Herman H. Heath to J. Sterling Morton, Washington, D.C., June 24, 30, 1866, Morton Papers; *Nebraska City News*, Sept. 15, 22, 1866; Brown, "George L. Miller," 41; Sheldon, *Nebraska*, I, 358–61; Morton and Watkins, *Nebraska*, I, 539–44; James C. Olson, *J. Sterling Morton* (Lincoln, Nebr., 1942), 145–46.

office.[45] Meanwhile, Heath and Train were pressing Johnson for appointment as territorial governor and secretary respectively. The president made no move. In September William A. Richardson, an Illinois Democrat, wrote to the president on Morton's behalf. "Let me call your attention to the importance of early removals of radical officials in the Territory of Nebraska. . . . We can carry the Territory if we have cordial co-operation of the federal officers there," he stressed, "but Democrats in Nebraska will not . . . fight . . . unless radical office holders are removed. . . . Unless these things are accomplished at once the effect of the fall elections will be lost." Later in the month Miller once again requested appointments for Democrats, and Heath and Train continued to pursue their own cause. But no changes were made, and in the October 9 election the conservative Republican-Democratic ticket lost by a substantial 700 votes. In the process Republicans also secured a two-thirds majority of both the territorial and state legislatures.[46]

It is doubtful whether the removal of radical officeholders would have changed the outcome of the election. The conservative-Democratic coalition was never strong, and with their increasing dislike for Morton's domination and his high rank on the ballot, many conservatives in the end chose to vote the radical ticket. While Heath was willing enough to work with Morton on the local level, he opposed his appointment to a territorial office. Morton discouraged an appointment for Heath as well.[47]

Endorsing no one, Johnson perhaps saw particular reason to overlook Morton. The Nebraskan had openly opposed the Republican

45. Morton Diary, Aug. 13, 19, 1866, T. T. Dwight to J. Sterling Morton, Quincy, Ill., July 12, 1866, both in Morton Papers.

46. William A. Richardson to Andrew Johnson, Quincy, Ill., Sept. 8, 1866, in LAR, Richardson File; George L. Miller to Johnson, Omaha, Sept. 22, 1866, in LAR, Miller File; George Francis Train to Johnson, Omaha, Oct. 3, 1866, Johnson Papers; *Kansas Tribune*, Oct. 17, 1866; Atchison *Free Press*, Oct. 17, 1866; S. M. Curren and others to Johnson, Omaha, Aug. 16, 1866, in LAR, Heath File; G. G. Marshall to William Seward, Plattsmouth, Nebr., Aug. 20, 1866, A. C. Dodge to Orville Browning, n.p., Sept. 3, 1866, both in TP: Nebraska.

47. Herman H. Heath to Andrew Johnson, Washington, D.C., Aug. 6, 1866, Heath to William Seward, Washington, D.C., Nov. 7, 1866, both in LAR, Heath File; J. W. Paddock to J. Sterling Morton, Omaha, Nov. 19, 1866, Morton Papers; "AYTCH" to editor, Brownville, Nebr., Sept. 16, 1866, in *Nebraska City News*, Sept. 22, 1866; Sheldon, *Nebraska*, I, 358–59.

prosecution of the war while the president had worked in its support. To confer territorial office now on Morton would only lay Johnson open to the charge of consorting with known "traitors," a term radicals were prone to throw at peace Democrats. As one Californian wrote, Johnson could not afford "to put old Copperheads into office." Moreover, the president had stipulated that appointees to federal office be Republicans and veterans with an honorable discharge. As a peace Democrat and a civilian in wartime, Morton met neither of these criteria.[48]

As for Heath, his qualifications did fall within the president's guidelines for appointment to office, but Nebraskans of every political persuasion viewed him with suspicion and considered him an opportunist. Informing Johnson of Heath's unpopularity, Algernon S. Paddock warned that his appointment as governor would shatter the conservative group. In addition, there was the question of why Saunders should be replaced at all. Editor August F. Harvey of the *Nebraska Statesman* for one was against it and argued that Saunders had bipartisan support. So competent was the governor in fact that Harvey, a Democrat, would consider it an "outrage" to dismiss Saunders for his political bias. "The party that removes Saunders ought to be and will be damned," concluded Harvey. In the end Heath was to be rewarded with an office but not in Nebraska. With the approval of J. Francisco Chaves, Johnson named Heath territorial secretary of New Mexico.[49]

Johnson made his patronage moves in Nebraska only after the October 9 election, and they must have disappointed both conservative Republicans and Democrats. The president retained Saunders as governor. Several conservatives and Democrats did receive nom-

48. T. T. Dwight to J. Sterling Morton, Omaha, June 18, 1866, Morton Papers.
49. Algernon S. Paddock to Andrew Johnson, n.p., Sept. 24, 1866, in TP: Nebraska; *Leavenworth Conservative*, July 25, 1866; *Nebraska Statesman*, Sept. 11, 1866; J. Francisco Chaves to Johnson, Washington, D.C., Dec. 29, 1866, in TP: New Mexico. Heath ran into difficulties in New Mexico when his enemies uncovered evidence that he had offered his services to Jefferson Davis in return for a commission in the Confederate army. Johnson chose not to dismiss Heath, but Grant, believing the Union general to have been dishonorably discharged for selling army horses, refused to retain him in office. J. Schofield to William Seward, Washington, D.C., June 26, 1868, Heath to H. St. Geo. Offuitt, Dubuque, Iowa, Apr. 9, 1861, Bureau of Claims Report dated June 30, 1868, Heath to Hamilton Fish, Santa Fe, Apr. 16, 1870, R. W. Taylor to Fish, Santa Fe, Apr. 23, 1870, all in TP: New Mexico; *New Mexican*, Mar. 30, Oct. 19, 1867.

inations to land office positions, but the Senate later rejected most of them. The only change of note was in the northern superintendency of Indian affairs at Omaha where H. B. Denman was awarded the post. Replacing E. B. Taylor as superintendent, Denman immediately began dismissing radicals.[50] To Morton and Train, Johnson offered nothing. Train left Nebraska to seek excitement elsewhere. Morton refocused his interest, now investing in railroads, establishing arboretums, and seeking to attract new settlers for Nebraska. Conservatives began to make amends to radicals, and together they were to reunite the state's Republican party.

Patronage problems in the West eased markedly with the passage of the Tenure of Office Act on March 2, 1867. Johnson was now required to show cause for removing a presidential appointee, and dismissal was effective only with Senate approval. The act itself, despite its later importance in Johnson's impeachment, received little editorial comment anywhere in the West. It was destined to be overshadowed by the first Reconstruction Act, which became law on the very same day. Most western editors had limited space for editorializing, especially in the weekly papers, and they chose instead to comment on the Reconstruction Act, in their view the more important of the two measures. Those Democrats who did offer comment labeled the Tenure Act as unconstitutional and an infringement on presidential prerogatives. To their mind, Congress had devised the act solely to restrict Andrew Johnson. They predicted its repeal once Democrats secured control of the federal government; even radicals would abandon it should they elect to the presidency an individual they could dominate. Ironically, some Democrats recalled their prediction as Republicans sought to repeal the act in the early months of Grant's administration. Indignant that their motive be challenged, Republicans in 1867 naturally denied the accusation and pointed to the act as a long-needed reform measure. In their defense they foreshadowed later demands of reform-minded Republicans for a civil service system. Even for a few non-Republicans, the party

50. *Senate Executive Proceedings*, XV, index; H. B. Denman to Thomas Ewing, Jr., Omaha, Dec. 7, 1866, Ewing Family Papers; J. W. Paddock to J. Sterling Morton, Omaha, Nov. 6, 1866, Morton Papers; Robert C. Farb, "Robert W. Furnas of Nebraska" (Ph.D. dissertation, University of Nebraska, 1949), 201–2; Morton and Watkins, *Nebraska*, I, 538.

gained new attraction in the Tenure Act. Matthew P. Deady praised Republicans for "trying to raise the country above . . . grovelling for public service."[51]

The patronage struggle took its toll on Johnson's popularity: it lost for the president support among western Democrats. His limited ability to maneuver within the patronage system before March, 1867, and the further restrictions of the Tenure Act after that time made it impossible for Johnson to fulfill Democratic expectations. In the wake of the elections of 1866 and during 1867 Democrats throughout the West were critical of congressional Reconstruction. Where they might have reaffirmed the president, they gave Johnson scant credit for his role in obstructing it. While there were a few remaining Democratic newsmen who continued to laud the president's every action, other Democratic editors gave him little notice. After all, said A. J. King of California, the president had sought Democratic support and had given nothing in return. A Nevadan, J. W. Avard, confirmed Democratic loss of faith. Johnson had no claim on Democratic sympathy, claimed Avard, and the party was "fully prepared to let [him] slide." Recalling Johnson's failure on all counts, Avard pointed to the president's inept handling of the patronage during 1866 and early 1867. Without benefit of the patronage, Avard offered, Andrew Johnson was like a poker player whose hand was so poor that it "couldn't beat a pair of deuces."[52]

In all likelihood the most disillusioned of Democrats was J. Sterling Morton. Never awarded office under Johnson, he retired from active politics in Nebraska and turned his attention elsewhere. Unfortunately at this point he gave up confiding his political thoughts in his diary; hence, his feeling toward Johnson after 1866 is not clearly evident. One observation, nonetheless, did emerge. As editor of the *Nebraska City News*, Morton mentioned the president less frequently as 1867 progressed. He broke a long silence in August, however. He noted Johnson's attendance at a "Schutzenfest" outside Washington,

51. *Colorado Transcript* (Golden), Feb. 13, 1867; *Sonoma Democrat*, Feb. 2, 1867; *Daily Reese River Reveille* (Austin, Nev.), Feb. 18, 1869; *Oregon State Journal*, Jan. 19, 1867; *Hastings* (Minn.) *Gazette*, Jan. 19, 1867; *Sacramento Union*, May 5, 1867; *Marysville Appeal*, Mar. 3, 1867; Sacramento *Bee*, Apr. 6, 1867, *Miner's Register*, Feb. 6, 1867; Matthew P. Deady to William Barnhart, Portland, Ore., Oct. 20, 1868, Deady Papers.

52. *Oregon Herald*, Oct. 16, 1867, Feb. 28, 1868; *Walla Walla Statesman*, Aug. 2, 1867; *Los Angeles News*, Oct. 5, 1866; *Esmeralda Union*, May 16, 1868.

D.C., and saw irony in the president's hitting two bull's eyes. "Such a bad marksman with the political rifle has Mr. Johnson shown himself to be," said Morton disdainfully, "that the public were about arriving at the conclusion that he could not hit a bull's-eye though it were as big as a barn door."

By late summer of 1867 one Oregon editor was to characterize Johnson's political position as "peculiar"—he was man almost alone.[53] He had alienated Republicans by his stubbornness and unwillingness to compromise on Reconstruction. Too many Democrats had placed their faith in presidential largesse only to come away empty-handed. Through the vagaries of his own action and the limits placed on his power, Andrew Johnson now stood politically isolated at the nation's helm.

53. *Nebraska City News*, Aug. 17, 1867; *Salem* (Ore.) *Daily Record*, Aug. 21, 1867.

CHAPTER FOUR

Congressional Reconstruction

"Congress has the right . . . to regulate . . . re-admission. . . ."
—Matthew P. Deady, Oregon

Republicans were unwilling to accept Johnsonian Reconstruction after mid-1866. Congress had refused to seat the southern representatives elected under Johnson's plan; therefore, to Congress itself fell the task of drafting guidelines for the restoration of the Union. Predictably there was dissent; just as Congress had taken issue with the president's plan, now Republicans found themselves at odds over the precise details of a Reconstruction policy. In 1866 Congress approved the Fourteenth Amendment and submitted it to the states for ratification, but not until March, 1867—two years after the war's end—did Congress pass the first Reconstruction Act. Swiftly the measure placed the South under military rule and outlined terms to be met by the seceded states for readmission. Three additional Reconstruction acts in 1867 and 1868 followed the first; each clarified ambiguous provisions in the original law. But from March, 1867, Reconstruction proceeded in an orderly manner, and within eighteen months most of the rebel states had conformed to Congress's demands.

Anxious for resolution of problems in the South, westerners watched the progress of events as Congress moved forcefully toward its own implementation of Reconstruction. As in the eastern portion of the nation, political groups in the West divided sharply over the intent and purpose of congressional Reconstruction. But whereas radical and moderate factions within the Republican party were readily discernible in the East, differences between the two groups over Congress's policy appeared less distinct in the West. Western radicals—those individuals who had been advocating black suffrage and some economic adjustment in the South—defended the congressional plan despite its failure to provide economic advantages for freedmen.

Along with moderates, radicals understood the compromise nature of congressional Reconstruction and yet welcomed the program. Countering this radical-moderate acceptance, conservative Republicans and Democrats showed less enthusiasm for congressional Reconstruction. Some conservatives could see its necessity and agree to certain aspects of Congress's plan, but as a group they denounced the new conformity which, in their view, the Republican party was now demanding. Democrats for their part saw nothing good in congressional Reconstruction but disagreed among themselves over its impact. While some members continued to declare it a scheme both debased and without precedent, others begrudgingly encouraged acceptance as the only means of restoring peace to the war-ravaged South.

The Democratic attack on congressional Reconstruction centered on two themes: Congress's plan constituted a bold assumption of power on the part of the national legislature in a move designed to reinforce Republican strength, and it sought to elevate the black at the expense of the white man. Airing and developing both ideas, Democrats in their correspondence to each other tended to emphasize Republican political designs. Democrats had a long-standing aversion to political equality among men of different races and saw little purpose in reiterating their prejudices among themselves.[1] They did, however, exploit the racial issue publicly when such action might serve to bolster their political image.

The major political thrust of congressional Reconstruction, according to Democrats, was to retain the Republican party in power. Throughout the West Democrats—along with some conservative Republicans—concluded that rather than seeking to achieve national reunification, Republicans were merely undertaking steps which would preserve their political party. Consequently, Democrats interpreted Congress's inability to devise a Reconstruction policy in 1866 as an attempt to prevent the return to Washington of delegations from the South. Republicans were afraid that southerners, again seated in Congress, would ally with northern Democrats and work together to frustrate Republican principles. Hence it was to their

1. V. Jacque Voegeli, *Free but Not Equal: The Midwest and the Negro during the Civil War* (Chicago, 1967), 54–56, 76–79, 142–44.

advantage, claimed Democrats, to keep the southern seats in Congress vacant. Developing this idea, E. F. Campbell of Kansas charged that Republicans might veil their goals under the words "freedom," "philanthropy," and "progress," but their purpose itself was less noble. Campbell compared leading Republicans to Jacobins and declared that through "some popular frenzy like the French revolution" they were attempting to establish a political control which "no humane power could stand before."[2]

Even as late as May, 1868, western Democrats attributed base motives to Congress's failure to readmit those states which had complied with the Reconstruction acts. By keeping these southern states out of the Union until after the November election, they pointed out, Republicans could discount their electoral votes—which would presumably be Democratic—and thus assure victory for their own presidential candidate. Pessimistic about the outcome of the election, Democrats foresaw no shift in power and viewed the impasse with dejection: Republicans had become masters at propaganda. They had persuaded most voters that they were acting in the public interest when, in fact, their primary concern was party. Instead of representing the people as they claimed, said Democrats, Republicans really held the masses in "contempt."[3]

Democrats also saw political design in the Republican call during 1866 for equal suffrage in the South. The dominant party, asserted its opposition, wanted to put the ballot in freedmen's hands only to establish Republican supremacy in the former Confederacy. It is true that certain Republicans, anxious to persuade the anti-Negro members of their party of the benefits of equal suffrage, did predict that the black vote would strengthen their party where blacks comprised a significant portion of the population; they believed former slaves would support the politicians who had emancipated them. Such statements encouraged Democrats like J. M. Bassett of California to declare that the Republican party could only hope to maintain itself through the black vote. "They found Cuffee," wrote Bassett deri-

2. James Nesmith to Matthew P. Deady, Washington, D.C., Oct. 2, 1866, Deady Papers; William A. Richardson to J. Sterling Morton, Quincy, Ill., May 6, 1866, Morton Papers; *Council Grove Democrat*, Mar. 2, 1866; *Oregon Statesman*, Mar. 19, 1866; *Idaho World*, May 19, 1866.

3. *Denver Daily Gazette*, Feb. 26, 28, May 20, 1868.

sively, "and now that Cuffee is free . . . they have mounted the hobby of negro suffrage, and on it are attempting to ride to power."[4]

Pursuing further the Republican party and its solicitude toward freedmen, some Democrats employed demagoguery. They charged that Republican benevolence extended only to blacks but not to poorer whites. Such an assertion denied the "free labor" concept which was an essential ingredient of Republicanism, but it also served as an effective appeal to prejudiced, economically hard-pressed white citizens. J. Sterling Morton ignored statistics in Republican newspapers indicating that whites in the South—not blacks—were receiving the larger share of rations distributed by the Freedmen's Bureau. In his view the federal government had no concern for poor whites; indeed, it "wrung [money] from white muscle" to feed the blacks of the South. Similarly, other Democrats chided Republicans for their lack of regard for the working man in the North. Not only did Republicans tax white wage earners to support the black man, but they remained oblivious to their poor working conditions and low standard of living. At the point of charging Republicans with prejudice against working-class whites, Democrats on the West coast claimed, "They see nobody but the nigger; they legislate almost entirely for the nigger." Democrats hastened to justify their assertion: Republican leaders were unwilling to improve the economic position of the laboring white classes because they were "the lords of the loom." Republicans were making enormous profits for themselves and their friends in the "aristocracy of wealth." Why should they risk improving the lot of the working man when it might affect their own profits? Republicans had eliminated black slavery in the agricultural South, but they remained purposely indifferent to "industrial slavery" in the North.[5]

A strong overtone of anti–New England prejudice colored Dem-

4. *Yreka Union*, Aug. 19, 1865, Aug. 11, 1866. See also *Montana Post*, May 5, 1866; *States Rights Democrat*, Sept. 1, 1866, Apr. 4, 1868; *Boise Democrat*, May 27, 1868; *St. Paul Pioneer*, June 21, 1865; *Daily Colorado Times* (Central City), Sept. 7, 1867.

5. *St. Paul Pioneer*, May 10, 1866; *Nebraska City News*, Apr. 6, 1868; *States Rights Democrat*, Apr. 25, 1868; *Placerville Democrat*, Feb. 2, 1867. For a discussion of the Republican "free labor" concept, see Eric Foner, *Free Soil, Free Labor, Free Men: The Ideology of the Republican Party before the Civil War* (New York, 1970), 11–40.

ocratic accusations as well. Western Democrats with a southern background, especially, equated and denounced New Englandism, puritanism, and radicalism as all part of one philosophy. For them this brand of Republicanism sought to elevate blacks to citizenship and reduce whites to vassalage, to maintain southern blacks in idleness, and to control the economy by draining off the money from the West for the enrichment of New England. As Congress was formulating the first Reconstruction Act and its provisions were made public, M. H. Abbott, an Oregon editor, reacted sharply. On the defensive, he labeled the measure as the essence of radicalism. By its provisions Congress planned to retain political control in the South through the black vote and to instigate racial warfare in which blacks would eliminate the white race. So outlandish were these predictions that Republicans in Oregon offered no rebuttals. However, California Republicans could not resist calling them "nonsense." There was simply no truth, they wrote, to statements which portrayed Republicans as "a roving bunch of barbarians who were waiting to devour all southern whites." Certainly the congressional policy was more harsh than Johnson's plan had been, but it was designed to benefit all the people of the South, not just the former ruling class.[6]

Once Congress passed the Reconstruction acts over Johnson's vetoes, Democrats in California lashed out even more angrily. The first three acts, passed between March and July, 1867, provided excellent campaign material for California Democrats seeking to wrest control of the statehouse and legislature from Republicans in the upcoming September, 1867, election. Describing the acts as "unconstitutional," "mad," "loathsome," and "repulsive," Democrats further characterized them as a "flagrant breach" of every Republican promise made about Reconstruction during the war. In the words of one Democrat, these congressional measures "crush[ed] beneath the iron heel of naked power every principle of right and freedom [for which] the revolution [had been] fought."

California Democrats objected most strongly to that provision of the first Reconstruction Act which imposed black suffrage on the former Confederacy. Unable to consider it a means of opening the political process to a previously denied race, the California contingent

---

6. *States Rights Democrat*, Dec. 1, 1866, Jan. 26, 1867; *Marysville Appeal*, June 14, 1868.

could only see equal suffrage as a Republican attempt to "Africanize" the South. Their illusion knew no bounds: Democratic editors were quick to accuse Congress of placing ten million whites under the rule of four million "ignorant, brutal, and naturally inferior" blacks. Radicals "say men are created equal," one declared, but "what they mean is that white men are inferior to negroes."[7]

Eugene Casserly, whom Democrats would elect to the U.S. Senate after their victory in September, 1867, took up the suffrage issue in most of his speeches from 1867 to 1870. Blacks, he said, were "incapable of suffrage because of their ignorance." To grant freedmen the ballot was, in effect, giving them political control of the South. Were not Republicans aware, asked Casserly, that these former slaves would elect twenty senators (presumably black) whose votes would have the same weight as those of twenty senators from the North? Blacks in the former Confederacy did need to be safeguarded from persecution by lower-class whites, conceded Casserly, but suffrage would not guarantee such protection. It could even lead to harsher treatment on the part of those whites who objected to voting with black men.[8]

It was for Henry Haight, Democratic candidate for governor, to make the most extended comment and to carry the fight into the statehouse after his election. Haight, in fact, would continue to oppose congressional Reconstruction well into the 1870s, long after many Democrats had turned their attention to other issues. But in 1867, when Democrats argued that Congress was surpassing its constitutional limitations, Haight chose to emphasize his own strong states' rights philosophy and champion a strict construction of the federal Constitution. By initiating congressional Reconstruction, he claimed, Republicans were destroying the sovereignty of all the states, not just those that had seceded. In his inaugural address on December 5, 1867, Haight gave primary emphasis to the subject of congressional Reconstruction. To the new governor the Reconstruction acts were "a violation of the fundamental principles of the Constitution and

7. Red Bluff (Calif.) *Weekly Sentinel*, Dec. 4, 1867; *Yreka Union*, Feb. 23, 1867; San Francisco *Daily Examiner*, Aug. 9, 1867; *Sonoma Democrat*, Jan. 19, 1867.
8. Lewis, "Los Angeles in the Civil War Decades," 8–10; Eugene Casserly, *The Issues of the Contest. Speech of Hon. Eugene Casserly in San Francisco, August 19, 1868, upon the Invitation of the Young Men's Central Democratic Club* (San Francisco, 1868), 9–11.

of liberty." By giving way to their anti-southern passions, Republicans had inflicted punishment on the whole people of the South, not just the guilty. By punishing without benefit of trial, he declared, they ignored the "innocent until proven guilty" precept. The entire congressional policy, beginning with the Freedmen's Bureau, had placed an undue financial burden on the nation. The need for money to carry on welfare programs and to occupy the South militarily had prevented any reduction in wartime tax assessments. Finally, Haight lashed out at black suffrage itself. "Inferior races" needed assurance against personal violence, but voting rights imposed by military rule gave no such guarantee.[9] Haight's speech had significance even though his ideas were not new. It made him the anti-black, states' rights spokesman for the West.

Elsewhere in the West Democrats echoed the same arguments, but, unlike obstinate party members in California, they counseled acceptance of congressional Reconstruction once the program had gone into effect. Strong in their denunciation when the first Reconstruction Act was passed, Democratic editors in Oregon, Colorado, and Minnesota began as early as May, 1867, to urge southerners to comply with the congressional demands. Not only was Congress determined to enforce its plan but the policy itself had gained general favor throughout the North, and only readmission into the Union could save the southern people from further disciplinary controls.[10] This acquiescence reduced solidarity among western Democrats. The party no longer posed united as the voice of opposition in the trans-Mississippi; now it claimed members who could not agree to congressional Reconstruction for any reason along with others who approved it as a *fait accompli*. Recognizing that Republicans were in control, Democrats like George West of Colorado saw little to be gained in obstructionism, and he encouraged fellow Democrats to focus on issues which might be more politically rewarding. Such a response confused Haight and, as will be shown later, he came to disparage the attitude of these more compliant members of his party.

9. Haight's inaugural is found in State of California, *House Journal, 1867–1868*, 97–100; H. H. Haight, *Speech of H. H. Haight, Esq., Democratic Candidate for Governor, Delivered at the Great Democratic Mass Meeting at Union Hall, Tuesday Evening, July 9, 1867* (n.p., n.d.).

10. See, for example, *States Rights Democrat*, May 11, 1867; *St. Paul Pioneer*, Mar. 5, 1867; *Denver Daily Gazette*, May 20, 1868.

The one distinguishing feature of western conservative Republican thought was its insistence that Reconstruction be an executive function. Like most wartime Republicans, western conservatives denied the legality of secession and maintained that the southern states had never left the Union. While believing Johnson's program for the South somewhat slack, still they insisted that the president, through his pardoning power, was the only person authorized to stipulate terms for the return of the South. Regarding themselves as political centrists, conservatives nonetheless took a less than moderate position on some issues involved in Reconstruction. At one extreme were Charles DeYoung of San Francisco and John Wright of Leavenworth, Kansas, conservative Republicans who advocated black suffrage as ardently as some radicals. Yet Wright thought himself conservative because, unlike most Kansas Republicans, he opposed disfranchising southern whites. At the other extreme San Francisco editors Elijah Rockwell of the *Call* and James Brooks of the *Golden Era* sounded as vehement as most Democrats in their denunciation of equal suffrage.[11]

Deploring lack of moderation and objectivity in the extremist elements, conservatives considered both radical Republicans and Democrats to be fanatical and intolerant. DeYoung recognized that among radicals there were "sincere, intelligent and high minded men," but as a group they wanted to accomplish too much, too fast. He likened radicals to young boys who, having planted an acorn one day, expected to find a full-grown oak tree the next. Decrying radical Republican zeal, western conservatives found far too much passion and anti-southernism in radical expression; radicals were calling for a vengeance which appealed to the "brutal elements of human nature" and which would retard the restoration of peace and harmony. John Miller Murphy in Washington Territory was clearly reflecting this view when he wrote, "We do not believe in radicalism of either extreme; ultra views are seldom sound and the class of men who hold them do the nation no good."[12]

Conservatives objected strenuously to Republican attempts to berate their position. Especially did conservatives resent implications

11. *Leavenworth Conservative*, Oct. 2, 1867; San Francisco *Chronicle*, Sept. 4, 1865; San Francisco *Golden Era*, Feb. 25, 1866; San Francisco *Call*, June 22, 1867.
12. San Francisco *Chronicle*, June 2, Sept. 4, 1865; *Chico Courant*, June 21, 1865; *Washington Standard*, June 17, 1865.

of disloyalty on their part because they opposed Congress's authoritarian role in Reconstruction after 1867. "Every citizen has the right
to question the laws of Congress even though he must obey them,"
wrote Elijah Rockwell, "but the ultras do not recognize this right. . . .
The idea of absolute subservience to the principles of the Congressional majorities, now so sedulously maintained . . . , logically leads
to a total destruction of all freedom of opinion, and it is violative
of the spirit of republican institutions." Nor was such thought confined to the West coast. When radical Republicans in Minnesota
accused R. A. Jones of Democratic sympathies, he replied with bitterness in a letter made public. Having never advocated any but
Republican policy, Jones saw his support of Johnson's plan as his
only deviation from fellow Republicans, ". . . but that," he concluded, "does not make me less a Republican than you."[13]

Besides deploring the Republican demand for political conformity,
conservatives and some Unionists resented the suspicious nature of
more ultra Republicans toward former Democrats. California Congressman John Bidwell, who was more moderate than conservative,
noted that it was unwise to question or "hesitate for a moment" in
anything involving Reconstruction. He who did was immediately
labeled a "Copperhead." Bidwell also believed prewar Democratic
political affiliation detrimental to the ambitions of postwar Republicans. Because he had campaigned for Stephen A. Douglas in 1860,
Bidwell considered his dream of a seat in the U.S. Senate doomed.
He doubted that he could ever secure enough Republican votes in
the California legislature to be elected to the Senate.[14]

Wilson Shannon, a former Democrat and second governor of territorial Kansas, is another case in point. Following his removal as
governor in 1856, Shannon established a law office in Lawrence,
where he mingled socially and professionally with the leading Republicans in the city. Although he was to remain in Kansas, Shannon
was by 1866 contemplating a move to Oregon. His reason, as he
expressed it, was political: "To be a Union man [in Kansas] is not
sufficient. It is necessary to be a radical, proscriptive abolitionist in

13. San Francisco *Call*, June 22, 1867; R. A. Jones to editor, Rochester, Minn.,
Oct. 6, 1866, in *Rochester Post*, Oct. 18, 1866.
14. John Bidwell to D. D. Harris, Washington, D.C., Apr. 28, 1866, Bidwell
Papers, CSUC; Bidwell to Annie E. Bidwell, Washington, D.C., June 18, July 5,
1867, Annie E. Bidwell Papers, CSL.

order to be recognized even in the social circle, as one entitled to respect." As late as 1869 Elwood Evans had his nomination for a territorial judgeship in Washington Territory withdrawn. To his misfortune he had served as a delegate to the National Union convention in 1866. Senator Henry Corbett of Oregon regretted his failure to secure the appointment, but as he reminded Evans, Republican colleagues in the Senate refused to consider individuals whose record was tarnished by political wavering.[15]

While western conservatives had reservations about congressional Reconstruction, their opposition proved ineffective because the group was a dwindling political element between 1865 and 1870. At the war's end the vast majority of western Republicans espoused presidential Reconstruction and thus would have considered themselves conservative. But as the break between Johnson and Congress materialized in 1866, most western Republicans began to side with Congress and refer to themselves as "radicals." Frank Hall and D. C. Collier of Colorado serve as examples of men who moved with the tide from conservatism to radicalism. In 1865 their newspaper, the *Miner's Register*, described the radicals as "by nature factionists" who regarded themselves as "leaders and lights of the world." Within a year, as Johnson became anathema to them, the two Coloradans began praising radical congressmen. There were, however, conservative Republicans like John Miller Murphy who felt no call to radicalism and drifted into the Democratic party. Those who were unable to accept either alternative remained in political limbo. They declined to participate in Republican-sponsored political functions or to support regular Republican nominees for local and national office. During the election of 1868 some conservatives returned to the Republican fold and recommended Grant's election, but their backing came too late to be of consequence.[16] Despite their brief gesture, conservatives remained outside the Republican mainstream.

By late 1866 most Republicans in the West had begun to think of themselves as radicals; in outlook they remained essentially mod-

---

15. Wilson Shannon to Matthew P. Deady, Lawrence, Kans., Jan. 17, 1866, Deady Papers; Henry Corbett to Elwood Evans, Washington, D.C., Apr. 7, 1869, Evans Papers.

16. *Miner's Register*, July 29, 1865, Oct. 21, 1866; *Washington Standard*, May 15, 1867; *Golden Era*, Oct. 31, 1868; San Francisco *Call*, Nov. 5, 1868.

erate, as historians have come to define the term. Unlike true radicals who extolled suffrage as an inviolate human right, most western Republicans more quietly accepted equal suffrage in the South as the necessary vehicle by which freedmen might protect themselves from abuse. They did not pursue economic reform for the South; they did not usually advocate the division and distribution of plantation lands among blacks. Whereas radicals were early champions of Congress's authority to direct Reconstruction, the majority of Republicans in the West accepted the idea only when the president's course proved unsatisfactory. Finally, western Republicans looked to restoration of the South as an end in itself; they were not pushing for broader, more widespread reforms as were many radicals in the East.[17] There were, of course, those Republicans in the West who conformed to the historical definition of a "radical"—for example, Congressman Ignatius Donnelly of Minnesota, editor Orville Brown of the Faribault *Central Republican,* and Jesse Applegate of Oregon. But Applegate's depiction of radicals as individuals seeking to "remove the rotten or defective timbers" in the national government was more overstatement than fact. Henry Pittock of Oregon and A. B. Balcombe of Nebraska gave a less emotional overview. To them radical demands included a more equitable basis than population for representation in the House of Representatives, a validation of the Union war debt by law, and the disqualification of former rebels from holding federal office. These were, however, little more than a reiteration of provisions in the Fourteenth Amendment. In the end, perhaps John Wright's assessment was most perceptive for the time. While Wright was able to distinguish the conservative Republican from the radical, he believed most western Republicans to be somewhere in between. Whatever the case, Wright continued, most of them preferred to be called radical because they had come to associate conservatism with the South and the Democratic party, and, therefore, found the word "hateful beyond expression."[18]

17. For historical definitions of radical and moderate Republicans, see W. R. Brock, *An American Crisis: Congress and Reconstruction, 1865–1867* (New York, 1963), 65–69; Rembert W. Patrick, *The Reconstruction of the Nation* (New York, 1967), 50–55. Mohr (ed.), *Radical Republicans in the North,* describes the general reform outlook of eastern radicals; see especially chs. 1 and 4.

18. The term "moderate Republican" has been adopted by historians to distinguish those who stood between radicalism and conservatism; however, contemporaries did not distinguish between radical and moderate Republicans. Jesse Applegate

Western Republicans could agree with reasonable certainty that Congress should have final authority over Reconstruction in order that the loyalty of the South be guaranteed; beyond that they were not so sure. For Balcombe, "equal rights in all the States to all loyal citizens, regardless of birth or color," was a national Republican aim. Pittock at the same time was assuring his more conservative readership that Congress would never impose black suffrage on the states that had remained loyal during the war. One Nevadan pronounced Republicanism opposed to distinctions of "caste and color," only to have his statement refuted by a fellow Republican. Two editors in Colorado, Ovando Hollister and L. M. Koons, prided themselves as loyal Republicans. Hollister disliked Johnson and opposed black suffrage; Koons favored the extension of suffrage and, although not pro-Johnson, objected to the president's impeachment. Ignatius Donnelly was the only Minnesota congressman to campaign for equal suffrage in his state in 1865, and he became so anti-Johnson that his wife warned him against being "too bombastic" in his denunciation of the president. Senator Alexander Ramsey seldom commented publicly on Andrew Johnson; still, Minnesotans considered him a radical because he voted for all measures improving the civil status of blacks. Each time Congress considered such a bill, however, Ramsey had to be assured that its provisions would not apply to Indians! Since each member of the Kansas congressional delegation was consistent in supporting congressional measures, Kansas Republicans at home considered their record beyond reproach. When Edmund G. Ross cast his vote for Johnson's acquittal in 1868, many Kansans felt themselves betrayed: Ross had ruined Kansas's reputation as "the most radicalized state in the Union."[19]

The extent of western radicalism might be measured in local Republican response to the two leading radicals in Congress, Charles

---

to Matthew P. Deady, Yoncalla, Ore., Sept. 4, 1865, Deady Papers; *Oregonian*, Mar. 5, 1866; *Nebraska Republican*, Aug. 27, 1866; *Leavenworth Conservative*, July 17, 1867.

19. *Nebraska Republican*, Aug. 27, 1866, Jan. 29, 1867; *Oregonian*, Mar. 5, 1866; *Carson Appeal*, Mar. 16, 20, 1866; *Mining Journal*, May 19, 1866; *Rocky Mountain News*, Nov. 12, 1868; *Denver Daily*, Dec. 22, 1867; *Daily Colorado Tribune* (Denver), Nov. 27, 1867; Kate Donnelly to Ignatius Donnelly, Nininger, Minn., Aug. 25, 1866, Donnelly Papers; Ridge, *Donnelly*, 100–103; John Clarence Haugland, "Alexander Ramsey and the Republican Party, 1866–1875: A Study in Personal Politics" (Ph.D. dissertation, University of Minnesota, 1961), 190.

Sumner and Thaddeus Stevens. When initially they favored presidential Reconstruction, western Republicans were leery of the eastern radical viewpoint. Nebraskans and Coloradans in particular objected to Sumner's crusade for equal rights. Both territories submitted constitutions in 1865 and 1866 limiting suffrage to white males, and it was Sumner's objection to these restrictions which delayed quick approval of statehood by Congress. Even when informed of the small, resident black population in Colorado and Nebraska, Sumner refused to yield. Thus did the *Nebraska Republican* describe Sumner's insistence on equal suffrage as "insulting" and declared him to be a "radical extremist" who lived "by promoting discord and ultra measures."

As congressional Reconstruction gained appeal and more western Republicans were persuaded of the necessity for equal suffrage in the South, they began to express greater appreciation for Sumner and his ideas. By February, 1867, D. C. Collier, who had been consistently critical of the Massachusetts senator, conceded that the eastern radical was "usually right." When Democrats in their turn attacked Sumner as a "Negroized wretch and monster," Republicans throughout the West rallied to his defense. Rejecting adverse criticism, the editor of the *Minneapolis Tribune* referred to Sumner as "earnest, honest, . . . and a man of convictions . . . found in advance of all reform issues." The senator also received letters of encouragement from others in the West praising him "in the noble position you occupy among our Statesmen" and for refusing to yield on the issue of equal rights. Asa Hatch of California congratulated Sumner, saying it was his inflexibility on black suffrage that had caused many Republicans in the West to reassess their own stand. "You [now] have hundreds of believers in your doctrine in this State where you had not one four years ago," wrote Hatch.[20]

For Thaddeus Stevens western Republicans felt somewhat less enthusiasm. Senator Edmund Ross of Kansas praised Stevens's prewar antislavery attitude. But of his radical career in the House, Ross

20. *Nebraska Republican*, Feb. 6, 1866; *Miner's Register*, Feb. 2, 1867; *Boise Democrat*, Dec. 18, 1867; *Idaho World*, Dec. 13, 1866; *Minneapolis Daily Tribune*, July 28, 1867; James L. Holmes to Charles Sumner, Lawrence, Kans., Feb. 27, 1866, Asa Hatch to Sumner, San Francisco, Feb. 16, 1866, William Lockwood to Sumner, ?, Nebr., Mar. 14, 1866, R. T. Lockwood of Washington Territory to Sumner, Washington, D.C., May 17, 1866, all in Sumner Papers; David Herbert Donald, *Charles Sumner and the Rights of Man* (New York, 1970), 251–52, 259, 281–84.

spoke only of Stevens's ineffectiveness due to advancing age and illness. Senator George Williams of Oregon, who regarded himself as radical, was not even that charitable. Years after, Williams would remember Stevens as "violent and vindictive in his attitude toward the South," unlikeable and unattractive as a person.[21] Like others who have recalled the period, Williams was fascinated with Stevens's physical infirmities and dour disposition and dwelled on these in detail. Apparently he found Stevens's radical ideas less compelling, for he gave them little notice.

Even in his own time Stevens's theories on Reconstruction found little acceptance among western Republicans. The *Marysville Appeal*, recognized as one of California's more radical dailies, balked at Stevens's approach. The editor advocated firmer treatment of the South but still could not accept Stevens's harsh suggestions for dealing with southern whites. The *Appeal* rejected as well Stevens's demand in August, 1867, for more stringent regulation of the southern states. Commenting on Stevens's new demand, which came several months after the passage of the first Reconstruction Act, the editor argued against further stipulations. In his view the federal government could more reasonably "afford to be generous" now that Reconstruction was firmly under Congress's control.[22]

Western Republicans generally resented Stevens's leadership in the House and his call for confiscation of southern lands and their division among former slaves. Although some Republicans realized that Stevens would not likely succeed in forcing his ideas on the House, others in the West feared his impact. Stevens was indeed to be criticized, asserted the moderate *Alta California*, for haranguing Congress about the president's inadequacies. No less worthy of reproach were Stevens's attempts to usurp the executive function by demanding the implementation of his own policy. Clearly Stevens was overstepping his bounds. After all, the editor reminded his readers, Stevens represented not all the people but one single district in Pennsylvania. Watching his behavior in Congress, western Republicans even began to fear his effect on the party. The *St. Paul Press*, usually

21. Edmund G. Ross, "Political Leaders of the Reconstruction Period," F, XX (Oct., 1895), 232; *Oregonian*, Dec. 10, 1905.

22. Stevens did have admirers in the West, although sources indicate they were few in number. See *Junction Union*, Dec. 22, 1866; Charles Durkee to Thaddeus Stevens, Salt Lake City, Feb. 20, 1866, Thaddeus Stevens Papers, LC; *Marysville Appeal*, Aug. 17, 28, 1867. For a statement on the radicalism of the *Appeal* see *Washington Standard*, June 17, 1865.

very liberal in its outlook, predicted that, short of dominating it, "this irate old man" would destroy the Republican party.

Despite the unlikelihood of Stevens's confiscation scheme being accepted as part of congressional Reconstruction, western Republicans were still sharply critical. Many of them found confiscation absurd and impractical. Not only would it impoverish a generation of southern upper-class whites, but it would lead to interminable feuds over land titles and boundaries. Others viewed confiscation of real property as a likely radical means to degrade the southern aristocracy. Since it would bring further humiliation and defeat, confiscation could hardly be consistent with Reconstruction's goal of securing once again the loyalty of the South. For those southerners who had worked hard to accumulate their land holdings, declared the San Francisco *Bulletin*, confiscation was "grossly unfair." Moreover, Stevens's plan was designed to aid only blacks, and it ignored the poverty of poor whites.[23] Stevens's stature among western Republicans improved

23. *Alta California*, Mar. 12, May 4, 1866; *Miner's Register*, Apr. 14, 1866; *St. Paul Pioneer*, May 16, 1866; *St. Paul Press*, May 16, 1866; *Winona Republican*, Sept. 18, 1865; Leavenworth *Times*, Dec. 29, 1865; San Francisco *Bulletin*, Mar. 20, 1867. By the time of his death in Aug., 1868, Stevens's stature had improved among western Republicans, but his ideas still were not widely accepted. Respectful of the congressman's zeal for his cause and his patriotism, Republicans nevertheless deplored his egotism and outspokenness. Orville Brown of Minnesota gave a fair and impartial assessment of Stevens's role in Reconstruction. While his "impulsive spirit and extreme radicalism had impaired his success as a party leader," Brown pointed out that Stevens's "radical firmness" counteracted "timid conservatism" in Congress. True, his more conservative colleagues had toned down Stevens's radicalism, but certainly he made Reconstruction more radical than it might have been. Faribault *Central Republican*, Aug. 19, 1868. Laudatory obituaries were printed in the *Nebraska Commonwealth* (Lincoln), Aug. 8, 1868 (this was three days before Stevens's death); *Alta California* and *Territorial Enterprise*, both Aug. 14, 1868; *Colorado Tribune*, *Miner's Register* (now renamed the *Central City Register*), *Carson Appeal*, and *Hastings Gazette*, all Aug. 15, 1868; Salem (Ore.) *American Unionist*, Aug. 17, 1868; *Mountain Champion* (Belmont, Nev.), Aug. 19, 1868; *Idaho Statesman*, Aug. 20, 1868; *Chico Courant*, *Yreka Journal*, and *Mankato Union*, (Minn.) all Aug. 21, 1868.

Western Democrats heartily disliked Stevens during the Reconstruction years and few took note of his passing. Among those Democrats who chose to acknowledge his death publicly, only George West in Colorado recognized Stevens's honesty of purpose and his role as a leader. Still, West denounced Stevens's principles. *Colorado Transcript*, Aug. 26, 1868. Other Democrats seemed almost relieved at his demise. The *St. Paul Pioneer* felt no inclination to shed tears "over the death of this bad old man," and M. H. Abbott of Oregon referred to Stevens as "unscrupulous, fanatical and malicious." *St. Paul Pioneer*, Aug. 13, 1868; *States Rights Democrat*, Aug. 22, 1868. See also *Montana Post*, Aug. 21, 1868; *Rocky Mountain Herald* (Denver), Aug. 22, 1868.

somewhat as Reconstruction progressed, but he never matched Sumner's popularity in the West.

The right of Congress to restore the nation was one concept which western Republicans, radical or moderate, came to accept without equivocation. Justifications for limiting presidential authority over Reconstruction were both political and personal. From the Far West Jesse Applegate and Matthew P. Deady spoke out most eloquently on the topic. Of the two, Applegate's opinions were the more radical and consistent with his long-held antislavery and pro–black suffrage views. Deady's argument resorted to legalism and contained elements of the moderate Republican stand. Their assessment, in its logic and forthright candor, is all the more significant since they were long-time residents of Oregon, one of the most conservative areas in the West.

The power to control the Reconstruction process lay inherently with the national legislators, in Deady's view. "I think myself," he wrote, "that Congress has the right, and it is its duty, to regulate the subject of re-admission. . . ." Because the Founding Fathers had empowered Congress to admit states, they also implied as well the right to "readmit" them. Johnson's only authority in Reconstruction lay in his power to veto acts of Congress. Deady readily acknowledged a long-standing sympathy for the South, strengthened by his awareness that in the events leading to the war and in the conflict itself, southerners "were as much sinned against as sinning." But this sympathy, he declared, "does not blind me to the fact of their actual condition and relation to the government of the United States, which is practically that of a conquered country." Further, Deady would deny Johnson a major voice in Reconstruction for his very inconsistency in handling the matter. Inasmuch as there were no constitutional guidelines, the program devised had specifically to be followed, and Johnson's past performance in Reconstruction showed inability to be firm in his demands.[24]

Answering a request that he come out publicly in support of Johnson's policy, Applegate chose instead to detail his reasons for not wishing to defend Johnsonian Reconstruction. Although he shunned an active political life, Applegate sustained a deep personal interest in public matters. His stature was such that friends often sought the

24. Matthew P. Deady to James Nesmith, Portland, Ore., Jan. 28, Oct. 30, 1866, Nesmith Papers.

opinion and backing of the "Sage of Yoncalla," as he was known locally. It was futile, wrote Applegate, to argue the validity of secession. Because the federal Constitution was silent on the subject, every opinion was as good as the next. But it was Applegate's personal contention that the southern states had left the Union and needed to be readmitted formally by Congress. In passing their ordinances of secession, citizens in the individual states had violated and nullified the federal compact, thereby transferring all governmental authority in their state to Congress. Hence, only the national legislature could remand it. Like Deady, Applegate considered Johnson's approach to Reconstruction untenable. With the president's actions belying his very words, he had forfeited his right to leadership. "I have no doubt of his ardent desire to restore peace and unity," Applegate noted, "yet . . . he has been a little too hasty in his clemency . . . by his free pardons he has in many cases put the loyal citizens in the power and under the control of their mortal enemies, and places the States in antagonism with the Union itself." Applegate specified that his refusal to write on the president's behalf was prompted not by personal antagonism but, rather, by Johnson's inconsistency and mishandling of the Reconstruction issue. "In short," Appleton concluded, "Mr. Johnson is not equal to the position he occupies. In a ruler lack of wisdom is a crime. . . ."[25]

Because western Republicans accepted the necessity for congressional Reconstruction, their representatives in Congress as well as leading Republican propagandists in the states and territories supported national legislative measures even though some westerners considered them less than advantageous to their own interests. This was especially true of the Fourteenth Amendment, passed only after six months' debate in Congress. As an inducement for eventual equal suffrage in the South, Charles Sumner proposed during the debate to change the basis for representation in the House. He suggested that, rather than by total population, the criterion for determining a state's representation in Congress be the actual number of voters in that state. Such a provision might encourage states to broaden the franchise. Since most Republicans in Congress were still unwilling

25. Benjamin F. Dowell to Jesse Applegate, Jacksonville, Ore., Nov. 11, 1865, Applegate Family Papers, OHS; Applegate to Dowell, Yoncalla, Ore., Nov. 12, 1865, Benjamin F. Dowell Papers, OHS. Bowles, *Across the Continent*, 176–77, offers an excellent pen-portrait of Applegate and an evaluation of his stature in Oregon.

to impose black suffrage in 1866, this partial gain was the best for which the senator could hope. Western radicals seized upon it as an excellent means of securing the ballot for southern freedmen, but the proposal was to take hold among other Republicans and some Democrats as well.[26] Given the high proportion of voting-age males within the total population of the West, every western state was guaranteed greater representation were such a scheme to be adopted.

Although most westerners favored the Sumner proposal, Californians were carried away in their zeal. Individuals throughout the state encouraged their congressmen to work in its behalf, and the California legislature passed a series of resolutions in approval. Anticipating congressional adoption, Frederick MacCrellish, editor of the *Alta California,* compiled his figures and announced prematurely that California's representation in the House would increase from three to eight members. He need not have exulted; the advantages to the West of basing representation on the number of voters was obvious to many, including James G. Blaine, representative from Maine. During the debate on the issue Blaine was to point out that the populations of California and Vermont were approximately equal at 350,000. Whereas California had 207,000 white males of voting age, Vermont could count only 87,000. Blaine reminded fellow congressmen that each state had three representatives at present; should Sumner's proposition become law, Vermont would lose and California would gain delegates. Persuaded by Blaine's argument, congressmen from the Northeast voted against the proposal and sent it to defeat.[27]

While the public in California and Nevada in particular responded bitterly to the defeat of the measure,[28] the failure to base represen-

26. James, *Fourteenth Amendment,* 23; DuBois, *Black Reconstruction,* 286; Howard P. Nash, *Andrew Johnson, Congress and Reconstruction* (Rutherford, N.J., 1972), 77; Faribault *Central Republican,* Sept. 20, 1865.

27. R. C. Gaskill to John Bidwell, San Francisco, Jan. 21, 1866, W. A. Elinson to Bidwell, Santa Rosa, Calif., Jan. 19, 1866, copies of "Concurrent Resolution XXIII (adopted March 2), 1866," all in Bidwell Papers, CSUC; *Alta California,* Oct. 26, 1865, Feb. 8, 1866; James, *Fourteenth Amendment,* 23–24; Nash, *Andrew Johnson,* 78; DuBois, *Black Reconstruction,* 286.

28. Senator William Stewart of Nevada, along with Congressmen Ashley of the same state and Higby of California, took the floor to denounce the defeat of Sumner's proposal. Editors in the West reiterated their arguments, that New Englanders had rejected the proposal because it threatened their own dominance over the nation. Together they labeled northeastern radicalism as selfish and restrictive. *Congressional Globe,* 39 Cong., 1 Sess., 426–28, 1103–7, 1314–16; *Oregon Herald,* Mar. 23, Sept. 2, 1866; *Washington Standard,* Apr. 7, 1866.

tation on the number of voters did not ultimately deter the ratification of the Fourteenth Amendment in the western states. The legislatures of Kansas, Nebraska, Minnesota, and Nevada approved it without significant opposition.[29] The Oregon legislature, too, was successful in ratifying even if it had to subvert Democratic opposition in the lower house. Initiated in the state senate, a resolution favoring ratification of the amendment received approval by a vote of thirteen to nine. Once in the assembly, the measure passed to the Republican-controlled Judiciary Committee, which quickly returned a favorable report. Little wonder, for its two Democratic members were given no chance to dissent. They were not even informed of the committee meeting held to consider the amendment. Republicans were no less willing to gamble on the resolution's outcome on the floor of the house. Conveniently, just long enough to secure ratification of the amendment by a vote of twenty-five to twenty-one, they delayed action on seating two Democrats from Grant County who were contesting Republican-held seats; quietly these Democratic contenders were seated the next day. The affair so angered Oregon Democrats that they rescinded the ratification during the next session of the legislature.[30]

California neither ratified nor rejected the Fourteenth Amendment. Rather than force the issue, Governor Frederick Low simply declined to call the Republican-controlled legislature into special session during 1866 that it might consider the amendment. By the time the next regular session convened in December, 1867, control of the lower house had passed to the Democrats and favorable action on the amendment was unlikely. Still, in his last message as governor Low recommended approval. Terming the amendment both "mild and lenient," he urged ratification as the only means of bringing peace to the South. In response, legislators offered two alternatives. A first resolution in the Republican state senate recommended rat-

29. James, *Fourteenth Amendment*, 186–96; State of Nevada, *House Journal, 1866–1867* (Carson City, 1867), 25, 51; Crawford, *Kansas in the Sixties*, 246; David Butler (governor of Nebraska) to Frederick Seward, Omaha, Oct. 16, 1867, Kennard Papers.

30. State of Oregon, *Senate Journal, 1866* (Salem, 1866), 25–26, 32, 34–35; *House Journal, 1866* (Salem, 1866), 55–57, 73, 76–77; *States Rights Democrat*, Sept. 29, 1866; *Oregonian*, Sept. 21, 1866; Charles H. Coleman, *The Election of 1868* (New York, 1971), 14–15.

ification; a second in the lower house called for rejection. Both died in committee.[31]

To the series of Reconstruction acts passed in 1867 and 1868 western Republican senators and representatives in Washington, D.C., gave strong and unified support.[32] Republicans at home cheered the passage of the first Reconstruction Act and fretted only at the loss of time between war's end and the implementation of Congress's plan. The Reconstruction law should "have been enacted as soon after the surrender of Richmond as possible," lamented one westerner. "We rejoice," agreed another, but "to the disgrace of the Government, it has taken nearly two years to commence its policy." A third added, "It is to be regretted that Congress has been so late in coming to a determination." Otherwise, Republicans discounted every Democratic criticism. The Reconstruction acts in no way violated the Constitution; rather, they were "conceived in patriotism and wisdom," in the words of a resolution passed by a Republican convention in California. Similarly, the Nevada legislature offered seven resolutions praising the acts as valid and condemning Johnson's past policy.[33]

The Reconstruction acts were acceptable to western Republicans because their scope was defined. They were intended merely to guarantee against future rebellion and to protect the loyal citizens of the South. The first Reconstruction Act, editoralized D. C. Collier, "insures justice, and good order and leaves the Southern people free to choose military rule, or reconstruction on the basis of universal loyalty." Collier did not think Congress motivated by hatred of the southern people. Its only intent, he believed, was to unify the nation and to perpetuate American institutions on the principles enunciated in the Declaration of Independence. Among themselves Republicans agreed that the South should cease complaining about Congress's requirements and indicate its good faith through compliance with

31. Frederick Low to Elihu Washburne, Sacramento, Nov. 16, 1866, Washburne Papers; State of California, *House Journal, 1867–1868*, 52–53, 601–11; *Senate Journal, 1867–1868*, 214; James, *Fourteenth Amendment*, 192; Moody, "Civil War," 351.

32. See Appendix.

33. *Western Home Journal*, Mar. 21, 1867; *State Atlas* (Minneapolis), Mar. 7, 1867; *Carson Appeal*, Feb. 20, 1867; *Proceedings of the San Francisco Union Ratification Meeting held at Union Hall, San Francisco, Tuesday Evening, June 25, 1867* (n.p., n.d.); State of Nevada, *House Journal, 1867*, 326–31.

the acts. As one Minnesotan phrased it, "the long-suffering people" of the North had waited long enough for the South to accept defeat; just as surely would they continue to watch with "sleepless vigilance" until southerners showed genuine repentance. Charles DeYoung of California urged the southern people to undertake whatever steps necessary to achieve readmission. He deplored "expressions of sullen vindictiveness" continuing from the North and South alike and wished all parties to concentrate their interests on the future, not the past. It was DeYoung's hope that "we [will] all yet be happy."[34]

Until southerners began to undertake steps indicating their willingness to abide by the Reconstruction acts, western Republicans feared resistance because every former Confederate state except Tennessee had rejected the Fourteenth Amendment. From the passage of the first Reconstruction Act to the readmission of seven southern states during the summer of 1868, therefore, western Republicans watched carefully for signs of southern reluctance to comply with congressional Reconstruction. More radical elements quickly noted any wavering on the South's part, but the mass of Republicans accepted in good faith every positive move by the South. It was with a sigh of relief and even righteous conviction that they welcomed back their "erring sisters." John Speer of Kansas found them "chastened, regenerated and redeemed." Somewhat prematurely the editor of the *Nebraska Commonwealth* announced that for these states Reconstruction had come to an end. The sole rationale for Reconstruction, to his mind, was the restoration of the southern states "to their proper relationship within the Union."[35]

Moderate western Republicans came to accept the right of Congress to restore the nation, but for some it was a step slowly taken. Whereas radicals began voicing doubts about Johnson's program in 1865, moderates did not seriously question his policy until 1866. But with the veto of the Freedmen's Bureau bill, individual Republicans began to come over to Congress, a move that would persist through the

34. *Miner's Register*, Mar. 10, 12, 1867; *Stars and Stripes*, Mar. 13, 1867; *Faribault Central Republican*, Mar. 6, 1867; *Idaho Statesman*, Feb. 28, June 25, 1867; *Sacramento Union*, Mar. 11, 1867; *Humboldt Times*, Feb. 23, 1867; *Minneapolis Tribune*, June 4, 1867; *San Francisco Chronicle*, May 15, 1867.

35. *Marysville Appeal*, Apr. 12, 18, Oct. 6, 1867; *Kansas Tribune*, June 25, 1868; *Nebraska Commonwealth*, June 27, 1868; *Nebraska Republican*, Nov. 22, 1867.

end of 1866. For his part the president contributed directly to this loss of support by his public demeanor and by his failure to implement a firmer Reconstruction policy. Johnson's activities, however, served mainly to foster uncertainty; other factors strengthened Republican acceptance of congressional control once the idea had taken hold. As they recognized the need to change the authority which would direct Reconstruction, Republicans in the West admitted that the policy adopted must take a new direction; it could not be a restatement of the program being rejected. As William Stewart explained, "The country will not justify a distinction without a difference," and the difference should lie in principle, not just policy.[36]

Republicans achieved a stunning victory in the congressional election in 1866, a victory which came to be regarded as a popular mandate for Congress to assume control over Reconstruction. For Frederick MacCrellish of California it was a turning point. Prior to the election MacCrellish had insisted that Johnson be responsible for Reconstruction. From the executive office had come direction in the war effort, and there was little justification for Congress, now that the war was over, to assert its authority and demand "the right to settle up matters." But faced with the results of the election, MacCrellish had a change of heart: the "loyal masses" had now determined who should direct Reconstruction and from that ultimatum there could be no appeal.[37] From this point Republicans ceased arguing that Reconstruction was an executive function. Thomas Foster of the *Minneapolis Chronicle* even termed the 1866 election a "referendum" in favor of Congress. He urged lawmakers to forsake idle dispute and get on with intitiating policy. "The lesson of this election," echoed Ovando Hollister from Colorado, "is that the North will complete the great work. . . . There is now no back seat possible. . . ." As Congress moved to finalize the provisions of the first Reconstruction Act, I. S. Kalloch of Kansas praised the national legislature for "doing . . . its whole duty." The results of the war were "just," he explained, and needed to be secured by law to future generations. Throughout the West Republicans took on a renewed optimism. "You are hardly aware of the intense feeling . . . around us, how we watch daily"; reflected Stephen Hewson of Minnesota,

36. *Congressional Globe*, 39 Cong., 1 Sess., 2803.
37. *Alta California*, Jan. 5, Nov. 8, 27, 1866.

". . . any move to ensure the safety of the Old Flag always elicits a feeling of joy."[38]

Western Republicans—moderate and radical alike—also concluded that the South would never agree to a voluntary Reconstruction program and that one had to be imposed upon her people. This thought stemmed from the failure of ten southern states to ratify the Fourteenth Amendment during 1866, a gesture deemed "foolish" by many, since denial of the amendment virtually ensured denial of readmission as well. True, Congress had offered no guarantee to readmit and had, in fact, rejected a bill proposing readmission for those states approving the amendment. But, as one Nevada Republican editor reminded his readers, the legislators had already established a precedent by admitting Tennessee once it ratified the document, and they could hardly deny any other state that took the same action. As a result, westerners encouraged southern citizens to approve the amendment without further hesitation, lest Congress adopt more drastic measures. Still the states continued to balk, and many of these same western Republicans began to show less patience; they came to believe the Reconstruction laws just retribution for southern stubbornness. ". . . since the south refused to accept the Constitutional Amendment," wrote Robert Nixon, "they only bit their own nose off." Only weeks before passage of the first Reconstruction Act D. C. Collier described its terms as harsh but concluded, ". . . it is the fault of the South alone. Congress had proffered lenient terms but they have been rejected." From Kansas to California Republicans united in their belief that "no rebel has a right to speak a complaint, or whisper a protest against [the first Reconstruction Act]. By their obstinacy . . . they are to receive their just reward."[39]

Western Republicans could not accept in any case that southerners found reason to object to the Fourteenth Amendment. They regarded it a compromise between extremes of Republican thinking, but one

38. *Minneapolis Chronicle*, Dec. 2, 1866; *Mining Journal*, Nov. 9, 1866; *Western Home Journal*, Jan. 24, 1867; Stephen Hewson to Ignatius Donnelly, Oxford, Minn., Dec. 28, 1866, Donnelly Papers.

39. *Alta California*, Nov. 4, 7, 1866; *Oregon City* (Ore.) *Enterprise*, Dec. 29, 1866; *Oregonian*, May 1, 1866; *Gold Hill News*, Oct. 23, Dec. 14, 1866; *Oakland News*, Dec. 15, 1866, Mar. 15, 1867; *Miner's Register*, Dec. 30, 1866, Feb. 9, 1867; *Yreka Journal*, July 19, 1867; *Topeka* (Kans.) *Tribune*, Mar. 6, 1867; *Marysville Appeal*, Feb. 17, 1867.

which tended toward moderation. Admitting that radicals indeed had reason to be disappointed in the final version, John Martin of Kansas nevertheless believed the document fair. He characterized its provisions as "nearly what the people desire and as nearly right as any that could receive the official sanction of the States." The amendment was, according to one Californian, both "conservative and radical enough to please all elements." Oregon's U.S. senator-elect, Henry Corbett, praised the document as one which "embodied all [the] guarantees and adjustments that will give justice to all." Further, as some westerners pointed out, the states of the West had gone ahead and ratified the amendment even though their favored representation-by-voters proposal had fallen by the way. Thus was Congress's demand for ratification a reasonable imposition upon the South, and failure to ratify looked upon as disloyal. As a result, the South was regarded with suspicion, for as one editor pointed out, "There is surely nothing in these measures that any loyal man can disapprove."[40]

Finally, congressional Reconstruction found favor with most western Republicans because of its moderation. Unlike some historians who have described Congress's policy as a harsh, radically conceived

40. *Atchison Champion*, June 29, 1866; *Monterey Gazette*, July 6, 1866; Corbett's speech is found in *Alta California*, Oct. 10, 1866; *St. Paul Press*, May 10, 1866. For additional favorable comment see Sacramento *Bee*, June 22, 1866; *Olathe Mirror*, Aug. 9, 1866; *Pacific Tribune*, Oct. 13, 1866. Democrats, of course, found fault with the amendment. For their reaction see *St. Paul Pioneer*, Oct. 6, 1866. In Nebraska Algernon S. Paddock, conservative Republican territorial secretary, expressed strong disapproval. Speaking before the territorial legislature in 1866, Paddock charged that the Fourteenth Amendment was designed to "perpetuate hatred, strife and discord." Under its terms, suggested Paddock, the loyalty of the South would never be secured. But the Nebraska legislature disagreed and, in a series of resolutions, disavowed the secretary's view and moved to endorse the amendment. Territory of Nebraska, *House Journal, 1866–1867* (Omaha, 1867), 17–18, 83. Democrats in California also brought out the implications of the Fourteenth Amendment for the Chinese among their population. Should the amendment be ratified, it would not immediately change the legal position of Asians, wrote James M. Bassett, but within a generation large numbers would be native-born citizens, and they would demand the right to vote. This possibility appalled Bassett, for he considered the Chinese so inferior that "all the philanthropic tinkering in the world will not change them one iota. . . ." *Yreka Union*, May 12, 1866. Just before the amendment was declared in force, Arizona officials asked the Justice Department for clarification; they wondered whether it granted citizenship to Indians. The department suggested that the answer be decided by the courts. See Richard McCormick to Henry Stanbery, Tucson, Mar. 14, 1868, and John Binckley to McCormick, Washington, D.C., Apr. 8, 1868, both in TP: Arizona, 1864–1872, NARG 59.

plan, western Republicans understood it to be a compromise between radical and moderate thinking. From 1865 on moderate western Republicans would point to the minority stance held by radical Republicans in Congress and remind critics that radicals themselves did not have the votes to secure extreme measures. Thereafter, Republicans acknowledged congressional measures on Reconstruction to be primarily temperate in their outlook and purpose. As Congress hammered out its final Reconstruction policy, there seemed little doubt among Republicans that it would be a program limited in its design.[41]

If congressional Reconstruction were moderate, according to westerners, it was the Republican party whose wide diversity of opinion made it so. While the more radical approved confiscation, some moderates were even opposed to black suffrage. Looking back, Cornelius Cole recalled that "various were the ideas of republicans"— so varying, in fact, that party unity was seriously threatened at times. Likewise, J. Francisco Chaves chastised Republicans of the post–Civil War era: "I have never seen such a damned set of fools for partizans in my life." Each Republican had his own ideas and seemed totally incapable of "supporting and properly sustaining the party." Frederick MacCrellish concurred; in 1866 he recognized that Republicans would never be "able to agree among themselves on any plan of reconstruction." Indeed, just before the passage of the first Reconstruction Act, another western Republican wondered whether the national legislature would ever take a stand. Differences among Republicans could easily give the impression that Congress was "unequal to the task at hand." Yet westerners, acknowledging the differences within the party, determined all the more to support the congressional plan. Failure to do so could jeopardize Reconstruction in its entirety, and such a possibility was untenable. As one westerner wrote, the "Republican party may not be all that it should be, and some of its members may be rash and reckless, [but] there is, I believe, no other organization through whose agency we can hope for . . . generous and just results.[42]

41. *Minneapolis Chronicle*, Feb. 26, 1867. For historical statements on the conservative nature of Reconstruction, see Patrick, *Reconstruction of the Nation*, 95–102, and Michael Les Benedict, "Preserving the Constitution: The Conservative Basis of Radical Reconstruction," JAH, LXI (Mar., 1975), 65–90.

42. Cole, *Memoirs*, 275; J. Francisco Chaves to Herman Heath, Washington, D.C., June 15, 1868, J. Francisco Chaves Papers, AHS; *Alta California*, Apr. 8, 1866; *Walla Walla Statesman*, Mar. 1, 1867; John Martin to Andrew Johnson, Atchison, Kans., Aug. 4, 1866, Johnson Papers.

To Cornelius Cole the greatest compromise aspect of congressional Reconstruction was its imposition of equal suffrage on the South. Against radicals arguing for confiscation of lands and other harsh punishment and conservatives demanding that suffrage qualifications be determined by states alone, moderates came to favor equality at the polls as a means of protecting freedmen's rights. Congress was having to tread carefully in extending suffrage to former slaves, observed the senator. Among many segments of the population there was intense hostility toward the southern white population, but legislators in Washington were just as cognizant of the northerner's "unconquerable aversion to free negroes." It was, therefore, with misgivings about their own political future that some congressmen voted for equal suffrage in the South.[43]

If Cole's presumption was correct, why then did western Republicans so readily approve a Reconstruction plan which stipulated black suffrage in the southern states? One year before Congress's passage of the first Reconstruction Act, the *Marysville Appeal* observed that "thousands of Unionists are opposed to forcing negro suffrage on the Rebel States. . . . They desire the fruits of victory may be secured without a resort to universal suffrage." Yet when it came, western Republicans did not argue the point. In the intervening months they had come to recognize black suffrage in the South a necessity. Through no other way but the ballot would southern blacks secure and retain a modicum of legal protection. "It being necessary as a war measure to give the colored race their freedom," declared J. W. Avard of Nevada, "it is equally necessary to protect them in their rights." If blacks of the South, explained another westerner, were expected to serve as a part of the productive community, they had to have the rights of all free men and such privileges as were guaranteed only by the ballot. Further justifying its extension, Frederick MacCrellish reminded his readers that suffrage was necessary to counteract southern white treatment of blacks. Individual proscription and racial disturbance in the South demanded action by Congress; had white southerners been more tolerant, they would not have brought upon themselves that which they feared the most—the imposition of black suffrage. Senator George Williams of Oregon noted that, given their present circumstance in the South, former slaves were incapable of protecting themselves. Although his opinion of

43. Cole, *Memoirs*, 255.

equal suffrage would become more conservative in later life, Williams defended the policy at the time that Congress implemented black suffrage in the South. "It would be an everlasting shame and disgrace to the country," he wrote, should the nation not offer a means for blacks to protect themselves.[44] Thus did many western Republicans come to regard equal suffrage as a necessity, if not a right. Ironically, many radicals in the West encouraged this thinking even though some took exception to it. For them the end was more important than the means.

In justifying the extension of equal suffrage to the South, some western Republicans insisted that it would never be imposed in the states which had remained loyal during the war.[45] Without specifically saying so, they implied that black suffrage was a form of punishment for southern whites, an idea that did not go unnoticed in the black communities. Democrats were not convinced; they rejected the notion that Congress was satisfied with its accomplishment and would overlook black suffrage for the North. As they read the recent past and witnessed the extension of equal suffrage during 1867 into the District of Columbia, the territories, and the former Confederacy, Democrats considered it only a matter of time before the reform would spread throughout the whole nation.

44. *Marysville Appeal*, May 1, 1866; *Reese River Reveille*, June 29, 1867; *Weekly Colusa* (Calif.) *Sun*, Nov. 11, 1866; statement by Sidney Clarke quoted in Caldwell, "Kansas," 111; *Esmeralda Union*, June 12, 1868; *Rocky Mountain News*, May 10, 12, 1867; *Alta California*, May 11, 1867; George H. Williams to Matthew P. Deady, Washington, D.C., June 20, 1866, Deady Papers; George H. Williams, *Speech of George H. Williams, United States Senator from Oregon, at Platt's Hall, San Francisco, Tuesday Evening, August 27, 1868* (San Francisco, 1868).

45. *Yreka Union*, July 27, 1867; McLaughlin, "Popular Reactions," 51.

CHAPTER FIVE

Black Suffrage—The Territories

"... the question is one that cannot rest."
—John Church, Nevada

The extension of voting rights to black men remained the most frequently discussed issue of Reconstruction between 1865 and 1870. The quarrel between Johnson and Congress created less excitement after the resounding Republican landslide in 1866, and the restoration of the seceded states became less compelling a topic as reunification appeared a tangible reality during the summer of 1868. But the suffrage question hovered with persistence until the promulgation of the Fifteenth Amendment in 1870. As the war came to a close and as adoption of the Thirteenth Amendment became a certainty, John Church of Nevada predicted that equal suffrage would replace abolition as the new, absorbing topic. Church recognized that differing opinions over suffrage, like those on slavery, would intensify debate and even delay a resolution of the issue; still, he anticipated an eventual decision. "It is clear," wrote Church, "that the question is one that cannot rest; it will be a living political issue in the country until it is disposed of definitely."[1]

Church was among the first to recognize the importance of the suffrage issue. Soon western Republicans and Democrats alike would be announcing that "Negro suffrage is . . . the question of the day," and "the question is coming. . . ." Reviewing the whole Reconstruction issue, Brigham Young mused, "The question of extending suffrage to the negro is a vexed one, and is likely to provoke a great amount of feeling throughout the nation." An astute observer who had watched the West develop around him, Young was aware of local attitudes toward national problems, but even he may have been

---

1. *Virginia* (City, Nev.) *Daily Union,* Apr. 15, 1865.

surprised at the ease with which westerners accepted black suffrage when it finally came.[2]

The "vexed" question, as Young termed it, was to surface in almost every western state and territory. In the five years following the war, equal suffrage was the topic of four different referenda held in Minnesota and Kansas, served as an impediment to quick approval of statehood for Nebraska and Colorado, and stood out as the chief campaign issue in the California legislative election of 1869. Everywhere gradations of opinion over black suffrage sharply distinguished Democrats from Republicans. For Republicans suffrage emerged as the most divisive issue within the party. Western Republican attitudes toward equal suffrage ranged from complete support to total aversion. On the whole the party was more liberal in its outlook than were the Democrats; still, a substantial number of Republicans remained unwilling to extend full civil rights to blacks. Minnesotans alone were to grant equal suffrage of their own volition but not before the question had been submitted to a public vote on three separate occasions. To the other western states and territories black suffrage was to come by direction of the federal government.

Congress enacted four measures between 1867 and 1869 which in their entirety enfranchised blacks throughout the United States. The bills extending the ballot in the District of Columbia (January, 1867) and in the South (March, 1867) did not directly affect the West; provisions of the Territorial Suffrage Act of January, 1867, applied to territories but to none of the western states. It was the Fifteenth Amendment that finally established suffrage in those states, along with all others throughout the country that heretofore denied the ballot to black men. The four acts gradually eliminated suffrage restrictions of whatever dimension. Because different circumstances dictated the need for each measure, westerners responded separately to each act, but in the end they were able to accept equal suffrage *per se*. Their justifications for doing so ranged from the humanitarian and the political, the desire to eliminate the issue from politics and the realization that, like it or not, black men were going to be given the right to vote.

2. *Osage Chronicle*, Jan. 13, 1866; *St. Paul Pioneer*, Aug. 30, 1865; *Oregonian*, Nov. 4, 1865; *Kansas Chief*, May 25, 1865; Brigham Young to William Hooper, Salt Lake City, Feb. 13, 1866, Young Papers.

Westerners took slight notice of Congress's action in January, 1867, extending the ballot to blacks in the District of Columbia. Democrats were busy condemning the various proposals for restoring the South then before Congress and, for the most part, they ignored the measure. Republicans passed lightly over the issue. Those who made comment noted that Congress governed the district by constitutional authority and therefore had the power to enfranchise blacks living there. But anti–black suffrage Republicans, like Ovando J. Hollister of Colorado, reacted negatively from the first introduction of the bill in 1866. Hollister considered enfranchisement of blacks in the district premature. In promoting the reform, he claimed, Congress was ignoring the fact that most blacks in Washington, D.C., had recently been slaves and had no familiarity with sophisticated political issues. It was radical pressure which had initiated the measure, charged Hollister, and it indicated the extremism of radical thought on racial matters. One would have hoped, he chided, "that slavery abolished, the Radicals would be somewhat disposed to be reasonable."[3]

Regarding the extension of black suffrage into the states and territories, western Republicans continually stressed the local nature of the question. At the close of the war it was their belief that suffrage lay within the jurisdiction of each individual state and territory. Because President Johnson's view on the issue was very nearly the same, his stand found wide acceptance, especially in the more conservative areas. As events in the South during 1865 and 1866 began to point toward the necessity of enfranchising blacks in the seceded states at least, western Republicans rationalized the granting of equal suffrage there. They justified suffrage in the former Confederacy as a reward for loyalty, a means of firmly establishing the Republican party throughout the South, and a method by which blacks might protect themselves from abuse and ill-treatment.[4] Some westerners, such as A. S. Smith of California, went further, declaring the imposition of suffrage a "punishment" levied upon the southern states for rejecting the Fourteenth Amendment.[5]

As more Republicans became committed to black suffrage in 1867

3. *Mining Journal*, Feb. 5, 1866.
4. *Ibid.*, Oct. 21, 1865; *Rocky Mountain News*, Jan. 27, 1866; *Oregonian*, Nov. 14, 1865, May 25, 1868; *Reese River Reveille*, May 29, 1868.
5. *Marysville Appeal*, May 27, 1868.

and as predictions of its spread to every state in the Union became commonplace, western Republicans put the onus on the South. One conservative Republican in Oregon, opposed to equal suffrage, lamented the passage of the first Reconstruction Act because it enfranchised all men in the South regardless of race. "Give the Southern negro the ballot," he cried, " and no State North dare exclude them from the polls." More liberal Republicans could accept the trend more graciously. William Stewart, Republican U.S. senator from Nevada, declared that blacks everywhere would be given the franchise. Speaking before an audience in Virginia City in September, 1867, Stewart said, "It is too late to war against negro suffrage." Congress had passed three acts toward its implementation and the enfranchisement of blacks was becoming "an accomplished fact." Anxious to deny any Republican responsibility, he hastened to add that "it grew out of the necessity of the case and the rebels and Copperheads created the necessity." But he was more likely catering to his audience. Just four months earlier Stewart had explained thus his pro-suffrage stand to colleagues in Washington: "When I found the Union party committed to it; when I was thoroughly convinced that it alone would protect the negro . . . , I was resolved to meet the issue, and meet it squarely."[6]

Western Republican humanitarians, Stewart among them, took care to minimize their party's role in the suffrage movement because of the unpopularity of equal suffrage. While it is true that most leaders expressed a relatively liberal viewpoint, the outcome of western referenda on black suffrage in strong Republican areas such as Kansas, Minnesota, and Colorado indicated the conservative inclination of many Republican voters. Both Republicans and Democrats recognized the diversity of opinion on the black suffrage question. "The Republican party is composed of two elements," wrote a California Democrat in 1865. "The radical element is . . . for negro suffrage. . . . The conservative element . . . is unalterably opposed to the extension of the right to suffrage to the negro." Echoing this assertion some three years later, a Nevada Republican remarked: "That these same men [who are against suffrage in the West] are quite content to have negro suffrage established by Congress in South Carolina, may be a little illogical, but nevertheless it is a good deal

6. *Salem Daily Record*, Aug. 17, 1867; *Territorial Enterprise*, Sept. 20, 1867; *Congressional Globe*, 39 Cong., 1 Sess., 2800.

so."[7] Aware of conservative reluctance, Republican spokesmen preferred to underplay their party's responsibility for the reform, lest the granting of equal suffrage work against them at the polls.

In the West itself the extremes of Republican thought have been preserved in two sources—private correspondence and newspaper editorials. In letters to family and friends Leland Stanford, prominent California Republican, aptly reflected the more radical viewpoint, while Cornelius Hedges of Montana was speaking for the most conservative when in candid appraisal of personal feeling he disavowed black suffrage even for the South. Hedges found little fault with the general fabric of congressional legislation on Reconstruction. Yet he was unable to accept the suffrage provision of the first Reconstruction Act. "I cannot really say that I am in favor of letting all the negroes in the south vote," he told his father. "It is letting in too much ignorance." Expressing sympathy for the plight of the southern freedman, Hedges nonetheless admitted the limits of his compassion. "I don't know that I have a much higher opinion of negroes than formerly," he observed quietly, "but I think they are better than rebels. I wish all the negroes could be returned to Africa, if they are not they will soon die out in this country. . . . I shall not mourn the result."[8]

Stanford, California's first Republican governor, was immediately more open to the idea. Writing to Cornelius Cole on the occasion of Cole's inauguration as a U.S. senator, Stanford digressed at length on equal suffrage. He characterized the Civil War as an "incomplete revolution" and looked forward to the time "not very far distant when every citizen will be considered and admitted to have equally one with another the right to a voice in the government. This is with me adopted as a principle and I want to see it carried out to all its legitimate consequences." He took pains to note that by "citizen" he meant women as well as men and would also grant them the right to vote. Rejecting most arguments put forth against black suffrage, Stanford conceded only the black man's inability to understand public issues. With Stanford personally, however, the point was unimportant, for the "poorer and more ignorant a man is, the more consequence that he should have the power to protect himself." The intelligent and wealthy of any country, noted Stanford, had

7. *Yreka Union*, Aug. 5, 1865; *Mountain Champion*, June 19, 1868.
8. Cornelius Hedges to his father, Helena, Sept. 9, 1867, Hedges Family Papers.

always shown the ability to defend themselves. The Californian was especially anxious for blacks in the South to be enfranchised: in his view the "conquered people" there would continue to be defiant, and only the black vote, combined with the loyal white vote, would offset latent feelings of rebellion.[9]

One of the more revealing discussions on black suffrage occurred among three Oregonians—Jesse Applegate, Matthew P. Deady, and Congressman James H. D. Henderson. Each man openly espoused congressional Reconstruction but varied sharply in his opinion of the black vote. Of the three, Applegate held the most radical view. For him the casting of a ballot was the same as providing a directive on how government should function; it was, therefore, "a right belonging to all who support it and obey its laws." To permit one man the vote while denying another was an injustice. No government in good conscience could approve a system which allowed a privileged few to direct policy affecting all persons. Deady's argument was more legalistic. He contended that the state had the authority to determine its electorate for state elections, but that the federal government should prescribe uniform qualifications for those voting in federal elections. Its failure to do so, Deady wrote, was a "solecism and contradiction of our whole system." He concluded that the state's authority in federal elections had been overextended. It was Deady's ardent hope that "the question of negro suffrage, or any other kind of suffrage, in the States for State purposes remain with the States[, but] the question of suffrage as far as the National Government is concerned be regulated by the whole people by a uniform rule throughout the United States."[10]

Henderson's perspective on equal suffrage was the more typical among his western Republican contemporaries and is interesting for its change over a year's time. In 1865 the congressman opposed the extension of suffrage to blacks, but by 1867 he had come to accept the reform. Many radicals at the war's end were declaring the ballot to be logical compensation for those blacks who had remained loyal to the Union or served in its military. But Henderson initially rejected such reasoning. "As to the debt that the government owes the negroes for their services in suppressing the rebellion," he asserted, "I think

9. Leland Stanford to Cornelius Cole, San Francisco, Feb. 9, 1867, Cole Papers.
10. Jesse Applegate to Matthew P. Deady, Yoncalla, Ore., July 7, 1867, Deady Papers; *Oregonian*, Apr. 12, 1866.

that has been overpaid in blood by white men in securing his liberty. There was perhaps tenfold more white blood spilled in securing the negro's freedom than the negroes spilled in sustaining our government. So, I do not consider that the government is in debt to the negro. . . ." To avoid continued friction, Henderson thought it best to let the states determine their own voting qualifications. But within thirteen months Henderson had come to change his mind and, indeed, he became a staunch defender of Congress's right to extend suffrage under federal law. Henderson readily admitted that, for him, the ideal racial solution would be to separate blacks from whites. But separation could only be achieved through deportation and that, declared the congressman, "would be almost as bad as forcing" blacks into slavery in the first place. Like so many western Republicans, he felt a personal repugnance to the presence of a black man. "But," Henderson concluded, "while he is here, God being my helper, I will do him justice."[11]

Republican editors, on the whole, tended to advocate equal suffrage, but their geographical placement as well as the political ramification of their comments sometimes tempered their outspokenness. In areas or cities of the West where the enfranchisement of blacks found a certain acceptance among the populace, editors printed pro–black suffrage editorials with some frequency. Along the Pacific slope, where the issue of the black vote was regarded with suspicion, only the more radical editors dared raise the subject with any regularity. In the Pacific Northwest, where it had found little welcome at all, Republican editors worked at avoiding the equal suffrage question whenever possible. Meanwhile Democrats were denouncing black suffrage in scathing editorials, and Republican editors, regardless of location, chose by and large not to acknowledge this opposition viewpoint. Their reluctance to comment gives the impression that they did not wish to publicize Democratic racial outbursts any more than necessary. To do so would have merely directed attention to the question.

The differences of thought on black suffrage among three Republican editors in Nevada reveal multiformity on the issue within a

---

11. James H. D. Henderson to Addison Gibbs, Washington, D.C., Dec. 16, 1865, Gibbs Papers; *Congressional Globe*, 39 Cong., 1 Sess., 571; John W. North to the Reverend Silvan Hawley, ?, Nev., n.d., in both *St. Paul Press*, Aug. 2, 1865, and Faribault *Central Republican*, Aug. 2, 1865.

closely confined geographic region. The two communities of Carson City and Virginia City are situated some twenty miles apart. The editors of the Republican newpapers in those towns, Joseph T. Goodman of the *Territorial Enterprise* and Henry Mighels of the *Carson Daily Appeal*, were among the strongest western advocates of equal suffrage. In between these communities lay the village of Gold Hill, whose Republican sheet, the *News*, steadily repudiated black suffrage until the promulgation of the Fifteenth Amendment in 1870.

In a unique contribution to the suffrage question, Mighels of the *Appeal* offered continued barbs at Nevada lawmakers. While the predominantly Republican Nevada legislature was most ardent in its support of congressional Reconstruction and pushed for national reform, still, its outlook was notably less generous at home. Consistently denying blacks the right to testify against whites, to vote, or to attend the same public schools as white children, its members spurned every attempt at revision of Nevada's anti-Negro laws. Goodman also criticized this double standard. Similarly he lashed out at lawmakers who were arguing for black suffrage in the South in the hope that it might broaden the Republican electorate there. The hypothesis was without merit, declared Goodman. Suffrage must never be extended for selfish reasons; rather, it should be given through obligation or right of citizenship. To do otherwise was proscriptive and unjust.

Charles A. Sumner, editor of the *News* from 1865 to 1867, was as adamant in his opposition to black suffrage as were his Republican colleagues in Virginia City and Carson City in their support. For every pro-suffrage argument, for every rumor of coming equality at the polls, Sumner offered quick retort. He saw no virtue, for instance, in the supposition that the Republican party would increase its strength in the South by enfranchising blacks. Freedmen were too ignorant, in Sumner's opinion, to understand the issues, and their votes could easily be influenced or purchased by those in power. Approving the Fourteenth Amendment, Sumner nevertheless denied that it would open the voting booth to blacks. In fact, he deplored the possibility and announced, "We object to the enfranchisement of the negro race." He believed blacks too inferior to vote and hold office. When Goodman criticized the Republican platform in 1868 for failing to advocate black suffrage throughout the nation, the *News* came out in support of the party's stand. Despite change in editorship, the *News* continued to argue that adoption of an equal suffrage plank would disappoint many and lead to a Democratic victory. The new editor also characterized as "absurd" the implication that his stand disqualified him as a "good Black Republican." "We don't believe this," he said, insisting that Republican ideals did not include the unqualified right of every man to cast a ballot.[12]

In every western state or territory there were Republicans who skirted the suffrage question by advocating the adoption of a literacy qualification. Chagrined at the success of Democrats in capturing the vote of enfranchised immigrants, these Republicans modified their definition of "literacy" to specify reading and writing of the English language only. They termed it unfair that foreign whites lacking fluency in English be permitted to vote while the ballot was denied to native-born educated blacks. Indeed, D. C. Collier of Colorado disclosed a greater conservatism than most in announcing his approval of any plan to restrict suffrage by means of a literacy test rather than expand the right to vote. Few in reality saw a literacy qualification as the ideal solution, however, as its enforcement posed even greater problems. Moreover, competency in reading and writing English was no guarantee that an elector would want to inform himself on the issues and vote with conscience; any literacy test imposed under this guise would be meaningless.[13]

12. *Carson Appeal*, Mar. 29, Sept. 17, 1867; *Territorial Enterprise*, Sept. 20, 1867; *Gold Hill News*, June 4, July 18, 19, 21, 1866, Sept. 16, 1867, May 25, 1868, Apr. 7, 1870. Other western Republican newspapers opposed to equal suffrage included the *Mining Journal* (until Jan., 1867), Mar. 1, 1866; *Washington Standard*, June 19, July 1, 1865; *Pacific Tribune*, June 24, 1865; *Salem Daily Record*, Feb. 26, 1868; *Oregon State Journal*, Dec. 30, 1865. Republican racial benevolence did not extend to Indians. Two Republican newspapers to espouse a lenient Indian policy were the urban San Francisco *Bulletin*, May 20, 1868, and the *Sacramento Union*, July 13, 1865. The Mormon-dominated *Telegraph* adopted a pro-Indian stance, but it appeared to be part of an anti-Gentile propaganda campaign. *Salt Lake* (City, Utah) *Daily Telegraph*, June 10, 1868. Among those Republicans calling for harsh treatment, even extermination, of Indians, were editors of the *Gold Hill News*, July 14, Aug. 26, 1865, Jan. 30, Feb. 26, 1867; *Carson Appeal*, Feb. 5, July 11, Aug. 9, 1867; Atchison *Free Press*, May 19, 1865, Jan. 22, 1867; *Leavenworth Conservative*, July 10, 1866, July 19, 1867, June 6, 1868; *Kansas Tribune*, Jan. 26, 1868; *Vedette*, Apr. 21, 1865; *Oregonian*, Aug. 30, 1865, Sept. 28, 1866; *Emporia News*, Jan. 26, 1867; *Junction Union*, Dec. 29, 1866; and *Rochester Post*, June 8, 1867.

13. Republicans who defended a literacy qualification on at least one occasion included editors of the *Marysville Appeal*, Apr. 30, 1865; *Oakland News*, Dec. 10, 1865; *Napa Register*, May 6, 1865; *American Unionist*, Dec. 3, 1866; *Salem Daily Record*, May 22, 1868; *Carson Appeal*, July 7, 1867; *Miner's Register*, Jan. 4, 1867; *Montana Post*, Feb. 12, 1869; *Atchison Champion*, June 17, 1865; *Nebraska Herald*,

Given the lack of unanimity on black suffrage, western Republican leaders avoided taking a positive stand or making the advocacy of equal suffrage a test of party loyalty. From 1865 through the election of 1868, they continued to deny equal suffrage as a national goal, and they tolerated party members voicing opinions both for and against the reform. In 1865 D. C. Collier recorded the trend: "Democratic leaders are more unanimous in their opposition to negro suffrage than the Republicans are in favor of it." And A. S. Smith of California added, "Universal suffrage is not a party question, and the Copperheads cannot make it one." The Republican position was so flexible as to allow every man to express his own opinion, argued Smith, no matter what it might be. Three years later, in 1868, Collier was still insisting that "impartial suffrage has never been authentatively made a test of Republicanism. There are many Republicans who do not believe it necessary or for the best. Whether we can afford to make it a party shibboleth remains to be seen. Only at present it is not so." Smith, for his part, had become an ardent champion of equal suffrage, but during the election he retreated somewhat, recognizing that "the black man, if admitted to franchise rights, will always remain subject to the political control of the white majority."[14]

While there were, of course, western Republicans who favored a positive commitment on equal suffrage by the party,[15] still the only state group which publicly advocated the ballot for all men was the Minnesota Republican organization. For other areas of the West Democrats played upon Republican ambiguity throughout the postwar years. Of a Republican territorial convention in Idaho during the summer of 1865, a Democrat criticized the party faithful for hedging on the black suffrage issue: "The Convention lacks the courage to

Dec. 26, 1867; *Nebraska Republican,* Nov. 14, 1865; *Minneapolis Chronicle,* Dec. 21, 1866; *St. Paul Press,* June 18, 1865. Opposed were *Emporia News,* June 3, 1865; *Sierra Advocate* (Downieville, Calif.), Feb. 9, 1867. There is every indication that blacks would have accepted a literacy qualification. For example, see comments by Philip Bell in *Elevator,* June 9, 23, 1865; by Lewis H. Douglass in *Colorado Tribune,* June 6, 1867; and by the Reverend John Turner in *Proceedings of the Colored Convention of the State of Kansas, Held at Leavenworth, October 13th, 14th, 15th & 16th, 1863* (Leavenworth, 1863), 4.

14. *Miner's Register,* Oct. 22, 1865, Jan. 7, 1868; *Marysville Appeal,* June 23, Aug. 22, 1865, July 25, 1868.

15. *Emporia News,* Feb. 15, 1867; *Kansas Tribune,* Sept. 15, 1867; *Leavenworth Conservative,* Aug. 25, 1867; *Mantorville Express,* Sept. 29, 1865; *Eastern Slope,* (Washoe City, Nev.), Oct. 19, 26, 1867.

meet the question squarely. It dare not pledge its candidates against it. It dare not come out openly before the people in favor of it." Similarly, a California Democrat wrote of a Republican convention in Placer County, "I was amused at the ingenious manner in which they dodged the only issue before the people at the present time; not daring to come out and say that they were in favor of negro suffrage, nor yet willing to go before the people and say that they were opposed to it, they referred the subject to a Committee on Resolutions, knowing that it would never be reported to the Convention; and now they have the brazen impudence to come before the people and say it is no issue!"[16]

Not only did Oregon's Republican organization dodge the suffrage issue, but office seekers consistently held back. Because black suffrage was so unpopular in the state, Republican candidates either refused to discuss it, claiming that equal suffrage had not been included in the party platform, or came out in clear opposition to it. Refuting several years later the Democratic charge that this Republican silence on equal suffrage was "peculiar," Henry Pittock, editor of the *Oregonian*, insisted that there was nothing at all "peculiar" about it. The Republican party, he retorted, had never adopted black suffrage as a principle. It had forced equal suffrage on the South but merely as a punishment for treason. "Very many earnest Republicans," Pittock continued, "still oppose it on principle, and only gave assent to it in the reconstruction acts on the conviction that it would . . . lead to a restoration of the Union and keep red-handed rebels out of Congress and prevent them from obtaining control of the country."[17]

Republicans in Kansas took pride in referring to their state as "the most radicalized state in the Union." Yet a number of these so-called "radicals" clearly embraced a concept of radicalism which supported Congress in its quarrel with the president and excluded equal suffrage. Most Republicans known to one editor in Kansas considered themselves "good radicals," but as of 1865 they were not willing to extend the ballot to black Kansans. An equal suffrage proposition put before the electorate at this time would, by his estimate, go down to defeat

16. *Idaho World*, July 9, 1865; "E. L. C." to editor, Georgetown, Calif., July 23, 1865, in *Placerville Democrat*, Aug. 5, 1865. See also R. C. Gaskill to John Bidwell, San Francisco, Jan. 21, 1866, Bidwell Papers, CSUC.

17. Matthew P. Deady to James Nesmith, Portland, Ore., June 11, 1866, Nesmith Papers; *Oregonian*, May 4, 1868; Salem (Ore.) *Weekly Democratic Review*, Mar. 12, 1866.

by a two-thirds margin. Even two years later other Kansas editors were continuing to stress the unpopularity of black suffrage and the lack of Republican commitment toward it. "The Republican party lacks unanimity on the question of negro suffrage," declared one. "It is useless to say that a man is not a republican because he opposes negro suffrage. . . . It is also altogether useless to say a man is not a republican because he favors negro suffrage."[18] Throughout the West, then, there was a hesitancy among Republicans to commit themselves firmly on black suffrage. Even though many party leaders personally favored the reform, they avoided the issue because of its political ramifications. Were they even tempted, they would have to face a Democratic opposition anxiously waiting to distort any Republican statement implying racial benevolence.

Democrats saw real political gain, after all, in portraying Republicans as seekers of racial equality. Democrats knew well enough the Republican stand regarding equal suffrage in the loyal states—that each state be permitted to decide the basis of suffrage for itself. But they preferred to misrepresent the position, giving the impression that Republicans wished to enfranchise every black man in the nation. Whenever Democrats met, claimed one western Republican, they "trotted out the negro question" and equated the liberality of a few extremists to the mood of the Republican party as a whole.[19] Because Democrats opposed black suffrage, they presumed Republicans to favor it. Republican candidates for office were not being honest with the public, insisted their Democratic opposition, when they remained silent on the question or spoke out against it.

Black suffrage, said western Democrats, would lead inevitably to social equality, and the elimination of all racial distinction between whites and blacks was the ultimate Republican goal. The charge was not new. Ever since the rise of militant antislavery in Jacksonian America, Democrats had been leveling the charge of racial equality against groups that sought to ameliorate the black man's position, and it had always proved an effective theme. From Los Angeles A. J. King warned, "The negro has such a hold on the radical party, they dare not stop short of complete equality." Even those Repub-

18. *Kansas Chief,* Nov. 23, 1865; *Border Sentinel,* Oct. 25, 1867; *Olathe Mirror,* Nov. 14, 1867, Mar. 5, 1868.
19. *Marysville Appeal,* May 26, June 10, 19, July 16, 1868.

licans who shunned blacks, said he, would have to face miscegenation should political equality be granted. Alarmed at the nativist thinking among some Republicans, a German immigrant in Nebraska charged all foreign-born Americans to vote Democratic. Should the Republican party continue to dominate the nation politically, he asserted, all foreigners—less favored still—would end up as house servants for blacks. Such exaggerations had no basis in fact, but they indicated the extent to which Democratic progagandists were willing to go. Said one San Franciscan pessimistically, "It . . . cannot stop at political and civil rights—it must take in as well social rights. It not only puts Sambo in the legislative halls, places him on the bench and arms him with the ballot, but it opens to him all places of amusement, our hotels, ball rooms, etc." Finally he alluded to the ultimate fear of many whites: "It does not restrict him in selecting his matrimonial partner to the dusky Dianahs of Africa, but allows him to revel as well in the charms of the fair daughters of Caucasis."[20]

Prior to and during the Civil War, Democratic harangues about Republican designs for racial equality had led to emotional outbursts. Pointing to the mulatto population in the South, western Republicans had at that time charged Democrats with favoring miscegenation; typically they referred to the Republican as the "white man's party."[21] During Reconstruction a few western Republicans fell back on this tactic in answering Democratic accusations, while others chose not to dignify the Democratic argument by responding to it. Those who did, like Orville Brown of Minnesota, referred to the Democratic contention as "a silly argument" because a republican form of government could never regulate the social lives of its people. Brown dismissed as preposterous the idea that blacks and whites in America would ever intermingle socially; "there is too much prejudice against the negro." In any case—prejudice or no—Republicans preferred the

---

20. *Los Angeles News*, Jan. 5, 1867; "Northwest" to editor, n.p., n.d., in *Nebraska City News*, Apr. 10, 1868; San Francisco *Examiner*, Dec. 29, 1866. For similar statements see *Oregon Herald*, Apr. 21, 1866, Oct. 1, 1867. Not all Democrats were as rigid in their prejudice against blacks, however. F. J. Stanton of Denver opposed black suffrage but conceded that "the negro has the right to live, move and . . . possess his freedom." M. H. Abbott of Oregon, concluding a long editorial against equal suffrage, wrote, "Because we do not want negroes to vote, . . . it does not follow that we hate them." *Denver Daily Gazette*, June 13, 1868; *States Rights Democrat*, Jan. 4, 1868.

21. For example, see Berwanger, *Frontier against Slavery*, 128–29.

argument that the government was obliged to protect all its people under the law and nothing further.[22]

But other Republicans replied in anger, denouncing Democratic charges of social equality and their anti-Negro comments as "indecent," "ungentlemanly," and "vulgar." On the West coast Republican editors characterized the Democratic attack as a "supreme humbug" and "a cry without foundation."[23] Democrats were stressing social equality only to excite prejudice and to secure political advantage, Republicans believed, and a few accurately predicted that Democratic politicians would find black men less objectionable once they were given the right to vote.

Blacks in the West responded to the suffrage debate according to their personal dictates, with either understanding or outright condemnation. Taking a pessimistic attitude, Thomas Detter of Idaho criticized the Republican party for keeping "the Jewels of Freedom and Justice" to itself. He concluded that in spite of their pronouncements that all men were equal, Republicans feared "negro supremacy. . . . Negro suffrage produced panic in their ranks." Philip Bell, editor of the *Elevator* in San Francisco, reacted with somewhat more optimism. Bell supported Republican candidates at the state level throughout the postwar years even though many were noncommittal on suffrage. Not all Republicans favored equal suffrage, Bell had to agree, but still he believed the party was moving in that direction "and to such conclusions [it] must ultimately arrive."

Bell assumed a less compliant attitude in responding to Democratic charges of social equality, denying that blacks desired any kind of social leveling with whites. In 1865 he recounted his daily contact with white editors in San Francisco. Describing these encounters as friendly and professional, Bell emphasized that "our social connection extends no further." Nor did he wish to be more familiar with his colleagues in the newspaper business. As Democrats began to vilify blacks during the campaign of 1868, Bell could feel nothing but contempt. Reminding his readers that "the highest condition of social equality is sexual intercourse," Bell with scathing incrimination called

22. *Rocky Mountain News*, June 16, 23, 1868; *Oregonian*, Apr. 21, 1868; Faribault *Central Republican*, Oct. 11, 1865; *Wathena Reporter*, June 6, 1867; *Carson Appeal*, Nov. 14, 1865.

23. *Nebraska Herald*, Sept. 26, 1867; *Humboldt Times*, Dec. 16, 1865; *Marysville Appeal*, Nov. 10, 1867; Sacramento *Bee*, Apr. 7, 1866; *Monterey Gazette*, May 14, 1868.

Democrats the "supreme hypocrites. The chief cornerstone of the institution of slavery had been adultery, until a virtuous female slave was almost considered an exception. . . . [Democrats] were willing that licentious white men should seduce our females, but they are struck with holy horror at the mere possibility of niggers marrying their daughters." Social and political equality were two different issues, argued Bell. A strong advocate of equal suffrage, he nonetheless believed that "we have never made any claim to social equality. We do not desire it. We are content with our own social status, and we ask no more." A convention of blacks, meeting in Lawrence, Kansas, in 1866, also shunned social intermingling. "We do not desire [it]," they declared, "but we demand equality before the law. We seek complete emancipation—absolute legal equality."[24]

Where the black population in western states and territories was concentrated or sufficiently large, blacks became active in seeking the franchise and removal of legal restrictions. For their loyalty during the war, their willingness to pay taxes and meet other obligations of citizenship, and because the national creed espoused the equality of man, they now demanded legal equality. Those in attendance at the Lawrence convention in 1866 offered a resolution: "Since we are going to remain among you, we believe it unwise or inhuman to continue discrimination. . . . Shall our presence conduce to the welfare, peace and prosperity of the state, or . . . be a cause of dissention, discord, and irritation." Blacks undertook to use whatever means available to publicize their demands. Holding local and state conventions to press for the repeal of anti-Negro laws, they presented petitions to legislatures in California, Nevada, Kansas, and Colorado on at least one occasion each between 1865 and 1867 requesting the right to vote.[25] Although Republicans dominated every legislature in question, the appeals went unheard. Black Americans were soon to learn that their own concerns were of minor importance before local politicians who, in their zeal to retain office, preferred not to take on unpopular causes.

24. "T. D." [Thomas Detter] to editor, Idaho City, Idaho, June 13, 1868, in *Elevator*, July 3, 1868; *Elevator*, May 19, 1865, Aug. 23, 1867, Aug. 14, 1868; *Kansas Tribune*, Oct. 28, 1866; Atchison *Free Press*, Oct. 26, 1866.

25. *Kansas Tribune*, Oct. 28, 1866. The *Elevator* contains detailed reports on public meetings in California and Nevada—see June 3, Oct. 27, 1865, Jan. 6, 12, Feb. 16, 1866, Feb. 2, 6, Oct. 11, 1867. Beasley, *Negro Trail Blazers*, 62–65; Elmer R. Rusco, *"Good Time Coming?" Black Nevadans in the Nineteenth Century* (Westport, Conn., 1975), 74–75; Caldwell, "Kansas," 108ff.

The only successful western black campaign for equal suffrage occurred in Colorado Territory. There blacks brought to the attention
of federal lawmakers the inconsistency between the radical philosophy
and the refusal of white Coloradans to enfranchise black men. In
remedying the situation, Congress passed the Territorial Suffrage Act,
granting the ballot to blacks in Colorado and in all other territories
as well.

Colorado blacks first began to press for equal suffrage in 1864 when
the territorial legislature attached a restrictive amendment to Colorado's voting law. Although election statutes enacted in 1861 had
extended the ballot to all "male persons" twenty-one years of age
or older, the amendment of March, 1864, declared that these "male
persons" did not include blacks and mulattoes; they were now expressly denied the right to vote. Local blacks angrily claimed that
the amendment deprived them of a privilege they had enjoyed until
its passage. White leaders denied the charge. When former territorial
governor John Evans in 1866 explained the legislature's action to
Congress, he merely observed that black men had not voted before
1864 and therefore the amendment had made no practical difference
in their political status.[26]

Intent on overturning the new discriminatory law, blacks in July,
1864, sent a small delegation to the state constitutional convention
where they lobbied unsuccessfully for equal suffrage. Because the
constitution was rejected at the polls, a second constitutional convention met in 1865. This time the convention submitted the suffrage
question, along with the constitution, to a public vote. On September
5, 1865, enfranchised Coloradans approved the constitution by 155
votes but rejected equal suffrage by a vote of 4,192 to 476. The
strongest opposition to enfranchising blacks came from the southern
part of the territory where many Mexican-Americans had settled.
The largest number of pro-Negro votes were cast in the heavily
populated regions around Denver and Central City, areas where most
blacks also lived.[27]

---

26. *General Laws of the First Session of the Colorado Territorial Legislature, 1861*
(Denver, 1861), 72–73; *General Laws of the Third Session . . . 1864* (Denver, 1864),
79–80; *Rocky Mountain News*, Feb. 8, 1866; Mothershead, "Negro Rights," 218–19.
27. *Congressional Globe*, 39 Cong., 1 Sess., 1351; *Rocky Mountain News*, Sept.
19, 1865. Both federal and territorial officials estimated the black population in
1866 to be about 150 persons. *Congressional Globe*, 39 Cong., 1 Sess., 1327.

Black Coloradans refused to accept the decision. Under the leadership of a group of barbers in Denver, including Edward Sanderlin, Henry O. Wagoner, and William J. Hardin, they urged Congress to delay Colorado's statehood until suffrage was guaranteed to all men. Especially outspoken was William Jefferson Hardin, who after his arrival in the Denver area in 1863 was quickly to become a leading civil rights figure. It was the rejection of equal suffrage in the 1865 referendum which angered him in particular and moved him to take up the campaign for equal justice in Colorado Territory. Throughout the fall and winter of 1865–66 he spoke before audiences on behalf of civil rights and actively challenged candidates for public office to debate the subject.

Hardin's efforts went well beyond speech-making. In a national appeal he wrote and telegraphed Senator Charles Sumner and Horace Greeley, editor of the *New York Tribune,* asking them to denounce publicly the lack of equal suffrage in Colorado and to use their influence against the territory's admission as a state so long as the suffrage restriction remained in effect. Basically Hardin argued for equal suffrage as an act of justice for blacks, and he objected to Colorado's admission with restricted suffrage lest it set a precedent for the postwar period. Privately he admitted to Sumner, "Slavery went down in a great deluge of blood, and I greatly fear, unless the american [sic] people learn from the past to do justice now, & in the future, that their cruel & unjust prejudices will, some day, go down in the same crimson blood." Responses to Hardin's appeal varied. Greeley spurned Hardin's call, insisting that black suffrage, while desirable, should never be a condition for granting statehood. Sumner reacted more favorably and, consistent with his avowed ideals, objected to Colorado's constitution because of the voting restriction.[28]

28. *Rocky Mountain News,* Nov. 4, 18, 1865, Jan. 15, 1866; William J. Hardin to Charles Sumner, Denver, Feb. 4, 1866, Sumner Papers; Hardin to Sumner (telegram), Denver, Jan. 15, 1866, in *Congressional Globe,* 39 Cong., 1 Sess., 2138; Hardin to Horace Greeley, Denver, Dec. 15, 1865, and Greeley's reply in *New York Tribune,* Jan. 15, 1866. Sumner consistently voted against statehood for Colorado during the first session of the Thirty-ninth Congress, even though some senators supported admission in order to secure additional votes in the quarrel with Johnson. Only with the passage of the Edmunds amendment, which stipulated equal suffrage as a condition for statehood, did Sumner agree to Colorado's admission. *Congressional Globe,* 39 Cong., 1 Sess., 1329–31, 1352, 1365; 2 Sess., 360–64.

The impact that Colorado black leaders had at the national level was limited by their own lack of prominence and their lack of personal acquaintance with national politicians. Locally they could do much more, and here blacks were able to enlist the aid of Alexander Cummings, territorial governor. On December 11, 1865, Hardin and several of his cohorts asked Cummings to forward to Congress a petition containing the names of 137 blacks who were angered by the voting restriction. To deny equal suffrage, they asserted, was to disregard "the bloody lessons of the last four years." Because the governor opposed Colorado's admission and thought the denial of black suffrage would forestall it, he forwarded the appeal to Secretary of State William Seward for transmittal to Congress.[29]

The petition sought to prevent statehood by arguing that the number of voters who approved the 1865 constitution was too small to indicate overwhelming sentiment for statehood. More important, insisted the petitioners, the state constitution ignored the recent rebellion by making color, not patriotism, the test for the right of suffrage. All restrictions against blacks should be removed, contended the signatories, and Congress should not admit Colorado into the Union "until the word *white* be erased from her State Constitution. . . . We ask for nothing but even handed justice," they concluded, "and we feel assured you will not turn a deaf ear to our humble and earnest appeal. . . ."[30]

During the next month, January, 1866, Hardin and four other blacks went to the governor with a second petition; this time they asked the territorial legislature to repeal the 1864 voting restriction. Cummings forwarded the document to the legislature along with a personal appeal for equal suffrage. United in their opposition, the legislators ignored both the petition and the governor's recommendation.[31]

29. Henry Wagoner, J. G. Smith, and William J. Hardin to Alexander Cummings, Denver, Dec. 11, 1865, Cummings to William Seward, Denver, Dec. 23, 1865, both in TP: Colorado Series, Vol. I, 1859–1874, NARG 59.
30. "Petition of Colored Citizens to Congress," n.d., in TP: Colorado, I. The territorial papers contain both printed and manuscript copies. They vary only in certain capitalizations and in the spelling of four signatures.
31. Territory of Colorado, *House Journal, 1866* (Black Hawk, 1866), 82–83; "Petition of Colored Citizens to the Territorial Legislature," Hardin, Wagoner, Albert Arbor, A. C. Clark, and W. Randolph to Alexander Cummings, Denver, Jan. 20, 1866, Cummings to William Seward, Denver, Jan. 29, 1866, "Special Message on Black Suffrage," all in TP: Colorado, I. The governor forwarded copies of the petition and his message to Seward.

The appeal of the blacks also failed initially to impress a majority of the Congress. Over radical Republican opposition to the restricted suffrage provision—with Charles Sumner in the fore—Congress voted in April, 1866, to admit Colorado. Statehood was not to be realized with congressional endorsement alone, however; Andrew Johnson vetoed the bill, arguing primarily that the territory had too small a population to be a state. Since this contention had earlier found support among many senators, it came as no surprise when the upper house failed to override the president's veto.[32]

Though Johnson's veto message ignored the civil rights argument in the blacks' petition, the document nonetheless had important consequences. Its exposure of the denial of black suffrage in Colorado Territory came at a time when equality at the polls was arousing much interest in Congress. Discussion among lawmakers from January to May, 1866, over the admission of the territory offered radical Republicans continuing opportunity to protest restricted suffrage there.[33] Finally, under their leadership and after months of legislative maneuvering, Congress in January, 1867, forbade restricted suffrage because of color in all U.S. territories.

The timing of and debate over the Territorial Suffrage Act indicated the influence of the Colorado situation on the measure. On May 15, 1866, Andrew Johnson vetoed Colorado's admission, a move which left the area a territory and, under the 1864 legislative restriction, limited voting to whites only. On the same day James Ashley of Ohio, chairman of the Committee on Territories, introduced in the House of Representatives a bill regulating territorial government. Of its nine provisions, five required territorial legislatures to pass laws severely restricting the activities of corporations within their boundaries, two concerned salaries of federal appointees in territories, one denied territorial governments the power to grant divorce, and the last gave all citizens (except Indians) the right to vote. Ashley characterized his bill as primarily an attempt to prevent special interest groups from securing unlimited favors in the newly settled regions. He did not refute two criticisms: one, that several of the provisions were illogical inasmuch as territorial legislatures

32. *Congressional Globe*, 39 Cong., 1 Sess., 2135–38, 2180; U.S. Congress, Senate, "Message of President Johnson Regarding the Admission of Colorado," *Senate Executive Documents*, 39 Cong., 1 Sess., Doc. 45 (ser. 1238); *Rocky Mountain News*, June 26, 1866.

33. *Congressional Globe*, 39 Cong., 1 Sess., 210, 1327–29, 2180.

could not be compelled to pass laws limiting their own powers; two, that the first eight provisions were a mere veil to force black suffrage upon the territories. The measure passed the House by a vote of ninety-seven to forty-three, with fifty-one members not voting. The Senate failed to take action before the close of the session.[34]

While Congress debated the Colorado Constitution, the predominantly Republican legislature in Nebraska Territory, at the suggestion of Governor Alvin Saunders, was preparing a state constitution which also limited suffrage to white men. Legislators included the restriction specifically to entice the approval of those Democrats who favored statehood but opposed equal suffrage. Approved by the slim majority of one hundred votes in June, 1866, the document was presented to Congress too late in the session to receive serious consideration.[35]

When Congress reconvened in December, 1866, Republicans were elated over the gains the party had made in the recent national elections. Interpreting their victory as a vote of confidence for congressional policy, Republicans determined to wrest control of Reconstruction from the president. In doing so they moved forward on suffrage. After overriding Johnson's veto of the bill enfranchising blacks in the District of Columbia on January 8, 1867, Congress within a week passed measures expanding suffrage in the West as well. The first two were amendments to separate bills admitting Nebraska and Colorado. Introduced by Senator George Edmunds of Vermont and called either the "fundamental condition" or the "Edmunds Amendment," they stipulated that each territory be admitted only when its respective legislature had inserted into the state constitution an irrevocable clause providing for equal suffrage, and at such time as the president had received formal notice of the action. Passed as amended, both statehood bills received a presidential veto. Congress overrode the Nebraska denial but sustained Johnson's objections to statehood for Colorado.[36]

34. Ibid., 2148, 2210, 2600–2603, 3476, 3525–29.
35. W. P. Polock to Charles Sumner, Brownville, Neb., Nov. 19, 1866, Sumner Papers; Thomas Kennard to Andrew Johnson, Omaha, July 1, 1866, Kennard Papers; Alvin Saunders to Johnson, Omaha, July 3, 1866, in TP: Nebraska; Sheldon, Nebraska, I, 341. Congress received the Nebraska Constitution on July 23, 1866, five days before the close of the session. Congressional Globe, 39 Cong., 1 Sess., 4044.
36. Morton and Watkins, Nebraska, II, 550, 559–60; Edward L. Pierce, Memoir and Letters of Charles Sumner, 4 vols. (Boston, 1893), IV, 284–86; Georges Clemenceau, American Reconstruction, 1865–1870, ed. Fernand Baldensperger (New

Inasmuch as Nebraska was the only territory admitted to statehood between the passage of the Edmunds amendment in 1867 and the promulgation of the Fifteenth Amendment in 1870, its legislature alone had to consent to the "fundamental condition." Republicans, anxious to secure statehood, supported the change but with little enthusiasm. Conservative Republican territorial secretary Algernon S. Paddock, although less opposed to equal suffrage than formerly, thought the 1867 condition too inclusive. Paddock favored suffrage for black veterans or educated blacks but not for every adult male. When Governor Saunders formally presented the Edmunds amendment to the legislature in February, 1867, he urged acceptance despite personal reservations about the political wisdom of requiring the lawmakers to assume the responsibility for black suffrage. Saunders thought it would have been wiser to submit the change to a referendum. Still, he said gamely, "we must meet the question as we find it, or as it has been presented by Congress."[37]

Nebraska Democrats were indignant. They railed against the "fundamental condition" as an "unconstitutional usurpation," an "invasion of the principles of States Rights and a dangerous encroachment upon the traditionary principles of our republican right to local self-government." But their argument lost force before the realization that black Nebraskans would vote whether or not the legislature accepted the condition. Congress had recently enfranchised blacks in all territories; should Nebraska fail to approve the Edmunds amendment, she would remain a territory and blacks would vote under the terms of the Territorial Suffrage Act. Republican advocates found a rallying point: if the legislature could accede now to federal demands, Nebraska would at least escape the odium of having black suffrage forced on her by Congress. With these thoughts in mind, the legislature unanimously approved the "fundamental condition" on February 21, 1867. Nine days later Nebraska was officially admitted into the Union.[38]

York, 1969), 80; *Colorado Transcript*, Feb. 20, 1867; *Rocky Mountain News*, Jan. 29, 1867; Lamar, *Far Southwest*, 261; *Congressional Globe*, 39 Cong., 2 Sess., 481, 487, 535–36, 1096, 1121, 1928.

37. Territory of Nebraska, *Council Journal, 1866–1867* (Omaha, 1867), 7, 17; State of Nebraska, *House Journal, 1867* (Omaha, 1867), 1–3; Sheldon, *Nebraska*, I, 364–65.

38. *Nebraska Advertiser*, Jan. 17, 1867; *Nebraska Herald*, Jan. 23, 30, Feb. 27, 1867; *Omaha Herald*, Mar. 2, 22, Apr. 12, 1867; State of Nebraska, *House Journal*,

A third measure enfranchising additional blacks in the West was the Territorial Suffrage Act. While the Senate was again debating the denial of suffrage to blacks in Colorado during January, 1867, Benjamin Wade resurrected Ashley's territorial bill. In his view it related to the lack of equal suffrage in Colorado; he hinted that it would solve the suffrage question in all territories. Amending Ashley's bill to strike all provisions except the one stipulating equal suffrage, Wade successfully maneuvered it to a final vote of twenty-four to seven in the Senate on January 10. Rushed to the House on the same day, the amended bill was approved within two hours. It became law without the president's signature on January 31, 1867.[39]

The Territorial Suffrage Act is one of the forgotten measures of Reconstruction history. The act has received very little notice in general studies on Reconstruction, and it has been skipped over in many western state histories—indeed, the extension of suffrage to blacks is mentioned in few of them. The failure to heed the act is unfortunate, for, along with the Edmunds amendment, it indicated the strength of will behind the congressional Republican stand on suffrage. New states and existing territories, at least, would no longer be permitted to adopt suffrage restrictions based on race. The precedent of disfranchising blacks in the western states (a pattern followed by every western state and territory since 1800) was to be reversed. If the states and territories failed to grant black suffrage of their own volition, then Republicans in Congress were determined that the federal government should do so. This new directive was not acceptable to all Republicans, especially congressmen from the West. Of the seventeen Republican representatives and senators from the western states, eight chose to absent themselves when the final votes

---

1867, 52; Sara L. Baisinger, "Nebraska and Reconstruction" (M.A. thesis, University of Nebraska, 1928), 100. After voting to accept the Edmunds amendment, Democrats in the legislature opposed a bill implementing equal suffrage. In order to keep this opposition from becoming a matter of public record, Republican officers in the legislature refused to recognize Democrats attempting to speak against the measure. J. Sterling Morton reported that authorities in Omaha, declaring the "fundamental condition" invalid, refused to let blacks vote in the municipal election on Mar. 4, 1867. Omaha newspapers failed to mention the matter. *Omaha Herald*, Mar. 1, 1867; *Nebraska City News*, Mar. 2, 16, 1867.

39. It should be noted, however, that twenty-one senators abstained. *Congressional Globe*, 39 Cong., 2 Sess., 364–65, 382, 398–99, 890; *Miner's Register*, Jan. 16, 1867.

were taken on the act.[40] Republican congressmen from the West gave less support to the Territorial Suffrage Act than to any other Reconstruction-related measure considered between 1865 and 1870.

Response to the Territorial Suffrage Act had interesting ramifications: it gave an indication of popular reaction should Congress impose equal suffrage in areas that had not engaged in rebellion. If radicals and pro-suffrage moderates in the national legislature feared a public rejection of a national suffrage law, those fears certainly must have been allayed by the response to the territorial act. Considering the bill's potential impact, reaction to it was surprisingly mild in the West. From the introduction of Ashley's bill in May, 1866, until final implementation of equal suffrage in the territories in 1867, Republicans in the West remained silent or expressed approval of the measure. Democrats and political independents, for their part, condemned every version of the bill. They wondered openly why so many congressmen were willing to impose black suffrage on territories when they were reluctant to approve it within their own states. Gloomily, W. B. Carter of Oregon predicted that black suffrage in the territories was only the first step. Next Congress would initiate suffrage in the southern states, he announced, and eventually extend it to every state in the Union. Carter himself regarded the Territorial Suffrage Act as unwise in view of the intense race prejudice in the territories; further, it completely disregarded the objections of whites to black suffrage. "No act could operate more injuriously to the best interest of the negroes," wrote Carter, and he assumed the people in the territories would "get up a war of extermination" before they would permit blacks to vote.[41]

Carter's conjecture proved wrong. Although chagrined, whites liv-

40. See Appendix.

41. For the Republican reaction see *Kansas Patriot*, May 26, 1866; *Mantorville Express*, June 1, 1866; *St. Paul Press*, May 24, 1866; Atchison *Free Press*, Jan. 14, 1867; *Atchison Champion*, Jan. 30, 1867; *Sacramento Union*, Jan. 31, 1867; *Kansas Tribune*, Jan. 15, 1867. Democratic comments are found in the *Oregon Herald*, May 25, 1866; *Corvallis* (Ore.) *Gazette*, May 26, 1866. Frederick MacCrellish, editor of the *Alta California*, described the Edmunds amendment as potentially more damaging than the Territorial Suffrage Act. While acknowledging the right of Congress to enfranchise blacks in the territories, MacCrellish denied that Congress could actually impose equal suffrage on new states. He disliked the phrase in the Edmunds amendment forbidding the denial of voting rights on account of race at any future time and declared that it disregarded the power of a state to amend its own fundamental law. *Alta California*, Jan. 17, 1867.

ing in territories generally accepted equal suffrage with decorum. Democrats in Washington Territory did issue an address criticizing Congress for amending its territorial law restricting suffrage after that law had been in effect for fourteen years, and Idaho Democrats complained that the suffrage act relegated the territories to the same status as the rebel states. Conservative Republicans who opposed equal suffrage found fault with the law too. But they did note one positive aspect of the bill—the territories could at least thank Congress for removing the suffrage question from territorial politics.[42]

The Territorial Suffrage Act voided all laws in conflict with it; still, two legislatures saw fit to respond to the bill's passage. Upon the advice of Governor Andrew Faulk, the Dakota legislature in 1867 revised the territory's voting law, striking out the word "white." Montana remained somewhat more defiant. Its legislature passed a bill prohibiting discrimination at the polls but voted to retain the phrase "all white male citizens" in the original election law. So angered were some radicals in Washington, D.C., by this resistance that they threatened to repeal Montana's organic act. Montana lawmakers, becoming more contrite in the next session, expunged the offending phrase from the statutes.[43]

Despite lingering objection locally, blacks voted without incident in the Montana election of 1867. Jack Simmons, a Nevadan visiting in Helena, estimated that between 200 and 400 black men in the territory cast their ballots. Describing their behavior as decorous, Simmons saw little drinking among the blacks; they merely recorded their vote and left the polling places. Most Montanans were in effect unconcerned about the imposition of black suffrage, wrote Simmons, and in its wake he doubted even a loss of twenty-five votes for the Republican party. Still, Simmons believed Montana Republicans to be conservative in their racial outlook. Although willing to let blacks vote, they were opposed to loosening other legal restrictions. They expected distinction between the races to continue, Simmons con-

42. *Washington Standard*, Jan. 26, 1867; *Walla Walla Statesman*, Feb. 8, 1867; *Idaho World*, May 25, 28, 1866; *Idaho Statesman*, June 12, 1866; *Salt Lake Telegraph*, Feb. 7, 1867.

43. TP: Dakota, 1861–1873, NARG 59; *Union and Dakotan* (Yankton, Dakota), Feb. 16, 21, 1867; William Gillette, *The Right to Vote: Politics and the Passage of the Fifteenth Amendment* (Baltimore, 1969), 30; Spence, *Montana*, 48–49; *Congressional Globe*, 40 Cong., 2 Sess., 781.

cluded, but in regard to equal suffrage, "all the injury it can do
. . . is passed."[44]

It was in Colorado that the most notable change in response to
territorial suffrage took place. White Coloradans, despite earlier and
strong objections to the enfranchisement of blacks, quietly accepted
equal suffrage when it came in 1867. Although rumors of mob action
to discourage blacks from voting in the municipal elections on April
1, 1867, circulated in Denver and Central City, no violence occurred.
Frank Hall, acting governor, was in part responsible. Sensing a possible confrontation, he had sent certified copies of the territorial act
to mayors throughout Colorado and informed each of his duty to
enforce the law. Local officials responded by deputizing additional
help; numbers of lawmen standing by at the polls may well have
played a role in discouraging opposition. Hall justified his action as
necessary, for "had a single riot occurred my administration would
have been branded with disgrace."[45]

But Coloradans may have been ready to accept black suffrage. For
some time journalists and politicians alike had been pointing to the
advantage of gaining black votes for one party or the other. Settlers
had begun to reconcile themselves to congressional authority—that
it took precedence when it came into conflict with territorial legislation and opinion. This same rationale may have been influential
in other areas as well, but in no other territory was it so clearly
detailed.

D. C. Collier claimed, simply, that Democrats in Colorado had
submitted to equal suffrage in order to entice the black vote. He was,
in effect, reflecting the editorial strategy of major Republican newspapers. Both the *Miner's Register* and the *Rocky Mountain News*,

44. Jack Simmons to a friend, Helena, Oct. 5, 1867, in *Eastern Slope*, Oct. 26,
1877. Excerpts from Simmons's letter were reprinted in *Elevator*, Nov. 29, 1867.
Davison and Tash, "Confederate Backwash," 54, note that the election of 1867
was not as peaceful as Simmons claimed. They recount that a white man killed a
black in Helena for attempting to vote. Although jailed, the defendant escaped and
no attempt was made to apprehend him. Unfortunately, I was not able to verify
the incident. I should also add that for Arizona and New Mexico editorial comment
on the Territorial Suffrage Act was of little value. Undoubtedly the few blacks in
these territories—less than 150 in 1870—lived unnoticed among the larger Indian
and Mexican-American population.

45. *Rocky Mountain News*, Apr. 1, 3, 1867; Frank Hall to his mother, Denver,
Apr. 14, 1867, Hall Papers, DWC.

during the two months preceding the municipal elections, exhorted blacks to recall demonstrated Republican sympathy when casting their votes. Hinting that the black vote had real significance, William Byers told blacks that suffrage offered them the chance to counter "the ignorant foreign vote" usually cast for Democratic candidates. Equally anxious to curry favor with black voters, Collier came out in support of the territorial suffrage law and praised blacks as "in-formed citizens." Though he believed that most southern freedmen were too unenlightened to vote, Collier contended that "in Colorado, negro suffrage is intelligent suffrage. . . . We believe the negro in this Territory fully capable of exercising the franchise." Collier's strong determination to capture the black vote for Republicanism caused his partisanship to become clearly evident. "We are sure [blacks] know which party always stood up for their manhood," he wrote, "and which party has rescued them from slavery and oppression which the Democracy shout to perpetuate."[46]

The final collapse of overt opposition to equal suffrage came as Coloradans realized Congress's determination to ensure equality at the polls. Republican editors during 1866 had regularly extolled the virtues of popular sovereignty and had expressed disdain for any federal measure which would stipulate unrestricted suffrage in the territory. They contended that Congress should legislate equal suffrage for the loyal states before forcing it upon the territories.[47] Yet as the Territorial Suffrage Act reached its final stages of debate in 1867 and as its passage became a certainty, they yielded to the inevitable. A most striking example of the change in attitude appeared in the *Rocky Mountain News:* "That Congress has full right and power to legislate for the Territories was argued and conclusively settled, affirmatively, . . . and no sane man who reads the Congressional reports, can doubt for a moment that Ashley's bill creating impartial suffrage will pass and become law in the present session. There is not the slightest doubt as to this fact, for Congress is determined to push this question to the wall, and forever nail it there. . . ." The *Miner's Register,*

46. *Rocky Mountain News,* Jan. 3, 6, 12, 1867; *Miner's Register,* Jan. 16, Mar. 18, 20, 1867.

47. *Rocky Mountain News,* Jan. 23, 27, 1866; *Miner's Register,* Jan. 27, 1866; *Mining Journal,* Jan. 31, Feb. 8, May 24, 1866.

reflecting a similar view, announced simply that the new suffrage act was law and must be obeyed. "Let those who are opposed to the measure," declared editor Collier, "remember that they gain nothing by opposition but will act far more wisely to accept the position and not combat the inevitable." Bitterly disappointed with the turn of events, George West, a leading Democratic journalist, nonetheless agreed with Republican editors: "We never can believe that any thing of the sort [equal suffrage] can take place here at present—but if our Congress does so enact we will bow our head to the laws and obey. . . ." Byers made perhaps the most concise appraisal of Colorado's attitude on black suffrage. Many would find suffrage distasteful, he consoled his readers, "yet it was coming to that and the issue may as well be accepted first as last."[48] Even though some white Coloradans lamented the loss of determining voting status for territorial residents, like Nebraskans, they acquiesced to Congress's demand. Groups in both areas did so with the realization that they had no choice in the matter and with the awareness that equal suffrage throughout the land was to be an inevitable result of Reconstruction.

In one sense Republicans in Colorado took solace in Congress's action. The suffrage question had embarrassed them since 1864 and Congress had relieved their dilemma. As Frank Hall informed Thaddeus Stevens, the Territorial Suffrage Act released "the Republican party of the State [from] any contest on the question of Negro suffrage."[49] Had Congress directed the legislature to amend the election law or demanded a referendum, the Republican party might well have suffered defeat over the issue. Now the party could quite truthfully maintain that it had played no role in enfranchising the territory's black population. Moreover, black suffrage was to work clearly to Republican advantage. In the 1868 congressional election, it was the black vote in Denver's Arapahoe County that determined a Republican victory. Allen Bradford secured a mere seventeen-vote margin over his Democratic opponent, David Belden—a victory made possible only by the 120 black votes cast in the city of Denver.[50]

48. *Rocky Mountain News*, Jan. 3, 6, 1867; *Miner's Register*, Mar. 24, 1867; *Colorado Transcript*, Jan. 16, 1867.
49. Frank Hall to Thaddeus Stevens, Denver, Apr. 13, 1868, Stevens Papers.
50. Walter Lumley Shelly, "The Colorado Republican Party: The Formative

This tight race committed Colorado Republicans even further to black suffrage. In November, 1868, Ovando Hollister, associate editor of the *News* since the failure of his own newspaper in Black Hawk, reminded his readership that contention on this very issue—equal suffrage—had posed the most recent and major impediment to statehood. Were black men to be disfranchised temporarily, suggested Hollister, perhaps Democrats and Republicans in the territory could unite to work for statehood. Republican editors immediately disclaimed the idea. ". . . we would lose our Republican majority," cried one. ". . . without the colored vote," wrote another, "Bradford would never have been elected. Now it is proposed to take the right of voting from the men who saved the Republican party." Hollister realized the absurdity of his scheme when even Democrats rejected it. The editor of the *Central Herald*, a paper described by Republicans as the "organ of Democracy in the Territory," labeled Hollister's plan ridiculous. "So far as we are concerned," the editor acknowledged, "negro suffrage is dead and buried, and while we could never be induced to vote for it, we have nothing further to say against it."[51] Undoubtedly many Democrats agreed with this sentiment.

Early in 1868 William Gagan of California, surveying recent advances in black suffrage, pointed out the uneven distribution of the black franchise in the United States.[52] Blacks were permitted to cast

---

Years, 1861–1876" (M.A. thesis, University of Colorado, 1963), 67–71; *Rocky Mountain News*, Oct. 16, 1868. The number of black and white voters in each territory in 1870 was approximately:

Territory	Black	White
Arizona	13	3,379
Colorado	197	15,318
Dakota	28	5,206
Idaho	38	5,519
Montana	108	11,415
New Mexico	85	22,357
Utah	36	10,111
Washington	67	7,835
For Nebraska the figure was	209	35,879

1870 Census, Population, 619, 623, 624, 626, 631, 632, 636, 637.
51. *Rocky Mountain News*, Nov. 10, 12, 1868; *Colorado Times*, Nov. 12, 1868; *Central Register*, Nov. 19, 1868; *Colorado Transcript*, Nov. 18, 1868; *Central Herald*, n.d., in *Rocky Mountain News*, Nov. 16, 1868.
52. *Oakland News*, Jan. 6, 1868.

ballots in the District of Columbia, in the territories, in parts of New England, and throughout the seceded states, but nowhere else. Admitting that there was extreme opposition to black suffrage in the remaining states, Gagan nevertheless foresaw the enfranchisement of blacks across the nation. He could not know that his supposition would become reality within twenty-six months.

CHAPTER SIX

Black Suffrage—The Western States

"*Gloria Triumphe!* We are free!"
—Philip Bell, California

Approximately 800 black men in the West were enfranchised through the Edmunds amendment and the Territorial Suffrage Act. There remained 6,400 blacks in five western states who were still denied the ballot because of their race.[1] In the Far West, California and Nevada legislators had spurned petitions requesting black suffrage. Republicans along the Pacific slope slighted the equal suffrage question whenever possible, with many believing it politically unwise to stress such an unpopular issue. Kansas Republicans viewed the extension of suffrage somewhat more favorably but, when pressed to a vote in 1867, Kansans voted to reject black suffrage in their own state. In the end, blacks in Kansas and the Far West would not cast ballots until 1870. Minnesota did enfranchise its black population in 1868, but only after the defeat of equal suffrage propositions on two previous occasions. Nonetheless, liberal Minnesotans could take heart: theirs was one of only two northern states—Iowa being the other—to grant suffrage freely during Reconstruction.[2]

If black suffrage was to be brought before the Minnesota electorate time and again, with defeat looming constant, its final acceptance was due largely to the determined efforts of one local official. Governor William R. Marshall was, in fact, the most ardent sponsor of equal suffrage in Minnesota. As a gubernatorial candidate in 1865 he spoke out for the reform after the legislature's call for a public

---

1. By state the figures were: California, 1,731; Kansas, 3,985; Minnesota, 246; Nevada, 203; and Oregon, 243. See Chapter 5, n. 50, for the black voting profile in the territories. These figures are based on 1870 computations of eligible voters in the states and territories. *1870 Census, Population*, 619.
2. Gillette, *Right to Vote*, 26; Dykstra, "Bright Radical Star," in Mohr (ed.), *Radical Republicans in the North*, 167–93.

vote on the question during the general election in November. Then, following his inauguration as governor, Marshall continued yearly to urge referenda on equal suffrage until 1868, when white Minnesotans finally approved the ballot for blacks.[3]

Initial lack of enthusiasm among Minnesota Republicans assured defeat for equal suffrage in 1865. Orville Brown, radical Republican in Faribault, did offer a vigorous editorial campaign but, on the whole, Republican editors showed little interest. Among prominent politicians, only Marshall and Congressman Ignatius Donnelly publicly advocated enfranchising blacks. Republican indifference prevailed, declared Brown, as it became apparent that the proposition would fail. Republicans understandably wished to dissociate themselves from a losing cause. In view of this apathy, Democratic opposition lacked the usual spark and emotionalism found in anti-Negro campaigns elsewhere. Democratic editors did publish articles exposing crimes committed by blacks in other areas of the country but seldom mentioned black suffrage as an issue in Minnesota.[4]

So the defeat of the 1865 referendum by a majority of 2,636 votes came as little surprise in Minnesota.[5] Both Republicans and Democrats were aware that approximately 4,000 of the 31,229 voters in the general election had chosen to ignore the suffrage proposition. Brown surmised as well that many Republicans cast their ballots for Marshall but against equal suffrage. The governor received a majority of the popular vote in seventeen of the twenty-four counties which in turn rejected black suffrage. Still, not all Republicans viewed the outcome of the referendum with dismay. D. Sinclair of Winona characterized the 12,000 votes cast in favor of black suffrage as an advance. "When we consider the state of the public mind on this question for the past four years," he wrote, "it becomes a matter of

3. William Watts Folwell, *A History of Minnesota*, 4 vols. (St. Paul, 1969), III, 7–8; Theodore C. Blegen, *Minnesota: A History of the State* (Minneapolis, 1963), 188–89.

4. Faribault *Central Republican*, Sept. 27, Oct. 11, Nov. 29, 1865; *Winona Republican*, Nov. 18, 1865; *St. Paul Press*, Nov. 16, 1865; *St. Paul Pioneer*, Oct. 14, 1865; Haugland, "Alexander Ramsey," 189–90; Ridge, *Donnelly*, 100–103.

5. The proposition received 12,196 votes in favor, 14,832 against. The figures cited are the official returns printed in the *Winona Republican*, Nov. 27, 1865. Tallies vary with almost every source. *The Tribune Almanac* for the years 1838 to 1868, 2 vols. (New York, 1868), II (1866), 55, lists the vote at 14,838 opposed and 12,170 for suffrage. Folwell, *Minnesota*, III, 7–8, and Blegen, *Minnesota*, 190, give different figures. See also Gillette, *Right to Vote*, 28.

congratulations . . . that . . . universal suffrage should have received so many votes in this State as it did."[6]

A second referendum in 1867 met a similar fate; it went down to defeat by 1,298 votes. Some 27,461 Minnesotans approved suffrage while 28,759 disapproved.[7] Having made a greater effort than in 1865 to publicize equal suffrage, Republicans this time were keenly disappointed. They were dismayed as well by lack of conviction among party regulars. State election returns indicated that Republicans were once again avoiding the issue. While Republican candidates for state office generally received 5,000 more votes than their Democratic opponents, 2,000 fewer Republicans chose to cast ballots on the suffrage question. A few Republicans attempted to blame the failure on the Democrats, who had intensified their campaign against equal suffrage in 1867. But Orville Brown felt the real criticism should be leveled against "weak-kneed Republicans, . . . upon whom the prejudice of caste still retains a strong hold. . . ."[8]

Determined in their quest, the Republican legislature called for a third referendum in 1868. Instead of presenting separate ballots as before, they now ordered the equal suffrage option printed right on the presidential ballot in the hope that Republicans would not again shun the issue. In addition, the proposition as stated asked the voters to approve a revision of section 1, article 7, of the state constitution. That such a change would, in effect, remove the word "white" from the suffrage article was mentioned neither in the legislature's call nor on the ballot. During the campaign a number of Republican editors urged an affirmative vote on the revision without elaborating the effect of the change. As a result black suffrage was approved by 9,372 votes.[9] Democrats labeled the victory a "swindle," but their charge lacked force in view of declining opposition to equal suffrage from 1865 on. Actually, Democrats showed themselves able to accept the

6. *Winona Republican*, Nov. 18, 27, 1865; Faribault *Central Republican*, Nov. 29, 1865; St. Paul *Pioneer*, Nov. 21, 24, 1865.

7. Again, figures vary. Those quoted here are the official returns printed in the St. Paul *Pioneer*, Jan. 9, 1868. But see *Mantorville Express*, Nov. 25, 1867, and *Tribune Almanac*, II, 70.

8. *Rochester Post*, July 20, 1867; *State Atlas*, Jan. 9, 1867; *Mankato Union*, Oct. 18, 1867; *Mantorville Express*, Nov. 25, 1867; Faribault *Central Republican*, Nov. 13, 20, 1867.

9. Minnesotans cast 39,493 votes for suffrage and 30,121 in opposition. *St. Paul Pioneer*, Jan. 7, 1869; *Minneapolis Tribune*, Oct. 25, 1868.

result of the referendum with good grace. John C. Wise, a Mankato editor who had been active in the campaign against suffrage, encouraged his readers: "as good citizens, it behoves [sic] all to cheerfully submit to the new decree." Even the *Pioneer*, the Democratic newspaper most opposed to equal suffrage, conceded, ". . . now that we have got it, we must make the best of it." True to the predictions of those Republicans who had insisted that Democrats would find blacks less objectionable once they were allowed to vote, Democrats in Minnesota now began visibly to entice the black vote by reporting every Republican infraction. They not only praised blacks for their political decorum and astuteness but pointed out that, under the Republican party, political offices were being given to whites only.[10]

Unlike most state Republican organizations in the North and the West, which preferred to avoid equal suffrage, Minnesota Republicans continued to raise the issue until resistance wore thin. Their success, when it came, bore on important demographic factors. Viewed in the national perspective, the three referenda show Minnesota's anti-Negro prejudice to have been less pronounced than in most areas of the country. Minnesotans cast a higher ratio of pro-Negro votes than any of the other eleven nonslaveholding states which held referenda on race-related issues between 1846 and 1869.[11] Favorable for the nation as a whole, Minnesota's suffrage results showed markedly less bias than for other areas of the West as well. Whereas Coloradans in 1865 rejected black suffrage by an overwhelming 90 percent, and 65 percent of Kansas's voters denied the ballot to black men in 1867, fewer still—an average of 51 percent—opposed equal suffrage at the polls in the three Minnesota referenda. This lower percentage was due in part to the presence of numerous settlers from New England and Wisconsin, areas of the nation where feeling against blacks was less evident. The 1870 population of nine Minnesota counties which had endorsed black suffrage in all three referenda— Dodge, Faribault, Fillmore, Freeborn, Martin, Mower, Redwood, Rice, and Steele—contained a higher percentage of individuals with

10. *Mankato Record*, Nov. 7, 1868; *St. Paul Pioneer*, Nov. 14, 1868, Jan. 1,5,1869.

11. McLaughlin, "Popular Reactions," 37, 71–73, 113; Felice A. Bonadio, "A 'Perfect Contempt of All Unity,' " and Philip D. Swenson, "Disillusionment with State Activism," both in Mohr (ed.), *Radical Republicans in the North*, 82–100, 104–15.

a New England or Wisconsin background than did most other counties in the state.

A second contributing factor was the largely agrarian, immigrant population from northern Europe. Although a detailed study of the foreign vote in Minnesota still awaits analysis by a quantitative historian, a preliminary conjecture may be drawn.[12] Minnesota was unique: for the West in 1870 it contained one of the largest, concentrated foreign elements, the majority of which had established residency in the state after 1865. The foreign-born population of Minnesota comprised nearly 39 percent of the whole, or 169,697 out of 439,706 people. Its principal foreign groups were Swedish-Norwegian (106,459), German (41,304), and Irish (21,419). In all three referenda there were forty-eight counties in the state participating; of these, fourteen might be classified as "foreign counties" in that the 1870 non-indigenous population of each was larger than 40 percent. Of these fourteen "foreign counties," seven contained a predominantly Swedish-Norwegian population—Chisago, Goodhue, Houston, Isanti, Pine, Renville, and St. Louis. The foreign population of three others—Brown, Carver, and Sibley—was mainly German, while the immigrant make-up of Nicollet and Washington counties was divided between Scandinavian and German groups. The two remaining counties contained a large Irish element. With the exception of Houston and Renville counties in 1865 only, the Swedish-Norwegian counties supported black suffrage in all three referenda. The German counties did not reach consensus—Brown approved while Carver and Sibley rejected suffrage in each referendum. The two German-Scandinavian counties opposed equal suffrage in 1865 but approved it when polled again in 1868. The counties with a large Irish population—Ramsey and Scott—rejected black suffrage each time it was put to a vote. Thus on the basis of voting it may be

12. Anti–black suffrage attitudes for other areas of the West resist quantification altogether, with the possible exception of Kansas—see below. Referenda on the topic were few (held only in Minnesota, Kansas, and Colorado), and reliable statistics are even fewer. In Colorado, for example, only the final tally in the Sept., 1865, election was forwarded to Congress; a local report printed in the *Rocky Mountain News*, Sept. 19, 1865, gives a breakdown so incomplete as to be meaningless.

Other factors prevail. The sparse population of Washington and Arizona would have been too limited a base for conclusions even had voter preference been polled. In California anti-Negro and anti-Chinese feeling very nearly merged, defying quantification for the black suffrage question alone. Even the validity of conclusions for Minnesota and Kansas in this chapter may lie in doubt, for they are based on population statistics for 1870 rather than for the years of the actual referenda.

concluded that, in the main, Scandinavian immigrants favored equal suffrage while the German faction split on the issue, and the Irish were least ready of all to share the franchise with the blacks.

The only real opposition to black suffrage in Minnesota was concentrated in the counties along the Mississippi River and in certain south-central portions of the state. In 1865 twenty-four of the state's forty-eight counties voted against equal suffrage; by 1868 this number had dwindled to ten. Predominantly Democratic Ramsey County (St. Paul) rejected black suffrage in all three referenda. The opposition vote cast in that county alone in 1867 could have accounted for the entire 1,298 majority against equal suffrage. In sharp contrast was neighboring Hennepin County (Minneapolis). Although the two counties each contained about 190 blacks, Hennepin supported the broader franchise proposal in every referendum. In fact, its vote in favor of black suffrage in 1868 equaled the ample 9,372 majority cast in the state. But on Hennepin County's more liberal attitude demographic statistics shed no light, for Hennepin's 30,000 residents in 1870 did not conform in background to other pro–black suffrage counties noted. Other counties endorsing equal suffrage in all the referenda invariably contained either a substantial New England or foreign-born component. Yet for Hennepin County—omitting those persons born within Minnesota itself—residents born within the United States tended to come either from New York or from states just north of the Ohio River. First-generation immigrants made up only 32 percent of the county's population, with the 2,900 Germans prevailing over the 2,000 Scandinavians and 2,000 Irish.[13] In the final analysis, St. Paul attracted a conservative, Democratic element whereas Minneapolis lured a more liberal, Republican population. For in those western states where referenda on enfranchising blacks were held between 1865 and 1868—Colorado, Kansas, and Minnesota—Hennepin was the only urban county consistently to approve black suffrage.

The Kansas referendum on equal suffrage in 1867 stood in sharp contrast to the referenda in Minnesota. The campaign was sparked by more agitation from the black community and grew more heated than any in Minnesota. It included the question of woman suffrage,

13. *St. Paul Pioneer*, Nov. 24, 1865, Jan. 9, 1868, Jan. 7, 1869; *1870 Census, Population*, 360.

which Republicans in Minnesota avoided until after black men had received the right to vote. Once equal suffrage had gone down to defeat, Kansas Republicans were loathe to press the issue before the public a second time.

From 1862 blacks regularly petitioned the Kansas legislature for the right to vote, and they held conventions yearly to seek the repeal of the state's other anti-Negro restrictions. Charles H. Langston, a black from Leavenworth, served as spokesman and chief advocate; among whites who supported these efforts was Daniel Wilder, some-time editor of the *Leavenworth Conservative* and later chronicler of Kansas history. The Republican-controlled Kansas legislature turned a deaf ear to the blacks' every appeal. During the war their petitions were tabled on the pretext that weighty matters should not be decided until Kansas's soldiers had returned from the battlefront. But an end came to the fighting, and still the legislature balked. Confronted once again with petitions in 1866 to broaden the franchise, lawmakers summarily decided that "the movement is premature . . . the people are not ready for the suffrage question." Some Republicans were critical of the delay, but others foresaw no change in any event. "Every intelligent man at all acquainted with the present feeling of our people," said one Republican resignedly, "knows that [black suffrage] will be defeated by a vote of at least 2 to 1."[14]

Blacks, along with white liberals, now turned to the Republican party for redress. A majority of Republicans attending the party's state convention in September, 1866, were willing to espouse broader suffrage; in response to black demands, they included in the platform a plank calling for the removal of the word "white" from voting requirements. Yet Governor Samuel Crawford and Congressman Sidney Clarke urged caution, for both felt such a strong position would be detrimental to their own re-election. Accordingly the convention amended the resolution and instead encouraged the legislature to submit equal suffrage to a popular vote. Once the gubernatorial election results were tallied in Crawford's favor and his second term assured, he moved forward with less reserve. Addressing the new legislature, Crawford recommended not only a referendum on black

14. State of Kansas, *House Journal, 1864* (Topeka, 1864), 218; *House Journal, 1866* (Topeka, 1866), 734–35; *Western Home Journal*, Jan. 21, Feb. 1, 1866; Atchison *Free Press*, Feb. 1, 1866; *Leavenworth Conservative*, Jan. 28, 1866; Caldwell, "Kansas," 108–9.

suffrage but also a second proposition to disfranchise all persons suspected of disloyalty during the war.[15]

Once the bill for an equal suffrage referendum actually came before the legislature, fierce opposition developed in the state senate. Anti-Negro senators attempted to kill the measure by attaching other, wholly inappropriate items. The only amendment to survive was one calling for a vote on woman suffrage. Accordingly the bill that emerged from the legislature asked Kansans to vote at the next general election in November, 1867, on three separate franchise propositions: one called for black suffrage by striking the word "white" from the voting qualification, a second provided for woman suffrage by removing the word "male," and the last denied the ballot to persons suspected of disloyalty.[16] While the latter proposition forbidding the vote to deserters stirred little controversy, the suffrage questions had an opposite effect, unleashing debate which continued over many months' time.

Samuel Newitt Wood originated the woman suffrage provision. Potentially a real advance for frontier women, the measure was spawned of a motive less noble. One Kansas historian has asserted that Wood's effort to secure the ballot for women was a device to bring attention to himself and to revive his own flagging political career. His contemporaries, however, believed it Wood's real intent to defeat black suffrage. As one editor said with open disdain, "This whole movement is one of the shabbiest and most disgusting of many tricks and shams for which Sam Wood has always been notorious." For Wood had taken an active anti-suffrage position, consistently voting to reject equal suffrage petitions in the legislature and encouraging other legislators to follow his example.[17] Now the plan was the same, under a different guise.

As Wood successfully maneuvered the woman suffrage referendum, pro-black Kansans voiced indignation at his tactic. From Wyandotte,

15. Atchison *Free Press*, Sept. 7, 1866; State of Kansas, *House Journal, 1867* (Topeka, 1867), 64–65.

16. State of Kansas, *Senate Journal, 1867* (Topeka, 1867), 340; Zornow, *Kansas*, 245–46; Atchison *Free Press*, Feb. 9, July 9, 1867; Plummer, *Frontier Governor*, 104–5.

17. *Leavenworth Conservative*, Apr. 6, 1867; G. S. Glick to Samuel N. Wood, Topeka, Mar. 22, 1866, Wood Papers; Caldwell, "Kansas," 123. Sister Jeanne McKenna, "With the Help of God and Lucy Stone," KHQ, XXXVI (Spring, 1970), 13–26, discusses Wood's aims and objectives in the suffrage contest.

R. B. Taylor, while not against women voting, thought the reform premature. It should be delayed, he cautioned, pending resolution of the black suffrage question. John Martin, a Republican from Atchison, agreed. " 'Sambo' has always had a hard time of it," he wrote. "And now when the people . . . stand freely to give him the rights of manhood, [he is to be burdened with woman suffrage.] Must the negro always be outraged, and his rights deferred until a more convenient time, which will never come."[18]

Reaction in the black community itself was mixed. Publicly blacks seemed unconcerned about the inclusion of woman suffrage on the referendum. At a convention called shortly after the legislature's passage of the bill providing for a public vote, blacks applauded the lawmakers' efforts. Privately, however, it was a different matter. Clearly blacks were furious and resented being pawns for Wood's scheme. Writing to Wood, Langston left no doubt as to his feelings. "I am exceedingly sorry to be compelled to say that your words and actions seem to me to be inharmonious—absolutely incompatible," he declared. "I feel that you are responsible, and you only for all the *dodging*, and all the unnecessary and embarrassing notions . . . in connection with the question of negro suffrage. I am not alone in this feeling. . . . If the measure is defeated, by these frivolous, *extraneous*, and distinctive motions, we the negroes shall hold you responsible."[19]

Unabashed, Wood went right on to organize his Impartial Suffrage Association, ostensibly a group formed to promote both black and woman suffrage. He persuaded Governor Crawford to serve as honorary president. For himself Wood retained the position of corresponding secretary and remained the driving force behind the group's efforts. He undertook a letter-writing campaign on behalf of impartial suffrage and was able to secure support for his movement from leading Republican politicians and elder statesmen of Kansas. He even invited nationally known Republicans and suffragettes to stump the state for impartial suffrage. Apparently few political leaders were attracted by his invitation, but Kansans were treated early to the presence of Lucy

18. *Wyandotte Gazette*, Mar. 16, 1867; *Atchison Champion*, Feb. 17, 1867. See also Atchison *Free Press*, Feb. 9, 1867; *Marysville* (Kans.) *Enterprise*, Mar. 2, 1867; *Kansas Tribune*, Feb. 2, 12, 1867.

19. Ms resolution in Crawford Papers; Charles H. Langston to Samuel N. Wood, Leavenworth, Feb. 10, 1867, Wood Papers.

Stone and her husband, H. B. Blackwell. They began touring Kansas in April, 1867, and by June the couple had spoken at some forty-five gatherings throughout the state. In ensuing months Kansans were favored by such other prominent woman suffrage speakers as Susan B. Anthony, Elizabeth Cady Stanton, Frances Gage, the Reverend Olympia Brown, and Bessie Bisbee. Even George Francis Train, no longer involved in Nebraska politics, came out to help the cause. On occasion these advocates of impartial suffrage would mention black men, but the burden of their song focused on the ballot for women. As one reporter who closely followed these "impartial" meetings remarked, "I have yet to hear one of their speakers, male or female, make an argument in favor of colored suffrage. They . . . ignore the subject or content themselves by a very faint expression in its favor."[20] Because of this emphasis, some Kansans saw woman suffrage becoming the more acceptable of the two referendum propositions.

Yet the outward enthusiasm for woman suffrage was misleading. The question had been thrust upon Kansans so quickly that many had no real opinion of their own. While Sallie Brown of Lawrence could regale "Auntie" with descriptions of the large crowds at woman suffrage gatherings, Sol Miller of White Cloud analyzed with greater accuity the audiences' basis for interest. Calling attention to notices of cancelled woman suffrage meetings, Miller insisted that the people attended these lectures only to hear and see the nationally known suffragettes; otherwise they stayed home.[21] Blinded by their own devotion, suffragists were unable to distinguish between true zeal for the cause and idle curiosity.

Such opposition as did develop against enfranchising women remained ineffective. Certain well-known local Republicans such as P. B. Plumb, John A. Martin, I. S. Kalloch, and state Attorney

20. *Address to the Voters of Kansas* (n.p., n.d.); Samuel Crawford to Samuel N. Wood, Topeka, May 1, 1868, Governor's Letterbooks, Crawford Papers; Charles Robinson to Wood, Lawrence, Apr. 6, 1867, Robinson Papers, KSHS; Wood to Charles Sumner, Cottonwood Falls, Apr. 26, 1867, Sumner Papers; John Stillman Brown to "dear Sister," Lawrence, Oct. 6, 1867, Sallie Brown to "dear Sister," Lawrence, Nov. 3, 1867, both in John Stillman Brown Family Papers, KSHS; *Wyandotte Gazette*, Apr. 12, 1867; *Wathena Reporter*, June 20, 1867; Rover to editor, Paola, July 24, 1867, in *Leavenworth Conservative*, July 28, 1867.
21. Sallie Brown to "Auntie," Lawrence, Sept. 8, 1867, Brown Family Papers; *Kansas Chief*, Aug. 22, 1867.

General G. W. Hoyt began speaking out against the measure, and caused the Republican state central committee to reconsider its stand. Earlier it had endorsed woman suffrage; now the committe asked that "side issues" not be allowed to prevent blacks' access to the ballot. "Let no other issue distract the party," it admonished, "but let every Republican come up to the mark on the . . . issue." Still others seeking to spark opposition to woman suffrage began to follow the gentlewomen about as they spoke and made light, publicly, of their personal lives.[22] Unfortunately the tactic worked against them; it served only to create more interest and excitement for the woman suffrage campaign.

In comparison to the hoopla over woman suffrage, the campaign to enfranchise black men seemed uninspired. Indeed, some advocates predicted defeat owing to the very lack of public enthusiasm. As if in echo to the Minnesota experience in 1865, a correspondent to the *Western Home Journal* warned that "our anti-slavery friends and progressive reformers have too much confidence in the righteousness of the question; or, in other words, that the people will do right. I assure you, without some active, energetic movement during the summer months, hundreds who are deemed good republicans, will dodge the question or vote against it."[23] Republican editors in Kansas were nearly unanimous in their support of black suffrage; still, their arguments on the black man's behalf lacked innovation.[24] Predictably they stressed his loyalty to the nation and to the Republican party, and declared that the responsibilities and rights of citizenship should be shared alike by all. Only with the passage of the first Reconstruc-

22. Wilder, *Annals of Kansas*, 456; *Kansas Tribune*, Oct. 20, 1867; *Emporia News*, Sept. 20, 1867; *Western Home Journal*, Sept. 26, 1867; Sallie Brown to "Auntie," Lawrence, Sept. 8, 1867, Brown Family Papers. Western Republicans outside Kansas were almost unanimous in their opposition to woman suffrage. See *Napa Register*, Jan. 26, 1867; *Oakland News*, Jan. 25, 1867; Sacramento *Bee*, Nov. 5, 1867; *Minneapolis Tribune*, June 9, 11, 1867; *Salem Daily Record*, Oct. 3, 1867. Democrats were divided on the issue. Those who favored it, like J. Sterling Morton of Nebraska, thought it preferable to enfranchise educated women instead of un-lettered black men. *States Rights Democrat*, Mar. 27, 1867; *Nebraska City News*, Oct. 28, 1868; *Southern Oregon Press* (Jacksonville), Feb. 2, 1867.

23. Unsigned letter to editor, n.p., n.d., in *Western Home Journal*, June 20, 1867.

24. Of the twenty-two Republican newspapers in Kansas surveyed for this study, eighteen advocated giving the ballot to black men. The files of the other four—*Chase County Banner* (Cottonwood Falls, Kans.), *Fort Scott* (Kans.) *Weekly Monitor*, *Allen County Courant* (Iola, Kans.), and Leavenworth *Times*—are incomplete for 1867, and their stand on the issue cannot be determined.

tion Act in March, 1867, did editors allude to the contradiction in forcing equal suffrage on the South while denying it in the North. John Speer of Lawrence among others spoke to the question: "We join in the general demand that the South shall . . . incorporate impartial suffrage into the new political fabric. . . . With what sincerity and consistency do we impose those requirements on our neighbors, which we omit to observe ourselves?"[25]

Although the campaign for black suffrage generally lacked vigor, Charles H. Langston worked relentlessly in its promotion. During the summer and fall of 1867 the Leavenworth black stumped the state and wrote letters advocating the ballot for all men. Langston stressed that blacks were citizens like the rest and that by refusing their enfranchisement whites were denying a segment of the population, not a racial group. Throughout the campaign he upheld the humanity of black people. When several editors began referring to him as "the great *colored apostle*," Langston fired back, "If I were Irish, or German, my race would not be thrown up at me." Commenting on the interrelationship of black and white races, however, Langston made it eminently clear to his audiences that "he asked no special privileges for his people, no social equality—simple justice and a fair show in the race of life, was all he demanded."[26]

During the campaign there were few sustained anti-black, anti-woman suffrage tirades. Indeed, the lack of strong, open opposition was a measure of public indifference and portended defeat. It is true that the Democratic state convention meeting in Leavenworth expressed forthright opposition, as did "Philo," who published a series of letters in Wyandotte newspapers denouncing both black and woman suffrage. Stinging with abuse, particularly toward black women, these missives produced rebuttals from Langston and Clarina Nichols, Kansas's most active female advocate of woman suffrage.[27]

25. Editorials favoring equal suffrage abound in Kansas newspapers throughout 1867. The most expressive are *Western Home Journal*, Apr. 25, June 20, Sept. 12, 1867; *Kansas Tribune*, Feb. 19, 26, Apr. 20, Oct. 30, 1867; *Olathe Mirror*, May 2, 1867; *Leavenworth Conservative*, Oct. 26, 1867.

26. Charles H. Langston to editor, Leavenworth, Aug. 19, 1867, in *Leavenworth Conservative*, Aug. 20, 1867; report of a Langston speech in *Wathena Reporter*, Aug. 15, 1867.

27. *Western Home Journal*, Sept. 12, 1867; *Wyandotte Gazette*, Apr. 27, May 4, 25, June 1, 8, 1867; Joseph G. Gambone, "The Forgotten Feminist of Kansas: The Papers of Clarina I. H. Nichols, 1854–1885 (Part IV, 1867–1868)," KHQ, XXXIX (Winter, 1973), 515–63.

But on the whole the opponents of equal suffrage did not have to become too vocal. The growing quarrel between woman's rights and black suffrage advocates undermined the concept of impartiality; what might have been a venture to mutual advantage was to end instead in open discord and disillusion before the public.

Disagreement between the pro-Negro and pro-woman groups flared almost from the beginning. Before long an open feud had developed between Wood and Langston, with Wood the more antagonistic of the two. At first he gently chided the black leader for his lack of sympathy in the women's cause. Wood alleged that "negroes of Kansas and their friends are claiming rights which they are not willing to give to mothers, wives, sisters and daughters of the state." Then in a campaign sheet entitled *The Banner of Liberty*, Wood abandoned pretense and denounced Langston outright for opposing woman suffrage. Langston held his temper: still not wishing to break with Wood's group, the black spokesman gave assurances of his good will. "You misrepresent me when you intimate that I think the friends of female suffrage are opposed to negro suffrage," he told Wood. "I have no dispute with you. . . . There shall be no antagonism between me and the friends of woman suffrage. I have never insisted that the friends of female suffrage are seeking the defeat of colored suffrage." Only a month before the November election Langston was able to persuade a black convention meeting in Highland, Doniphan County, to pass resolutions denying any conflict between blacks and suffragists, and advocating impartial suffrage without regard to sex or color.[28]

Despite Langston's overtures, the friends of female suffrage seemed increasingly less tolerant of the black suffrage campaign. Like suffragists in other parts of the nation, those in Kansas rejected the notion that former slaves should be enfranchised before the same consideration were given educated women. Their motivation came partly from the belief that black men opposed ballots for women, partly from race prejudice itself. Sallie Brown, for one, truly believed that ". . . if the negroes get the ballot there will be no chance for us, for they are all opposed." The Reverend Olympia Brown, speaking before an audience in Fort Scott, was wholly disdainful of black

28. Charles H. Langston to Samuel N. Wood, Leavenworth, Apr. 7, 1867, Woman Suffrage Papers, KSHS; *Kansas Patriot*, Oct. 5, 1867; *Emporia News*, Apr. 19, 1867; *Leavenworth Conservative*, Aug. 20, 1867.

suffrage and "disclaimed against placing the dirty, immoral, degraded negro before a white woman."[29] Others gave vent to their prejudice privately. R. W. Massey of Paola promised Wood his support for female suffrage because women would add "moral strength and power to our political system." Conversely, Massey rejected black suffrage because it would add "degradation and filth and dirt to a system already degraded and corrupt." While not all of Wood's correspondents in favor of woman suffrage were motivated by anti-Negro prejudice, they did share a common goal; they all preferred to give the ballot to women before extending it to black men.[30]

Not wishing to get caught in the crossfire between the two pressure groups, political leaders began to shun the referendum campaign altogether. Where initially they had offered their support to impartial suffrage, now they found it more convenient to absent themselves. In the weeks prior to the election Senator Ross and Governor Crawford remained in the western part of the state on an "Indian expedition," while Senator Pomeroy chose to devote himself to personal business in Boston. Their absence was conspicuous and provoked comment. Said John Wright of Leavenworth, "Where is Senator Pomeroy? Where is Senator Ross? Where are the score or more of other prominent Republicans who see the cause of manhood suffrage trembling in the balance?" [31]

Several weeks before the referendum individual Kansans were predicting the defeat of black suffrage, with the result that pro–black suffrage editors made last-minute appeals to muster support for the

29. Sallie Brown to "Auntie," Lawrence, Sept. 8, 1867, Brown Family Papers; *Kansas Chief,* Aug. 22, 1867; *Border Sentinel,* Sept. 17, 1867; Atchinson *Free Press,* Oct. 25, 1867.

30. R. W. Massey to Samuel N. Wood, Paola, Kans., May 16, 1867, John Stillman Brown to Wood, Lawrence, June 26, 1867, O. Brown to Wood, Olathe, n.d., H. B. Norton to Wood, Emporia, Aug. 14, 1867, Samuel Reader to Wood, Indianola, Kans., May 14, 1867, P. P. Elder to Wood, Ottawa, Kans., Apr. 27, 1867, Joel Moody to Samuel Crawford, Pleasant View, Kans., Aug. 1, 1867, all in Woman Suffrage Papers. For a discussion of the anti–Negro suffrage attitude in the national post–Civil War feminist movement, see Forrest G. Wood, *Black Scare: The Racist Response to Emancipation* (Berkeley, Calif., 1968), 94–97. Ellen Carol DuBois asserts in *Feminism and Suffrage, 1848–1869* (Ithaca, N.Y., 1978), 102–4, that tension between feminists and pro–black suffrage supporters in Kansas resulted in the withdrawal of woman suffrage advocates throughout the nation from the Equal Rights Association.

31. Samuel Crawford to Samuel N. Wood, Topeka, May 1, 1867, Governor's Letterbooks, Crawford Papers; *Address to the Voters of Kansas,* 4; *Leavenworth Conservative,* Oct. 9, 1867.

reform.[32] But their pleas went unheard. Sixty-five percent of the Kansas electorate voted to retain the suffrage restriction against blacks. While 10,438 voters conceded the right of black men to the ballot, 19,421 Kansans did not. The northeastern counties with the urban centers and the largest black population—Atchison, Doniphan, Jefferson, and Leavenworth—returned the strongest anti-Negro majorities. Only seven of the state's forty-four counties—Allen, Cherokee, Lyon, Osage, Ottawa, Riley, and Waubansee—approved equal suffrage, and, excepting Cherokee County, they all lay to the south and to the west of Lawrence, a region of earlier antislavery settlement. Daniel Wilder offered a terse but accurate description of Kansas's attitude on black suffrage: "Talk for it, vote agin it."[33] Woman suffrage also went down to defeat. Of the 29,927 votes cast on the proposition, 69 percent, or 19,857, rejected female suffrage. The third and lesser proposition to disfranchise disloyal persons easily passed with a majority of 4,000 votes.[34]

Some were disheartened. Sallie Brown conceded that "politics are indeed dreadfully demoralizing." Partisan editors sought to blame Democrats, but more astute Republican observers knew better. Lingering anti-Negro prejudice was undoubtedly one factor, they had to admit; the negative influence exerted by the suffragists was another. For others the cause seemed not altogether lost. Blacks once again convened in Leavenworth, this time to convey appreciation to those whites who had supported them and to urge an equal suffrage amendment to the federal Constitution. Sam Wood, for his part, had no thought of reconciling himself to the vote. He proposed that a state impartial suffrage convention put the issue on the ballot again in 1868. Governor Crawford rejected the plan. "I think the less of side issues we have in the next canvass, the better it will be for the Republican Party," he replied. Once again party leaders were affecting

32. Everard Bierer to Andrew Johnson, Hiawatha, Kans., Oct. 14, 1867, Johnson Papers; *Leavenworth Conservative*, Nov. 5, 1867.

33. Wilder, *Annals of Kansas*, 468. Unlike the situation in Minnesota, the foreign-born element in Kansas probably had little impact on the final outcome. Slightly more than 13 percent of the whole, the non-indigenous population was distributed rather evenly throughout the state. Only Davis and Saline counties in 1870 had a foreign population surpassing 40 percent; it comprised Irish, German and Scandinavian groups more or less equal in number. *1870 Census, Population*, 335.

34. Wilder, *Annals of Kansas*, 463. Different totals are printed in *Topeka* (Kans.) *State Record*, Dec. 9, 1867.

indifference toward equal suffrage, and S. C. Smith noted that politicians always enlist in a cause until it "burns [their] fingers." With some political spokesmen in Kansas having reversed themselves so unexpectedly on the suffrage issue, mused Smith wryly, "I should have supposed that [they] w'd have broken [their] neck in the operation."[35] The people had made known their wishes, and politicians, excepting Wood, clearly understood the mandate. The "most radicalized state in the Union" had shown the limitations of its radicalism. For the real test of radical inclination during Reconstruction was equal suffrage, and in this test Kansas Republicans were found wanting.

Ratification and acceptance of the Fifteenth Amendment remained the final step toward enfranchisement of western blacks who lacked the right to vote. Recognizing the amendment's potentially strong impact, western Republicans expressed their approval but in subdued terms. During the earlier years of Reconstruction editors of even the smallest newspapers focused their attention on national politics. In the year that the Fifteenth Amendment was before the nation, from its submission to the states in late February, 1869, to its promulgation in March, 1870, many Republican editors mentioned it briefly but appeared reluctant to elaborate.[36] This seeming disinterest may have stemmed from a devloping conservatism which became evident just before and during the course of Johnson's impeachment trial, or from a desire not to feed the Democratic propaganda machine. After all, in those western states where they controlled the legislatures, Republicans stood to gain nothing by taking a public stand and unduly attracting Democratic rebuttal.

Western Republican arguments in favor of the Fifteenth Amendment sought to lessen fears about the amendment's impact: the mea-

35. Sallie Brown to "Auntie," Lawrence, Nov. 5, 1867, Brown Family Papers; *Kansas Tribune*, Nov. 10, 1867; Atchison *Free Press*, Nov. 15, 1867; Sidney Clarke to D. W. Houston, Washington, D.C., Nov. 20, 1867, in *Kansas Tribune*, Dec. 7, 1867; *Junction Union*, Nov. 16, 1867; *Border Sentinel*, Nov. 15, 1867; *Topeka State Record*, Nov. 13, 1867; *Atchison Champion*, Nov. 9, 1867; Samuel Crawford to Samuel N. Wood (telegram), Topeka, Apr. 13, 1868, Crawford Papers; S. C. Smith to Charles Robinson, n.p., Feb. 4, 1868, Robinson Papers, KSHS.

36. William Stewart of Nevada played a key role in the formulation of the amendment. For Stewart's somewhat embellished assessment of his part, see his *Reminiscences*, 231–34. William Gillette's concise treatment of the amendment's passage through Congress also evaluates Stewart's importance. Gillette, *Right to Vote*, 46–78.

sure was necessary to guarantee continued black suffrage in the South, it did not grant everyone the right to vote, and it would ensure political calm. Along the West coast, where many individuals became concerned lest the amendment enfranchise the Chinese, Republicans again and again noted the three reasons for which suffrage could not be denied—"race, color, and previous condition of servitude." Every state was still free to impose voter qualifications on the basis of literacy, property holdings, taxes paid, birthplace, or whatever. Ironically, Frederick MacCrellish, whose own Republicanism fluctuated between moderation and conservatism, realized the amendment's shortcomings and declared it "maimed." By approving a measure which permitted the imposition of any suffrage qualification at all, Congress had failed to deal effectively with the problem, he wrote. As if looking into the future, one Minneapolis Republican predicted, ". . . we may be very sure that . . . the southern states . . . will disfranchise their blacks under the permission to proscribe property or educational qualifications."[37]

Western proponents of the amendment went further, devising two political arguments to encourage its acceptance. To Republicans they announced that the Fifteenth Amendment would effectively remove the franchise issue from politics. Said one Republican in Nevada with obvious relief, "The adoption of the Amendment will place the whole vexed question of suffrage at rest. . . ." Reviewing the effect of Democratic racial propaganda against their party for the past decade, Republicans knew in fact that the equal suffrage issue had to be settled before their dominance in western politics could be assured. Failing that, the party would remain vulnerable. Congress was the only agency to settle the suffrage question. For state Republican organizations it remained too divisive an item, and a deterrent to party strength. There could even be advantages in the amendment for Democrats, as some Republicans noted. Dissolution of black suffrage as a political issue would encourage discussion of new topics. While blacks would most likely vote Republican for a number of years, some would in time ally with Democrats on certain problems; thus Democrats might hope to entice a portion of the black vote.[38]

37. *Oregonian*, Feb. 10, 1869; *Marysville Appeal*, Feb. 13, 28, 1869; *Oakland News*, Feb. 1, 1869; *Oregon State Journal*, Aug. 14, 1869; *Mankato Union*, Feb. 5, 1869; *Alta California*, Feb. 2, 1869; *Minneapolis Tribune*, Mar. 4, 1869.

38. *Territorial Enterprise*, Feb. 28, 1869; *Kansas Tribune*, Nov. 12, 1868; *Marysville Appeal*, Mar. 4, 1869. See also *Humboldt Times*, Feb. 27, 1869; *Oakland News*, Mar. 8, 1869.

In their own campaign against the amendment Democrats raised the usual charges of Negro inferiority and racial equality. But as ratification became more certain, they resorted less often to the racial argument. Instead they turned on the Republican party, emphasizing its failure to adhere to its 1868 platform. Republicans had promised to let every loyal state decide the suffrage issue for itself, Democrats recalled; yet now that their presidential candidate had been elected, they proposed to extend black suffrage to every state. "How can the people have confidence in this lying, hypocritical and shameless organization?" charged Robert Ferrall of California. "Its leaders make a business of deception and advocate today what they denounced yesterday." To some, perhaps dissatisfied themselves, his logic made sense. At least one "Old Line Republican" did announce his withdrawal from the party and for those very reasons. Since 1866 national Republican leaders had been disclaiming intent to enfranchise northern blacks; now the Fifteenth Amendment with its equal suffrage provision was on the way to making indiscriminate franchise a reality.[39]

For Democrats seeking complete control of the California legislature in September, 1869, the Fifteenth Amendment offered a ready-made political issue, as had the first Reconstruction Act in 1867. Rather than emphasize black suffrage, Democrats redirected the focus to the Chinese, the larger and more important minority group in the state. Thus when Democrats convened in June, 1869, for their state convention, they stressed that adoption of the amendment would enfranchise Asians. Republicans could not miss the devastating implications of this argument and reaffirmed, just as quickly, their opposition to citizenship and the ballot for the Chinese. They minimized black suffrage by maintaining that the question was no longer viable politically.[40]

The potential impact of the Chinese vote, merely by virtue of its numbers, was clearly frightening to white Californians. Whereas the 4,272 black residents amounted to less than 1 percent of the state's population, the 49,310 Asians made up one-tenth of the whole.

39. *Sonoma Democrat*, Feb. 6, 1869; "Old Line Republican" to editor, n.p., n.d., in San Francisco *Examiner*, Feb. 16, 1869. Other comments on the inconsistency of Republican policy can be found in *Boise Democrat*, Mar. 17, 1869; *Oregon Herald*, Feb. 12, 1869; *Placerville Democrat*, Feb. 20, 1869; *Red Bluff Sentinel*, Mar. 20, 1869; San Francisco *Examiner*, Jan. 12, Mar. 5, 12, 1869.

40. Davis, *Political Conventions*, 290–94; *Sacramento Union*, Aug. 30, 1869.

Beyond that they were predominantly male. Blacks could count only 1,731 men over twenty-one years of age, but 36,890 Asians fell into that category. Therefore, the possibility of these men becoming voters overshadowed black suffrage as an issue as the campaign progressed. Republicans termed as "ridiculous" Democratic charges that they favored Chinese suffrage and pleaded with the electorate to understand that the amendment would enfranchise citizens and no others. The whole force of the Republican national policy since the end of the war had been to elevate black or mulatto citizens. Of no concern, at any time, were civil rights for foreigners, and the party would never give the ballot to Asian-born immigrants.[41]

Democrats had the upper hand in any case and exploited the Chinese issue with cleverness and advantage. As in the 1867 campaign, their chief spokesmen were Henry Haight and Eugene Casserly. Governor Haight condemned Republican policy for attempting "indiscriminate suffrage regardless of race, color, or qualification." He reminded voters further of the lower living standard of Asians, whose population he estimated at 50,000. So used to working for cheap wages were they, he said, that even twenty-five cents would seem like a large sum to them. In all likelihood, said the governor, their vote could be bought for just that little. By Haight's calculation, the party which had the $12,500 to purchase the Asian vote could win an election. Even more effective, perhaps, was Haight's contention that Chinese suffrage would give control of California politics to the Central Pacific Railroad. Employing some 10,000 coolies, the Central Pacific, as the theory went, could direct their vote under threat of dismissal and thus sway the results of an election.[42]

Senator Casserly rejected the contention that Republicans opposed enfranchisement of Asians. Comparing Republican disavowals of black suffrage with their laws which extended the reform, Casserly could put no faith in Republican assurances. It was impossible to trust Republicans, he stated flatly, because they had broken so many previous promises. Casserly and his Democratic supporters, along with

41. *1870 Census, Population*, 15–16, 606–9, 619; *Marysville Appeal*, Feb. 13, Apr. 9, 28, May 1, July 15, Aug. 25, 1869; *Oakland News*, Aug. 12, 1869; *Yreka Journal*, Feb. 26, Mar. 12, 1869. Some Republicans did voice approval of enfranchising those Chinese who assimilated into American society.
42. Moody, "Civil War," 348; H. Brett Melendy and Benjamin F. Gilbert, *The Governors of California: Peter H. Burnett to Edmund G. Brown* (Georgetown, Calif., 1965), 152.

some conservative Republicans, insisted that Californians dare not accept the Fifteenth Amendment because of the state's racial diversity.[43]

Evidently the voters were listening. Democrats easily won control of the state legislature by a majority of 15,000 votes. Republicans lost the upper house, and the twenty-two Republicans in the 1869–71 legislature were in no position to offer meaningful resistance to their eighty-two Democratic colleagues. It is the contention of at least one student of California history that the Central Pacific played a vital role in the 1869 election—but not because it could tell its coolie laborers how to vote. Rather, the transcontinental railroad had just been completed and the company had released a flood of Chinese workers. Looking for work, these coolies were a glut on the California labor market and provided fierce competition for newly arrived white laborers seeking jobs. Democrats interpreted the election results as a mandate against the Fifteenth Amendment and determined that California should withhold its consent. Republicans acknowledged the amendment as doomed in California but still hoped for sufficient ratification in other states. Reviewing the current Republican rate of election failures in California, the *Marysville Appeal* offered a cryptic assessment: the sooner that equal suffrage was decided, the better it would be for the Republican party.[44]

Four of the six western areas which had achieved statehood by 1870 were to ratify the Fifteenth Amendment. In Minnesota and Nebraska endorsement was a foregone conclusion since blacks already had the vote in both states. Yet ironically, assent was not a step hastily undertaken by officials in either locale. Anxious that their state be the first to ratify the amendment, Minnesota's congressional delegation telegraphed the text of the document to the legislature once Congress approved the amendment. Democratic opponents in the assembly, however, introduced a resolution to the effect that ratification would imply Minnesota's willingness to surrender her sovereignty to the federal government. Republicans, rather than argue the point on the floor, dropped the issue for the session and adjourned without taking action on the amendment. Evidently Democrats saw

43. Eugene Casserly, *Speech on the Fifteenth Amendment and the Labor Question, Delivered in San Francisco, California, July 28, 1869* (n.p., n.d.), 1–7; San Francisco *Call*, Mar. 7, Aug. 11, 1867; *Sonoma Democrat*, July 20, 1867.

44. *Sonoma Democrat*, Sept. 11, 1869; Hubert Howe Bancroft, *History of California, 1860–1890*, vol. XXIV, *The Works of Hubert Howe Bancroft* (San Francisco, 1890), 363; Moody, "Civil War," 362; *Marysville Appeal*, Sept. 28, 1869.

little reason for continued resistance, for they abandoned their ploy in the next session and ratification was quickly secured. Still, because of Democratic obstruction in 1869, Minnesota was the twenty-second state instead of the first to sanction black suffrage by federal enaction.[45]

Nebraska was even slower. It was her approval which gave the three-fourths vote needed to incorporate the amendment into the federal Constitution, but it came only at the prodding of federal officials. Governor David Butler had been reluctant to convene the legislature into special session. Lawmakers in Nebraska were not scheduled to meet again until January, 1871, and the governor was unwilling to incur the expense of an interim session. Butler specified that he would call his legislature only if ratification looked doubtful. Several Republican editors voiced support for the governor's stand because they objected to expending further time and money to ratify the amendment. In the view of one such editor, the nation had already contributed enough of its monetary and human resources toward improvement of the black man's status. Suffrage would come, he wrote, but as for the amendment, "we can get along just as well without as with it."

It was President Grant who finally roused Butler. In the fall of 1869 ratification still seemed remote; Grant asked Butler to "consider the propriety of convening the legislature into extra session . . . , and if the proposition should meet with your views, I request that a proclamation be issued to that effect at as early a period as you deem expedient." Butler submitted to Grant's request and summoned the legislature in mid-February, 1870. In a brief opening statement the governor advocated ratification as a "simple act of justice to the national freedmen," but otherwise refrained from comment. Aware of the events that had led to their meeting, the legislators acted quickly. Within fifteen minutes they had approved the amendment with only four dissenting votes.[46]

Ratification in Kansas and Nevada came as a victory for the Re-

45. State of Minnesota, *House Journal, 1869* (St. Paul, 1869), 134; *House Journal, 1870* (St. Paul, 1870), 29; *Senate Journal, 1870* (St. Paul, 1870), 9, 21.

46. David Butler to Charles Sumner, Lincoln, Nebr., Oct. 30, 1869, Sumner Papers; *Nebraska State Journal* (Lincoln), Feb. 5, 19, 1870; U. S. Grant to Butler, Nov. 23, 1869, quoted in Gillette, *Right to Vote*, 146; State of Nebraska, *House Journal, Special Session, 1870* (Omaha, 1870), 19; *Senate Journal, Special Session, 1870* (Omaha, 1870), 18.

publican party rather than as an expression of the popular will. Pro-suffrage Republicans in Kansas considered the amendment as the only means, in face of public opposition, of securing the ballot for black men. Representative Sidney Clarke entertained the same hope as his colleagues from Minnesota; he wanted Kansas to be the first to ratify, and immediately upon positive action by Congress, he telegraphed the text of the amendment to Topeka. There Republican legislators pushed ratification before opposition could form. Unfortunately, Clarke in his haste had transmitted an incorrect copy of the text. Kansas's act of approval was, therefore, invalid and had to be re-considered in the 1870 session. By this time Democrats had mar-shalled some resistance, if ineffective. Just as in Minnesota, they condemned the amendment as a surrender of authority to the central government and, paraphrasing Governor Haight of California, warned of the importation of thousands of Chinese by unknown railroad entrepreneurs in order to dictate state politics. The threat was without foundation and had no effect on the Kansas legislature. It consented to the amendment for a second time in January, 1870.[47]

To Nevada, finally, went the honor of being the first state to ratify the Fifteenth Amendment. But it was scarcely a distinction for the legislature inasmuch as it had rejected every effort since 1864 to repeal discriminatory legislation. Indeed, given the prevalence of anti-Negro sentiment in the state, one Nevadan expressed surprise at the support rallied there for congressional Reconstruction, let alone black suffrage. William Stewart may be credited with spearheading Nevada's speedy assent. Proud of his own role in formulating the amendment, the senator used his influence to pressure Republicans at home into quick action. Still, opposition did arise. In the face of possible rejection by the party, eleven Republicans in the assembly withheld their consent, arguing that ratification would violate the 1868 Republican platform. The six dissenting senators entered their protest in the senate *Journal*. Declaring ratification out of order until such time as the president had officially submitted the amendment, they criticized the legislature for its "haste and undignified action." They objected as well that voting qualifications be set by the federal government and not by the states. With quiet disdain they submitted

47. *Kansas Tribune*, Feb. 28, 1869; Wilder, *Annals of Kansas*, 501; State of Kansas, *House Journal, 1869* (Topeka, 1869), 911–12; *House Journal, 1870* (Topeka, 1870), 135, 137–38, 175.

finally that Nevadans, while assuredly pro-Republican, were certainly not pro-Negro.[48]

Democrats in Oregon in a gesture of perverse defiance rejected the amendment in October, 1870, fully six months after its incorporation into the federal Constitution. On October 26 the state senate initiated and passed a resolution which declared the amendment in violation of Oregon's sovereignty, an illegal interference by Congress in Oregon's right to establish voting qualifications, and a change in law forced on the nation by the bayonet. Without fanfare, the lower house sanctioned the resolution immediately after its arrival from the senate.[49]

As expected, lawmakers in California rejected the Fifteenth Amendment by a vote of eighty-one to sixteen. Demoralized by the Democratic victory in 1869, Republicans could offer little resistance. Legislative denial was a fact; more intriguing was Governor Haight's curious theory, presented in his annual message, that Congress lacked authorization to recommend changes in the federal Constitution. The U.S. Constitution was merely an instrument through which the states might delegate authority to the federal government, he argued. The states might expand the powers of the national government, but in Haight's view the latter could not seek to extend its own authority. Were the federal government empowered to initiate action which broadened its own power, "the people of a section of the country could be deprived of every vestige of self-government, and held in a condition of provincial servitude."[50] While many in the West were reconciling themselves to expanded congressional jurisdiction, Governor Haight clearly remained on the defensive, convinced that any directive out of Washington constituted interference in state affairs.

Other California officials, perhaps influenced by Haight's opinion, attempted for a brief time to resist black suffrage. Despite promul-

48. George A. Nourse to Lyman Trumbull, Carson City, Apr. 7, 1866, Lyman Trumbull Papers, LC; *Gold Hill News*, Mar. 1, 1869; *Territorial Enterprise*, Mar. 4, 1869; *Carson Appeal*, Feb. 28, 1869; State of Nevada, *House Journal, 1869* (Carson City, 1869), 243–44; Elliott, *History of Nevada*, 388; William Hanchett, "Yankee Law and the Negro in Nevada, 1861–1869," WHR, X (Summer, 1956), 241–49.

49. State of Oregon, *Senate Journal, 1870* (Salem, 1870), 654; *House Journal, 1870* (Salem, 1870), 512.

50. State of California, *Senate Journal, 1869–1870* (Sacramento, 1870), 245; *House Journal, 1869–1870* (Sacramento, 1870), 168–76, 295–96; Henry Haight, *Speech of Governor Haight, at the Democratic State Convention at Sacramento, June 29, 1869* (San Francisco, 1869), 4–5.

gation of the amendment in March, 1870, county clerks in Sacramento, San Joaquin, Santa Clara, and San Francisco counties refused to register blacks as voters. Jo Hamilton, state attorney general, praised these officials as defenders of the state constitution. California law, in his judgment, took precedence over the federal amendment, and blacks could not vote until the state had passed legislation to implement the change in the federal Constitution. Opponents, on the rebound, took the attorney general to task. Hamilton's opinion, they maintained, was dictated by his prejudice rather than by his legal training. Moreover it was worthless; as a state official he lacked authority to decide the validity of federal law.[51] Persuaded by the force of the Republican argument, recalcitrant county clerks soon began permitting blacks to register.

Outspoken Democratic resistance to the Fifteenth Amendment was not limited to California alone. Throughout the western half of the nation, but especially along the West coast, Democrats characterized the Fifteenth Amendment as "conceived in iniquity and sent through the forms of adoption by fraud, force and villainy. By every known rule . . . it is binding neither in law nor in conscience." But not all Democrats were so grudging in their acceptance. George O. Kies, editor of the *Placerville Democrat*, did not believe the amendment illegal. The suffrage provision, in Kies's view, had been added to the federal Constitution in a lawful manner. "If it is a little black in the face," he wrote, "that only betrays its partisan paternity, and does not affect its Constitutional legitimacy . . . its adoption has been duly and even enthusiastically celebrated. . . . Having conscientious scruples to fighting against numerical odds, we always accept the decision of the sovereign majority."[52] Like Democrats in the territories three years earlier, Kies accepted federal law even though he per-

---

51. *Sonoma Democrat*, Apr. 16, 1870; *Sacramento Union*, Apr. 8, 11, 1870; San Francisco *Chronicle*, Apr. 8, 9, 11, 12, 13, 1870; *Humboldt Times*, Apr. 15, 1870; *Stars and Stripes*, Apr. 14, 1870; Sacramento *Bee*, Apr. 9, 1870; *Marysville Appeal*, Apr. 8, 9, 12, 13, 1870; *Alta California*, Apr. 9, 13, 1870. Democrats in Oregon sought to have votes cast by blacks in the June, 1870, election thrown out on the grounds that the Oregon Constitution prohibited black suffrage. Rejecting the request, the Oregon Supreme Court ruled instead that the state constitution was in violation of the Fifteenth Amendment. John Marby Mathews, *Legislative and Judicial History of the Fifteenth Amendment* (Baltimore, 1909), 97–99.

52. *Idaho World*, Apr. 21, 1870; *Placerville Democrat*, Apr. 16, 1870. See also *Boise Democrat*, Apr. 16, 1870; *Red Bluff Sentinel*, Apr. 23, 1870; *Oregon City Enterprise*, Mar. 19, 1870; *St. Paul Pioneer*, Apr. 1, 1870.

sonally opposed the change it brought. But this acceptance, if not always given with enthusiasm, was another reason why the Republican quest to enfranchise blacks succeeded.

And what of the western blacks, the people most directly affected by the Fifteenth Amendment? They celebrated its promulgation with unrestrained elation. As its adoption became a reality, Philip Bell exclaimed, "*Gloria Triumphe!* We are free!" From March to May, 1870, Bell filled the columns of the *Elevator* with reports of celebrations in California, Oregon, and Nevada. Even in Colorado, where they had voted since 1867, blacks met to commemorate the promulgation. In Kansas blacks held a statewide convention in Leavenworth. During the first half of the program the audience prayed, sang, and listened to speeches. Then, as evening approached, the participants took the festival to the streets in a torchlight parade.[53] For western black leaders the Fifteenth Amendment was the culmination of their desires. They had not advocated social leveling between the races, nor had they sought to uplift western blacks economically. In their quest for equality before the law, their goal had been adequate guarantee of their rights within the political structure. With the ratification of the Fifteenth Amendment they believed these rights secured.

In the aftermath, few western Republicans justified giving the black man in the loyal states the right to vote. Clearly they had rationalized the need for equal suffrage in the South and recognized Congress's right to impose it in the territories, yet their eloquence failed them in 1870. Earlier, with the passage of the first Reconstruction Act in 1867, Frederick MacCrellish had anticipated the Fifteenth Amendment. Common sense, said MacCrellish, dictated that in a democracy all the people be permitted to participate in the governmental process. Equal suffrage would out of necessity become fact throughout the nation once implemented in the South. "What most of the Northern and Western States are willing to impose on the South, but are so loath to accept themselves, they will learn to think better of after it has been proved. . . . This suffrage concession is deemed a necessity to safe reconstruction . . . and not at all the choice of the people. But evil or not, it is a necessity, and therefore, it will become the law of the republic . . . first at the South . . . and afterward

53. *Elevator*, Feb. 11, 1870; *Rocky Mountain News*, May 3, 1870; Moore Journals, Apr. 7, 1870.

at the North, where popular political logic is against this sort of proscription."

Like MacCrellish, Samuel Bowles believed suffrage must come—but for a more selfish reason. Editor of the Springfield, Massachusetts, *Republican* and widely traveled in the West, Bowles declared civil advances for both blacks and Chinese inevitable because of the scarcity of "cheap and reliable labor" along the West coast. The need to cultivate and sustain these minority groups as a work force would ease the more blatant racial restrictions. Said Bowles in cold appraisal of the situation, ". . . our national democratic principle, of welcoming hither the people of every country and clime, aside, the white man needs the negro and the Chinaman more than they need him; the pocket appeal will override the prejudice of his soul—and we shall do a sort of rough justice to both classes, because it will pay."[54]

By the end of 1870 black men were voting in every western state and territory. They still faced discrimination, and their participation in politics was limited to casting the ballot. Only in Colorado, where their vote was deemed crucial, did blacks regularly serve as delegates to Republican territorial conventions in the late 1860s and early 1870s. But the tendency toward a more liberal view would overtake the West, even in areas where the black vote made little difference in election results. In the 1880s Nevada and Kansas were to delete racial restrictions from their voting laws, an advance untenable in earlier decades. Although their move merely recognized a *fait accompli,* the Oregon legislature in 1959 and the California legislature in 1962 ratified the Fifteenth Amendment.[55]

Only Wyoming, in the West, never restricted by law black participation in the political forum. Blacks voted in the territory from its inception in 1868, and soon after organizing, the territorial legislature enfranchised women as well. The first black to be elected to high public office in the West sat in the Wyoming legislature from 1879 to 1882. It is perhaps fitting that the man was William Jefferson

54. *Alta California,* Apr. 2, 1867; Bowles, *Across the Continent,* 243–44.

55. Elmer Ellis, *Henry Moore Teller, Defender of the West* (Caldwell, Idaho, 1941), 88; Henry Wagoner to Elihu Washburne, Denver, Nov. 10, 1867, Washburne Papers; Rusco, "*Good Time Coming?*" 47; Zornow, *Kansas,* 127; Gillette, *Right to Vote,* 85.

Hardin. There had been pitfalls along the way, but Hardin's political horizon had expanded significantly since 1866 when he wrote: "Sir, it is a solemn fact, before God & man, that I have never voted in all my life. Is it strange then that I should contend for the right to suffrage? Sir, I leave the question for you and every lover of justice to answer."[56]

56. William J. Hardin to Charles Sumner, Denver, Feb. 4, 1866, Sumner Papers. For details on Hardin's post-Colorado career see Berwanger, "William J. Hardin," 64–65.

CHAPTER SEVEN

Western Politics and Reconstruction

"We feel ourselves to be offshoots of the nation. . . ."
—Ignatius Donnelly, Minnesota

Reconstruction issues served to revitalize the Democratic party in the West. Increase in Democratic strength varied, of course, in the different states and territories. In areas where the party had never been strong—Kansas and Colorado, for example—Democrats merely added to their representation in the state legislatures. These were minimal gains which, coupled with the lack of effective party leadership, precluded the development of meaningful opposition to Republicans in power. But in California and Oregon, where the Democratic party had been a viable organization with active party leadership during the 1850s, Democrats knew greater success. Here they were able to regain control of state politics in the late 1860s, relegating Republicans to a minority position and providing an effective challenge to their program.

The resurgence of the Democratic party along the West coast paralleled a similar movement occurring along the eastern seaboard. Where a trend toward conservatism became noticeable in New York and Connecticut in 1867, it was at that point, and for many of the same reasons, that California returned to the Democratic fold. Oregon followed suit and selected a Democratic legislature only a year later. Clearly, Democrats who had joined the Union-Republican coalition established during the war were dismayed by 1866 with the radical Republican stand on Reconstruction and black suffrage. In California especially former Democrats were feeling like second-class members of the Union party, for old-line Republicans dominated state patronage and were making a concerted effort to exclude war Democrats. Throughout the West people were uneasy over Republican taxation policy and federal spending, causing many former Democrats to seek shelter once again in the party they had forsaken. Conservative Republicans, too, disillusioned with their own party platform, began supporting the Democrats while Republicans were displaying more political apathy generally. Taken all together, these factors weighed in favor of the Democrats when it came time to vote. Whereas in 1865 all eight congressmen from the West had been elected under the Union-Republican label, by 1869 fully one-half of the western congressional delegation was acknowledging Democratic affiliation.[1]

As their party gained in areas of the West, some Democratic leaders began to reaffirm the doctrines of states' rights and popular sovereignty. While California Democrats were the most vocal, party loyals in the Oregon legislature were just as strong-willed and used the states' rights concept as their rallying cry against national legislation. Demands for local autonomy arose in Utah and Montana territories as well but from local rather than national issues. Yet underlying the particulars in each case was the radical Republican attempt to exert more federal authority over these territories. This was not a new phenomenon; Congress had previously negated territorial laws or stipulated conditions for statehood. Nevertheless, when Congress sought to eliminate polygamy in Utah and annulled laws passed by the Montana territorial legislature, individuals directly affected by the legislation regarded Congress's action as a threat to popular government. Lacking the power to obstruct passage of the laws in Congress itself, these people relied instead on the popular sovereignty concept as their one means of self-defense. To be sure, their criticism had little impact on strong-minded Republicans in Washington, D.C. Bent on securing their way, Republican leaders in the nation's capital either ignored or effectively countered Democratic moves in the West. But Republican success, while impressive, was not total. During the immediate post–Civil War period radicals got nowhere at all in

1. The four Democratic congressmen included Samuel Axtell and James Johnson of California, Joseph S. Smith of Oregon, and Eugene Wilson of Minnesota. In 1865 James McDougall from California was the sole western Democrat in the Senate, although Union-Republicans James Nesmith of Oregon and Daniel Norton of Minnesota usually voted with the Democrats. Cornelius Cole replaced McDougall in Mar., 1867, giving California two Republican senators until Eugene Casserly took John Conness's seat in Mar., 1869. John Niven, " 'Poor Progress' in the Land of Steady Habits," and James C. Mohr, "The Depoliticization of Reform," both in Mohr (ed.), *Radical Republicans in the North*, 28–31, 61; Hubert Howe Bancroft, *History of Oregon, 1848–1888*, vol. XXX, *The Works of Hubert Howe Bancroft* (San Francisco, 1888), II, 667; Bancroft, *California, 1860–1890*, 326–27.

their drive to do away with polygamy, to Republicans as devastating a social evil as slavery.

The impact of Reconstruction on western politics differed within each state and territory. In the more populous, politically mature areas which had direct telegraphic communication with the East, Reconstruction played a most influential role. In the outlying territories national issues were of lesser importance. While federal policy and implementation did have a part in campaign oratory, for these areas the national question was so entwined with political rivalries, personal jealousies, and local issues that it became difficult to separate one from the other. The dominating factor in New Mexican politics, for instance, was rivalry between leading Spanish-surnamed families whose political ideals were determined by their own crass economic interests or by their anti-Americanism. Only nominally did representatives of these families serving in the territorial legislature or as delegates to Congress refer to themselves as Republican or Democrat, and these men took notice of national legislation only insofar as it affected New Mexico. J. Francisco Chaves, New Mexico's Republican delegate to Congress from 1865 to 1871, was typical of the native New Mexican politician. In Congress he worked above all to defend the territory's own system of peonage. Chaves leaned toward conservatism with respect to Reconstruction; he supported Johnson long after most Republicans had abandoned the president. Yet radicals in New Mexico were aware of Chaves's influence with the powerful Pino family and, as a result, they dared not criticize his lack of radical orthodoxy. Instead they backed his candidacy for Congress with vigor. States' rights Democrats in the territory did take Chaves to task for his conservatism, but their attack only proved his stand to be substantially the same as theirs.[2]

In Arizona, Republicans shunned national politics, even to the point of avoiding use of the term "Republican." Aware that the voting power lay in the hands of Mexican-Americans and Democrats, Republicans also underplayed Reconstruction and attempted to garner support from the white population by emphasizing local Indian troubles. This tactic did not prevent opposition to congressional Reconstruction from surfacing, however. Six months after the passage of

2. Lamar, *Far Southwest*, 132–35; *Santa Fe Gazette*, Apr. 6, 17, 1868, Feb. 27, 1869; Hubert Howe Bancroft, *History of Arizona and New Mexico, 1530–1888*, vol. XVII, *The Works of Hubert Howe Bancroft* (San Francisco, 1889), 707–9.

the first Reconstruction Act in 1867, Democrats purchased the *Arizona Miner* and began to denounce Congress's policy. As the new editor explained, Arizona Democrats were attempting to do their part in preserving the "freedom of . . . every white American" and in crippling "the monster [the Republican party] that had grown fat upon the misfortunes of our country." Although such opposition caused concern among Republican officials in the territory, they need not have worried. From 1863, when Arizona Territory was created, to 1875, delegates to Congress were consistently Republican.[3]

Reconstruction as a political issue was more evident in Dakota Territory, where the Republican party divided along ideological lines as early as 1866. Delegate Walter Burleigh and Governor Andrew Faulk led the conservative group, taking a strong pro-Johnson stand. As vocal expressions of this support gradually declined through 1868, the radical Republican element in turn took up a vigorous campaign on behalf of congressional Reconstruction. Still, the underlying difference between the two groups was more petty rivalry than political substance. The radicals hoped to wrest control—and the patronage—from the Burleigh-Faulk Republicans. The radicals in fact had been unable to make inroads, for Dakota Democrats, declining to nominate a slate for public office, consistently voted the conservative ticket during the immediate postwar years. Only in 1868 did the conservative-Democratic coalition break down when Democrats decided to put up their own candidate. A lively campaign ensued, with Reconstruction the focus, and radical candidate Solomon Spink captured the delegateship to Congress. Yet when victory came for the radicals, according to Dakota historian Howard R. Lamar, it was more realistically due to the tenor of national affairs than to politics unique to the territory. As Johnson's prestige dimmed, radical Republican popularity increased in the territory. At the same time Dakota was experiencing a Grant boom even though its citizenry could not cast a presidential vote. Dakota's steady influx of new settlers, for the most part Union veterans who were inclined to endorse the radical

3. *Arizona Miner*, Sept. 21, 1867; Richard McCormick to Charles Sumner, Tucson, Jan. 20, 1868, Sumner Papers; Howard R. Lamar, "Carpetbaggers Full of Dreams: A Functional View of the Arizona Pioneer Politican," AW, VII (Autumn, 1965), 192; Kelley, *Arizona*, 17; Wagoner, *Arizona Territory*, 36, 77; Lamar, *Far Southwest*, 443; U.S. Congress, Senate, *Biographical Directory of the American Congress, 1774–1971* (Washington, D.C., 1971), 197.

Republican ticket and Grant, only reinforced the growing tendency toward radicalism in the territory.[4]

Republicans early secured a firm hold on Colorado, Nebraska, Minnesota, and Kansas and throughout the Reconstruction period retained that strength. Democratic support did increase in each area except for Nebraska, but still the party was unable to topple its Republican opponents. In Nebraska there was actual decline in Democratic showing at the polls, most likely caused by J. Sterling Morton's withdrawal from politics and by his personal feud with George Miller, next to Morton the most prominent Democrat in the state. In Colorado Democratic hopes for victory peaked with the party's narrow defeat in 1868; thereafter Democratic strength ebbed as Republican-oriented settlers began immigrating into the territory from the older Middle West.

In terms of actual numbers of voters, the Democratic party outdistanced Republican growth in Minnesota. While Republican strength increased between 1864 and 1867 by some 10,000 votes, Minnesota Democrats realized an even greater surge of 12,000 votes for the same period. New settlement was in part responsible, but since the increase was most apparent in counties largely Democratic prior to the conflict, war Democrats were likely returning in droves to their former political allegiance. In recording so strong a Democratic vote, citizens were no doubt protesting Republican Reconstruction policy, for on local questions Democrats and Republicans seldom took issue in Minnesota.

Still the party did not benefit from the gain: because the Democratic electorate was concentrated in St. Paul and in the counties along the Mississippi River, their growing numbers had little effect on statewide politics. Republicans continued to dominate the legislature, and with the creation of legislative districts in the newly settled western portions of the state, the Republican majority in the capital was significantly reinforced. In the 1866 legislature Republicans held the advantage by twenty-three seats; their number had expanded to thirty-nine by 1868 despite the greater increase in Democratic votes.

Democrats nonetheless were able to elect Eugene Wilson to Congress in 1868. His victory was made possible by a split in the state Republican party when Ignatius Donnelly decided to make a bid for

4. Kingsbury, *Dakota*, I, 434–40; Lamar, *Dakota Territory*, 112–16; *Directory of the American Congress*, 524, 1736–37.

Alexander Ramsey's seat in the U.S. Senate. Upon becoming aware of Donnelly's intention, Ramsey wielded his influence to have Donnelly denied the regular Republican nomination for the House of Representatives. Undaunted by the setback, Donnelly ran anyway— as an independent—and split the Republican vote. Because the district contained a growing number of Democrats, the division among Republicans offered Wilson an easy victory.[5]

In Kansas the Republican party was the state's only viable political organization during the Civil War. Even so, political feuding was intense, with differences most often arising between pro–James Lane and anti-Lane Republicans. Prior to 1866 Democrats apparently sensed the futility of nominating their own candidates and typically threw their support in statewide races to conservative Republicans. But in that year they did run candidates for the state legislature and secured eleven out of the 105 seats. Encouraged by growing opposition to congressional Reconstruction and black suffrage, Democrats stepped up their campaign in 1867. Perhaps to their surprise, they increased their number to twenty-five in the legislature and won a significant number of county offices throughout the state.

While the practical effect of these Democratic gains in 1867 was negligible, Republican editors could not resist speculating on the implications. Some went out on a limb and flatly predicted the dissolution of the state Republican party; others attributed the growing vigor of the Kansas Democracy to dissatisfaction among Republicans over congressional policy, and equal suffrage in particular. Jacob Stotler of Emporia indicted Republican voters, too, but for their apathy. The party had dominated Kansas politics for so long that many of the rank and file saw little reason to participate in a race whose outcome was certain. In addition, he believed, the referendum on black suffrage had discouraged many Republicans from coming to the polls; they wanted no part of it. But to a greater degree the matter hearkened to national politics; said Stotler flatly, "Congress is largely to blame for Republican defeats." The southern policy had left Kansas radicals disappointed and less willing to support the national legislature, while conservatives opposed to congressional Reconstruction were beginning to vote Democratic. Whatever the

5. *Winona Republican*, Jan. 2, 1866, Nov. 14, 21, 1867, Nov. 6, 1868; *St. Paul Pioneer*, Nov. 22, 1865, Nov. 27, 1866; Haugland, "Alexander Ramsey," 240, *passim*.

case, Stotler declared, Reconstruction was responsible for the Republican decline in Kansas.[6]

In the northern and central intermontane West, between the Continental Divide and the Sierra Nevada–Cascade ranges, only the state of Nevada sustained congressional Reconstruction. Between 1865 and 1870 Republicans were normally receiving 55 percent of the vote, and this slight edge encouraged them to proclaim Nevada's radicalism. Yet some Nevada Republicans evidently did not consider themselves "radical" and in 1870 threw their support to the Democratic slate. Democrats in that year, with the help of conservative Republicans, elected a Democratic governor and congressman. Continued Republican domination of the state legislature, however, enabled the party to keep Republicans in the U.S. Senate.[7]

On the Pacific coast Washington Territory remained Republican only by the narrowest of margins. Republicans won the delegateships to Congress in 1867 and 1869 by less than 200 votes in each case. In 1870 Republicans held just three more seats in the territorial legislature than did the Democratic contingent.[8] Still largely unsettled Washington Territory was, in effect, a weak Republican enclave in the Pacific Northwest. To the east lay Democratic Idaho and Montana; to the immediate south, more populous Oregon. The Beaver State and its southern neighbor, California, comprised the stronghold of Democracy in the West.

The political wars between Republicans and Democrats in Idaho and Montana were a continuous struggle to determine which party might prevail in the territories. Reconstruction issues were involved, to be sure, but they were peripheral to the central theme. In the post–Civil War era "Democrats were to Republicans," says historian

6. *Emporia News*, Nov. 15, 22, 1867; *Topeka State Record*, Nov. 13, 1867; *Atchison Champion*, Nov. 6, 1867; *Kansas Tribune*, Dec. 8, 1867; *Topeka Tribune*, Nov. 17, Dec. 4, 1866; *Leavenworth Conservative*, Oct. 31, 1866, Nov. 15, 1867; J. Bowles to Mary Lane, Leavenworth, Kans., Jan. 15, 1865, Lane Papers, KU; Zornow, *Kansas*, 124; Caldwell, "Kansas," 20–30.

7. Myron Angel, *History of Nevada* (Oakland, Calif., 1881), 89–90; Hubert Howe Bancroft, *History of Nevada, Colorado, and Wyoming*, vol. XXV, *The Works of Hubert Howe Bancroft*, (San Francisco, 1890), 189–90. For an evaluation of conservative Republican and Democratic cooperation, see J. L. Bennett to Andrew Johnson, Washoe City, Nev., Dec. 13, 1867, Johnson Papers.

8. *Oregonian*, June 13, 1867; *Vancouver Register*, June 19, 1869; *Pacific Tribune*, June 30, 1870; Bancroft, *Washington, Idaho, and Montana*, 265, 280.

Paul Buck, "and Republicans were to Democrats, not opponents to be persuaded, but enemies to be remorselessly pursued and destroyed."[9] For nowhere in the West than in these two northernmost territories is his statement more apt.

Basically, Democrats and Republicans shared the responsibility for governing the two territories and neither was happy with the arrangement. Republicans, sent out from Washington, D.C., under the patronage, dominated the executive and judicial branches of territorial government, while Democrats, elected by the local constituency, controlled the legislature. In itself complex, this Democratic element contained northerners who had fled conscription during the war and rebel southerners who had served in the Confederate army. Somehow the many Democrats in both territories who had served in the Union army and whose loyalty was beyond question were less conspicuous, and Republicans were soon regarding all Democrats as traitors.

Idaho politics during the first three years of the territory's existence, 1863–66, were marked by relative calm. Democrats held all but one seat in the legislature, and the Republican governors and territorial secretaries kept their distance. Caleb Lyon and Horace Gilson serving in 1865 were no exception. Neither offered any opposition to the legislature's action, and, in turn, neither commanded any particular attention from the lawmakers. They had reason to avoid notice, for they were soon to abscond with $80,000 in federal and territorial funds and flee the United States. Presently another set of officials arrived on the scene, this time setting a different mood: the new governor, David Ballard, and secretary, Solomon Howlett, at once ran afoul of the Democratic legislature. Delegates frankly resented the appointment of Ballard, an Oregonian. While in the long run Ballard was to prove his mettle as governor, for the moment he was suspect for taking action where his predecessors had not. The legislators viewed Howlett with even greater distrust, for the Idaho appointee was known as a staunch Republican who considered all Democrats disloyal and worthy of disdain.[10]

The lawmakers themselves sparked the feud when they devised a

9. Paul H. Buck, *The Road to Reunion, 1865–1900* (New York, 1937), 75.

10. *Idaho World*, Dec. 16, 1865; Caleb Lyon to William Seward, Boise, Feb. 10, 1866, in TP: Idaho; *Idaho Statesman*, Feb. 6, 1866; Wells, "Ballard," 5; Bancroft, *Washington, Idaho, and Montana*, 469–70; William B. Daniels to William Seward, Lafayette, Ore., Nov. 22, 1865, in LAR, W. H. Wallace File.

bill to cut Ballard's and Howlett's salaries in half. The federal compensation for Idaho's officials and legislators was modest, so much so that the first legislature in 1864 had deemed it necessary to match the federal stipend from the territorial treasury. But now local political leaders were feeling less generous and proposed in 1866 to eliminate the territorial portion of the governor's and secretary's salaries, effectively reducing their compensation from $4,000 to $2,000. Not without guile, the governor, in a special message to the legislature, praised its members for seeking to reduce expenditures; carefully he assured the group that he did not believe their proposed measure to be motivated by personal animosity. Then Ballard suggested quite as seriously that an additional $12,000 saving could be realized if extra compensation paid legislators were also eliminated. Taken aback, the lawmakers expressed "indignation and contempt" at Ballard's remarks and resolved to return to the governor any further messages containing similar, unsolicited advice. Knowing that a veto would have little effect except to produce further wrath, Ballard quietly signed the bill upon its passage.[11]

Howlett became involved in an even more spirited controversy with Idaho legislators. Congress in 1862 had stipulated that all persons elected or appointed to a position under the United States government sign a loyalty oath; territorial lawmakers were generally believed subject to the provision since they were paid, in part or in full, out of the U.S. Treasury. Locals had no objection to a loyalty oath *per se*, but many could not verify under oath the appended clause—that they had never countenanced or supported the Confederacy. Actually Idaho legislators were embarrassed: a number among them had expressed strong sympathy for the southern cause or even served in the Confederate army. To subscribe falsely would deprive them, if convicted of perjury, of all future honor under the United States; to refuse could mean automatic removal from office. They therefore decide to take matters into their own hands. Representatives worked out their own oath which omitted any reference to sympathy or aid for the South. Governor Ballard vetoed the measure, declaring it to be in violation of the 1862 federal law and invalid. Legislators easily overrode his veto but then faced a showdown with Howlett.[12]

11. Wells, "Ballard," 7–10; "Ballard's special message to the legislative council," in ITER, ISHS; *Idaho Statesman*, Dec. 18, 1866, Feb. 26, 1867.
12. Wells, "Ballard," 10; Ballard's veto dated Dec. 24, 1866, in ITER.

Like Ballard, the territorial secretary found the compromise oath unacceptable. But unlike the governor, he had the means to call the legislators' bluff: either they take the federal oath or forego their salaries. Secretary of the Treasury McCulloch had in fact released $20,000 for legislative compensation but with instructions to pay only those who signed the oath. Some legislators began to relent, with a few signing the federal oath in secret, but the majority remained adamant in their refusal. On the eve of adjournment these members confronted Howlett directly. To their demand for payment, Howlett allegedly replied, "You ought to be shot, you damned Rebels, for asking money from a government you detest. Not a cent do you get until you subscribe and hand me the iron clad oath." Howlett then ordered the legislative hall locked, whereupon several of the more impetuous legislators broke into the chamber and destroyed lamps and furniture. Determined to prevail, the secretary requested help of federal troops in nearby Fort Boise, ostensibly to protect government property. With the arrival of the military, lawmakers at last recognized the futility of their situation and agreed to let the territorial supreme court arbitrate the dispute. The judges decided in Howlett's favor and legislators subscribed the federal oath before final adjournment.[13]

Idaho remained Democratic, even though the more rabid pro-southern element began filtering out of the territory in 1867—some to return South, others to seek their fortune elsewhere in the West. Fortunately for Ballard and Howlett, who retained office through the remainder of Johnson's term, the legislature grew more receptive to their efforts and once again began providing the governor and secretary additional compensation out of the territorial treasury.[14] Ballard himself was responsible. In handling the 1866–67 legislature, for instance, the governor consistently played down differences between

13. Solomon Howlett to William Seward, Boise, n.d., Austin B. Farnsworth statement, n.d., both in TP: Idaho; *Idaho World*, Jan. 19, 1867; San Francisco *Bulletin*, Jan. 30, 1867; Bancroft, *Washington, Idaho, and Montana*, 469; Donaldson, *Idaho*, 248. A similar impasse developed in Montana in 1865. John H. Rogers, representative from Deer Lodge, could not as a known former Confederate soldier subscribe to the oath without committing perjury. He devised an oath of his own which Governor Sidney Edgerton in turn refused to accept. Rogers resigned from the legislature; re-elected in 1866, he was seated without question. Spence, *Montana*, 25; Athearn, "Civil War and Montana Gold," 65–66.

14. David Ballard to Benjamin Wade, Boise, June 13, 1867, Wade Papers; *Idaho World*, Sept. 30, 1868; Bancroft, *Washington, Idaho, and Montana*, 471–72.

himself and Idaho lawmakers. At the same time Ballard avoided mention of national affairs in his annual messages, thus de-emphasizing issues which could easily have antagonized the legislature. More important, Ballard worked at handling his own problems and chose not to resolve local crises with federal intervention. In Montana, by contrast, where territorial Republicans were having to face an even more strong-minded Democratic legislature, Republican leaders turned to Congress for help when they found themselves powerless to impose their own will. The resultant congressional response created a bitter and lingering enmity in local Democratic circles.

From its earliest days as a territory Montana was a political thorn in the side of Republicanism. The first legislature was so overwhelmingly pro-southern and Democratic that Thomas Dimsdale, editor of the *Montana Post*, described it as a body of "secessionists, openly proclaiming to be citizens of Dixie." The territory itself contained such a large number of Democrats from Missouri that even the most optimistic Republicans could only envision defeat at the polls. Reflecting his distaste for the party in power, a Montana Republican characterized the territory as "the solitary example of an unredeemed people" and "the black sheep" of territories. But Republicans had reason to hope, at least, for a turnabout. In sparse numbers settlers were beginning to arrive from the Old Northwest, many of them Union veterans. Political observers anticipated that their numbers would swell, providing in time a new, more Republican-oriented population whose force might overshadow Democratic strength at the polls.[15]

Democrats, too, foresaw a change in the political complexion of the territory and, like Idaho Democrats, they were wary of the Republicans sent to administer Montana at the territorial level. To gain that final measure of autonomy and thus rid themselves of Republican appointees, Democrats were intent on achieving statehood quickly. Unfortunately, Republican governor Sidney Edgerton stood as an obstacle to their plan. Edgerton opposed statehood and would never have considered summoning a constitutional convention. The legislature itself might have called a convention but the governor refused

15. *Montana Post*, Nov. 5, 1864; Mary Edgerton to Martha Carter, Bannack, Mont., Aug. 27, 1865, Edgerton Family Papers; Cornelius Hedges Diary, Sept. 4, 1865, Hedges Family Papers; *Helena Herald*, Feb. 28, 1867; George B. Wright to John Sherman, Fort Benton, Mont., Oct. 6, 1866, Sherman Papers.

to convoke even that body, claiming it had ceased to exist. Montana's organic act had provided only for an initial meeting of the territorial legislature, stipulating that lawmakers divide the territory into electoral districts before holding additional sessions. When Democrats gerrymandered the territory in their favor, Edgerton reacted in anger to their partiality and vetoed the bill. As a result, no districts were established. With the legislature's subsequent move to adjourn, the governor declared the body legally terminated.[16]

In the fall of 1865 Thomas F. Meagher arrived in Montana to assume the duties of territorial secretary, and Edgerton rushed back to Washington to discuss the difficult political situation. Democrats appealed to Meagher, now acting governor, to reconvene the legislature. At first Meagher refused, believing disloyal sentiment too strong among the Democrats. But soon the secretary reversed himself. In January, 1866, he not only convoked the legislature but summoned a constitutional convention as well. Defending his about-face, Meagher claimed to have been mistaken about Montana Democrats. They were not suspect and could be relied on by the national administration. In any case, Meagher was concerned that territorial citizens be given the chance to voice their feelings about statehood.[17]

In the months following Meagher's decision to side with the Democrats, events moved rapidly. The constitutional convention met but adjourned shortly without framing a document. The legislature convened and carried out a normal session. Republicans voiced an official protest, and to their appeal Justices Hosmer and Munson of the territorial supreme court responded by declaring the acts of the second session invalid. In a fighting mood the legislature met a third time and this time passed a bill not only assigning the two justices to almost uninhabited judicial districts on the eastern plains but requiring that they live there as well![18]

By now it had become apparent to Republicans that "Meagher's Mob" was too powerful to be reasoned with or controlled; they decided to appeal to Congress. Wilbur Fisk Sanders, leader of the

16. Robert Edwin Albright, "The Relation of Montana with the Federal Government, 1864–1889" (Ph.D. dissertation, Stanford University, 1933), 71–76.

17. Thomas Meagher to William Seward, Virginia City, Mont., Dec. 11, 1865, Feb. 20, 1866, both in TP: Montana; Meagher to Andrew Johnson, Virginia City, Jan. 20, 1866, Johnson Papers; Athearn, *Meagher*, 149–52.

18. Thomas Meagher to Andrew Johnson, Virginia City, Mont., Jan. 20, 1866, Johnson Papers; Athearn, *Meagher*, 154–55.

territorial Republican party, and Robert Fisk, editor of the *Helena Herald,* quickly departed for the national capital where they used their every personal and political contact to seek the repeal of all acts passed by the second and third sessions of the legislature. They did their work well. Through private conversation and public testimony before the House and Senate territorial committees, the two men persuaded Republicans in Congress that Montana was in a state of anarchy. Moved by their testimony, Congress on March 2, 1867, invalidated the acts of the legislature and abolished its authority to regulate territorial courts. Dealing a final blow, it called for the election of a new legislature.[19]

Reaction in Montana divided along party lines, but Republican jubilance faded as the results of the territorial election came in. For during the campaign Democrats had repeatedly denounced federal interference in local affairs, and their message obviously hit home: once again Montana voters threw their weight toward an overwhelmingly Democratic legislature. Buoyed with their success, Democrats promptly—and unceremoniously—ousted the one lone Republican who had managed to secure a seat. The lawmakers then resolved the acts of the two preceding sessions to have been "just, equitable and beneficial"; simultaneously they demanded the resignations of Justices Hosmer and Munson.[20] Had they expected Congress's support to boost their own chance to control the territory, Montana Republicans must now have felt sadly deceived.

Congressional annulment of the two sessions, wrote Martin Maginnis, delegate to Congress from Montana in later years, was "the most unjust act ever perpetrated by the United States on a Territory." Undoubtedly western congressmen also questioned the wisdom of the action, for only two California representatives voted to approve the bill. With reference to Congress's attitude, John Goodwin, Republican delegate from Arizona, deemed national lawmakers too political in governing the territories, more readily influenced by oratory than by facts, and too hasty in their decisions. Montana historians have generally agreed with Goodwin's assessment: in nullifying the legis-

19. A. W. White and others to James Ashley, Helena, Dec. 26, 1866, Sanders Papers; *Congressional Globe,* 39 Cong., 2 Sess., 1816–17, 2368; Spence, *Montana,* 45.

20. Bancroft, *Washington, Idaho, and Montana,* 668–69; Spence, *Montana,* 46–47.

lative acts, they maintain, Congress legislated specifically on behalf of the Republican party in Montana and with no regard for the popular will. Should men opposing congressional strategy be permitted to control a territorial legislature? Congress apparently thought not.

Congress may indeed have been showing its partisan colors in the Montana misadventure. At least when faced with a similar situation in New Mexico Territory shortly thereafter, congressional Republicans chose not to follow their own, most recent precedent. During the absence of pro-Johnson governor Robert Mitchell, his radical territorial secretary W. F. M. Arny approved laws passed by the New Mexican legislature and appointed radicals to territorial office. Mitchell, upon his return, dismissed the appointees and declared the laws invalid. Arny appealed to Congress, which, this time sympathetic, reversed the governor's decision on March 26, 1867.[21] The two situations—Montana and New Mexico—offer a startling contrast; in both cases the legality of an action taken by an official governmental body or representative was at issue. In Montana the Republican opposition saw no validity to the acts of the second and third sessions of the legislature, since the first session had not met provisions of the territory's organic act. Further, acting governor Meagher had apparently exceeded his authority in convening the legislators at all; certainly he had overstepped his bounds, to the Republican way of thinking, by providing the legal means by which Montana Democrats might frustrate their political enemies. In New Mexico Mitchell argued that President Johnson had relieved Arny of his office as territorial secretary, and that as such Arny could not assume the governorship under any guise. Congress accepted the argument of Montana Republicans in nullifying the laws of a Democratic legislature and, by implication, rejected Meagher's authority to call the legislature into session. Three weeks later Congress adjusted its reasoning in favor of a radical Republican in New Mexico and permitted Arny's appointees to retain their public office.

If radical Republican congressmen were tempted to settle political disputes in favor of their partisans in the territories, some appeared

---

21. Martin Maginnis, "Thomas Francis Meagher," MtHSC, VI (1907), 106; *Congressional Globe*, 39 Cong., 1 Sess., 2369–70; Spence, *Montana*, 48; Calvin Horn, *New Mexico's Troubled Years: The Story of the Early Territorial Governors* (Albuquerque, 1963), 119.

just as determined to destroy polygamy in Utah. As early as 1856 Republicans had condemned the "twin relics of barbarism," slavery and polygamy. In part they were hoping to force the Democratic administration to interfere in Utah Territory and thus contradict its own stand on popular sovereignty. Still, Republican aversion to plural marriage remained sincere and was to be overshadowed only by the slavery question. With the coming of the war Utah once again came into focus and, with it, the issue of polygamy. In 1862 Congress took a formal stand and declared bigamous marriages in the territories a federal offense, but to little avail. Lincoln personally preferred a hands-off policy toward Utah, partly because of his reluctance to interfere in their religious doctrine and partly to avoid stirring up the Mormons, who had expressed sympathy for the southern cause. Their attitude was more a reaction against federal authority than an affinity for southern institutions, although some did hold slaves. In any case, the president's posture won him the respect of the Mormon community, and Utahans mourned his assassination as deeply as did the rest of the nation.[22]

Andrew Johnson inclined to follow Lincoln's example toward Utah. Not many in Washington shared his feeling, and Brigham Young was prompted to write, "We are pleased to notice the disposition to deal fairly with us which is manifested by President Johnson. It is so rarely that men in authority in these days manifest independence and fairness enough to do us at least justice that it is worthy of notice." Specifically Young was speaking of Congress, whose members were known to be less reasonably disposed toward the Utah question. Ironically, Young saw anti-Mormonism most ardently among members of the territorial committees of each house.[23]

Radical Republican animosity was in fact responsible for a series of unsuccessful measures from 1865 to 1870 designed to eradicate polygamy. Up for debate at the same time that Congress was dealing with Reconstruction in the South, these antipolygamy bills conformed with Reconstruction theory: Congress had authority to eliminate polygamy just as it had abolished slavery; Congress could interfere

22. Roy Franklin Nichols, *The Disruption of American Democracy* (New York, 1948), 109; William Alexander Linn, *The Story of the Mormons: From the Date of Their Origin to the Year 1901* (New York, 1902), 543–51; Arrell Morgan Gibson, *The West in the Life of the Nation* (Lexington, Mass., 1976), 506.

23. Brigham Young to William Hooper, Salt Lake City, June 16, 1866, Young Papers.

in local government to achieve its end. Later, with the Edmunds Act of 1882, Congress more clearly defined its policy toward Utah, disfranchising the nonconformists and governing Utah by commissions as it had governed the South for a short time through military rule. The implementation of the Edmunds Act did indeed destroy polygamy, but its harshness has caused one historian to equate federal policy toward Utah with Congress's policy toward the Reconstruction South.[24]

Beginning in 1866 with a bill introduced by Benjamin Wade and until 1870, various other proposals were introduced in Congress to eliminate polygamy. The Wade measure would have made probate judges in Utah appointive instead of elective officials. Further, it would have required U.S. marshals to challenge the swearing of jurors who were polygamists, and taxed all Mormon church property in excess of $20,000. The bill failed, but in December, 1867, Senator Andrew Cragin of New Hampshire presented a second measure which included the main points of Wade's bill. Cragin's proposal also forbade all but civil marriage ceremonies and stipulated fines and prison terms for persons guilty of practicing polygamy or performing polygamous marriages. In a final gesture it declared all children of polygamous marriages illegitimate. The Cullom bill followed in 1870: incorporating the previous restrictions, it further disqualified polygamists from public office as well as from jury duty. Mormons back home protested more vigorously than usual and their delegate to Congress, William Hooper, reminded his colleagues from the floor of the House that the passage of the measure would imperil the very sanctity of religious freedom. The House passed the bill by a vote of ninety-four to thirty-two but, despite staunch support from some radical senators, the bill was never brought to a vote in the upper house.[25]

The reaction of western Republicans to these measures indicates a direct relationship between radicalism and antipolygamy sentiment. Conservative Republicans seldom mentioned the problem of plural marriage in Utah; instead, they expressed concern at congressional Republican efforts to stamp it out. Inasmuch as polygamy was part of Mormon religious doctrine, conservatives worried that the bills

---

24. Richard Poll, "The Political Reconstruction of Utah Territory, 1866–1890," *PHR*, XXVII (May, 1958), 111–26.

25. *Congressional Globe*, 39 Cong., 1 Sess., 3750; 41 Cong., 2 Sess., 2181, 3582, and appendix, 173–79; *Deseret Evening News* (Salt Lake City, Utah), Dec. 14, 1867, Jan. 2, 1868, Jan. 25, Feb. 4, Apr. 14, 1870.

proposed in Congress were a violation of the First Amendment. Radicals, on the other hand, were oblivious to violation of religious freedom. Two leading radical newspapers in California, the *Marysville Appeal* and the *Oakland News*, scathingly referred to Mormonism as a "cancer upon the body politic which cannot be cured otherwise than by cauterization." Both wrote of Brigham Young in most vile terms and characterized polygamy as "another name for lechery." Kansas radicals thought so too, adding that polygamy was degrading to women and made them "serfs, ministering to the lusts of men." From all appearances, few radical Republicans would have questioned Utah editor P. L. Shoaff's indictment of polygamy as "an unclean, abominable thing."[26] Striving to achieve racial equality, the true radical was committed to purging moral evil wherever he saw it.

Mormons replied in kind to the flood of radical accusations. Predictably, they denied charges of immorality and defended polygamy as part of their religious belief. Relying on an argument more likely to weigh in their favor, Mormons denounced all attempts to dictate their institutions as a violation of popular sovereignty. In Brigham Young's words, Mormons were asking only the right to govern themselves, but this Republicans "have withheld and denied us." George Cannon, editor of the *Deseret News*, expressed the Mormon viewpoint more bluntly by saying, "Congress has no right, constitutionally, to object . . . because our domestic institutions may not accord with those of other places." From Pine Valley another believer urged Congress to stop proclaiming its desire to make government republican until it could offer Mormons and southerners the same degree of self-determination which it had given northerners. It was "wicked and unconstitutional," he charged, to impose "reconstructed military governments" on the South and to refuse Utah "state rights."[27]

The call of these church faithful for local self-government with little federal interference was to be a fading dream in the postwar years. True, Congress was able to impose significant restraint on the

26. San Francisco *Chronicle*, Feb. 25, 1869; George Price to John Bidwell, Salt Lake City, Feb. 4, 1866, Bidwell Papers, CSUC; Donaldson, *Idaho*, 55–56; *Marysville Appeal*, Oct. 18, 1866; *Oakland News*, Aug. 12, 1866; *Atchison Champion*, Apr. 8, 1866; Atchison *Free Press*, Jan. 26, 1866; *Vedette*, Aug. 16, Sept. 6, 1865. For a critical but fair evaluation of polygamy, see Bowles, *Across the Continent*, 105–30.

27. *Salt Lake Telegraph*, Jan. 13, Mar. 12, 1867; *Deseret News*, Dec. 30, 1867, Mar. 15, 1870; Brigham Young to William Hooper, Salt Lake City, Dec. 5, 1865, Mar. 15, 1870, both in Young Papers; William Snow to editor, Pine Valley, Utah, May 24, 1868, in *Rio Virgin Times* (St. George, Utah), May 31, 1868.

Mormon subculture only with the passage of the Edmunds Act in 1882. But while Democrats in the 1850s had espoused the idea of minimal federal involvement, postwar Republicans were more freely inclined to manifest their will and, in the case of Utah, to rectify what they considered a moral wrong.

Democratic victories in California (1867 and 1869) and Oregon (1868) were among the most stunning political reversals in the nation in the immediate postwar years. Whereas the Union party in 1864 held 90 percent of the seats in the Oregon legislature, Democrats had gained remarkably by 1868 and won a full 62 percent control. With a dramatic increase in representation from seven members in 1864 to fifty-six in 1868, they lacked a two-thirds majority in each house by only one vote. Oregon, moreover, was one of the first northern states to return to the Democratic fold after the war. While the year 1866 saw overwhelming Republican victories throughout the nation, in Oregon the opposite was true: Democrats missed capturing control of the legislature by a mere four seats.[28]

In California the political tables turned between 1864 and 1869. Republican candidates for Congress in 1864 had received an average of 6,000 votes in excess of those tallied for the opposition; by 1867 the electorate was giving the same edge to Democrats running for state office. Gubernatorial candidate Henry Haight fared even better; he received 9,546 more votes than his leading Republican opponent. Republicans in 1865 held 65 percent of the seats in the legislature. Democrats tipped the scale with a majority of twenty-two votes in the assembly in 1867, while Republicans still controlled the senate but only by two votes. Finally the Democratic opposition routed Republicans altogether in the legislative election of 1869 and, as a result, secured two-thirds of the seats in the senate and three-fourths in the assembly.[29]

28. *Oregon Statesman*, June 11, 1866; *Oregonian*, June 22, 1866; David Ballard to George Drew, Boise, June 30, 1866, Ballard Papers; Woodward, *Political Parties in Oregon*, 250; Coleman, *Election of 1868*, 66–67. See Gillette, *Right to Vote*, 33, for a brief discussion of Democratic gains in the Northeast and the Midwest in 1867.

29. The 1869–70 California legislature was composed as follows: Senate—26 Democrats, 11 Republicans, 3 Independents; Assembly—66 Democrats, 11 Republicans, 3 Independents. Bancroft, *California, 1860–1890*, 327–31, 363; San Francisco *Bulletin*, Sept. 7, 8, 1868; *Sacramento Union*, Sept. 7, 8, 1865; *Alta California*, Nov. 1, 1867; Davis, *Political Conventions*, 212, 267.

Realignment of the political parties at their base was a factor in the postwar Republican decline in both Oregon and California. Both states prior to the war had contained a thoroughly organized Democratic party. Secession splintered it and the pro-Union or war faction united with Republicans under the Union party label. But war Democrats came to find their position in the Union party untenable as radicalism became more pronounced in 1866. They were not, in the main, advocates of equal suffrage nor did they favor stern measures for the South; in addition, they now spurned fiscal policies previously accepted as war measures and rejected the Republican tendency to increase national authority. For these reasons they drifted back into the Democratic party to become critics of radical Reconstruction.

In Oregon antipathy toward continued federal taxation along with thoughts of Negro equality drove war Democrats to their old allegiance posthaste. Even James Nesmith expressed surprise at the burgeoning Democratic support as the legislative election of 1866 drew near. ". . . the democratic ticket," wrote the senator, was so pro-southern as to be "one as Jeff Davis would select." Republicans were dismayed at the trend. They could not believe that their more radical philosophy held so little attraction for their recent allies. Trying to pinpoint the cause, they blamed the sudden reverse on increasing Democratic immigration from Missouri. But one editor found this explanation wholly inadequate. It could possibly have accounted for the 6,000 Democratic vote increase in the eastern counties, but failed to justify Democratic advances in more settled western Oregon. There the surge in Democratic votes did not tally with population growth; clearly, Unionists were switching parties.[30]

The breakup of the Union organization in California was to be prolonged and bitter. Triggered in 1864 over a quarrel to redistrict San Francisco, it ended with the total disruption of the Union party in 1867. Underlying the issues which arose to deepen the rift in the party was a fundamental difference in political makeup. One group of Unionists, the "Long Hairs," consisted of regular Republicans who dominated state patronage. The other faction, the "Short Hairs," were former Democrats who resented both their exclusion from political appointments and the arrogance of the Long Hairs. As Fred-

30. James Nesmith to Matthew P. Deady, Washington, D.C., May 20, 1866, Deady Papers; *Yreka Union*, July 7, 1866; *Oregonian*, July 12, 1868.

erick MacCrellish, editor of the *Alta California*, explained, "The original Republicans [Long Hairs] have been jealous and suspicious of those liberal Democrats [Short Hairs] who, with them, formed the Union party at the beginning of the war. The original Republicans have never forgotten that they were 'original,' and have kept up the clannish divisions of former times."[31]

The Short Hairs supported Unionist Governor Frederick Low for the U.S. Senate in the legislative election of 1865. Hoping to entice Democratic votes, these former Democrats also came out against equal suffrage. Those in Yuba County, for example, wanted to make themselves perfectly clear: "While we are willing to extend to the African or negro race . . . all their natural rights . . . we still believe this to be a 'white man's government' and that allowing or permitting the negro to vote would be the introduction of a system unnatural, impolitic, and degrading." Long Hairs chose to ignore the suffrage question and focus instead on Low's candidacy, which they opposed. To be sure, the suffrage issue was real in 1865, but it remained in the background as the two factions argued over sending their governor to Washington, D.C. Anxious to heal the breach and reunite Unionist factions, Low withdrew from the Senate race. The ploy did not work. Democrats only improved their position in the legislature. Their gains were such, according to one outside observer, as to stimulate hope for a revival of the Democracy in the Far West.[32]

Unfortunately for the California Union party the rift widened further in 1867. Again personalities—not issues—were responsible. The Short Hairs, led by Senator John Conness, arrived at the Union state convention determined to nominate George C. Gorham, a former Douglas Democrat, for governor. Congressman John Bidwell was the Long Hairs' preference. When the Short Hairs prevailed and Gorham got the bid, a contingent of Long Hairs bolted, establishing a separate ticket. Bidwell was no longer interested in the gubernatorial nomination, he said, and their choice fell to Caleb T. Fay, a perennial candidate for office. Thus the Unionists went into the election a

31. *Alta California*, Sept. 6, 1867.

32. Benjamin Edson to Robert Moir, LaPlata, Nev., Oct. 31, 1865, HEH Miscellaneous Collection; Bancroft, *California, 1860–1890*, 317–20; Malone, "Democratic Party in California," 5–17; Moody, "Civil War," 325–26; *Placerville Democrat*, Aug. 26, 1865; Royce Delmatier and others (eds.), *The Rumble of California Politics, 1848–1970* (New York, 1970), 31–33, 58–59.

party divided. Gorham's followers were calling themselves Union Republicans; Fay's supporters became the National Republicans. Only on the issue of subsidies to railroads, which the National Republicans opposed, was there anything to distinguish the two groups. Each in turn endorsed congressional Reconstruction, black suffrage in the South, and the eight-hour workday. Both were notably less enthusiastic on the subject of Chinese suffrage.[33]

When defeat came for National and Union Republicans alike, both groups emphasized the split as the reason for the September, 1867, debacle. After all, major Republican newspapers including the San Francisco *Bulletin* and the *Sacramento Union* had not sustained Gorham; many other Republican editors in the state had given him only half-hearted support. Regular Republicans who remained with the Gorham group—but were Long Hairs by inclination—had campaigned indifferently for his cause. Bidwell might have had some influence had he chosen to work on Gorham's behalf, but he kept his distance; he still resented having been denied the Union party gubernatorial nomination in the first place. From the nation's capital Senator Cole could only surmise that Conness's attempt to bring the Union party under the control of former Democrats had created extreme animosity and, ultimately, disaster. Indeed, the Gorham-Fay factions expended so much energy feuding among themselves that their campaign against the Democrats was mild by comparison, leaving the door wide open for a Democratic victory.[34]

Party realignment not only fostered dissent but induced apathy and a defeatist attitude as well among Republicans. In Oregon Republicans were reluctant to campaign in the 1868 legislative election when everyone was predicting a Democratic victory. According to Henry Pittock, editor of the *Oregonian*, the gains in 1866, plus the overwhelming Democratic victory in California in 1867, had stilled Republican enthusiasm generally and made "Republican Union people of Oregon seem to be the only ones in the United States who are not wide awake." They simply could not erase the thought of a

33. *Sacramento Union,* June 12, 1867; *Napa Register,* June 15, 1867; Davis, *Political Conventions,* 247, 260.

34. John Bidwell to Annie E. Bidwell, Chico, Calif., June 18, 27, 1867, Annie E. Bidwell Papers; Cornelius Cole to Addison Gibbs, Washington, D.C., Sept. 28, 1867, Gibbs Papers; Sacramento *Bee,* Sept. 6, 1867; San Francisco *Bulletin,* Sept. 6, 1867; *Yreka Journal,* Sept. 13, 1867; *Marysville Appeal,* Sept. 14, 1867.

Democratic victory. As a result, in California 13,000 fewer votes were cast in 1867 than in 1864. Fully one-sixth of Sacramento's registered voters failed to appear at the polls, and some 5,000 eligible men in San Francisco did not vote. Of those who did, most went Democratic: the Bay City contributed an ample 4,000 votes to Haight's 9,500 majority for the state.[35]

While population changes, party realignment, and purely local problems explain revitalization of the Democratic party in Oregon and California, they do not reveal the entire story. Just as important were opposition to radical Republican demands on the South and the ever-present fear of black enfranchisement. Few Republicans were willing to admit publicly that Reconstruction issues were responsible for their party's decline. Because they had avoided the divisive question of black suffrage and Reconstruction during their campaigns, Republicans, once the votes were tallied, refused to acknowledge that these same issues could have led to their defeat. Fully two years passed before Oregon Republicans would accept the fact that national problems had played so pivotal a role in their state elections. From 1866 to 1868 they continued to believe increases in Democratic strength were due to the influx of southerners into the state. Finally in 1868 S. A. Clarke, a Republican editor in Salem, assessed the facts for what they were: the recent Democratic sweep of the legislature could only be viewed as a reaction against radical policy, high taxes, and black suffrage. Many Oregonians had come to believe that wartime tax levels were being maintained in the postwar era in order to support former slaves who refused to work. Rumor of ill-treatment of blacks in the South had convinced still others that freedmen needed the ballot to secure their civil rights. But few of these same people could understand why Congress had imposed equal suffrage on the territories in 1867 and, by the Edmunds amendment, had required new states to grant blacks the right to vote.[36] In short, Oregonians had come to distrust national Republican pronouncements on suffrage and Reconstruction, and they reacted by supporting

35. A. W. Brown to Mrs. H. C. Tucker, Portland, Ore., May 17, 1868, OHS Miscellaneous Collection; *Oregonian*, June 5, Aug. 14, 1868; Ossian J. Carr to Daniel Bagley, Salem, Ore., June 15, 1868, Daniel Bagley Papers; *Alta California*, Sept. 7, 1867; *Sacramento Union*, Sept. 7, 1867.

36. *Salem Daily Record*, June 5, 1868.

Democratic candidates. Indeed, Oregon was the only western state to cast its electoral vote for Horatio Seymour in 1868.

The anti–black suffrage mood in Oregon, while not without precedent, takes on added perspective given the state's small black population of 346 and its distance from the South. Locally, the enfranchisement of blacks would hardly have had any influence on state politics in the 1860s and 1870s, and certainly Oregon was not a popular destination for black immigration in the postwar years. Yet the fear of black suffrage apparently was more prevalent in Oregon than in other western states. Said Orange Jacobs of the average voter in Oregon: "There is a large class of Union men afraid of the nigger. They start up affrighted at the idea of a negro voting. Negro equality is their dread. If he is enfranchised they are perfectly certain that they will be compelled to sleep with him. You may as well bay at the moon as to reason with such men. A few men think and are governed by reason . . . the mass feel and act from their predjudices [*sic*]."[37] Jacobs was an admitted radical Republican who sensed the injustice of racial discrimination more keenly than most. But it is easy to conclude from his testimony why settlers would have shied from voting for Republican candidates: better to side with the Democrats who were saying consistently and in no uncertain terms that they opposed suffrage for blacks.

California Republicans were just as disbelieving and credited their defeat in 1867 to local problems. Yet they had little controversy strictly local in nature. The two Republican groups and the Democratic party all reflected a surprisingly similar stand. In order to entice the labor vote, Republicans espoused the Democratic eight-hour plank, and all three groups rejected Chinese suffrage. Only on national issues did the opposing parties show divergence. Democrats condemned congressional Reconstruction and black suffrage while Republicans at first spoke out in their defense. As the campaign progressed, both Republican factions became more reluctant to discuss these national questions. Congress, they contended with a gesture of impatience, had settled the southern problem by the passage of the recent Reconstruction acts, and equal suffrage nationwide was

37. *1870 Census, Population*, 606–9; O[range] Jacobs to Benjamin F. Dowell, Jacksonville, Ore., Oct. 23, 1867, Dowell Papers.

not an issue. Steering consciously away from radical goings-on in Washington and having little of import locally to argue, both Union and National Republicans spent their campaign mostly questioning the loyalty of Democrats or bickering with each other.[38]

Both sides were aware nonetheless that the 1867 election would serve as something of a referendum on congressional Reconstruction, since it was to provide the first polling of opinion since 1865. Of course, Republicans later publicly denied any influence of national affairs on their defeat and stressed instead the split in the party. It seemed that the more strongly Democrats equated their own landslide with popular disapproval of Reconstruction and black suffrage, the more vigorously Republicans objected.

Privately, however, Republicans were more candid. "Negro suffrage hurt us here very considerable," F. B. Shannon was forced to admit. "A great many of our party here are weak enough to want it in the South & not in the North." Another Republican attributed his party's defeat to fear of black suffrage even though Republicans had sought to keep the issue under cover. Democrats had manipulated the issue with great skill, especially among the working classes. They had, in effect, succeeded in convincing laborers that a Republican victory would result in equality at the polls and economic improvement for blacks at the workingman's expense. Even among blacks there was the feeling that, at the heart of the campaign, lay the question of enfranchisement of their race. "The issue was as plain as daylight," wrote the editor of the *Pacific Appeal.* With parties freely discussing black suffrage at the beginning of the campaign, Republican factions had dropped the issue resolutely once it was deemed injurious to their cause. What their tactic proved, concluded the editor sagely, was that "Negro suffrage is as hard a dose for some of our pretended Union friends to swallow as it is for some of our avowed political enemies."[39]

Once again in power, Democrats in the Far West were encouraged to reassert their pre–Civil War states' rights philosophy. Prior to the

38. *Alta California,* Sept. 6, 13, 1867; *Marysville Appeal,* June 22, 1867.

39. *Marysville Appeal,* Apr. 30, May 16, June 8, 1867; *Petaluma Journal & Argus,* Aug. 22, 1867; *Oakland News,* July 3, Aug. 2, 31, 1867; F. B. Shannon to Elihu Washburne, San Francisco, Oct. 27, 1867, Washburne Papers; Cornelius Cole to E. Burke, Washington, D.C., Oct. 2, 1867, Cole Papers; Thomas Robinson to William Pitt Fessenden, San Francisco, Sept. 20, 1867, William Pitt Fessenden Papers, LC; *Pacific Appeal,* n.d., in San Francisco *Call,* Sept. 17, 1867.

war many had held firm to the idea of local control: it was the state which delegated authority to the federal government, and any expansion of federal power without state consent was a violation of a "sacred" pledge. During the war the federal government had extended its authority over the individual through conscription and taxes. Further, Congress had involved itself in business with new banking laws and minor regulation of railroads, and in the expansion of money.[40] Accepted as a wartime necessity, these burdens—the continuance of heavy taxes and the decline in the value of paper money, and the persistent desire of some Republicans to involve government in business—were now considered irksome by the Democratic party. In the West Democrats were especially agitated about congressional Reconstruction and expansion of black suffrage by national fiat. They declared the former an unjustifiable intervention in southern state governments and the latter a privilege which only the states could grant.

Certain that they had a mandate from the electorate, Democrats in the 1868 Oregon legislature proceeded with alacrity to undo Republican wrongs where they saw them. Shortly after convening, the lawmakers instructed George Williams and Henry Corbett to resign from the U.S. Senate. In quick order of succession, they rescinded the previous session's ratification of the Fourteenth Amendment even though the amendment itself had been promulgated some months earlier. Their reversal of the Fourteenth Amendment came in part out of their dislike for Congress's authoritarian ways. More particularly, Oregon Democrats were challenging the validity of the amendment, whose ratification had depended on the endorsement of southern states. Legislatures there had been established by military despotism and were not empowered to function as normally elected bodies, claimed the lawmakers. There was a personal reason for the reversal as well: Oregon Republicans in the previous session had deliberately refused to seat two Democratic members in the assembly until after the body had secured enough Republican votes to ratify the amend-

---

40. Historians do not agree that this intervention in personal and business affairs necessarily led to centralization during and after the war. Allan Nevins, *The War for the Union: The Improvised War, 1861–1862*, 2 vols. (New York, 1959), I, 240–43, presents a case for centralization, while Harold Hyman, *A More Perfect Union: The Impact of the Civil War and Reconstruction on the Constitution* (New York, 1975), 379–90 *passim*, argues against it.

ment. In an additional bit of perversity, the state senate assigned the resolutions rescinding the Fourteenth Amendment to its committee on foreign relations rather than to the more appropriate federal relations committee.

Senators Williams and Corbett were Republican and thus might have failed legislative scrutiny under any of a variety of pretexts. In this instance the two were accused, in a series of resolutions, of misrepresenting the people of Oregon. The senators had voted for the Reconstruction acts and for President Johnson's removal from office under the impeachment charges. Yet the Reconstruction acts, declared the resolutions, "were in plain and palpable violation of the constitution of the United States," and Johnson's impeachment was "actuated by unworthy partizan motives." Both sets of resolutions passed the legislature by strict party vote. The thirteen Democrats in the senate and twenty-seven of the thirty in the assembly approved them: each and every Republican in the legislature was opposed. The U.S. Senate, in its turn, rejected the resolutions; Williams and Corbett duly served out their terms. Although the legislature had ordered state officials to forward notification of their rescission of the Fourteenth Amendment to Washington, no evidence exists to indicate compliance.[41]

Democrats were able successfully to impose their will in the Oregon legislature but seriously antagonized their Republican colleagues in the process. Twelve representatives subsequently resigned from the assembly in protest. They were frustrated when Democrats removed a number of Republicans from their seats in the house and senate; they were embarrassed about the Democratic partisanship which so dominated the proceedings that "Oregon now stands impeached of a deliberate attempt to nullify" the federal Constitution. Plainly they no longer wanted their names associated with such an endeavor, lest their own political futures be jeopardized. Moreover, Oregon state

41. State of Oregon, *Senate Journal, 1868* (Salem, 1868), 32–37, 101–4, 107–8, 131, 164, 168; *House Journal, 1868* (Salem, 1868), 123–27, 144–45, 169, 181; *Oregonian*, Sept. 18, 1868; *Oregon Herald*, Sept. 29, 1868; Robert W. Johannsen, "The Oregon Legislature of 1868 and the Fourteenth Amendment," OHQ, LI (Mar. 1950), 3–12. In going through state legislative journals, I have not come across the existence of other committees on foreign relations. Whether this was a standing committee or one created especially to consider the rescinding resolution is not clear.

business, the legislators' first responsibility, had been left unattended while the Democratic majority worked at condemning national policy. In the view of those who could stand the abuses no longer, the session was a dismal failure because the legislature had "done little but make speeches and it treated the minority in an underhanded fashion."[42]

Assertion of states' rights among Democrats in California became commonplace between 1865 and 1870.[43] But it was Governor Henry Haight who served as chief states' rights advocate for California and the West. He began publicly denouncing centralization during his gubernatorial campaign in 1867 and persevered throughout his administration. In his inaugural address in December, 1867, Haight, although born in New York, paraphrased ideas expressed by John C. Calhoun during the 1830s and 1840s. Limitations had been imposed upon the federal government in the first place to protect the minority from oppression by the majority. Now in the passion of the postwar era, Congress had dared expand its own authority over the southern states and indirectly over the nation as a whole. To permit this unbridled extension of legislative power, charged the governor, was to ignore a fundamental truth—that Congress was the creature, not the creator, of the U.S. Constitution. A Congress failing to respect the Constitution for its limitations as well as for its privileges was advancing toward tyranny. From the nation's inception the federal government had held only delegated authority, with the states retaining all undelegated power, especially in their own local concerns. For its basic political strength, the nation must now continue to

42. *Address to the People of Oregon, by the Retiring Members of the Legislative Assembly, Giving Their Reasons for Their Resignation in That Body* (Salem, 1868), 1–12.

43. See, for example, *Los Angeles News*, July 24, 27, 1866; *San Francisco Examiner* Aug. 7, 11, 1865, Jan. 4, 1869; *Sonoma Democrat*, Mar. 12, 1866, Mar. 2, 1867; *Placerville Democrat*, Jan. 13, 1866, Jan. 30, 1869; Horace Hawes, *Horace Hawes . . . His Reply . . . on the Congressional Policy of Reconstruction and Other Political Questions* (San Francisco, 1867), 14–16; E[dward] J. Lewis, *Speech of Hon. E. J. Lewis on Reconstruction . . .* (n.p., n.d.), 13–15; Casserly, *Issues of the Contest,* 4–5; "Minority Report of the Committee on Federal Relations Concerning Electoral Votes of States Organized under the Reconstruction Acts of Congress," in State of California, *Appendix to Journals of Senate and Assembly of the Seventeenth Session of the Legislature of California* (Sacramento, 1868), Doc. 10, 3–6; *Colusa Sun,* June 3, 17, 1865; *Sierra Advocate,* June 10, 1867.

practice the concept of divided sovereignty; in Haight's opinion, Congress was wholly incapable of governing in all respects a country as vast as the United States.[44]

Two years later, in 1869, Haight would recommend the rejection of the Fifteenth Amendment. Aside from its enfranchisement of blacks, which he had so long opposed, the governor condemned the amendment for increasing congressional authority. The national legislature, by enabling itself to pass laws to enforce the amendment's provisions, had made Congress the sole judge of the propriety of such enforcement legislation. Both the Fourteenth and Fifteenth Amendments, announced Haight, reflected such strong tendency toward centralization that they were by their very nature unconstitutional. Through the amendments Congress had usurped power from the states and thus altered the basic form of government established by the Founding Fathers.[45]

Haight's private correspondence indicates his concern to have been sincere and deep-rooted. Writing to John Bigler in May, 1868, the governor remarked, "A strict construction of the federal constitution & a proper reverence of its authority—a jealous regard for the right of each state to regulate its domestic affairs—uncompromising opposition to all centralizing tendencies—these are sources of indestructible vitality. . . ." Later in the year Haight voiced his disapproval of the national Democratic slate. Horatio Seymour and Francis P. Blair, Jr., had not, as far as Haight could determine, revealed a true sympathy for established Democratic principles; rather, they seemed motivated solely by desire for office. Even as late as 1870 Haight was still objecting to congressional Reconstruction and anxious to see its downfall. But he was just as pessimistic about its realization, for younger Democratic party members seemed unable to counter effectively the Republican argument. Their failure, in Haight's mind, lay either in their misunderstanding of traditional

44. State of California, *House Journal, 1867–1868,* 93–96. Reaction to the governor's remarks varied. California Republican editors tended to be critical of Haight for emphasizing national affairs in his address. However, the governor received letters echoing strong support for his stand. As examples, see *Alta California,* Dec. 5, 1867; Joseph B. Crockett to Henry Haight, San Francisco, Dec. 14, 1867, Samuel Wilson to Haight, San Francisco, Dec. 19, 1867, Matthew McAllister to Haight, San Francisco, Jan. 2, 1868, all in Henry Haight Papers, HEH.

45. State of California, *House Journal, 1869–1870,* 174–76.

Democratic political philosophy or in their willingness to accept centralization as complementary to their own political advancement.[46]

Haight failed to secure a large following in the West for two reasons: younger Democrats wished to abandon Reconstruction as a political issue, and most westerners did not fear the growth of federal power. National Democrats had fought the election of 1868 squarely on the issue of Reconstruction and had lost. Thereafter, they gave up their negative attitude of noncompliance and went after more rewarding political issues. When Haight complained that younger Democrats were acquiescing to Republican policy, he was revealing his own isolation from his party. In announcing their willingness to comply with federal legislation on black suffrage, for instance, such Democrats as George West of Colorado and George O. Kies of California were not giving their approval. They were merely following the national Democratic leaders and acceding to a trend they could not reverse. In his attitude of nonacceptance and vocal denunciation, Haight was moving in a direction which most Democrats had abandoned. Indeed, his became a voice alone in its plea to retain political concepts which were fading.

Nor were most westerners excited by Haight's tirades against the growth of federal power. Democrats like Peter Burnett, California's first governor, regarded increasing federal authority a natural consequence of the war. In abolishing slavery, claimed Burnett, the federal government had assumed automatically the responsibility of protecting the black man's liberty. Because government had to treat all citizens equally, this guarantee of liberty had to be extended to whites as well as to blacks. Thus emancipation by national fiat would encourage federal politicians to "govern the individual in every respect." Senator James Nye of Nevada agreed with Burnett's ideas. Speaking against the states' rights concept, Nye declared it dangerous for its encouragement of local despotism. To avoid such an occurrence, the federal government had to act as overseer of laws affecting all citizens.[47]

46. Henry Haight to John Bigler, San Francisco, May 7, 1868, Haight to William Tell Coleman, San Francisco, Oct. 20, 1868, both in Haight Papers; Haight to Lafayette Grover, Sacramento, Nov. 14, 1870, Lafayette Grover Papers, OHS.

47. Buck, *Road to Reunion*, 92–93; Peter Burnett to James Nesmith, San Francisco, Feb. 27, 1866, Nesmith Papers; *Congressional Globe*, 39 Cong., 1, Sess., 1078.

There were two broader factors contributing directly to the new acceptance of federal authority. The first was a Union-wide growth of nationalism. During the war northerners had fought to save the Union; as a result, the idea of a stronger, more cohesive central authority was replacing the old concept of the United States as a collection of semisovereign states. Whereas prior to the war Americans had referred to their country in the plural (the United States "are"), now they were stressing instead the singular (the United States "is"). Political tracts of the time as well as postwar literature tended to bear out this new sense of pride and affinity to the whole. Further, Thomas Jefferson and his earlier states' rights doctrine in the Kentucky Resolutions of 1798 began to suffer a noticeable decline in esteem. Americans of the post–Civil War era gave greater credence to Alexander Hamilton's nationalistic ideals as expressed in Federalist political philosophy. This newly fortified nationalism not only made states' rights seem an anachronism but strengthened the concept of more ample federal power as well.

In any case, the states' rights concept may have been destined to failure in the West from the outset because federal control had preceded statehood throughout the region. In the words of Ignatius Donnelly, "We who come . . . from the far West have not that deep and ingrained veneration for State power which is to be found among the inhabitants of some of the older States. . . . We feel ourselves to be offshoots of the nation. . . . We are willing to trust the nation. We have never received aught at its hands but benefits. We need erect no bulwark of State sovereignty behind which to shelter ourselves from the gifts which it so generously and bountifully showers upon us." Donnelly went on to explain his preference for strong central authority. Tradition mattered little to him; the federal government had become sovereign over the states and by that mere fact had the right to continue to exercise its powers.[48] For men like Donnelly the fears expressed by Henry Haight of California could pose no real threat.

The revitalization of the western Democracy in the Reconstruction era was a partial advance. In those regions where it could secure the votes, the Democratic party controlled the political process. Still,

48. *Congressional Globe*, 38 Cong., 2 Sess., 2037; David Herbert Donald, *Liberty and Union* (Lexington, Mass., 1978), 214–18, 263–72; Merrill D. Peterson, *The Jefferson Image in the American Mind* (New York, 1962), 209–26.

it could not persuade its adherents to embrace the old states' rights principles. Haight may have looked with suspicion upon the younger Democratic element, but it was this contingent, less bound by tradition, which would adapt more readily as the Republican philosophy began to prevail. As Donnelly ventured, the West in this respect was indeed a frontier open to change.

CHAPTER EIGHT

The West, Ross, and Impeachment

"It will go as I turn my hand. . . ."
—Edmund G. Ross, Kansas

The acquittal of Andrew Johnson in May, 1868, marked the culmination of a stubborn and prolonged effort to remove the president from office. The initial move was made seventeen months earlier, in December, 1866, when James Ashley of Ohio requested that the House of Representatives look into Johnson's behavior to determine whether he had committed an impeachable offense. The House failed to vote on the motion, but Ashley was not to be dissuaded. In January, 1867, he went a step further and introduced a formal resolution charging the president with "high crimes and misdemeanors." This time the House took notice and ordered the Judiciary Committee to investigate. For six months the committee reviewed accusations which could seldom be substantiated by fact, and reported in June, 1867, its failure to find evidence supporting Ashley's resolution. Despite this conclusion, the House ordered the investigation continued.

The imbroglio deepened during the summer of 1867 as Johnson himself precipitated action which would lead to his impeachment. At the president's urging Attorney General Henry Stanbery issued an opinion in June narrowly interpreting the Reconstruction acts and severely restricting the authority of voter registrars and military commanders in the South. In response Congress passed the third Reconstruction Act, over Johnson's veto, in July. Angered by his discovery that Edwin Stanton, secretary of war, had collaborated on the bill, Johnson suspended Stanton in August, 1867, and as required by the Tenure of Office Act informed the Senate of the reasons for his action. In succeeding months he dismissed several military commanders in the South as well as certain Freedmen's Bureau officials.

Still, when the House convened in December, 1867, its members were hesitant and voted against a recommendation to impeach the president.

Then within weeks impeachment became a certainty. The Senate refused to concur with Johnson's suspension of Stanton and reinstated him on January 13, 1868. Affronted by the decision, Johnson was determined to replace his radical secretary of war. Casting about in the meantime for an individual willing to take over the cabinet post, the president again suspended Stanton on February 21. The House delayed no further. Three days later, on February 24, 1868, its members approved a resolution declaring that Johnson be "impeached of high crimes and misdemeanors in office" and accepted shortly thereafter eleven articles of impeachment. Therein the representatives charged the president with intent to violate the Tenure of Office Act and the Command of the Army Act, and intent to hinder a duly appointed officer from performance of his duties. Finally they declared Johnson guilty of inappropriate conduct and injurious remarks against certain radicals, and of degrading the presidency itself.

The trial of Andrew Johnson, the only U.S. president to be impeached, began in March, 1868. Two months later, on May 16, the Senate voted on article eleven, a summary of the previous ten; meeting again on May 26, it recorded opinion on articles two and three. In every instance the senators acquitted Johnson of the charges by a vote of thirty-five to nineteen, one vote short of the necessary two-thirds required for conviction; each time, seven of those nineteen voting to retain Johnson in office were Republicans. The focus of this chapter is to survey western reaction to the entire impeachment struggle and to assess the motives of Edmund G. Ross, U.S. senator from Kansas—the only westerner among the seven Republicans who voted to acquit the president.[1]

Western Democrats assumed a strong stand against impeachment, but for the most part their position did not include a defense of Andrew Johnson himself. It is true that until the winter of 1867 some western Democrats continued to justify the president's every action. Especially in more conservative Oregon, proponents saw John-

1. Further description of the impeachment charges and trial remains outside the scope of this study. For conflicting analyses of Johnson's impeachment, see McKitrick, *Andrew Johnson and Reconstruction*, 486–509, and Benedict, *Trial of Andrew Johnson*.

son's attempts to frustrate the progress of congressional Reconstruction and his suspension of Stanton as heroic deeds.[2] As impeachment became a reality in early 1868, however, such laudatory comments were to dwindle significantly.

Several factors stimulated this change in attitude. By 1868 a number of western Democrats were thinking Johnson too defiant toward Congress and therefore at least partly responsible for his dilemma. George West of Colorado, for one, agreed that the radicals had pushed legislative authority to its limits in forcing Johnson to justify dismissal of even his own cabinet members. The Coloradan could sympathize with the president in his differences with Stanton. Yet West would have liked the president to practice a little more restraint. "Knowing the pertinacity of the party in power," he wrote, "discretion on his part would have been the better part of valor. . . . It does seem as if the President has gone a little out of his way to bring [impeachment] about, and if it comes, he has nobody to thank for it but himself."[3]

Other Democrats as well warned Johnson against incurring the anger of Congress. Shortly after the Senate's reinstatement of Stanton in January, 1868, Henry Haight of California advised Johnson "to persevere in a course of moderation & forbearance." Concerned about reports from the nation's capital that Johnson was still determined to replace Stanton, Haight cautioned the president a second time. Given the "excited state of feeling . . . at Washington," counseled the governor, "forbearance [will] serve our cause better than forcible resistance." Future generations would recognize the president's hand in preserving American institutions, said Haight, but should Johnson now be removed from office, it would very likely undo every achievement credited thus far to the postwar administration.[4]

An old mistrust of Johnson also encouraged western Democrats to dissociate themselves from him just before and during the trial; others perhaps stepped back in fear of being too closely aligned with a cause now so clearly unpopular. Musing over the situation, F. J. Stanton of Denver summed up the current Democratic attitude: "Our

2. *Santa Fe Gazette*, Dec. 1, 1866; *Northwestern Chronicle* (St. Paul, Minn.), Jan. 19, 1867; *Oregon Herald*, Oct. 26, 1867; *Boise Democrat*, Nov. 30, 1867.

3. *Colorado Transcript*, Sept. 18, 25, 1867.

4. Henry Haight to Andrew Johnson, Sacramento, Jan. 18, Feb. 15, 1868, Johnson Papers.

only sympathy with [Johnson] lies in the fact that he is a little less objectionable a radical than the party opposed to him." Stanton conceded that while Democrats might praise the president for his executive ability and his firmness in dealing with radicalism, never would they forgive his defection from the party during the war. Stanton observed that "instead of having a party to back him" Johnson stood alone, and the Democrats were saying that it "served him right."[5]

Whatever the case, most western Democrats had come to regard Johnson as a political liability, and they feared that a show of personal support might endanger their hopes for success in the election of 1868. Thus, when the House actually passed the resolution to impeach the president in February, 1868, western Democrats attacked the move but with a curious restraint. Conventions meeting in Kansas and Oregon censured the radicals for stripping the "Presidential office of its constitutional authority," and the Democratic assembly of California passed resolutions openly condemning the radicals. Yet for all their criticism of the radicals and concern for the viability of the presidency, western Democrats had little to say for Johnson; they chose to endorse him neither as a man nor as a politician. J. Sterling Morton, for instance, chastised the Senate as "self-satisfied," "self-righteous," and a body of "Jacobins" in his Nebraska editorials on the impeachment trial. But Morton seldom mentioned the office of the presidency and then did not print anything favorable about Johnson. One editor in Albany, Oregon, found nothing unusual in this response. Simply, Democrats were cautious and even begrudging because "we can never forget how basely he betrayed us in our hour of trial."[6]

Henry Haight took the same cool view of Johnson's fate. Earlier, as tension grew between the chief executive and his Congress, Haight had seen fit to advise Johnson. Now, with impeachment a reality, he did not seek to justify the president. Rather, he directed the force of his opposition against Congress for its wanton abuse of power. Haight became involved at the local level when the Republican California senate passed a series of resolutions praising Congress for

5. *Denver Daily Gazette*, Mar. 5, 14, May 16, 1868.
6. Wilder, *Annals of Kansas*, 475; *Oregonian*, Mar. 10, 1868; State of California, *House Journal, 1867–1868*, 533–34; *Sacramento Union*, Mar. 4, 1868; *Nebraska City News*, Feb.–May, 1868 *passim*—see especially Feb. 26, Mar. 18, Apr. 10, 1868.

its impeachment articles and reprehending Johnson for violating the Tenure of Office Act. Senators then requested that Haight, as governor, transmit copies of the statement to the House of Representatives and the Senate in Washington, D.C. Haight was indignant and wasted little time denouncing the whole endeavor. In a special message the governor termed the resolutions out of order and denied the senate's request. At this point the governor might have gone on to defend Johnson but he did not; instead, he merely denounced Congress for assuming too much power and the state senate for assessing the president's guilt prematurely. Following the lead of other Democrats in the West, Haight avoided any statement that might reveal a personal sympathy for the president.[7]

Rather than offer a defense for Johnson, most western Democrats seemed impassive to his plight and clearly preferred to remain aloof from his troubles. Noting the passage of the final impeachment resolution by the House, a Kansas Democrat wrote stoically, "I guess Andy will go up this time. Democrats don't care a d—d as it is none of our funeral." An editor in St. Paul, Minnesota, echoing a similar attitude, spelled out even further the Democratic reaction to Johnson's impeachment. "As between the present Republican President and the present Republican Congress," he insisted, "the Democratic party has neither lot or part in the quarrel. [It has] greater interests to serve, and higher objects to gain, than any that are personal to President Johnson."[8]

There were Democrats, of course, who were saddened at this lack of compassion within their party. Ruefully John T. Knox of Washington Territory confessed to the belief that "the Democracy is making a mistake for not giving Johnson a more hearty support." But he understood the reasons for dissociation from the president. Already unpopular before his impeachment, Johnson now was finding even less favor in the public eye. Certainly Democrats did not want to give any impression that Johnson might be their presidential can-

7. [Henry Haight], *Message of the Governor in Relation to Senate Resolutions Condemning the Course of President Johnson, March 4, 1868* (Sacramento, 1868); *Sonoma Democrat*, Mar. 7, 1868; *Sacramento Union*, Mar. 4, 1868; *Protest by the Democratic Senators of the Legislature of California, on the Resolutions Condemning the President and Indorsing Congress* (n.p., n.d.).

8. Moore Journals, Feb. 24, 1868; *St. Paul Pioneer*, Mar. 3, 1868. See also O. E. Babcock to Edward L. Plumb, Washington, D.C., Feb. 25, 1868, Edward L. Plumb Papers, SU.

didate in the upcoming election. Still, Knox hoped that Democrats would not altogether foreswear Johnson as a candidate should he be acquitted. He might possibly be as attractive as any of the other aspirants who were coming forth now to seek the nomination.[9] Such a hope, however, was never to become reality, for during the impeachment trial Democrats in the West made it abundantly clear that they wanted nothing further to do with Andrew Johnson.

Western Republicans, for their part, wavered on the issue of impeachment but in the main tended toward conservatism on the question. Their response seemed to follow three distinct phases. Initially Republicans were wary of the whole idea, from December, 1866, to June, 1867—months when the House was investigating grounds for impeachment but failed to find any. But when Johnson gave them cause in the fall of 1867 by seeking to remove Stanton, they hesitated no longer and urged the House to act. Adamant in their concern, still they were to retreat once again: with the beginning of the trial they questioned whether Johnson was guilty at all and worried lest his removal make the presidential office subservient to the legislative branch.

Republicans urged extreme caution during the initial investigation by the House Judiciary Committee. The Tenure of Office Act, passed midway through the investigation, was not at issue. The only substantive charges against Johnson were for his vetoes and for his inappropriate behavior and remarks. True, the president's opposition to Congress and lack of decorum were reason enough for some westerners to demand his removal. But the majority of Republicans doubted that Johnson was guilty of any impeachable offense; similarly they questioned his removal as a reasonable means of resolving the differences between Congress and the president. By their attitude they echoed the desire of most western Republicans to treat the office of the presidency with respect and to avoid placing their party in a position in which it could be accused of political proscription.

For a while, in fact, radicals and conservatives alike shared this view. Early in 1867, for example, A. S. Smith of the radical *Marysville Appeal*, pondered the enormity of the situation and declared, "The impeachment of the President would be a high-handed act." The

9. John T. Knox to William W. Miller, Olympia, Wash. Terr., Apr. 16, 1868, Miller Papers.

country was already in a "disordered condition," noted Smith, and the president's removal from office would add substantially to the confusion. Throughout California both radicals and conservatives wondered at Ashley's vindictiveness toward the president and believed that a congressman so obsessed with destroying Johnson must surely be directed "from passion rather than from reason.[10]

Republicans in other parts of the West found themselves at odds with Ashley's resolution as well. Said D. C. Collier of Colorado, "We deprecate the measure as being impolitic and unwise and can but consider it doubtful whether such an impeachment can be presented as will be sustained by the Senate." Republicans in Kansas, Nebraska, and Minnesota similarly were not convinced. J. W. Wines of the *Olathe Mirror* spoke for the general attitude. Radical Republicans, declared Wines, were confusing indiscretion in the political forum with actual misconduct in office. He doubted that any real basis for impeachment existed; "that [Johnson] is guilty of such maladministration as will make him guilty of high crimes and misdemeanors is a serious question."[11]

Reluctant themselves to rush into impeachment, western Republicans likewise urged their national representatives to exercise care and moderation. While a few disappointed office seekers understandably did advocate the president's removal from office, most Republicans preferred a less drastic course. Writing to Congressman Elihu Washburne of Illinois, Governor Frederick Low of California clearly revealed his apprehension. Given the need for two-thirds approval to convict in the Senate, Low urged that Senate response to the charges be determined as closely as possible in advance. "If this cannot be ascertained before hand," he cautioned, "impeachment had better not be attempted as it would have an injurious effect to make the attempt and fail."

One among Ignatius Donnelly's correspondents, an E. F. Drake, was concerned for the implications of impeachment and was prompted to poll local Republicans in his home town. He informed Donnelly

10. *Marysville Appeal,* Jan. 3, 1867; *San Francisco Chronicle,* Jan. 19, 1867; *Oakland News,* Jan. 12, 1867; *Chico Courant,* Dec. 4, 1866.

11. *Miner's Register,* Jan. 11, 1867; *Leavenworth Conservative,* Feb. 6, 1867; *Border Sentinel,* Feb. 1, 1867; *State Atlas,* Jan. 16, 1867; *Fairbault Central Republican,* Nov. 21, 1866; *Nebraska Advertiser,* Nov. 22, 1866, Jan. 21, 1867; *Olathe Mirror,* Dec. 6, 1866.

that half of those Republicans he queried definitely opposed impeachment, while "the balance hesitate." These Republicans, according to Drake, believed that "any act of cruelty will give [Johnson] strength. Expose him and his acts as they deserve, but lay no hand on him." Similarly, Joseph A. Wheelock, co-editor of the *St. Paul Press*, thought the Senate should restrain the more impetuous and radical House before it embarrassed the party. "My impression is," he wrote, "that impeachment is not popular." Finally, Olive Cole confided to her diary, "God and the nation knows [Johnson] has done enough to convict him, but whether it will be considered best to impeach him, I do not know."[12]

Republican congressmen may have been listening to the criticism from home, for certain among them were showing discretion and evident restraint. Senator James Nye of Nevada, speaking before an audience in San Francisco just after the Judiciary Committee began to investigate the president in January, 1867, refused to sanction impeachment. Nor would Nye speak disrespectfully of Johnson. The presidency was a position which commanded respect, said Nye, and it should not be assailed without good reason. Following Stanton's reinstatement on January 13, 1868, George Williams apprised Matthew P. Deady of the mood in the upper house. Senators had refused to tolerate Stanton's dismissal and worked effectively to counter Johnson's move. Even at that late date, however, they were not inclined to press for indictment on a larger scale, and of the Senate membership in general, said Williams, "there were really very few in favor of [impeachment]."[13]

Republican hesitancy began to diminish during the fall and winter of 1867. Western Republicans were increasingly disquieted with Johnson's attempts to frustrate Reconstruction; further, his suspension of Stanton and dismissal of military commanders in the South persuaded many of the necessity for action. Voices urging restraint became fewer

12. William H. Wallace to Perry, Washington, D.C., Feb. 6, 1867, Wallace Papers; Frederick Low to Elihu Washburne, Sacramento, Nov. 16, 1866, Washburne Papers; E. F. Drake to Ignatius Donnelly, n.p., Jan. 14, 1867, Donnelly Papers; Joseph A. Wheelock to Alexander Ramsey, St. Paul, Dec. 1, 1867, Ramsey Papers; Olive Cole Diary, Mar. 4, 1867, quoted in Catherine Coffin Phillips, *Cornelius Cole, California Pioneer and United States Senator: A Study of Personality and Achievements Bearing upon the Growth of a Commonwealth* (San Francisco, 1929), 151.

13. *Sacramento Bee*, Jan. 31, 1867; George H. Williams to Matthew P. Deady, Washington, D.C., Jan. 14, 1868, Deady Papers.

and almost inaudible among the clamor for the president's removal. Of the many western editors who were watching local response, William Byers of Colorado explained the shift in thought as cogently as any: "Hitherto we have considered the impeachment of Andrew Johnson as unnecessary. To-day, we are of the opinion that it is necessary. If Andrew Johnson will not execute the laws, as president, the constitution provides for removing him, and for placing a man there who will do his duty." Anxious for something definitive now that they had resolved the question in their minds, western Republican editors welcomed the House resolution of February 24, 1868. The California senate, as stated, readily echoed its support, even if the governor of the state could not; the legislatures of Minnesota and Kansas presently signified their approval as well.[14]

Despite consensus on the issue, an apparent lack of enthusiasm began to manifest itself in the West as Johnson's trial progressed. During the early weeks of March, 1868, editors followed the impeachment proceedings in minute detail. But as the weeks passed from April into May, they merely speculated from time to time as to the outcome of the trial. On every front there was evidence to support the observation that "impeachment is growing stale." The same lack of conviction expressed prior to the summer of 1867 began to surface again. Westerners once more feared that Johnson's impeachment might be regarded as political proscription, or that the Senate might not convict. L. M. Koons of Colorado, who considered himself a radical, became less convinced of the whole endeavor. Republicans in their haste to rid themselves of Andrew Johnson, he lamented, might well have set a precedent for removing future presidents unwilling to bow to the wishes of Congress. By early May, 1868, many western Republicans were perhaps ready to admit that "the suspense [of impeachment] is becoming painful," or that "impeachment has demoralized everyone."[15]

14. *Rocky Mountain News*, Aug. 26, Sept. 6, 1867. Pro-impeachment editorials during the autumn of 1867 were numerous and repetitious. For samples see: *Marysville Appeal*, June 26, 1867; Sacramento *Bee*, Sept. 25, 1867; *Alta California*, Aug. 15, 1867; *Hastings Gazette*, Dec. 14, 1867; Fairbault *Central Republican*, Aug. 27, 1867; *Gold Hill News*, Sept. 9, 1867; *Atchison Champion*, Aug. 22, 1867; *Miner's Register*, Aug. 16, 20, 21, 1867. [Haight], *Message of the Governor*; State of Minnesota, *House Journal, 1868* (St. Paul, 1868), 212; State of Kansas, *House Journal, 1868* (Topeka, 1868), 780; *Senate Journal, 1868* (Topeka, 1868), 485.

15. C. K. Cleveland to Ignatius Donnelly, Mankato, Minn., Apr. 17, 1868,

The change in Republican attitude reflected a growing distaste for Reconstruction generally—a trend that first became noticeable in portions of the West during the fall of 1867. While this departure is to be the subject of the final chapter, it is apropos to state here that growing conservatism did affect western reaction to the impeachment proceedings. Strong in their support of the first Reconstruction Act of March, 1867, some western Republicans began to have doubts even as Congress passed supplemental acts later in that year. Besides reinforcing the impression that Congress lacked a firm course in Reconstruction, the supplemental acts tended to place more authority into the hands of the military governments. The third Reconstruction Act, in fact, clearly gave precedence to military commanders in the South over civilian officials by declaring existing state governments in the region illegal and by permitting commanders to override the opinion of any civil officer of the United States.[16] With the thought that radicals could be undermining the very structure of southern state government, Republicans feared that Congress could be attempting to bring the executive department under its control as well.

Stricken with conscience once again over the fate of the presidency, westerners heard the news of Johnson's acquittal with both disappointment and relief. The more radical among Republicans refused to concede Johnson's innocence. ". . . the acquittal is to us a bitter disappointment," wrote William Gagan, editor of the *Oakland News*. "We regard Andrew Johnson as an obstinate and willful disturber of the public peace. Of his moral guilt we have not now, and have never had a particle of doubt. . . . His acquittal by the Senate does not change our view of this point, and it does not whitewash his crimes."[17] But the more moderate characterized the Senate's ver-

---

H. D. John to Donnelly, St. Paul, Feb. 26, 1868, and Donnelly to "my dear friend," Washington, D.C., May 17, 1868, all in Donnelly Papers; C. Rogers to Alexander Ramsey, St. Paul, Mar., 11, 1868, Ramsey Papers; *Colorado Tribune*, May 5, 1868; Cornelius Cole to E. Burke, Washington, D.C., May 14, 1868, Cole Papers.

16. James G. Randall and David Donald, *The Civil War and Reconstruction*, 2d ed. (Boston, 1961), 598–99.

17. *Oakland News*, May 30, 1868. See also *Marysville Appeal*, May 19, 1868; *Stars and Stripes*, May 21, 1868; *Humboldt Times*, May 30, 1868; Sacramento *Bee*, May 20, 1868; *Sacramento Union*, May 18, 1868; *Miner's Register*, May 20, 1868; *Mantorville Express*, May 22, 1868; Faribault *Central Republican*, June 3, 1868; *Montana Post*, May 22, 1868; *Gold Hill News*, May 30, 1868.

dict as sound. Certainly it eased anxiety about undue congressional strength in later administrations. Similarly it calmed fears that Johnson's removal would offer Democrats political propaganda in the upcoming election. Moreover, added William Byers, there was little cause now for deposing Andrew Johnson. The Reconstruction "policy has begun to culminate in the South," he wrote, "seven of the ten states have virtually accepted it. . . . There are no longer sufficient political reasons, in our judgment, for his removal."[18]

Those Republicans who approved the outcome of impeachment saw in Johnson's trial the ultimate challenge to the American political system, and believed it had met the test successfully. For them the verdict refuted charges as well that the Republican party was determined in and of itself to punish Andrew Johnson for his political obstinacy. In the end, Frederick MacCrellish was optimistic: "Viewed as a judicial question, the acquittal of the President will have no other effect on the country than to add new weight to the accumulated testimony of years to the stability and security of republican institutions." MacCrellish and others wanted particularly to make their readers aware that in rendering the verdict, the Republican members in the Senate had not cast a united vote. Whereas every one of the twelve Democratic senators voted to acquit the president, seven of the forty-two Republicans diverged from their political colleagues. Democrats—not Republicans—were guilty of casting a party vote. Republican senators, in the editors' belief, had voted their conscience.[19] The Republican party now stood vindicated of any charge of political proscription.

Kansas Republicans of the Reconstruction era considered Edmund G. Ross's vote to be critical in securing Johnson's acquittal, and occasionally historians have speculated about the reasons for Ross's decision. Of the twelve senators from the West, only two, Daniel S. Norton of Minnesota and Ross of Kansas, voted in the president's favor. Norton's vote came as no surprise, since he had staunchly upheld the administration all along; Ross's vote was somewhat less expected and angered many Kansas Republicans, especially those who were counting on their senator to side with the radicals. Ross was

18. *Rocky Mountain News*, May 13, 1868.
19. *Alta California*, May 17, 19, 30, 1868; *Sacramento Bee*, May 16, 1868 *Petaluma Journal & Argus*, June 4, 1868.

certainly not alone among Republicans to vote for acquittal; several votes hung in the balance until the actual roll call. But interestingly Ross is the one who has been singled out most often as "the man who saved the President." And the image was to linger: until the late 1950s historians continued to picture him as a fearless, principled man—a politician who ruined his own career to save the nation from the ambitions of ruthless "Jacobins." Others, upon closer examination, have found Ross wanting and believe that he sold his vote for a slice of the federal patronage.[20] More accurately, Ross may lie somewhere between these two extremes.

"Ross the martyr," "Ross the persecuted," and "Ross the hero of the impeachment trial" were facets of an image created by Edmund G. Ross himself. From May 16, 1868, when he cast his first vote to acquit Johnson, until his death in 1907, Ross was to portray himself repeatedly in this light. Clearly the senator from Kansas gloried in his role as he perceived it at the trial. "This storm of passion will soon pass away," he wrote at the time to his wife, "and the people, the whole people, will thank and bless me for having saved the country by my single vote from the greatest peril through which it ever passed, though none but God can ever know the struggle it cost me. Millions of men are cursing me today, but they will bless me tomorrow." Honesty may have been one of Ross's attributes; humility was not. He was to elaborate on the theme as he spoke before the Senate on July 27, 1868. "I have been singled out as the object of assault," he said, "doubtless because I am a new member here, unskilled in debate, unknown to national politics, and comparatively without means of self-defense. I am conscious of these disadvantages, as well as the strength and malignity of my accusers. . . . I have but a feeble voice here backed, however, by a never failing

20. The other Republican senators who voted "not guilty" were William Pitt Fessenden of Maine, Joseph S. Fowler of Tennessee, James W. Grimes of Iowa, John B. Henderson of Missouri, Lyman Trumbull of Illinois, and Peter G. Van Winkle of West Virginia. For a while it was thought that Cornelius Cole of California, Henry Corbett of Oregon, and even James Nye of Nevada would vote for acquittal; however, in his recent study *The Presidency of Andrew Johnson* (Lawrence, Kans., 1979), 193, Albert Castel characterizes such rumors of vote-switching as based on secondhand and unreliable sources. Trefousse, *Impeachment of a President*, 167; Welles, *Diary*, III, 358; John F. Kennedy, *Profiles in Courage* (New York, 1955), 126–51; William A. Dunning, *Reconstruction, Political and Economic, 1865-1877* (New York, 1907), 107; Charles A. Jellison, "The Ross Impeachment Vote: A Need for Reappraisal," SQ, XLI (Sept., 1960), 150–55.

source of strength, my own consciousness of rectitude and patriotic, honest purpose." [21]

The many who have accepted Ross at his word have perhaps done so because Ross aired his role before the public time and time again. In the 1890s Ross compiled his memoirs in a book-length account; he offered a number of shorter reminiscences as well on the Reconstruction era. [22] When he spoke of the impeachment trial in these writings, Ross quite predictably magnified his own heroism and role. Indeed, in reading Ross it is easy to forget that there were six other Republican "recusants." The emotion surrounding his vote for the president's acquittal had scarcely dimmed for him even twenty-five years later: "Conscious that I was at the moment the focus of all eyes . . . it is something of a simile to say that I literally looked down in my open grave. Friends, position, fortune . . . were about to be swept away. . . . Realizing the tremendous responsibility which an untoward combination of conditions seemed to have put upon me . . . the verdict came—'Not guilty.' . . . The die was cast. The best or the worst was known. The historical trial of the age was practically ended." Ross gave a final version of his self-perceived role in the trial in a letter to R. S. Hoxie in 1896. He described a conversation held on the eve of the first Senate vote and quoted Thomas Ewing, Jr., as asking, "Well, Ross, how is this thing going to-morrow?" Ross recalled answering, not without pride, "It will go as I turn my hand, . . . but no living person will know what my verdict will be until he hears it from my lips at my desk." [23]

Ross's vote did come as a surprise to some people. Governor Crawford of Kansas seemed taken aback. "My God, Ross, what does it mean[?]" he telegraphed the senator. ". . . don't betray the party in casting your votes on the other articles." But Crawford could not

21. Edmund G. Ross to his wife, Washington, D.C., May 22, 1868, quoted in Edward Bumgardner, *The Life of Edmund G. Ross: The Man Whose Vote Saved a President* (Kansas City, Mo., 1949), 89; *Congressional Globe*, 40 Cong., 2 Sess., 4513.

22. Edmund G. Ross, *History of the Impeachment of Andrew Johnson, President of the United States, by the House of Representatives, and His Trial by the Senate for High Crimes and Misdemeanors in Office, 1868* (Santa Fe, N.Mex., 1896); Ross, "A Previous Era of Popular Madness and Its Lessons," F, XIX, (July, 1895), 595-605; Ross, "Historic Moments: The Impeachment Trial," SM, XI (April, 1892), 517-24; Ross, "Political Leaders," 218-34.

23. Ross, "Historic Moments," 523-24; Edmund G. Ross to R. S. Hoxie, Santa Fe, Nov. 2, 1896, Vinnie Ream Hoxie Papers, LC.

have been too surprised. The senator was reported to be "shaky" on impeachment as early as February, 1868, and reports of his wavering filtered back to Kansas all during the trial. His refusal to attend Republican councils and his open association with Thomas Ewing, Jr., administration confidant, further aroused suspicions that Ross was leaning toward acquittal. These reports prompted a group of Kansas radicals to plead with Ross for a vote of "guilty." Gideon Welles reported intense pressure on the senator from radicals on the one hand and Johnson's friends on the other.[24] It cannot be denied that, by Ross's own admission, spectators in the Senate chamber and fellow senators were anxiously awaiting the moment when Ross would announce his decision. But Ross's final move was very likely anticipated by some.

Radical editors back home were furious and saw their good faith in Ross betrayed. As a result the Kansas press subjected Ross in turn to scourging criticism, as many historians have shown. Moderate as well as radical Republican editors labeled Ross a modern Judas. A sampling of editorials shows Ross to have been "cowardly," "craven," "contemptible," and "a man who sold his vote to the highest bidder."[25] Given the intense censure leveled against the senator, it is easy to accept Ross's own theory that he was one of the most maligned public figures in the nineteenth century.

In among the scathing criticism, however, Ross did receive scattered praise from Democrats and even some Republicans. Kansas Democrats met in Paola for the sole purpose of adopting resolutions commending Ross's vote. Numerous Republicans in Topeka openly endorsed Ross's decision of May 16, and some telegraphed him to "stand firm" when the Senate faced another vote on May 26. T. C. Hill, a Kansas Republican, argued for Ross's privilege to decide. "You have . . . as much a right to render a verdict according to law & evidence as any juror," wrote Hill. "I cannot [condemn] you for doing what your judgment dictated to you was right." Another cor-

24. Samuel Crawford to Edmund G. Ross, Topeka, May 16, 1868, Crawford Papers; Ross, "Previous Era," 603–5; *Kansas Tribune*, Feb. 28, 1868; *Leavenworth Conservative*, May 17, 1868; Welles, *Diary*, III, 359, 362; Ross to R. S. Hoxie, Santa Fe, Nov. 2, 1896, Hoxie Papers.

25. L. D. Bailey to Edmund G. Ross, n.p., May 16, 1868, in *Leavenworth Conservative*, May 17, 1868; *Emporia News*, May 20, 1868; *Osage Chronicle*, May 23, 1868; *Kansas Chief*, June 4, 1868; *Olathe Mirror*, May 21, 1868; *Manhattan Independent*, May 23, 1868; *Marysville Enterprise*, May 23, 1868.

respondent and friend to the senator assumed that Mrs. Ross must find the barrage of criticism disheartening. Attempting to console her in a letter, John Horner reminded her that the scurrilous commentary would be short-lived and that her husband's fine reputation would prevail. Even his worst enemies could not continue to repeat the charge of bribery against Ross. "His record," said Horner, "is too pure and unsullied to be tarnished thereby."[26]

Horner was correct. Typically, Republican editors leveled abuse at the senator for a week or two and then ceased to show further concern.[27] So soon after the trial, Ross's critics certainly had not forgiven him, but they refrained from vilifying him over an extended period. Ironically, within a year some of the sharpest critics of Ross's impeachment vote were praising his work in Washington. Writing for the *Osage Chronicle* in 1868, for instance, Marshall Murdock was vehemently opposed to the senator's stand: "Ross sinks beneath our contempt." But in 1869 Murdock remarked, ". . . Ross has . . . labored for the best interest of his state without fee or reward above his salary." The *Leavenworth Conservative* did a similar about-face. While in 1868 it had considered Kansas "betrayed and outraged by this creature Ross," in 1869 it allowed Ross to be "the most creditable representative that Kansas has had in the national capitol." In his

26. *Kansas Tribune*, May 26, 1868; *Kansas Chief*, May 28, 1868; T. C. Hill to Edmund G. Ross, Americus, Kans., June 12, 1868, John Horner to Mrs. Ross, Baldwin City, Kans., May 24, 1868, both in Ross Papers, KSHS.

27. Criticism of the seven Republicans generally did not last long in the West. While Ross was the chief target of the Kansas press, he hardly received mention in other western areas. The *St. Paul Dispatch* did pick up the topic, only to label unfair the campaign being waged against Ross in his home state. With Senators Fessenden and Trumbull, and not Ross, lay the blame for Johnson's acquittal: ". . . these two lawyers furnished a too ready excuse for the others." Their stature, in the editor's opinion, encouraged lesser men like Ross to follow their example. *St. Paul Dispatch*, May 25, 1868. In the West the seven recusants were criticized most strongly in Minnesota, Nebraska, and Kansas. In addition to the Kansas papers cited, see *Minneapolis Tribune*, May 17, 29, 1868; *Rochester Post*, May 23, 1868; *Nebraska Commonwealth*, May 28, 1868. Republican editors along the West coast were almost unanimous in their defense of the seven. Even William Gagan, editor of the *Oakland News* and bitterly disappointed in Johnson's acquittal, found the courage to write, "We believe that the leading Republican Senators who have voted against the impeachment . . . are governed by purely conscientious motives." *Oakland News*, May 16, 1868. See also *Napa Register*, May 20, 1868; San Francisco *Bulletin*, May 18, 29, 1868; *Petaluma Journal & Argus*, June 4, 1868; *Alta California*, May 17, 19, 1868; *Salem Daily Record*, May 19, 1868; *Rocky Mountain News*, May 13, 15, 16, 1868.

first editorial following Johnson's acquittal, Sol Miller held nothing back: "Does Ross not know he is a contemptible ass?" Yet a year later he was to write unabashedly, "Ross is the best and most honest [representative] Kansas has in Congress. . . ." Thus Ross faced an intense but relatively brief period of persecution at home. By the end of his Senate term in 1871 Kansas newspapers were commending both Ross's devotion to duty and his efforts on behalf of the state. There were even rumors that conservative Republicans favored Ross's re-election to the Senate for a second term.[28] He did not, however, receive serious consideration by Kansas legislators. His vote on the impeachment may have been a factor, but his failure to secure the post was more likely due to the venal nature of Kansas politics in the post–Civil War era.

Contemporaries and anti-Ross historians have generally favored one of two reasons given for Ross's decision to vote for acquittal. In the months immediately following the trial persons opposed to his stand very commonly equated his vote with personal corruption. It was evident, they said, that the Kansas senator and his fellow recusants had been bribed. But a House committee charged with investigation and chaired by Benjamin F. Butler failed to substantiate the accusation.[29]

Andrew Johnson's own papers have cast a different light on the affair. Historians with access to them have discovered letters implying that, by voting as he did, Ross hoped to acquire control of federal patronage in Kansas and in the Southwest. As historian Charles Jellison has explained it, the letters reveal no specific arrangement between Ross and the president, but they do show that the senator "lost little time in 'cashing in' on his vote after the President's acquittal."

What makes the accusation damaging is the evident lack of correspondence between Ross and Johnson prior to the trial. Following the acquittal there were four letters written in quick succession,

28. *Osage Chronicle*, May 23, 1868, May 8, 1869, Dec. 14, 1871; *Leavenworth Conservative*, May 17, 1868; *Leavenworth Conservative and Times*, June 2, 1869; *Kansas Chief*, June 4, 1868, June 10, 1869, June 9, 1870; *Emporia News*, July 19, 1870; Ralph J. Roske, "The Seven Martyrs?" AHR, LXIV (Jan., 1959), 327-28.

29. U.S. Congress, House of Representatives, "Raising of Money to be used in Impeachment," *Reports of Committees of the House of Representatives*, 40 Cong., 2 Sess., Report 75 (ser. 1358), 4-13.

between June 6 and July 10, 1868—all requesting patronage appointments. Ross did seek two posts in the South—one for his brother William and another for Perry Fuller, a close personal friend—but in every other case Ross sought to place his own men in jobs where they could use their influence to augment the senator's political strength back home in Kansas. Johnson may have been a willing partner, for he acceded to most of Ross's requests. In one instance the president even removed a man avid in Johnson's support as southern superintendent of Indian affairs and gave the office to Newton Robinson, one of Ross's cohorts.[30]

The supposition that Ross "cashed in" on his vote finds support in his correspondence with Johnson. The drawback lies in its failure to answer one obvious question: why should Ross, whose relationship with Republican colleagues in the Senate was apparently amicable, suddenly seek favors from a president whose public image was at its lowest point? True, Johnson designated nominees for federal posts, but senatorial consent was required before appointments could take effect. Thus it seems odd that Ross would have sided with Johnson solely for the purpose of securing more influence over patronage. He could just as readily have encountered defeat in the Senate had his colleagues suspected him of intrigue. Moreover, Ross already had an ear to the administration through Thomas Ewing, Jr., and relied on his influence in securing appointments. Ewing even continued to work on Ross's behalf after the impeachment trial was over.[31] But with the close of the trial Ross apparently found this roundabout arrangement too limiting and shortly began his urgent appeals to Johnson. The reason, involving the patronage to be sure, nonetheless lay primarily in an imbroglio among the Kansas congressional delegation.

Kansas during the 1860s sent two senators and one representative to Washington: normally theirs was a politically diverse group even though its members consistently were Republican. Senator James H.

30. Edmund G. Ross to Andrew Johnson, Washington, D.C., June 6, 23, July 1, 10, 1868, Johnson Papers; *Senate Executive Proceedings*, XVI, 274, 430, 741; Jellison, "The Ross Impeachment Vote," 153–54; Trefousse, *Impeachment of a President*, 167–68.

31. Edmund G. Ross to Thomas Ewing, Jr., Lawrence, Kans., May 31, 1867, Ewing Family Papers; Ewing, Jr., to Andrew Johnson, Washington, D.C., June 30, 1868, Johnson Papers.

Lane, because of his domination of federal patronage in Kansas, could usually count on the political backing of the representative. As a result, Senator Samuel Pomeroy was the odd man out. In 1866 the Kansas delegation consisted of Lane, Pomeroy, and Congressman Sidney Clarke. Upon Lane's death in July Governor Crawford appointed Ross to fill the seat, and when the legislature next convened in 1867, Ross was duly elected to the post. Clarke was displeased to see Ross take hold so rapidly, for the representative had ambitions of his own to serve in the Senate. Particularly ominous was the fact that he and Ross both resided in Lawrence; it seemed unlikely that the legislature would ever elect two U.S. senators from the same locale, much less from the same city. Consequently Clarke turned to Pomeroy, in the hope that together they might work to reduce Ross's influence. By the spring of 1868 they were firmly united in common front against Ross. At least it was at this point that Ross discovered the alliance and its purpose. Furious, Ross hesitated only briefly before taking the offensive and casting his lot in such a way as to alter his career. For just before the vote on Johnson's impeachment, according to Henry C. Whitney in a letter to S. S. Prouty of the *Kansas Patriot*, Ross learned that Pomeroy and Clarke were conspiring "to turn all of Ross's friends out of office as soon as Wade should don the 'imperial purple.' This 'furnishing a club to beat his own brains with' was not relished by our young Senator and so he slaughtered the conspiracy and the impeachment together." Not only did Ross very expressly give a pro-Johnson vote in response—and a vote against Wade—but, by Whitney's account, the senator now moved in "to secure the patronage of the State." He was angry and intent on destroying Clarke and Pomeroy; short of that, he wished at least to have Kansas federal patronage under his control before "Pomeroy gets a chance at it under Grant's administration."[32] This, Whitney claimed, was the essential explanation for Ross's impeachment vote.

The validity of Whitney's statement is contingent upon three factors—his credibility as a witness, his relationship with Ross at the time, and the plausibility of his conjecture in terms of Ross's later activities. Earlier a political colleague of Lincoln's in central Illinois

32. Henry C. Whitney to S. S. Prouty, Washington, D.C., June 13, 1868, in *Kansas Patriot*, June 20, 1868.

during the 1850s, Whitney had on occasion visited Washington and the president during the war when serving as paymaster in the army; very possibly he met leading Republicans in this way. He became acquainted with Kansas politics at war's end when he transferred his law practice from the Midwest to Lawrence, Kansas. He spent May and June, 1868, in Washington, D.C., lobbying against the Osage Indian treaty, a document that gave to certain Kansas railroad interests preferential terms for the acquisition of large tracts of Indian territory while practically excluding settlers from the same lands. Ross and Pomeroy favored the treaty, Sidney Clarke opposed it. Whitney at this point would not likely have been partial to Ross, given their difference of opinion on the treaty. Nor was it Whitney's purpose in writing the letter to justify Ross's behavior: the revealing paragraph on Ross came only at the conclusion of a detailed description of Whitney's own lobbying activities. Yet Whitney was not alone in his supposition on Ross's incentive; at the time, three Kansas editors hinted at the same motive but failed to elaborate. In the emotionalism of the moment they could only conclude that the senator was guilty of corruption. Still, the impression that political rivalry weighed heavily in Ross's vote remained strong with Whitney. At least, in 1869 he informed the senator of his own successful efforts to block in the Kansas legislature a series of Clarke-inspired resolutions declaring Ross guilty of corruption during the impeachment trial and requesting his resignation from the Senate.[33]

Further, Whitney's assertion is relevant in its clarification of certain points in Ross's letters to Johnson, especially those in reference to Clarke. To Johnson Ross spoke of the animosity shown toward him by the House of Representatives as "fostered by the member from Kansas, who omits no opportunity to take advantage of it to serve

33. Whitney remained in Kansas into the 1870s, serving one term in the legislature. Shortly thereafter he returned to Chicago, where he established a law practice and wrote several biographies on Lincoln. Historians have questioned Whitney's interpretation of Lincoln and his era, but his veracity as a political observer has not been challenged. See Basler (ed.), Lincoln Works, IV, 33n, 35n, 79n, 145, 543, V, 433n, VII, 120; Emanuel Hertz, The Hidden Lincoln (New York, 1940), 388–91; Carl Sandburg, Abraham Lincoln: The War Years, 4 vols. (New York, 1939), II, 217. Paul Wallace Gates, Fifty Million Acres: Conflicts over Kansas Land Policy, 1854-1890 (Ithaca, N.Y., 1954), 194–208; Leavenworth Conservative, May 21, 1868; Emporia News, May 29, 1868; Junction Union, May 23, 1868; Kansas Patriot, June 6, 1868; Henry C. Whitney to Edmund G. Ross, Topeka, Jan. 19, 1869, Ross Papers, KSHS.

his own purpose. . . ." But the senator did not want for spirit and made known his desire for revenge: "Clarke comes up for re-election in the fall, and I am determined he should not be re-elected. The [southern superintendency of Indian affairs] in the hands of my friends will enable me to defeat Clarke." Later he was to elaborate. "I am aware," said Ross quietly to the president, "that I am asking a good deal of you, but I feel constrained to do so by the persistent efforts that are being made for my destruction."[34]

Faced with unexpected and dramatic obstinacy from the junior senator, Clarke and Pomeroy redoubled their efforts at home to subdue Ross. From time to time Clarke's supporters in the Kansas legislature introduced resolutions requesting the senator's resignation, but Ross's friends were successful in getting them tabled. Still they could do little to forestall Clarke and Pomeroy, who, once Grant was secure in office, launched an all-out effort to remove every Ross appointee in Kansas and gain control for themselves. It was only Ross's direct appeal to the Senate at this point that induced the senators to retain Ross's backers in their federal posts.[35] Ross must certainly have felt a sense of relief and victory when Clarke failed to be renominated for a fourth term to Congress in 1870.

Whitney's statement also bears out Ross's insistence that the impeachment trial had developed into a scheme by some Republicans to retain control of the nation through patronage. Perhaps not by chance, Ross focused repeatedly on Pomeroy as the most unscrupulous of the western senators. Senator Ross himself faced the accusation of selling his vote for promise of patronage, but as he chided the Senate in July, 1868, "If true, there may be two sides to that also." While he did not deny the possibility, he effectively silenced his accusers with the hint that they themselves might be guilty of the same crime. After his retirement from the Senate in 1871 Ross established a newspaper in Coffeyville, Kansas. Therein he editorialized on Johnson's impeachment, and he stressed the patronage theme in particular. Every federal position from the presidency down to the smallest post office had been "farmed out," he wrote scathingly; "impeachment . . . degenerated long before its close into a stupen-

34. Edmund G. Ross to Andrew Johnson, Washington, D.C., June 6, July 10, 1868, Johnson Papers.
35. State of Kansas, *Senate Journal, 1869*, 74, 86; Caldwell, "Kansas," 154.

dous and damnable conspiracy for the robbery and plunder of this Government."[36]

Ross had Pomeroy yet to contend with, and it was no coincidence that as the senior senator came up for re-election in January, 1872, Ross recalled two damaging letters written by Pomeroy. These missives had surfaced at the time that the House was investigating charges of bribery in the impeachment trial. The first, dated April 16, 1867, advised a close friend of Pomeroy's, one James Legate, to request the postmastership at Leavenworth, Kansas, from Postmaster General Alexander Randall. ". . . if he will give it to you to-day," said Pomeroy as he parlayed favors, "he may count on my support . . . & should either himself or the President get in trouble, even if it be Impeachment, they can count on me . . . and you may so say to him." The second letter, written a year later during the impeachment trial, to Edmund Cooper, the president's secretary, was even more incriminating. In Ross's version Pomeroy had offered his own and the votes of two other senators to acquit the president if Cooper could reach a "suitable arrangement" with the bearer of the letter, William Gaylord, Pomeroy's brother-in-law. The "suitable arrangement" turned out to be a remuneration of $40,000, as Cooper was later to testify before the House committee. But the plan fell through when Cooper insisted on paying part of the agreed amount by check; understandably, Gaylord preferred cash to avoid detection by a third party. Legate actually came before the committee for questioning on both letters, and he was able to corroborate Cooper's testimony. Legate had apparently met up with Gaylord, who, after recounting the ill-fated bargain, tore the letter into pieces in Legate's presence and threw them away. Unfortunately for Gaylord—and for Pomeroy—Legate retrieved the pieces, pasted them together again, and had them photographed.

Pomeroy maintained his innocence. During the investigation he steadfastly denied responsibility for either letter, and the committee in the end determined them to be forgeries. As Ross recounted the affair in 1872, the letters were indeed genuine; however, Butler, chairman of the House investigating committee, offered to de-emphasize their importance if Pomeroy would give evidence implicating

36. *Congressional Globe*, 40 Cong., 2 Sess., 4514; *Ross's Paper* (Coffeyville, Kans). Jan. 19, 1872.

Ross in bribery. This Pomeroy agreed to do, said Ross, at Butler's threat to ruin him if he refused. Ross also took the opportunity to level a charge directly at Pomeroy: the latter had even tried to tempt him with a sum of $50,000, he said, for the guarantee of a vote to convict Johnson. His colleague, insisted Ross, could promise such a large sum because upon Wade's becoming president Pomeroy was to receive control of all patronage positions concerned with the collection of internal revenue.[37]

Ross's version of the tale, coming as it did somewhat after the fact, probably caused little excitement. Pomeroy, nonetheless, could not let it pass. "You are the only man I know who vacillated," he wrote, "and at this late period, the less you say about impeachment, the better for you." Pomeroy had long since been cleared of wrongdoing, but several facts still continued to hint at some guilt on his part. He remained Legate's close friend, for instance, and even tried to solicit other federal appointments for him. The letter to Cooper must have bothered Pomeroy, for reportedly he paid $25,000 for the negative and all pictures of the item even though it had been declared a forgery. The amount may have seemed exceptional, but Pomeroy was not above using cash sums to further his own purposes. He lost his bid for re-election in 1872 only after a state senator accepted a $7,000 bribe to vote for him and then exposed the whole affair before the Kansas legislature.[38]

Thus Ross's vote to acquit Johnson came of a complexity of motives. He may well have wished to dissociate himself from a number of radicals who, in his belief, had grown corrupt and were using the impeachment for base purposes. But concern for his own political future also motivated Ross to vote for acquittal. As of June, 1868, he had every intention of seeking a second term in the Senate, and he concluded he would not be successful were the radicals, including Pomeroy and Clarke, to prevail. But in attempting to save his own career, Ross miscalculated the vagaries of Kansas politics. Although he received a smattering of votes for re-election in 1871, Ross did

---

37. U.S. Congress, House of Representatives, *Reports of Committees*, Report 75, 4–13; Samuel C. Pomeroy to James Legate, U.S. Senate Chamber, Apr. 16, 1867, true copy certified by Cornelius Wendell, Johnson Papers—there is also a typewritten copy in the Samuel Clarke Pomeroy Papers, KU; *Ross's Paper*, Dec. 22, 1871, Jan. 12, 19, 1872.

38. *Ross's Paper*, Jan. 12, 1872; Plummer, *Frontier Governor*, 147; Caldwell, "Kansas," 161–62.

not come close to obtaining a second term in the Senate.[39] Historians have credited this defeat solely to his vote to acquit Johnson. True, Clarke, despite his failure to secure renomination for the House in 1870, remained a power in Kansas politics, and he used his position to vent his hatred against Ross. But as important a factor were the Leavenworth business interests. Members of that group selected Alexander Caldwell as their candidate and by contemporary account succeeded in purchasing Caldwell's election. Against such odds Ross never had a chance.

While Ross suffered malign and personal defeat, the real casualty of the impeachment struggle was Andrew Johnson. Ross's vote may have saved the president from removal, but for Johnson it did little else. There was no likelihood that he could regain his credibility with the electorate of either party at this point. From the close of the trial to the inauguration of Grant in March, 1869, western Republicans and Democrats alike waited anxiously for Johnson's departure from the White House. The Republican *Marysville Appeal* of California began to count the final days of his presidency a full month before its completion: "On March 4th next, one month from tomorrow, Andrew Johnson . . . becomes a private citizen . . . so hated and despised that the people would refuse to elect him to the lowest office within their gift." Later in the month Charles Slocum, editor of the *Mankato Union*, printed a headline proclaiming, "Six More Days of Andrew Johnson." With his readers Slocum reveled in the thought that "the long night of our mourning will be ended. The nation will then throw off the vile sack cloth and ashes worn since the martyrdom of Abraham Lincoln. . . ."[40]

Democrats were hardly more kind. Wrote Beriah Brown of the *Sonoma Democrat*: Johnson "fought a great fight, and his name will go into history as a statesman and a patriot [but] like [most] Democrats, . . . we have too often thought . . . he had 'a happy faculty for doing the right thing at the wrong time.' " And finally came the testimony of James O'Meara, avid Democrat and newsman from Idaho: "He has gone from the Chief Magistracy of the nation, and

39. Henry C. Whitney to S. S. Prouty, Washington, D.C., June 13, 1868, in *Kansas Patriot*, June 20, 1868; Wilder, *Annals of Kansas*, 548.

40. *Marysville Appeal*, Feb. 3, 1869; *Mankato Union*, Feb. 26, 1869.

. . . we think we shall never cease to rejoice that Andrew Johnson is no longer President of the United States."[41]

Seeking to give perspective in the aftermath of the impeachment, Frederick MacCrellish of the *Alta California* offered poignant insight on Johnson the man. During the Johnson administration MacCrellish had alternately praised and questioned the president's Reconstruction policy and his actions. An advocate of impeachment, MacCrellish had nonetheless come to accept Johnson's acquittal. Upon the president's subsequent retirement from office, the editor offered a lengthy and personal reflection: ". . . an honest spasm of pity passes over the popular heart as his magnificent opportunities misspent, and exalted station disgraced, are recalled to mind. Andrew Johnson will carry into his retirement the good-will of no considerable portion of his fellow men, but only the hatred and contempt of many. . . . The cause of Mr. Johnson's utter failure is simple enough . . . he lacked the teachableness which makes a man truly great. . . . Andrew Johnson of 1869 is the identical Andrew Johnson of 1866. . . . His personal opinions have been to him the supreme law; and he retires into private life, an awful example of untaught and unteachable egotism."[42] In terms of his image as a man and a president, the impeachment of Andrew Johnson may not have been completely without meaning.

41. *Sonoma Democrat*, Mar. 6, 1869; *Idaho World*, Mar. 11, 1869.
42. *Alta California*, Mar. 4, 1869.

CHAPTER NINE

The Waning of Reconstruction

". . . the Republican party . . . has undertaken too much."
—I. S. Kalloch, Kansas

Interest in Reconstruction began to decline in certain portions of
the West during the fall of 1867. As concern for national reunification diminished, western Republicans quietly retreated to a more
conservative position—a shift which became apparent throughout
the region toward the end of the impeachment trial and which
intensified during 1869 and 1870. The trend was not peculiar to the
West; a similar movement was occurring in the North at the same
time. Nor was it limited to average, less politically aware individuals.
Just as the voting public turned its attention away from national
problems, northern and western congressmen began arguing for moderation, and by 1870 western representatives in Washington were
among the most vocal advocates for ending Reconstruction. Demanding the readmission of southern states along guidelines established in the Reconstruction acts, western Republican senators
strongly opposed requiring more of Virginia when the Senate reviewed
her constitution in 1870. From the radical standpoint of a few years
earlier they might have accepted harsher measures, but now the
western contingent balked when a few radicals demanded a clause
denying Virginia the right, ever, to retract black suffrage. Thomas
Tipton of Nebraska, among others, spoke out. Virginia had met every
stipulation outlined by Congress, announced the senator firmly, and
he would consider any additional requirement to be a breach of faith.
Similarly William Stewart of Nevada argued two months later against
further stipulations on Georgia. Declared Stewart: "Reconstruction
has been under consideration for five years, the country wants it
terminated. . . . We want an end of reconstruction."[1]

1. Western senators opposed to the codicil on Virginia's constitution were Re-

In the West Republican editors, no longer finding the topic so vital, increasingly turned their attention elsewhere. While their personal concerns may have been changing, they were in their unanimity reflecting part of the larger trend and a growing dissatisfaction with national affairs. At the same time Democratic response to Reconstruction decreased markedly. Without Republican impetus there was little cause for debate, for editors in the nineteenth century expressed themselves most freely and candidly when attacking a viewpoint or offering rebuttal. Clearly the lack of commentary indicated that westerners were beginning to redirect their focus on public issues and that problems in the South were fading in importance.

It is true that westerners watched national developments during the presidential election of 1868 with concern, but in the wake of Grant's inauguration their interest fell off sharply and the trend to emphasize state and local affairs prevailed. The Fifteenth Amendment did bring editorial comment while in Congress during 1868–69 and upon its promulgation in 1870, but relative to the extensive news coverage on the Fourteenth Amendment two years before, interest in the Fifteenth was nominal. While the daily newspapers briefly explored the rise of the Ku Klux Klan in the South and reviewed passage of the Enforcement Act in 1870, the weeklies said nothing. Earlier they had given most detailed coverage to national affairs despite lack of space; now their silence on southern resistance to federal directives and on Congress's rejoinder left a curious void.

The shift came earlier in some portions of the West, later in others. In Kansas the decline of interest in Reconstruction was evident as early as 1867, when a number of editors abruptly curtailed coverage of events in Washington during the summer months and played up instead the local campaign for black and woman suffrage. The suffrage issue was likely more compelling for the time, but a new pattern was emerging as well. Even after the suffrage referendum met defeat in November, 1867, these mostly Republican editors continued to stress local news. When R. B. Taylor of the *Wyandotte Gazette* deigned to inform his readers of Johnson's impeachment in 1868, it was his

---

publicans Cole, Corbett, Nye, Ross, Stewart, Tipton, and Williams, and Democrats Casserly and Norton. Republicans Pomeroy, Ramsey, and Thayer supported the move. *Congressional Globe*, 41 Cong., 2 Sess., 2822; *Nebraska State Journal*, Feb. 5, 1870; *Fremont* (Neb.) *Weekly Tribune*, Feb. 24, 1870; Hoogenboom, *Outlawing the Spoils*, 39; Donald, *Charles Sumner*, 420.

first mention of the president to any extent for almost a year. Sol Miller, one of the more politically aware newsmen in the state and editor of the *Kansas Chief*, showed similar reluctance. He directed editorial efforts in 1867 to the suffrage issue; thereafter, he focused on county politics. Miller diverged only to give several editorials on Ross's role in acquitting the president.[2] While no one in the media undertook to explain this shift of emphasis locally, a theme of caution prevailed and it is not difficult to conclude from editorial comments that growing Democratic strength was at its base: Republican editors believed that Democratic gains in the election of 1867 had been due to increasing popular discontent with Reconstruction, and they retreated to issues less virulent.

For Democrats along the Pacific coast it was politically expedient to keep Reconstruction issues alive well into 1870. In Oregon they were in fact successful in parlaying the Reconstruction topic to regain their power in 1868. Even so Oregon Democrats were not immune to the trend and before long were backing off, looking more typically at local issues. During the remainder of the nineteenth century political ascendancy in Oregon was to shift back and forth between Republicans and Democrats, but no longer were political issues to be shaped or dominated by national politics.[3]

In California Democrats made full use of both restoration in the South and equal suffrage to gain and strengthen their political control in 1867 and again in 1869. But their effort paled somewhat as California Republicans regrouped. Shattered by Reconstruction issues, Republicans now worked zealously at local concerns in order to stage a political comeback. Aware of Republican strategy, Democrats dropped Reconstruction altogether as a political issue by 1871. Thereafter both parties addressed themselves instead to land reform and to the problems of Chinese immigration along the Pacific coast.[4]

As Reconstruction became less vital and less political a topic, so too were westerners increasingly weary of the whole affair. A shift in management and editorial policy of the radical *Appeal* of Marysville, California, plainly bears out this fact. Throughout the Reconstruction years to 1870, the *Appeal* retained strong concern for

2. *Wyandotte Gazette*, Feb. 29, 1868; *Kansas Chief*, July, 1867–May, 1868 *passim*.
3. Woodward, *Political Parties in Oregon*, 265.
4. Ralph J. Roske, *Everyman's Eden: A History of California* (New York, 1968), 377; Davis, *Political Conventions*, 298.

national affairs. Until the election of 1868 editor A. S. Smith consistently stressed federal problems and politics with only brief respite during the state election campaigns. Even with Grant's accession to the presidency, this emphasis on national news continued, except during the statewide election of 1869. Thereupon the *Appeal* in a conscious move switched its focus from the national scene to the local political arena. When F. W. Cross replaced Smith upon his retirement in 1870, the shift became acknowledged fact. Declaring his acquiescence to pressure from local citizens and the newspaper's owners as well, Cross spelled out the new editorial policy. In the future, said Cross, the *Appeal* would devote itself to furthering the interests of northern California.[5] Thus the *Appeal*, which had served as a steady outlet for radical views since 1865, now reflected minimal concern for news outside its own area.

Westerners themselves could not fail to notice the change and sought on occasion to explain it. To Democrats the emotionalism of impeachment was the significant, contributing factor, with Andrew Johnson's acquittal signaling doom for radicalism. Seeing the charges as the first step to a general Republican decline, one editor in Washington Territory felt certain "that the impeachment plot has resulted in the complete discomfiture" of its radical proponents. Another in Nevada agreed, writing that impeachment "killed radicalism. It is of no importance for the moment whether Johnson goes or stays."[6] Yet in perspective it is one of the ironies of western Reconstruction history that Democrats came to place so much importance in one event for which they had professed so little interest.

Republicans, on the other hand, tended to minimize the importance of impeachment. Rather, they viewed the readmission of seven southern states in June, 1868, as the greater determinant in the call for conservatism. In light of the western concept of the purpose of Reconstruction, Republicans had the better argument. Most westerners conceived its aim as restoration of the seceded states with guarantees for their loyalty, and little else beyond. Civil rights and suffrage for blacks did become a facet of the larger issue—indeed, the racial question overshadowed it at times—but pursuing reunification always remained the primary goal for westerners. Thus, to

5. *Marysville Appeal*, Apr. 26, 1870.
6. *Washington Standard*, May 28, 1868; *Silver Bend Weekly Reporter* (Belmont, Nev.), May 16, 1868.

many western Republicans the return of the "erring sisters" signified the resolution of the problems in the South and, correspondingly, the end of Reconstruction. Idaho Republicans, meeting in July, 1868, expressed this attitude most succinctly. They praised Congress for its role in bringing about reunification and called for an end to federal authority in the readmitted southern states. Even the *Marysville Appeal* in 1868 had to acknowledge that Congress had accomplished its work insofar as the majority of the southern states were concerned. For the radical *Appeal*, however, Congress had not achieved all that it might, and it had left a legacy of ill will between North and South. But, reasoned editor Smith, one could scarcely expect the hatreds engendered by a civil war to be erased in the lifetime of its participants.[7]

There was more to the growth in conservatism than outwardly evident. Westerners frankly were experiencing disillusion with their political leaders generally and with the idea of political reform in particular. Democrats, first of all, had been leveling charges of corruption against the Republicans, and the effect was not lost on the public: many now believed the party unworthy. While Democrats did not impugn the honesty of national Republican leaders, they did question the integrity of many lesser Republican officeholders. Administrative personnel in Indian agencies especially were retiring from office with fortunes far in excess of sums lawfully accrued.

Republicans themselves began showing alarm about the corruption among their numbers, and there was evidence to support their concern. Predictably following every senatorial election in Kansas between the years 1867 and 1872, the legislature was called upon to investigate election practices and bribery; during the same years several state officials were charged with misappropriation of public funds. Congressman Clarke and Senators Pomeroy and Caldwell in turn were accused of securing office through illegal use of funds. Clarke was never convicted, but Pomeroy and Caldwell fared less well. Upon indictment, Pomeroy failed to survive a re-election bid for a third term in 1872, and Caldwell was forced to resign from the Senate in 1873. California government during the same time was acknowledged to be even more corrupt. According to one California historian, legislators in the post–Civil War years utterly lacked "a sense of

7. *Idaho World*, July 4, 1868; *Marysville Appeal*, June 30, 1868.

political honor," with the entire California state government marked by "a moral laxness that frequently assumed the proportions of open scandal."

Less is known about dishonesty in territorial government, but charges of graft and corruption surfaced often. Indeed, it was to stem such problems that James Ashley, chairman of the House Committee on Territories, proposed his territorial bill in 1866, a bill which, when amended, became the Territorial Suffrage Act. In particular he wished to revoke the right of territorial legislatures to grant charters of incorporation. During a recent trip to the West Ashley had seen too many legislators using their power to secure special privileges for themselves or their friends, and elected officials too easily bribed by individuals or groups seeking to control aspects of territorial economy.[8] Before such evidence westerners could not fail to react, and the credibility of their officials—elective and appointive—fell dramatically.

Too often these officeholders were Republican, with radical leanings, and radicalism became suspect. Local Republicans came to conclude that radicals in Congress were retaining appointees in office solely for their support of radical aims, with little regard for personal integrity or capability. Job security, in turn, permitted officeholders to use their position for private gain. As early as October, 1867, J. Tyler Carr of Washington Territory was blaming Republican losses on corruption. The Republican party, he remarked, "is an unweeded garden, full of grass grown to seed . . . and if it does not wake itself up & weed itself out . . . God only knows what the next years of our history will have in store for us."[9] Carr feared above all that corruption among Republican officials would work to Democratic advantage, and he could envision every Republican achievement of the Reconstruction era needlessly wiped out.

Corruption was one source for concern; factionalism was another. Most notable for the West was the schism within the California

8. *Nebraska City News*, Nov. 20, 1867; Wilder, *Annals of Kansas*, 458–601 *passim*, especially 570; Robert Glass Cleland, *A History of California: The American Period* (New York, 1923), 405; *Congressional Globe*, 39 Cong. 1 Sess., 2601–2.

9. J. Tyler Carr to Clarence Bagley, Olympia, n.d., Clarence B. Bagley Papers, UWa. The correspondence most likely dates from Oct., 1867. Carr's letter, by his own acknowledgment, is a reply to Bagley's note of Sept. 5, 1867, wherein he refers to a letter just received from Eugene Semple, dated Oct. 4, 1867. See also Sayre to editor, Walla Walla, Dec. 1, 1867, in *Boise Democrat*, Dec. 11, 1867.

Republican party, but internal strife elsewhere was more usual than not. The Donnelly-Ramsey feud in Minnesota, along with the Pomeroy-Clarke attempt to deprive Ross of patronage in Kansas, the division between the pro- and anti-statehood Republicans in Colorado, and intraparty friction in Dakota—all serve as examples. Assessing the impact of party feuding, one California Republican firmly believed it responsible for the Democrats' return to power. California's support for Grant in 1868 was not to be misunderstood, he maintained. It was a personal victory for the general and nothing more, for "the same election showed a majority against the Republicans."

The western electorate in general and even many among the Republican faithful were uneasy before the marred Republican image. J. Francisco Chaves reported candidly that "the rank and file [of Republicans] are disgusted with their leaders, and I don't wonder." Republicans in Congress, he said, seemed incapable of consensus on their own legislation. From Chaves's vantage point, Democrats in Congress were having more influence than might otherwise have been expected, since they were able to present a united front. "Democrats always vote in a solid phalanx for their men and measures," wrote Chaves, almost too boldly, while Republicans "are utterly incapable of supporting and properly sustaining their party."

While many looked to faults within the Republican party as they attempted to pinpoint their disillusion, others bemoaned the quality of leadership generally—irrespective of party. One Oregon citizen saw decline in legislative leadership at both the state and national level, for politicians were abandoning principles and precedent as they sought to retain their own power. In Nebraska Henry Gere likewise saw no reason for confidence in the nation's leaders: "What a disaster it is to be accounted great in this country. Our mediocre . . . statesmen pursue the even tenor of their way, are elected to fat offices & attain great glory . . . ," while more capable individuals went without recognition.[10] Always a point of vulnerability in public officials, corruption and factionalism in this era appear to have been more than idle concern.

---

10. *Marysville Appeal*, Sept. 4, 1869; J. Francisco Chaves to Herman Heath, Washington, D.C., June 15, 1868, Chaves Papers; William G. T'Vault to Benjamin F. Dowell, Jacksonville, Ore., May 3, 1868, Dowell Papers; Henry Gere to ——, Omaha, May 9, 1868, Gere Family Papers. See also *Rocky Mountain Herald*, Feb. 29, 1868.

The growing dissatisfaction with Reconstruction developed out of less altruistic motives also. Tiring of federal reform efforts in the South, especially on behalf of blacks, westerners began to resent the time Congress was spending on southern matters. Specifically they begrudged the numerous acts designed to ensure southern loyalty and protect freedmen. By 1868 a number of westerners were complaining about the lack of federally sponsored improvements in the West, and they found their culprit in Reconstruction. One Los Angeles resident, for example, categorically described the Far Southwest as the most neglected portion of the United States. He knew the reason; only when Reconstruction in the South had ceased to absorb their attention would federal lawmakers likely improve communications and deal effectively with Indian problems in the more remote West. Similarly Utah residents were displeased that Congress by 1867 had not yet reduced the heavy wartime tax burden. The editor of the *Salt Lake Telegraph* laid the blame directly on the national legislature and its undue concern with Reconstruction. In seeking to resolve problems in the South, he charged, Congress had virtually ignored the rest of the nation.[11]

From the charge that Congress was giving too much time to the South rose a parallel indictment—that Congress was seeking to change the South too rapidly. While I. S. Kalloch in Kansas had at first staunchly defended congressional Reconstruction, by February, 1868, he was thinking that Congress had moved too quickly. "The great . . . blunder of the Republican party," decided Kalloch, "has been up to this point [too much legislation]. It has undertaken too much. It has legislated too rapidly, and therefore unsatisfactorily, both to itself and the people." Congress had been presumptive, enacting legislation without sufficient investigation and debate: it "hardly gets a reconstruction measure on its legs, before it starts another after it, and presently puts a swifter one on the track of both." Congress did not understand, said Kalloch, that "it was not within the range of its power to prevent all the ills, relieve all the difficulties, smoothe all the roughnesses, and heal all the wounds produced by our late fearful fraticidal war." Congress should have known, he argued further, that "four million slaves . . . could not all be enlightened as to their civil condition [and] preserved from

11. *Los Angeles News*, Nov. 27, 1868; *Salt Lake Telegraph*, Oct. 17, 1868.

every indignity, and ushered into the political millennium" by a Freedmen's Bureau and a civil rights act. In Kalloch's view national lawmakers ought better to "have left some things to time, the great restorer as well as the destroyer." Nor was this contention limited to Kalloch. Others were reaching the same conclusion, such as the Utahan who declared that never in the nation's history had "so many measures, fundamentally modifying the governmental institutions of the country [been] broached, urged and carried . . . since the advent of the Republican party to the controlling power."[12]

Antipathy toward reform generally was another facet of western response; simply stated, westerners of the Reconstruction era were not reform-minded. Unlike Republicans in several eastern states, particularly Massachusetts, who were motivated to alleviate wrongs where they saw them, western Republicans had virtually no desire to get involved in establishing prohibition, eradicating prostitution, or regulating business. In the East these were questions carrying moral and social import; in the West they were, more accurately, facts of life. The less stringent personal morals often associated with the new West, while condemned by some, carried no special implication for others. Attitudes would change as areas became more settled, but that time had not yet arrived for large portions of the West by 1870. In areas newly populated, local leaders tended to ignore business abuse, especially questionable practices involving railroads. Avid in their desire to secure these vital transportation links to the outside, officials often winked at such matters as excessive charges or rate discrimination. While state and territorial leaders did suggest reform legislation from time to time, their proposals garnered little support and usually carried no party endorsement. Reform efforts were minimal even in more settled areas like California and Kansas. Despite the call of both Republicans and Democrats in the California gubernatorial campaign of 1867 for an eight-hour working day, the legislature took no action to secure the advance. Indeed, the eight-hour platform was forgotten until the more radical California Workingmen's party revived it in 1872. In Kansas, while Samuel Wood's effort on behalf of woman suffrage was laudable, his incentive was not; he saw it as a means to defeat the black suffrage referendum. What better way to ensure the rejection of voting rights for blacks

12. *Western Home Journal*, Feb. 27, 1868; *Salt Lake Telegraph*, May 20, 1868.

than by tying the issue to the even more unpopular subject of ballots for women!

Labeling western Republicans as nonreformers does not impugn the motives or deny the sincerity of those in the West who truly advocated reform. It merely acknowledges that western Republicans fell behind eastern Republicans in their desire for social and economic change. In any case, Republicans tended to play down reform ideals which would likely interfere with party success at the polls. Governor Crawford understood the political barometer and was unwilling to promote black and woman suffrage in Kansas once these issues had suffered rejection in 1867; Republicans generally were unwilling to discuss black suffrage wherever it was unpopular. Much has been made of the most significant post–Civil War reform in the West— securing the ballot and the right to hold office for Wyoming women in 1869. But Republicans could take none of the credit. To a man, every member of the legislature which enacted the woman suffrage bill was a Democrat.[13]

With their interest in Reconstruction fading and their reticence on reform so evident, western Republicans spoke out less frequently about broadening civil rights for the nation's black citizens. To be sure, the more radical had not abandoned their quest for equal suffrage and offered unlimited praise for the Fifteenth Amendment when it came. To many Republicans from Oregon to Nebraska, the guarantee of manhood suffrage showed "a realization that all men are equal" and "the genius of American nationality." Still, others were growing weary of all the excitement, of the deference accorded black suffrage as an issue. Republican editor Marshall Murdock of Kansas, for one, was frankly relieved. "The Fifteenth Amendment," he wrote, "is at last the law of the land. So the colored man is no better than the rest of us . . . we hope now he may by both parties be let alone to work out his own political and social salvation without hindrance or extra laudation."[14]

---

13. Mohr (ed.), *Radical Republicans in the North*, *passim*; John Walton Caughey, *California* (New York, 1940), 453–56; T. A. Larson, *History of Wyoming* (Lincoln, Neb., 1965), 78–79; T. A. Larson, *Wyoming: A Bicentennial History* (New York, 1977), 76–77. Despite the apparent liberalism implied in woman suffrage, Larson points out that Wyoming seldom advanced the cause of women's rights in other respects. Indeed, it has often lagged behind other western states.

14. *Oregonian*, Apr. 1, 1870; *Carson Appeal*, Apr. 1, 1870; *Nebraska State Journal*, Apr. 16, 1870; *Osage Chronicle*, Apr. 2, 1870.

Westerners understood the concept of black equality to be limited within the perspective of Reconstruction: it prescribed equality before the law, nothing more. Thus even editors with radical leanings could regard the Fifteenth Amendment as a "final triumph." To their way of thinking, the quest for racial equality had been satisfied with the granting of the right to vote. Among the many who editorialized on the advent of equal suffrage, only John Speer of Kansas seemed aware that equality involved economic reassurance as well. Suffrage was only the first step; blacks needed education and economic advance just as urgently. Were they to remain illiterate and poor, asserted Speer, blacks would only serve as "mudsills" in society and their "suffrage will be a mere sentimental gratification or an article of merchandise for sidewalk politicians."[15]

On the racial question westerners were inhibited by their own perspective as well: many white westerners who advocated equal suffrage for blacks in the South had no desire to extend the same generosity to blacks elsewhere in the nation. Instead they focused upon southern blacks who, as former slaves, were being proscribed by southern whites, former rebels. Thus while radical Republicans in the West were urging equality before the law on humanitarian grounds, the less radical viewed it as a base for Republican expansion in the South or a means by which southern whites might be made to feel the power of the federal government. Still others saw suffrage as the key to preventing mistreatment of southern blacks. But as politicians and editors were aware, many of these same individuals were reluctant to enfranchise blacks in the West; they could not accept for themselves the same racial reforms they were willing to impose on the South. Minnesota did grant suffrage in 1868, but Colorado in 1865 and Kansas in 1867 each in turn refused to yield. It is true that once equal suffrage came it met almost no resistance in the West. But the mere fact that the reform had to be imposed from the outside rather than given at home indicates a double standard on racial views. Old prejudices still lingered even though the more liberal attitude of the era had done much to lessen them.

Western black spokesmen were keenly aware of the ambivalence in western racial thought, even to the point of challenging supposed

15. *Oregonian*, Apr. 1, 1870; *Carson Appeal*, Apr. 1, 1870; *Kansas Tribune*, Mar. 14, 1869.

Republican benevolence. In 1870 Henry Wagoner, Jr., of Denver pointed out that the right to vote in no way signaled the end of discrimination. Blacks themselves, said Wagoner, must now learn to compete with whites intellectually and not just at the polls. Thomas Detter in Nevada was not satisifed either. For him it was not enough that blacks had the vote; inequality would be a fact so long as there were laws excluding blacks from public health institutions and privately owned businesses. He found Republicans wanting in commitment toward broadened civil rights, and as the federal 1875 civil rights bill came up for passage, Detter was to issue a challenge from the West coast: "The great work of freedom is not completed. Nor is the mission of the Republican national party ended." Detter was severely disappointed when Congress failed to pass the bill, and he characterized the Republican party as lacking in moral courage: it "wink[ed] at" discrimination even though it had the power to remedy the evil. Still, most western blacks continued to place their confidence in the Republican party, despite its shortcomings. Indeed, they knew western Republican racial thinking to be limited but recognized too that the party had advanced civil rights further than had any previous political organization.[16]

Western leaders of the Reconstruction era were later to become critical of both national leadership and legislation for the postwar years, and tended to reflect their disillusion in personal memoirs written some twenty and thirty years afterward. Typically they regarded the quarrel between Johnson and Congress as the outstanding political development of the period and passed off the racial issue as inconsequential. George Williams of Oregon was unique among westerners in recalling the suffrage question to any extent. Strongly partisan toward the Fifteenth Amendment at the time of its passage, Williams would admit after the turn of the century that the amendment had been the most unpopular of Congress's Reconstruction measures; he questioned whether such an "unchangeable rule as to suffrage" really belonged in the Constitution at all. Blacks indeed deserved a voice in national politics, said Williams, and should several now be elected to Congress, "no harm would be done." But through

16. *Rocky Mountain News*, May 3, 1870; Rusco, *"Good Time Coming?"* 106–9; Atchison *Free Press*, Aug. 2, 1867.

the years he had come to "appreciate the feelings of white people" in the South; he could understand their wish to disfranchise blacks in areas where through their numbers they might determine local elections or serve as elected officials over whites.

With the passage of time also came a lessening of Williams's vindictive attitude toward Andrew Johnson. In 1868 Williams had attributed Johnson's acquittal to "base and treacherous influence." By 1904, however, Williams could agree that Johnson's acquittal had not been "seriously damaging to the public interest." From the vantage point of nearly forty years, he could see that Johnson's impeachment was more the result of emotionalism than any wrong the president himself had committed. Yet Williams still reproached Johnson for his numerous vetoes, which lay at the heart of his difficulties with Congress. It was ironic, thought Williams, that the president should have been impeached for violating the Tenure of Office Act— in Williams's view the least defensible measure of the era. Presidents from Washington on had regularly dismissed appointed officials without Senate approval, and Johnson in relieving Stanton of his duties "had the practice of the government . . . to back him up in his position."[17]

Cornelius Cole of California likewise blamed the impeachment crisis on overheated emotions. Johnson's quarrel with Congress had come of "the chaotic conditions of the country politically that followed the rebellion," and ought to have been avoided. Congressmen, in Cole's opinion, could better have controlled the president by placing more rigid limitations on his power. Johnson was "eccentric, impulsive and obstinate," but the ex-senator still credited him with a "kindly disposition." Cole had painful memories of the trial itself: "I voted with the majority to sustain the accusations. . . . I so decided with no pleasure and have since been glad the trial turned out as it did."[18]

Edmund G. Ross, when he was not vaunting his own role, remembered the impeachment trial primarily as an attempt by radical legislators to subordinate the chief executive to their will. But he did not exonerate the president totally. To Ross, Johnson "lacked

17. George Williams to Matthew P. Deady, Washington, D. C., June 3, 1868, Deady Papers; *Oregonian*, June 27, 1895, Jan. 7, 28, Mar. 18, June 24, Oct. 24, 1906.

18. Cole, *Memoirs*, 275–78.

his predecessor's . . . ability to direct public opinion. . . . it is not a matter of surprise that he failed to satisfy expectations, or that he passed into history as the most generally hated man by his political opponents that ever sat in the Presidential chair."[19]

William Stewart of Nevada remained adamant in his dislike for Andrew Johnson; always he begrudged the president his veto of the Civil Rights Act despite promise of support. Sometime afterward, upon Johnson's return to the Senate in 1875, the two had a chance encounter. Meeting Johnson face to face in the Patent Office, Stewart was suddenly so angered that he very nearly attacked the ex-president physically; only the intervention of clerks at hand prevented a scandal. Stewart expressed no remorse in recalling the scene years later, so firm was his disregard for Johnson. Said he, "The world will never know the extent of the misfortune to which the people of the United States, particularly to the South, sustained by the substitution of Andrew Johnson for Abraham Lincoln. Lincoln was the wisest, kindest, most impartial and just man I ever knew; Johnson was the most untruthful, treacherous, and cruel person who ever held place or power in the United States. I voted to impeach him, and I would do it again."[20]

As freely as they discussed Johnson in retrospect, few western leaders criticized the Republican party itself. Most simply remained within its ranks and loyal to its cause. Edmund Ross did not prove so faithful; he drifted into the Democratic party and was eventually to serve as governor of New Mexico Territory under Grover Cleveland. On radicals and their quest for impeachment, the embittered Ross did not mince words: ". . . political leaders of the time were ill equipped to meet the issue." They were, according to Ross, unable to divorce themselves from party dictates, and they acted with ill-timed haste and too much emotion. Among the rank and file of Republicans were many who could accept Ross's assessment because they had believed it themselves for years. George W. Brown was one: a militant antislavery editor in Kansas during the 1850s, he was an outspoken propagandist for the early Republican party in the state. But from 1868 on, Brown admitted, he had "never voted for the party." His disdain came partly from the attempt to remove Johnson

19. Ross, "Political Leaders," 219, 234.
20. Stewart, *Reminiscences*, 200–201.

from office, partly from the belief that leading Republicans had become too political and less than reform-minded.[21] Brown's defection, like Ross's, was of little importance as far as Republican political dominance in the West was concerned, but, written in 1901, it attested to the lasting enmity which postwar Republicanism had inspired among some of its early and most ardent followers.

Amidst the complexity of thought on Reconstruction—much of it critical toward Johnson and the radicals—emerged a note of confidence. Richard Chute of Minnesota envied congressmen their role in the Thirty-eighth and Thirty-ninth Congresses. Glowingly he praised their accomplishments and exclaimed, "What history has been made in that epoch!" George Cannon, a Mormon and editor of the *Deseret News*, actually found little to applaud in Congress's Reconstruction policy or in its attempts to control polygamy. But still he could evaluate the era optimistically: "Whatever may be said in the future of the present long domination of the Republican party, in the legislation of the nation, commencing with the first term of Abraham Lincoln, one thing is certain, it will ever be memorable in the history of the country as the period during which slavery in the Union was abolished, and during which the millions of emancipated blacks were enfranchised and raised to the status, in the eyes of the law, equal with that of the white man."[22]

Few would disagree. Despite its power struggles and emotionalism, the Republican party did indeed bring to the nation humanitarian reform significant for its time. Western Republicans had done their part in making the reform possible. With only nominal resistance from Democrats, westerners serving in the national legislature gave their full backing to Reconstruction measures. Perhaps this support appears surprising inasmuch as western Republican attitudes on Reconstruction varied so widely; still, in this respect the West differed little from the North. In neither sector did the Republican electorate always know its own mind on Reconstruction. Its radicalism or conservatism might depend upon the issues involved, and its ideals change with the progression of time. Yet westerners were proud,

21. Ross, *History of the Impeachment*, 20; George W. Brown to Edmund G. Ross, Rockford, Ill., Dec. 19, 1901, Edmund G. Ross Papers, NMRC.

22. Richard Chute to Ignatius Donnelly, St. Anthony, Minn., Jan. 27, 1868, Donnelly Papers; *Deseret News*, Apr. 7, 1870.

sometimes defiant but vitally concerned as the nation moved toward resolution of its postwar problems.

Contrary to the West of legend and popular history, the post–Civil War West was cognizant of national affairs, with its citizenry active and speaking out on the issues. Westerners were, after all, tied to the East by birth. From the midwestern and eastern quadrants and, to a lesser extent, from the rebel South they had come, for whatever reason, to relocate in the West. It was only natural that they retain concern for developments in the eastern part of the country. But there was more. In displaying so avid an interest for the nation restored, westerners reflected not so much their own disparate backgrounds as a feeling for the whole. Like their countrymen in the North and Unionists in the South, westerners were in fact experiencing the new nationalism characteristic of the time.

Appendix

VOTES OF WESTERN REPRESENTATIVES IN CONGRESS
ON RECONSTRUCTION MEASURES

SYMBOLS:
X = Yea vote   R = Republican
O = Nay vote   U = Unionist
A = Absent or no vote   D = Democrat
given

Thirty-eighth Congress

VOTE NUMBER

SENATE:	1	2	3	4	5	6	7	8	9	10	11	12	13	14	15	16	17
John Conness, R, Calif.	x																
James McDougall, D, Calif.	x																
Samuel Pomeroy, R, Kans.	x																
James Lane, R, Kans.	x																
Morton Wilkinson, R, Minn.	x																
Alexander Ramsey, R, Minn.	x																
James Nesmith, U, Ore.	o																
Benjamin Harding, R, Ore.	o																

HOUSE:																	
Cornelius Cole, R, Calif.	x																
William Higby, R, Calif.	x																
Thomas Shannon, R, Calif.	x																
A. Carter Wilder, R, Kans.	x																
Ignatius Donnelly, R, Minn.	x																
William Windom, R, Minn.	x																
John McBride, R, Calif.	x																

Thirty-ninth Congress

VOTE NUMBER

SENATE:

	1	2	3	4	5	6	7	8	9	10	11	12	13	14	15	16	17
John Conness, R, Calif.	x	x	x	x	x	x	x				x		x		x		
James McDougall, D, Calif.	o	o	o	o	o	o	A				A		o		A		
Samuel Pomeroy, R, Kans.	x	x	x	x	x	x	x				A		A		x		
James Lane, R, Kans.	A	x	A	x	o	x											
Edmund G. Ross, R, Kans.							x				A		x		x		
Alexander Ramsey, R, Minn.	x	x	x	x	x	x	x				A		x		x		
Daniel Norton, U, Minn.	A	o	o	o	o	o	o				A		A		A		
William Stewart, R, Nev.	x	o	x	x	x	x	x				x		x		x		
James Nye, R, Nev.	x	x	x	x	x	x	A				A		A		A		
James Nesmith, U, Ore.	A	o	o	o	o	o	o				A		A		o		
George Williams, R, Ore.	x	x	x	x	x	x	x				x		x		x		

HOUSE:

	1	2	3	4	5	6	7	8	9	10	11	12	13	14	15	16	17
Donald McRuer, R, Calif.	x		x	x	x	x	x	A	x				x		x		
John Bidwell, R, Calif.	x		x	x	x	x	A	x	x				x		x		
William Higby, R, Calif.	x		x	x	x	x	x	x	x				x		x		
Sidney Clarke, R, Kans.	x		x	x	x	x	x	x	x				x		x		
William Windom, R, Minn.	x		x	x	x	x	x	x	x				x		x		
Ignatius Donnelly, R, Minn.	x		x	x	x	x	x	x	x				x		x		
Delos Ashley, R, Nev.	x		x	A	x	x	x	o	A				x		x		
James Henderson, R, Ore.	x		x	A	x	x	x	A	A				x		x		

Fortieth Congress

VOTE NUMBER

SENATE:	1	2	3	4	5	6	7	8	9	10	11	12	13	14	15	16	17
John Conness, R, Calif.													X	A	A		X
Cornelius Cole, R, Calif.													X	X	X		X
Samuel Pomeroy, R, Kans.													A	X	X		A
Edmund G. Ross, R, Kans.													X	A	X		A
Alexander Ramsey, R, Minn.													A	X	X		X
Daniel Norton, U, Minn.													A	O	A		O
John Thayer, R, Nebr.													X	X	X		X
Thomas Tipton, R, Nebr.													X	X	X		X
William Stewart, R, Nev.													X	A	X		X
James Nye, R, Nev.													X	X	X		X
George Williams, R, Ore.													X	A	X		X
Henry Corbett, R, Ore.													X	A	X		A

HOUSE:	1	2	3	4	5	6	7	8	9	10	11	12	13	14	15	16	17
William Higby, R, Calif.													A	A	A	X	X
Samuel Axtell, D, Calif.													A	A	O	O	O
James Johnson, D, Calif.													A	A	O	O	O
Sidney Clarke, R, Kans.													A	X	X	X	X
William Windom, R, Minn.													X	X	A	X	X
Ignatius Donnelly, R, Minn.													X	X	A	X	X
John Taffee, R, Nebr.													A	X	X	X	X
Delos Ashley, R, Nev.													X	A	X	X	X
Rufus Mallory, R, Ore.													X	A	A	X	O

VOTE NUMBERS:

1. Wade-Davis bill (HR244). Passed House, May 4, 1866; passed Senate, July 1, 1864. *Congressional Globe*, 38 Cong., 2 Sess., 2180, 3461.
2. Extension of the Freedmen's Bureau bill (S60). Passed House, Feb. 6,

1866; passed Senate as amended by House, Feb. 8, 1866. *Ibid.*, 39 Cong., 1 Sess., 688, 747.

3. Vote to override Johnson's veto of Freedmen's Bureau bill. On Feb. 20, 1866, Johnson returned the bill along with his objections to the Senate, the house of origin. Because senators were unable to secure the two-thirds vote needed to override, action terminated in the upper house. *Ibid.*, 943.

4. House resolution to reconsider Johnson's veto of the Freedmen's Bureau bill and a call to override the veto (HR613). Passed both houses, July 16, 1866. *Ibid.*, 3842, 3850.

5. Civil Rights Act (SB61). Passed Senate, Feb. 2, 1866; passed House, Mar. 13, 1866. *Ibid.*, 606–7, 1367.

6. Vote to override Johnson's veto of the Civil Rights Act. Vote in the Senate taken on Apr. 6, 1866, in the House on Apr. 9, 1866. *Ibid.*, 1809, 1861.

7. Fourteenth Amendment (HR127). Passed Senate, with amendment, June 8, 1866; House accepted Senate version on June 13, 1866. *Ibid.*, 3042, 3149.

8. Act granting equal suffrage in the District of Columbia (S1). Passed Senate, Dec. 13, 1866; passed House, Dec. 14, 1866. *Ibid.*, 39 Cong., 2 Sess., 109, 138.

9. Bill to regulate government in the territories, including the granting of equal suffrage (HR508). Passed House, May 15, 1866; tabled in Senate and no roll call vote taken. *Ibid.*, 39 Cong., 1 Sess., 2602–3, 3525.

10. Territorial Suffrage Act (HR508 amended). An amended version of the previous bill which deleted all provisions except the one granting equal suffrage in all territories. Passed both houses, Jan. 10, 1867. *Ibid.*, 39 Cong., 2 Sess., 382, 399.

11. Tenure of Office Act (S453). Votes recorded were taken on motions in the Senate (Feb. 23, 1867) and in the House (Feb. 19, 1867) to accept the version of the bill as reported by a joint conference committee. *Ibid.*, 1340, 1518.

12. First Reconstruction Act—final vote (HR1143). Passed House with amendments, Feb. 15, 1867; Senate approved House amendments, Feb. 20, 1867. *Ibid.*, 1400, 1645.

13. Second Reconstruction Act (HR33). Passed Senate with amendments, Mar. 16, 1867; House accepted amended bill, Mar. 18, 1867. *Ibid.*, 40 Cong., 1 Sess., 171, 190.

14. Third Reconstruction Act (HR123). Passed Senate with amendment, July 13, 1867; House accepted amended bill, July 13, 1867. *Ibid.*, 628, 638.

15. Fourth Reconstruction Act (HR214). Passed Senate with amendment, Feb. 25, 1868; House accepted amended bill, Feb. 26, 1868. *Ibid.*, 40 Cong., 2 Sess., 1417, 1453.

16. Vote in the House of Representatives to impeach President Johnson, Feb. 24, 1868. *Ibid.*, 1400.

17. Fifteenth Amendment (SR8). Votes recorded were taken on motions in the House (Feb. 25, 1869) and in the Senate (Feb. 26, 1869) to accept the amendment as reported by a joint conference committee. *Ibid.*, 40 Cong., 3 Sess., 1564, 1641.

Bibliography

Manuscript Sources

COLLECTIONS AND PAPERS

Anderson Family Papers. Kansas State Historical Society.
Applegate Family Papers. Oregon Historical Society.
Clarence B. Bagley Papers. University of Washington.
Daniel Bagley Papers. University of Washington.
William W. Bailey Letter. Huntington Miscellaneous Collection, Huntington Library.
David W. Ballard Papers. Beinecke Library.
Annie E. Bidwell Papers. California State Library.
John Bidwell Papers. Bancroft Library.
John Bidwell Papers. California State University at Chico.
Francis P. Blair Family Papers. Manuscript Division, Library of Congress.
Henry Goode Blasdel Papers. Nevada State Historical Society.
James Madison Bowler and Family Papers. Minnesota Historical Society.
John Stillman Brown Family Papers. Kansas State Historical Society.
William Newton Byers Letterbooks. Western Collection, University of Colorado.
Zachariah Chandler Papers. Manuscript Division, Library of Congress.
Samuel M. Chapman Papers. Nebraska State Historical Society.
Salmon P. Chase Papers. Manuscript Division, Library of Congress.
J. Francisco Chaves Papers. Arizona Historical Society.
Henry Harmon Clark Papers. Montana Historical Society.
Joseph and Elvira Cody Papers. Kansas Collection, University of Kansas.
Cornelius Cole Papers. University of California at Los Angeles.
Henry W. Corbett Papers. Oregon Historical Society.
David Watson Craig Papers. Oregon Historical Society.
Samuel Crawford Correspondence. Governor's Papers, Kansas State Historical Society.
George Law Curry Papers. Oregon Historical Society.
Samuel R. Curtis Papers. Beinecke Library.
Cushman Kellogg Davis and Family Papers. Minnesota Historical Society.
Matthew Paul Deady Papers. Oregon Historical Society.
Walter W. DeLacy Papers. Montana Historical Society.
James Denver Papers. Kansas Collection, University of Kansas.
Ignatius Donnelly Papers. Minnesota Historical Society.

James Rood Doolittle Papers. Manuscript Division, Library of Congress.
Alfred Doten Diaries and Papers. University of Nevada.
Benjamin F. Dowell Papers. Oregon Historical Society.
John Van Deusen DuBois Papers. Beinecke Library.
Sidney Edgerton Family Papers. Montana Historical Society.
Edward Eggleston Papers. Minnesota Historical Society.
Elwood Evans Papers. Beinecke Library.
Thomas E. Ewing Family Papers. Manuscript Division, Library of Congress.
Thomas Ewing, Jr., Papers. Kansas State Historical Society.
Andrew Jackson Faulk Papers. Beinecke Library.
William Pitt Fessenden Papers. Manuscript Division, Library of Congress.
Andrew Jackson Fisk Papers. Montana Historical Society.
Fisk Family Papers. Montana Historical Society.
Robert W. Furnas Papers. Nebraska State Historical Society.
Selucius Garfielde Papers. University of Washington.
Charles Henry Gere Family Papers. Nebraska State Historical Society.
Addison Crandall Gibbs Papers. Oregon Historical Society.
Isaac T. Goodnow Papers. Kansas State Historical Society.
Handford L. Gordon Papers. Minnesota Historical Society.
Lafayette Grover Papers. Oregon Historical Society.
Henry Haight Papers. Huntington Library.
William D. Hale and Family Papers. Minnesota Historical Society.
Frank Hall Papers. Colorado State Historical Society.
Frank Hall Papers. Western Collection, Denver Public Library.
Samuel T. Hauser Papers. Montana Historical Society.
Cornelius Hedges Family Papers. Montana Historical Society.
Vinnie Ream Hoxie Papers. Manuscript Division, Library of Congress.
David Jacks Papers. Stanford University.
Andrew Johnson Papers. Manuscript Division, Library of Congress.
Thomas Perkins Kennard Papers. Nebraska State Historical Society.
William Smith King Papers. Minnesota Historical Society.
Franklin Kirkaldie Papers. Montana Historical Society.
James H. Lane Papers. Kansas Collection, University of Kansas.
James H. Lane Papers. Kansas State Historical Society.
Louis E. Larson and Family Papers. Minnesota Historical Society.
Charles B. Lines Papers. Kansas State Historical Society.
Robert R. Livingston Papers. Nebraska State Historical Society.
James Lomax Papers. Montana Historical Society.
Hugh McCulloch Papers. Manuscript Division, Library of Congress.
Thornton F. McElroy Family Papers. University of Washington.
John McGilvra Papers. University of Washington.
John Rogers Maltby Papers. Nebraska State Historical Society.

Samuel Maxwell Papers. Nebraska State Historical Society.
Thomas Francis Meagher Papers. Montana Historical Society.
John F. Miller Papers. Stanford University.
William Winlock Miller Papers. Beinecke Library.
Frederick William Mitchell Papers. Beinecke Library.
Thomas Montogomery Papers. Minnesota Historical Society.
Thomas Moonlight Papers. Beinecke Library.
J. Sterling Morton Papers. Nebraska State Historical Society.
James Willis Nesmith Papers. Oregon Historical Society.
James Warren Nye Papers. Nevada State Historical Society.
E. O. C. Ord Papers. Stanford University.
Oregon Historical Society Miscellaneous Collection.
William Pickering Papers. Beinecke Library.
Edward L. Plumb Papers. Stanford University.
Samuel Clarke Pomeroy Papers. Kansas Collection, University of Kansas.
Samuel Clarke Pomeroy Papers. Kansas State Historical Society.
Charles D. Poston Papers. Arizona Historical Society.
Alexander Ramsey Papers. Minnesota Historical Society.
William G. Ritch Collection. Huntington Library.
Charles Robinson Papers. Kansas Collection, University of Kansas.
Charles and Sara T. D. Robinson Papers. Kansas State Historical Society.
William S. Rosecrans Papers. University of California at Los Angeles.
Edmund G. Ross Papers. Kansas State Historical Society.
Edmund G. Ross Papers. New Mexico Records Center and Archives.
Wilbur Fisk Sanders Papers. Montana Historical Society.
Eugene Semple Papers. University of Washington.
William Shafter Papers. Stanford University.
George M. Shearer Papers. Idaho State Historical Society.
John Sherman Papers. Manuscript Division, Library of Congress.
Edwin McMasters Stanton Papers. Manuscript Division, Library of Congress.
Frederick Steele Papers. Stanford University.
Thaddeus Stevens Papers. Manuscript Division, Library of Congress.
James and Granville Stuart Papers. Beinecke Library.
Charles Sumner Papers. Houghton Library.
Lyman Trumbull Papers. Manuscript Division, Library of Congress.
John Palmer Usher Papers. Kansas State Historical Society.
Benjamin Franklin Wade Papers. Manuscript Division, Library of Congress.
William Henson Wallace Papers. Idaho State Historical Society.
Elihu Washburne Papers. Manuscript Division, Library of Congress.
William F. Wheeler Papers. Montana Historical Society.
George A. Whitney Papers. Nevada State Historical Society.
Augustus Wildman Papers. Beinecke Library.

George H. Williams Papers. Oregon Historical Society.
William Windom Papers. Manuscript Division, Library of Congress.
Woman Suffrage Papers. Kansas State Historical Society.
Samuel Newitt Wood Papers. Kansas State Historical Society.
George Burdick Wright and Family Papers. Minnesota Historical Society.
Brigham Young Papers. Beinecke Library.

STATEMENTS AND JOURNALS

Christopher Columbus Andrew Diary. Minnesota Historical Society.
John Bidwell Diary. Bancroft Library.
John Bidwell Diaries. California State Library.
John Rudd Brown Diaries. California State Library.
Sara E. Canfield Diary. Montana Historical Society.
William Berry Cross Diaries. California State Library.
Cornelius Hedges Diaries. Montana Historical Society.
Henry Mills Moore Journals. Beinecke Library.
James and Granville Stuart Diaries. Beinecke Library.
Recollections of George L. Woods. Bancroft Library.

OFFICIAL MANUSCRIPTS

Idaho, Territory of. Executive Records of Idaho Territory from March, 1863, to October, 1874. Idaho State Historical Society.
————. Idaho Territorial Papers. Idaho State Historical Society.
U.S. Bureau of the Census. "Population Schedules of the Ninth Census of the United States, 1870: Colorado." National Archives, Record Group 29.
U.S. Congress, Senate. Territorial Papers of the U.S. Senate: Arizona, 1857–1865. National Archives, Record Group 46.
————. Territorial Papers of the U.S. Senate: Colorado, 1860–1868. National Archives, Record Group 46.
————. Territorial Papers of the U.S. Senate: Dakota, 1858–1873. National Archives, Record Group 46.
————. Territorial Papers of the U.S. Senate: Idaho, 1863–1871. National Archives, Record Group 46.
————. Territorial Papers of the U.S. Senate: Montana, 1863–1869. National Archives, Record Group 46.
————. Territorial Papers of the U.S. Senate: Nebraska, 1853–1867. National Archives, Record Group 46.
————. Territorial Papers of the U.S. Senate: Oregon, 1824–1871. National Archives, Record Group 46.
————. Territorial Papers of the U.S. Senate: Utah, 1849–1870. National Archives, Record Group 46.

————. Territorial Papers of the U.S. Senate: Washington, 1853–1868. National Archives, Record Group 46.

————. Territorial Papers of the U.S. Senate: Wyoming, 1869–1871. National Archives, Record Group 46.

————. Records of the U.S. Senate: Nomination Files from 39 Congress (39B-A4). National Archives, Record Group 46.

————. Records of the U.S. Senate: Nomination Files from 40 Congress (40B-A5). National Archives, Record Group 46.

U.S. Department of Interior. Interior Department Territorial Papers: Dakota, 1863–1887. National Archives, Record Group 48.

————. Interior Department Territorial Papers: Washington, 1854–1902. National Archives, Record Group 48.

U.S. Department of Justice. General Records of the Department of Justice: Records Relating to the Appointment of Federal Judges, Marshals and Attorneys, 1853–1901: Nebraska. National Archives, Record Group 60.

————. General Records of the Department of Justice: Records Relating to the Appointment of Federal Judges, Marshals and Attorneys, 1853–1901: Nevada, Colorado, Arizona, New Mexico. National Archives, Record Group 60.

U.S. Department of State. Domestic Letters of the Department of State, 1865–1870. National Archives, Record Group 59.

————. Letters of Application and Recommendation during the Administrations of Abraham Lincoln and Andrew Johnson, 1861–1869. National Archives, Record Group 59.

————. State Department Territorial Papers: Arizona, 1864–1872. National Archives, Record Group 59.

————. State Department Territorial Papers: Colorado Series, vol. I, 1859–1874. National Archives, Record Group 59.

————. State Department Territorial Papers: Dakota, 1861–1873. National Archives, Record Group 59.

————. State Department Territorial Papers: Idaho, 1863–1872. National Archives, Record Group 59.

————. State Department Territorial Papers: Montana, 1864–1872. National Archives, Record Group 59.

————. State Department Territorial Papers: Nebraska, 1854–1867. National Archives, Record Group 59.

————. State Department Territorial Papers: New Mexico, 1851–1872. National Archives, Record Group 59.

————. State Department Territorial Papers: Utah, 1860–1873. National Archives, Record Group 59.

————. State Department Territorial Papers: Washington, 1859–1872. National Archives, Record Group 59.

————. State Department Territorial Papers: Wyoming, 1868–1873. National Archives, Record Group 59.

U.S. Department of the Treasury. General Records of the Treasury Department: Records Relating to Assessors of Internal Revenue: California. National Archives, Record Group 56.

————. Office of the Director of the Mint. Records of the Bureau of the Mint: Appointments and Removals, April, 1873–February, 1879. National Archives, Record Group 104.

Newspapers

ARIZONA

Prescott *Daily Arizona Miner.*
Prescott *Weekly Journal-Miner.*
Tucson *Weekly Arizona Citizen.*
Tucson *Weekly Arizonian.*

CALIFORNIA

Auburn *Stars and Stripes.*
Chico *Weekly Courant.*
Weekly Colusa Sun.
Downieville *Sierra Advocate.*
Eureka *Humboldt Times.*
Los Angeles Semi-Weekly News.
Marysville *Daily Appeal.*
Monterey *Gazette.*
Napa (City) *Register.*
Napa *County Reporter.*
Oakland *Daily News.*
Oroville *Weekly Union Record.*
Petaluma *Journal & Argus.*
Placerville *Mountain Democrat.*
Red Bluff *Weekly Sentinel.*
Sacramento *Daily Bee.*
Sacramento Daily Union.
San Francisco *Daily Alta California.*
San Francisco *Daily Dramatic Chronicle.*
San Francisco *Daily Examiner.*
San Francisco *Daily Morning Call.*
San Francisco *Elevator.*
San Francisco *Evening Bulletin.*

San Francisco *Golden Era.*
Santa Rosa *Sonoma County Democrat.*
Yreka Journal.
Yreka Union.

COLORADO

Black Hawk *Daily Mining Journal.*
Central City *Daily Colorado Times.*
Central City *Daily Miner's Register.*
Denver Daily.
Denver *Daily Colorado Tribune.*
Denver *Daily Gazette.*
Denver *Daily Rocky Mountain News.*
Denver *Rocky Mountain Herald.*
Golden *Colorado Transcript.*

DAKOTA

Yankton *Weekly Dakotan.*
Yankton *Union and Dakotan.*

IDAHO

Bannock *Boise News.*
Boise Democrat.
Boise *Idaho Tri-Weekly Statesman.*
Idaho (City) *World.*
Lewiston Journal.
Silver City *Owyhee Avalanche.*
Silver City *Semi-Weekly Tidal Wave.*

ILLINOIS

Chicago Tribune.

KANSAS

Atchison *Champion & Press.*
Atchison *Daily Champion.*
Atchison *Daily Free Press.*
Atchison *Freedom's Champion.*
Burlingame *Weekly Osage
 Chronicle.*
Burlington *Kansas Weekly Patriot.*
Coffeyville *Ross's Paper.*
Cotton Falls *Chase County Banner.*
Council Grove *Democrat.*
Emporia News.
Fort Scott *Weekly Monitor.*
Iola *Allen County Courant.*
Junction City Union.
Lawrence *Kansas Daily Tribune.*
Leavenworth *Daily Conservative.*
Leavenworth *Daily Times.*
Manhattan *Independent.*
Marysville *Enterprise.*
Mound City *Border Sentinel.*
Olathe *Mirror.*
Ottawa *Western Home Journal.*
Topeka *Kansas Farmer.*
Topeka *State Record.*
Topeka *Tribune.*
Troy *Weekly Reporter.*
Wathena Reporter.
White Cloud Kansas Chief.
Wyandotte Commercial Gazette.

MINNESOTA

Brownsville *Western Progress.*
Faribault *Central Republican.*
Hastings Gazette.
Mankato Union.
Mankato *Weekly Record.*
Mantorville Express.
Minneapolis Chronicle.

Minneapolis Daily Tribune.
Minneapolis *State Atlas.*
Owatonna Journal.
Rochester Post.
St. Charles *Herald.*
St. Paul *Daily Pioneer.*
St. Paul *Dispatch.*
St. Paul *Northwestern Chronicle.*
St. Paul *Press.*
St. Paul *Rural Minnesotian.*
Shakopee Spy.
Wabasha Herald.
Winona Daily Republican.

MONTANA

Helena Herald.
Helena *Montana Radiator.*
Virginia City *Montana Democrat.*
Virginia City *Montana Post.*

NEBRASKA

Arago *Southern Nebraskian.*
Brownville *Nebraska Advertiser.*
Fremont *Weekly Tribune.*
Lincoln *Nebraska Commonwealth.*
Lincoln *Nebraska State Journal.*
Nebraska City News.
Nebraska (City) Statesman.
Omaha *Daily Nebraska Republican.*
Omaha *Republican.*
Omaha *Weekly Herald.*
Plattsmouth *Nebraska Herald.*

NEVADA

Aurora *Esmeralda Union.*
Austin *Daily Reese River Reveille.*
Belmont *Mountain Champion.*
Belmont *Silver Bend Weekly
 Reporter.*
Carson (City) *Daily Appeal.*
Carson City *Nevada State Journal.*
Elko Independent.
Gold Hill Daily News.

Virginia City *Daily Territorial Enterprise.*
Virginia (City) *Daily Union.*
Washoe City *Eastern Slope.*

NEW MEXICO

Santa Fe *New Mexican.*
Santa Fe *Weekly Gazette.*

NEW YORK

New York Times.
New York Tribune.

OREGON

Albany *States Rights Democrat.*
Corvallis *Gazette.*
The Dalles *Weekly Mountaineer.*
Eugene *Guard.*
Eugene *Oregon State Journal.*
Jacksonville Reveille.
Jacksonville *Oregon Reporter.*
Jacksonville *Southern Oregon Press.*
Oregon City Enterprise.
Portland *Morning Oregonian.*
Portland *Oregon Herald.*
Salem *American Unionist.*

Salem Daily Record.
Salem *Oregon Statesman.*
Salem *Weekly Democratic Review.*

UTAH

Corrine *Utah Reporter.*
St. George *Rio Virgin Times.*
Salt Lake City *Daily Union Vedette.*
Salt Lake City *Desert Evening News.*
Salt Lake Daily Telegraph.

WASHINGTON

Olympia *Commercial Age.*
Olympia *Daily Tribune.*
Olympia *Echo.*
Olympia *Pacific Tribune.*
Olympia *Territorial Republican.*
Olympia Transcript.
Olympia *Union Guard.*
Olympia *Washington Standard.*
Port Townsend *Weekly Message.*
Seattle *Weekly Gazette.*
Seattle *Weekly Intelligencer.*
Vancouver Register.
Walla Walla Statesman.

Published Sources and Documents

Address to the People of Oregon, by the Retiring Members of the Legislative Assembly, Giving Their Reasons for Their Resignation in That Body. Salem, 1868 (Pamphlet, Beinecke Library).

Address to the Voters of Kansas [on the proposed Amendments to the State Constitution, 1867]. N.p., n.d. (Pamphlet, Beinecke Library).

Ballard, David W. *Governor's Veto Message* [of the Bill Prescribing the Legislative Loyalty Oath]. Boise, Idaho, 1866 (Pamphlet, Beinecke Library).

Basler, Roy P. (ed.). *The Collected Works of Abraham Lincoln.* 9 vols. New Brunswick, N.J., 1953.

Bigelow, John (ed.). *The Letters and Literary Memorials of Samuel J. Tilden.* 2 vols. New York, 1908.

Blaine, James G. *Twenty Years of Congress: From Lincoln to Garfield.* 2 vols. Norwich, Conn., 1893.

Blegen, Theodore (ed.). *The Land of Their Choice: The Immigrants Write Home*. Minneapolis, 1955.

Bowles, Samuel. *Across the Continent: A Summer's Journey to the Rocky Mountains, the Mormons, and the Pacific States*. Springfield, Mass., 1865.

Brace, Charles Loring. *The New West: Or, California in 1867–1868*. New York, 1869.

California National Union State Central Committee. *Address of the National Union State Central Committee, September 26, 1866*. San Francisco, 1866 (Pamphlet, Bancroft Library).

California, State of. *Journal of the House of Representatives of the State of California*, 1865–66, 1867–68, 1869–70 (Title and imprint vary).

————. *Journal of the Senate of the State of California*, 1865–66, 1867–68, 1869–70 (Title and imprint vary).

————. "Minority Report of the Assembly Committee on Federal Relations Recommending the Adoption of a Substitute for the Assembly Concurrent Resolution No. 58, approving the action of the majority of the United States Senate in Refusing to Sanction the President's Veto of the Freedmen's Bureau Bill," in *Appendix to the Journals of the Senate and Assembly of the Sixteenth Session of the Legislature of the State of California*, No. 52. Sacramento, 1866.

————. "Minority Report of the Committee on Federal Relations concerning Electoral Votes of States organized under the Reconstruction Acts of Congress," in *Appendix to Journals of the Senate and Assembly of the Seventeenth Session of the Legislature of California*, No. 10. Sacramento, 1868.

Casserly, Eugene. *Speech on the Fifteenth Amendment and the Labor Question, Delivered in San Francisco, California, July 28, 1869*. N.p., n.d. (Pamphlet, University of California at Los Angeles).

————. *The Issues of the Contest. Speech of Hon. Eugene Casserly in San Francisco, August 19, 1868. . . .* San Francisco, 1868 (Pamphlet, Bancroft Library).

Cole, Cornelius. *Memoirs of Cornelius Cole, Ex-Senator of the United States from California*. New York, 1908.

Colorado, Territory of. *General Laws, Joint Resolutions, Memorials, and Private Acts . . . of the Legislative Assembly*, First Session (1861), Third Session (1864), Fourth Session (1865), Fifth Session (1866), and Sixth Session (1867) (Title and imprint vary).

————. *Journal of the Legislative Council of the Territory of Colorado, Fifth Session*. Central City, 1866.

————. *Journal of the House of Representatives of the Territory of Colorado*, 1866, 1867, 1868, 1870 (Title and imprint vary).

————. *Provisional Laws and Joint Resolutions . . . of the General Assembly of Jefferson Territory*. Omaha, 1860.

Constitution of Freedom's Defenders of the State of California. San Francisco, 1867 (Pamphlet, Beinecke Library).

Cox, Samuel S. Union—Disunion—Reunion. Three Decades of Federal Legislation, 1855–1885. San Francisco, 1885.

Crawford, Samuel J. Kansas in the Sixties. Chicago, 1911.

Davis, Winfield. History of Political Conventions in California, 1849–1892. Sacramento, 1893.

The Federal Cases Comprising Cases Argued and Determined in the Circuit and District Courts of the United States. Vol. XXIV. St. Paul, Minn., 1896.

Gorham, George C. Speech Delivered by George C. Gorham of San Francisco, Union Nominee for Governor at Platt's Hall, San Francisco, July 10, 1867. San Francisco, 1867 (Pamphlet, Bancroft Library).

Goulder, W. A. Reminiscences: Incidents in the Life of a Pioneer in Oregon and Idaho. Boise, 1909.

[Haight, Henry]. Message of the Governor in Relation to Senate Resolutions Condemning the Course of President Johnson, March 4, 1868. Sacramento, 1868 (Pamphlet, Huntington Library).

———. Speech of Governor Haight, at the Democratic State Convention at Sacramento, June 29, 1869. San Francisco, 1869 (Pamphlet, University of California at Los Angeles).

———. Speech of H. H. Haight, Esq., Democratic Candidate for Governor, Delivered at the Great Democratic Mass Meeting at Union Hall, Tuesday Evening, July 9, 1867. N.p., n.d. (Pamphlet, Bancroft Library).

Hawes, Horace. Horace Hawes, Independent Candidate for Joint Senator for the City and County of San Francisco and County of San Mateo. His Reply. . . . San Francisco, 1867 (Pamphlet, Bancroft Library).

Hollister, Ovando J. The Mines of Colorado. Springfield, Mass., 1867.

Julian, George W. Political Recollections, 1840–1872. Chicago, 1884.

Kansas, State of. Journal of the House of Representatives of the State of Kansas, 1864, 1866, 1867, 1868, 1869, 1870 (Title and imprint vary).

———. Journal of the Senate of the State of Kansas, 1867, 1868, 1869, 1870 (Title and imprint vary).

Kendrick, Benjamin G. The Journal of the Joint Committee of Fifteen on Reconstruction. New York, 1914.

Layres, Augustus. A Defense of the Reconstruction Act of Congress. San Francisco, 1868 (Pamphlet, Huntington Library).

Lewis, E[dward] J. Speech of Hon. E. J. Lewis on Reconstruction, Delivered in the Senate of the State of California, March 2, 1868. N.p., n.d. (Pamphlet, Bancroft Library).

Low, Frederick F. Some Reflections of an Early California Governor Contained in a Short Dictated Memoir between Governor Low and Hubert Howe Bancroft. Sacramento, 1883.

Mallory, Rufus. *Speech of Hon. Rufus Mallory, of Oregon, on the Impeachment of the President*. Salem, 1868 (Pamphlet, Beinecke Library).

Mass Meeting of the Friends of President Johnson [in Helena, Montana]. N.p., n.d. (Broadside, Beinecke Library).

Minnesota, State of. *Journal of the House of Representatives of the State of Minnesota*, 1868, 1869, 1870 (Title and imprint vary).

———. *Journal of the Senate of the State of Minnesota*, 1868, 1869, 1870 (Title and imprint vary).

Murray, Donald M., and Robert M. Rodney. "The Letters of Peter Bryant, Jackson County Pioneer: First Installment, 1862–1902." *Kansas Historical Quarterly*, XXVII (Winter, 1961), 469–96.

Nebraska, State of. *Journal of the House of Representatives of the State of Nebraska*, 1867, Special Session 1870 (Title and imprint vary).

———. *Journal of the Senate of the State of Nebraska*, Special Session 1870. Omaha, 1870.

Nebraska, Territory of. *Journal of the House of Representatives of the Territory of Nebraska, 12th Session*. Omaha, 1867.

———. *Journal of the Legislative Council of the Territory of Nebraska, 12th Session*. Omaha, 1867.

Nevada, State of. *Journal of the House of Representatives of the State of Nevada*, 1866, 1867, 1869 (Title and imprint vary).

———. *Journal of the Senate of the State of Nevada*, 1869. Carson City, 1869.

Oregon, State of. *Journal of the House of Representatives of the State of Oregon*, Special Session 1865, 1866, 1868, 1870 (Title and imprint vary).

———. *Journal of the Senate of the State of Oregon*, 1866, 1868, 1870 (Title and imprint vary).

Pierce, Edward L. *Memoir and Letters of Charles Sumner*. 4 vols. Boston, 1893.

Pratt, Richard Henry. *Battlefield and Classroom: Four Decades with the American Indian, 1867–1904*. Ed. Robert M. Utley. New Haven, Conn., 1964.

Proceedings of the Colored Convention of the State of Kansas, Held at Leavenworth, October 13th, 14th, 15th, & 16th, 1863. Leavenworth, 1863 (Pamphlet, Beinecke Library).

Proceedings of the San Francisco Union Ratification Meeting held at Union Hall . . . June 25, 1867. N.p., n.d. (Pamphlet, Bancroft Library).

Protest by the Democratic Senators of the Legislature of California, on the Resolutions Condemning the President and Indorsing Congress. N.p., n.d. (Pamphlet, Huntington Library).

Radical Reconstruction on the Basis of One Sovereign Republic. . . . An Address

Delivered at an Interior Town in Nevada. . . . Sacramento, 1867 (Pamphlet, Bancroft Library).

Review of the Official Acts of Our Delegation in Congress [Kansas]. N.p., n.d. (Pamphlet, Beinecke Library).

Richardson, James D. (ed.). *A Compilation of the Messages and Papers of the Presidents, 1789–1897.* 10 vols. Washington, D.C., 1896–99.

Ross, Edmund G. "A Previous Era of Popular Madness and Its Lessons." *Forum,* XIX (July, 1895), 595–605.

————. "Historic Moments: The Impeachment Trial." *Scribner's Magazine,* XI (Apr., 1892),517–24.

————. *History of the Impeachment of Andrew Johnson, President of the United States, by the House of Representatives, and His Trial by the Senate for High Crimes and Misdemeanors in Office, 1868.* Santa Fe, N. Mex., 1896.

————. "Political Leaders of the Reconstruction Period." *Forum,* XX (Oct., 1895), 218–34.

Stewart, William M. *Reminiscences of Senator William M. Stewart of Nevada.* Ed. George Rothwell Brown. New York, 1908.

This Pamphlet is True!! It is a History of the Manner in which Nebraska became a State, Elected its State Officers and its First U.S. Senators, and Entered the American Union. Omaha, 1866 (Pamphlet, Beinecke Library).

The Tribune Almanac for the Years 1838 to 1868. 2 vols. New York, 1868.

Union League of America. *The Record. The Republican Party vs. the False Democracy!* N.p., n.d. (Pamphlet, Bancroft Library).

U.S. Bureau of the Census. *Eighth Census of the United States: 1860, Population.* Washington, D.C., 1864.

————. *Ninth Census of the United States: 1870, Population.* Washington, D.C., 1872.

U.S. Congress. *Congressional Globe,* 39, 40, 41 Congresses, 1865–71.

————, House of Representatives. "Raising of Money to be used in Impeachment," *Reports of Committees of the House of Representatives,* 40 Cong., 2 Sess., Report 75 (ser. 1358).

————, Senate. *Biographical Directory of the American Congress, 1774–1971.* Washington, D.C., 1971.

————, Senate. *Journal of the Executive Proceedings of the Senate.* Vols. XIV, XV, XVI (1865–69). Washington, D.C., 1887.

————, Senate. "Returning Bill to Admit Colorado into the Union." *Senate Executive Documents,* 39 Cong., 2 Sess., Doc. 7 (ser. 1277).

————, Senate. "President of the United States . . . Objections to the Admission of Colorado." *Senate Executive Documents,* 39 Cong., 1 Sess., Doc. 45 (ser. 1238).

————, Senate. "Federal Census—Territory of New Mexico and Territory of Arizona." *Senate Miscellaneous Documents,* 89 Cong., 1 Sess. (ser. 12668–1).

U.S. Department of Interior. *Register of Officers and Agents, Civil, Military and Naval in the Service of the United States, on the Thirtieth of September, 1865.* Washington, D.C., 1866.

———. *Register of Officers . . . on the Thirtieth of September, 1867.* Washington, D.C., 1868.

———. *Register of Officers . . . on the Thirtieth of September, 1869.* Washington, D.C., 1870.

Washington, Territory of. *Journal of the House of Representatives of the Territory of Washington, 1867–1868.* Olympia, 1868.

Welles, Gideon. *The Diary of Gideon Welles.* 3 vols. Boston, 1911.

Wilder, D. W. *The Annals of Kansas, 1541–1885.* Topeka, 1886.

Williams, George H. *Speech of George H. Williams, United States Senator from Oregon, at Platt's Hall, San Francisco, Tuesday Evening, August 27, 1868.* San Francisco, 1868 (Pamphlet, Bancroft Library).

Secondary Accounts

Albright, Robert Edwin. "The American Civil War as a Factor in Montana Territorial Politics." *Pacific Historical Review,* VI (Mar., 1937), 36–46.

———. "The Relations of Montana with the Federal Government, 1864–1889." Ph.D. dissertation, Stanford University, 1933.

Angel, Myron. *History of Nevada.* Oakland, Calif., 1881.

Athearn, Robert G. "The Civil War and Montana Gold." *Montana, the Magazine of Western History,* XII (Apr., 1962), 62–73.

———. "Civil War Days in Montana." *Pacific Historical Review,* XXIX (Feb., 1960), 19–33.

———. *Thomas Francis Meagher: An Irish Revolutionary in America.* Boulder, Colo., 1949.

Baisinger, Sara L. "Nebraska and Reconstruction." M.A. thesis, University of Nebraska, 1928.

Bancroft, Hubert Howe. *History of Arizona and New Mexico, 1530–1888.* Vol. XVII, *The Works of Hubert Howe Bancroft.* San Francisco, 1889.

———. *History of California, 1860–1890.* Vol. XXIV, *The Works of Hubert Howe Bancroft.* San Francisco, 1890.

———. *History of Nevada, Colorado, and Wyoming.* Vol. XXV, *The Works of Hubert Howe Bancroft.* San Francisco, 1890.

———. *History of Oregon, 1848–1888.* Vol. XXX, *The Works of Hubert Howe Bancroft.* San Francisco, 1888.

———. *History of Utah, 1540–1886.* Vol. XXVI, *The Works of Hubert Howe Bancroft.* San Francisco, 1889.

———. *History of Washington, Idaho, and Montana, 1845–1889.* Vol. XXXI, *The Works of Hubert Howe Bancroft.* San Francisco, 1890.

———. "The Life of Matthew Paul Deady." In *Chronicles of the Builders of the Commonwealth.* 2 vols. San Francisco, 1892.

Barsness, Larry. *Gold Camp: Alder Gulch and Virginia City, Montana.* New York, 1962.

Baumgardner, James Lewis. "Andrew Johnson and the Patronage." Ph.D. dissertation, University of Tennessee, 1968.

Beale, Howard K. *The Critical Year: A Study of Andrew Johnson and Reconstruction.* New York, 1958.

Beasley, Delilah L. *The Negro Trail Blazers of California.* Los Angeles, 1919.

Benedict, Michael Les. *A Compromise of Principle: Congressional Republicans and Reconstruction, 1863–1869.* New York, 1974.

———. *The Impeachment and Trial of Andrew Johnson.* New York, 1973.

———. "Preserving the Constitution: The Conservative Basis of Radical Reconstruction." *Journal of American History,* LXI (Mar., 1975), 65–90.

Berwanger, Eugene H. *The Frontier against Slavery: Western Anti-Negro Prejudice and the Slavery Extension Controversy.* Urbana, Ill., 1967.

———. "Reconstruction on the Frontier: The Equal Rights Struggle in Colorado, 1865–1867." *Pacific Historical Review,* XLIV (Aug., 1975), 313–29.

———. "Three against Johnson: Colorado Republican Editors React to Reconstruction." *Social Science Journal,* XIII (Jan., 1976), 149–58.

———. "William J. Hardin: Colorado Spokesman for Radical Justice, 1863–1873." *Colorado Magazine, Quarterly of the State Historical Society of Colorado,* LII (Winter, 1975), 52–65.

Billington, Ray Allen. *Westward Expansion: A History of the American Frontier.* New York, 1960.

Blackmar, Frank. *The Life of Charles Robinson, the First State Governor of Kansas.* Topeka, 1902.

Blegen, Theodore C. *Minnesota: A History of the State.* Minneapolis, 1963.

Bogue, Allan G. *From Prairie to Corn Belt: Farming on the Illinois and Iowa Prairies in the Nineteenth Century.* Chicago, 1963.

Bonadio, Felice A. *North of Reconstruction: Ohio Politics, 1865–1870.* New York, 1970.

Bowers, Claude G. *The Tragic Era: The Revolution after Lincoln.* Boston, 1929.

Brock, W. R. *An American Crisis: Congress and Reconstruction, 1865–1867.* New York, 1963.

Brodie, Fawn M. *Thaddeus Stevens: Scourge of the South.* New York, 1959.

Brown, Wallace. "George L. Miller and the Struggle over Nebraska Statehood." *Nebraska History,* XLI (Dec., 1960), 299–318.

Bruyn, Kathleen. *"Aunt" Clara Brown: Story of a Black Pioneer.* Boulder, Colo., 1970.

Buck, Paul H. *The Road to Reunion, 1865–1900.* New York, 1937.

Bumgardner, Edward. *The Life of Edmund G. Ross: The Man Whose Vote Saved a President.* Kansas City, Mo., 1949.

Burlingame, Merrill G., and K. Ross Toole. *A History of Montana.* New York, 1957.

Caldwell, Martha Belle. "The Attitude of Kansas toward Reconstruction, before 1875." Ph.D. dissertation, University of Kansas, 1933.

Carey, Charles H. *A General History of Oregon prior to 1861.* 2 vols. Portland, 1936.

Carmen, Harry J., and Reinhard Luthin. *Lincoln and the Patronage.* New York, 1943.

Carroll, John M. *Black Military Experience in the American West.* New York, 1971.

Castel, Albert. "Civil War Kansas and the Negro." *Journal of Negro History,* LI (Apr., 1966), 125–39.

———. *A Frontier State at War: Kansas, 1861–1865.* Ithaca, N.Y., 1958.

———. *The Presidency of Andrew Johnson.* Lawrence, Kans., 1979.

Castle, Henry A. "Reminiscences of Minnesota Politics." *Collections of the Minnesota Historical Society,* XV (1915), 553–98.

Caughey, John Walton. *California.* New York, 1940.

Clarke, Dan E. "The Movement to the Far West during the Decade of the Sixties." *Washington Historical Quarterly,* XVII (Apr., 1926), 105–13.

Cleland, Robert Glass. *A History of California: The American Period.* New York, 1923.

Clemenceau, Georges. *American Reconstruction, 1865–1870.* Ed. Fernand Baldensperger. New York, 1969.

Coben, Stanley. "Northeastern Business and Radical Reconstruction: A Re-examination." *Mississippi Valley Historical Review,* XLVI (June, 1959), 67–90.

Cochrane, William Ghormley. "Freedom without Equality: A Study of Northern Opinion and the Negro Issue, 1861–1870." Ph.D. dissertation, University of Minnesota, 1957.

Colebank, Kenneth. "Civil Rights Legislation, 1866–1875." Ph.D. dissertation, University of Kentucky, 1968.

Coleman, Charles H. *The Election of 1868.* New York, 1971.

Cox, LaWanda and John H. *Politics, Principle & Prejudice, 1865–1866: Dilemma of Reconstruction America.* New York, 1963.

Craven, Avery. *Reconstruction: The Ending of the Civil War.* New York, 1969.

Curry, Richard O. (ed.). *Radicalism, Racism, and Party Realignment: The Border States during Reconstruction.* Baltimore, 1969.

Curtis, George H. *The Governors and Secretaries of Idaho Territory together with Other Matters Relating to Early Idaho History.* N.p., n.d. (Pamphlet, Beinecke Library.)

Davison, Stanley R., and Dale Tash. "Confederate Backwash in Montana Territory." *Montana, the Magazine of Western History,* XVII (Oct.,1967), 50–58.

Delmatier, Royce, and others (eds.). *The Rumble of California Politics, 1848–1970.* New York, 1970.

Doig, Ivan. "John J. McGilvra: The Life and Times of an Urban Frontiersman, 1827–1903." Ph.D. dissertation, University of Washington, 1969.

Donald, David Herbert. *Liberty and Union.* Lexington, Mass., 1978.

———. *Charles Sumner and the Rights of Man.* New York, 1970.

———. *The Politics of Reconstruction, 1863–1867.* Baton Rouge, La., 1965.

Donaldson, Thomas. *Idaho of Yesterday.* Caldwell, 1941.

Dorris, Jonathan Truman. *Pardon and Amnesty under Lincoln and Johnson: The Restoration of the Confederates to Their Rights and Privileges, 1861–1898.* Chapel Hill, N.C., 1953.

Douglas, Jesse S. "Origins of the Population of Oregon in 1850." *Pacific Northwest Quarterly,* XLI (Apr., 1950), 95–108.

DuBois, Ellen Carol. *Feminism and Suffrage, 1848–1869.* Ithaca, N.Y., 1978.

DuBois, W. E. B. *Black Reconstruction in America, 1860–1880.* New York, 1935.

Dunning, William A. *Reconstruction, Political and Economic, 1865–1877.* New York, 1907.

Durham, Philip, and Everett L. Jones. *The Negro Cowboys.* New York, 1965.

Elliott, Russell R. *History of Nevada.* Lincoln, Nebr., 1973.

Ellis, Elmer. *Henry Moore Teller, Defender of the West.* Caldwell, Idaho, 1941.

Ellison, Joseph. *California and the Nation, 1850–1869: A Study of the Relations of a Frontier Community with the Federal Government.* Berkeley, 1927.

Farb, Robert C. "Robert W. Furnas of Nebraska." Ph.D. dissertation, University of Nebraska, 1949.

Farish, Thomas Edwin. *History of Arizona.* 5 vols. Phoenix, 1916.

Fishel, Leslie H., Jr. "Northern Prejudice and Negro Suffrage, 1865–1870." *Journal of Negro History,* XXXIX (Jan., 1954), 8–26.

Fite, Gilbert C. *The Farmers' Frontier, 1865–1900.* New York, 1966.

Folwell, William Watts. *A History of Minnesota.* 4 vols. St. Paul, 1969.

Foner, Eric. *Free Soil, Free Labor, Free Men: The Ideology of the Republican Party before the Civil War.* New York, 1970.

Gambone, Joseph G. "The Forgotten Feminist of Kansas: The Papers of

Clarina I. H. Nichols, 1854–1885 (Part IV, 1867–1868)." *Kansas Historical Quarterly*, XXXIX (Winter, 1973), 515–63.

Gates, Paul Wallace. *Fifty Million Acres: Conflicts over Kansas Land Policy, 1854–1890*. Ithaca, N.Y., 1954.

Gibson, Arrell Morgan. *The West in the Life of the Nation*. Lexington, Mass., 1976.

Gillette, William. *Retreat from Reconstruction: A Political History, 1867–1878*. Baton Rouge, La., 1979.

———. *The Right to Vote: Politics and the Passage of the Fifteenth Amendment*. Baltimore, 1969.

Gleason, Mercedes S. "The Territorial Governors of the State of Washington, 1853–1889." M.A. thesis, University of Washington, 1955.

Goff, John S. "The Arizona Career of Coles Bashford." *Journal of Arizona History*, X (Spring, 1969), 19–36.

Hafen, LeRoy R. *Colorado and Its People: A Narrative and Topical History of the Centennial State*. New York, 1948.

Hall, Frank. *History of the State of Colorado*. 4 vols. Chicago, 1889.

Hamilton, James McClellan. *From Wilderness to Statehood: A History of Montana, 1805–1900*. Portland, Ore., 1957.

Hammond, Carl. "California and the Civil War." Ph.D. dissertation, Indiana Unversity, 1950.

Hanchett, William. "Yankee Law and the Negro in Nevada, 1861–1869." *Western Humanities Review*, X (Summer, 1956), 241–49.

Haugland, John Clarence. "Alexander Ramsey and the Republican Party, 1866–1875: A Study in Personal Politics." Ph.D. dissertation, University of Minnesota, 1961.

Hertz, Emanuel. *The Hidden Lincoln*. New York, 1940.

Hinkston, Eugene R. "California's Assertion of States' Rights: A History of Jurisdictional Controversies with the Federal Government." Ph.D. dissertation, University of Southern California, 1960.

Hoogenboom, Ari. *Outlawing the Spoils: A History of the Civil Service Reform Movement, 1865–1883*. Urbana, Ill., 1961.

Hoover, Herbert Theodore. "History of the Republican Party in New Mexico, 1867–1952." Ph.D. dissertation, University of Oklahoma, 1966.

Horn, Calvin. *New Mexico's Troubled Years: The Story of the Early Territorial Governors*. Albuquerque, 1963.

Hunt, Rockwell D. *John Bidwell, Prince of California Pioneers*. Caldwell, Idaho, 1942.

Hyman, Harold. *A More Perfect Union: The Impact of the Civil War and Reconstruction on the Constitution*. New York, 1975.

Hynding, Alan A. "The Public Life of Eugene Semple: A Study of the Promoter-Politician on the Pacific Northwest Frontier." Ph.D. dissertation, University of Washington, 1966.

Jackson, W. Turrentine. "Montana Politics during the Meagher Regime." *Pacific Historical Review*, XII (June, 1943), 139–56.

———. "The Appointment and Removal of Sidney Edgerton, First Governor of Montana Territory." *Pacific Northwest Quarterly*, XXXIV (July, 1943), 293–304.

James, Joseph B. *The Framing of the Fourteenth Amendment*. Urbana, Ill., 1956.

Jellison, Charles A. "The Ross Impeachment Vote: A Need for Reappraisal." *Southwestern Social Science Quarterly*, XLI (Sept., 1960), 150–55.

Johannsen, Robert W. "The Oregon Legislature of 1868 and the Fourteenth Amendment." *Oregon Historical Quarterly*, LI (Mar., 1950), 3–12.

Johnson, Harrison. *Johnson's History of Nebraska*. Omaha, 1880.

Katz, William Loren. *The Black West*. Garden City, N.Y., 1971.

Keleher, Wiliam A. *Turmoil in New Mexico*. Santa Fe, 1952.

Kelley, George H. (comp.). *Legislative History of Arizona, 1864–1912*. Phoenix, 1926.

Kelsey, Harry E., Jr. *Frontier Capitalist: The Life of John Evans*. Denver, 1969.

Kennedy, John F. *Profiles in Courage*. New York, 1955.

Kingsbury, George W. *History of Dakota Territory*. 5 vols. Chicago, 1915.

Lamar, Howard R. "Carpetbaggers Full of Dreams: A Functional View of the Arizona Pioneer Politician." *Arizona and the West*, VII (Autumn, 1965), 187–206.

———. *Dakota Territory, 1861–1889: A Study in Frontier Politics*. New Haven, Conn., 1956.

———. *The Far Southwest, 1846–1912: A Territorial History*. New York, 1970.

———. "Statehood for Utah: A Different Path." *Utah Historical Quarterly*, XXXIX (Fall, 1971), 307–27.

Larson, Robert W. *New Mexico's Quest for Statehood, 1846–1912*. Albuquerque, 1968.

Larson, T. A. *History of Wyoming*. Lincoln, Nebr., 1965.

———. *Wyoming: A Bicentennial History*. New York, 1977.

Lewis, Albert Lucian. "Los Angeles in the Civil War Decades, 1850–1868." Ph.D. dissertation, University of Southern California, 1970.

Limbaugh, Ronald Hadley. "The Idaho Spoilsmen: Federal Administrators and Idaho Politics, 1863–1890." Ph.D. dissertation, University of Idaho, 1966.

Linden, Glenn M. *Politics or Principle: Congressional Voting on the Civil War Amendments and Pro-Negro Measures, 1838–69*. Seattle, 1976.

Linn, William Alexander. *The Story of the Mormons: From the Date of Their Origin to the Year 1901*. New York, 1902.

Lyon, Peter. "The Wild, Wild West." *American Heritage*, IX (Aug., 1960), 33–48.

McFarland, Carl. "Abraham Lincoln and Montana Territory." *Montana, the Magazine of Western History*, V (Oct., 1955), 42–56.

McGee, Lee Albert. "History of Colorado Territory." Ph.D. dissertation, University of Texas, 1932.

McKenna, Sister Jeanne. "With the Help of God and Lucy Stone." *Kansas Historical Quarterly*, XXXVI (Spring, 1970), 13–26.

McKitrick, Eric L. *Andrew Johnson and Reconstruction*. Chicago, 1960.

McLaughlin, Tom LeRoy. "Popular Reactions to the Idea of Negro Equality in Twelve Nonslaveholding States, 1846–1869: A Quantitative Analysis." Ph.D. dissertation, Washington State University, 1969.

McMahon, Adrian Michael. "The Concept of Freedom and the Radical Abolitionists, 1860–1870." Ph.D. dissertation, University of Texas at Austin, 1970.

Mack, Effie Mona. "James Warren Nye." *Nevada Historical Society Quarterly*, IV (July, 1961), 1–59.

Maginnis, Martin. "Thomas Francis Meagher." *Historical Society of Montana Contributions*, VI (1907), 102–24.

Malone, Thomas E. "The Democratic Party in California, 1865–1868." M.A. thesis, Stanford University, 1949.

Manning, Edwin C. "The Kansas State Senate of 1865 and 1866." *Transactions of the Kansas State Historical Society*, IX (1906), 359–75.

Mantell, Martin E. *Johnson, Grant, and the Politics of Reconstruction*. New York, 1973.

Marsh, Ronald Russel. "The Republican Party of Washington Territory: 1867–1872." M.A. thesis, University of Washington, 1966.

Mathews, John Marby. *Legislative and Judicial History of the Fifteenth Amendment*. Baltimore, 1909.

Melendy, H. Brett, and Benjamin F. Gilbert. *The Governors of California: Peter H. Burnett to Edmund G. Brown*. Georgetown, Calif., 1965.

Milton, George Fort. *The Age of Hate: Andrew Johnson and the Radicals*. New York, 1930.

Mohr, James C. *The Radical Republicans and Reform in New York during Reconstruction*. Ithaca, N.Y., 1973.

——— (ed.). *Radical Republicans in the North: State Politics during Reconstruction*. Baltimore, 1976.

Montgomery, David. *Beyond Equality: Labor and Radical Republicans, 1862–1872*. New York, 1967.

Moody, William Penn. "The Civil War and Reconstruction in California Politics." Ph.D. dissertation, University of California at Los Angeles, 1950.

Morton, J. Sterling, and Albert Watkins. *Illustrated History of Nebraska*. 3 vols. Lincoln, 1905–13.

Mothershead, Harmon. "Negro Rights in Colorado Territory, 1859–1867." *Colorado Magazine, Quarterly of the State Historical Society of Colorado*, XL (July, 1963), 212–23.

Murphy, Lawrence R. "Crusader in the West: The Life of W. F. M. Arny, 1813–1881." Ph.D. dissertation, Texas Christian University, 1968.

———. "Reconstruction in New Mexico." *New Mexico Historical Review*, XLIII (Apr., 1968), 99–115.

———. "William F. M. Arny, Secretary of New Mexico Territory." *Arizona and the West*, VIII (Winter, 1966), 323–38.

Nash, Howard P. *Andrew Johnson, Congress and Reconstruction*. Rutherford, N.J., 1972.

Nevins, Allan. *The War for the Union: The Improvised War, 1861–1862*. 2 vols. New York, 1959.

Newmark, Maurice H., and Marco R. Newmark (eds.). *Sixty Years in Southern California, 1853–1913*. Los Angeles, 1970.

Nichols, Roy Franklin. *The Disruption of American Democracy*. New York, 1948.

Norby, Charles H. "The West in the Civil War Decade." Ph.D. dissertation, University of Iowa, 1935.

Nugent, Walter T. K. *Money and American Society, 1865–1880*. New York, 1968.

Olson, James C. *J. Sterling Morton*. Lincoln, Nebr., 1942.

Parkhill, Forbes. *Mister Barney Ford: A Portrait in Bistre*. Denver, 1963.

Patrick, Rembert W. *The Reconstruction of the Nation*. New York, 1967.

Paul, Rodman Wilson. *Mining Frontiers of the Far West, 1848–1880*. New York, 1963.

Peterson, Merrill D. *The Jefferson Image in the American Mind*. New York, 1962.

Phillips, Catherine Coffin. *Cornelius Cole, California Pioneer and United States Senator: A Study of Personality and Achievements Bearing upon the Growth of a Commonwealth*. San Francisco, 1929.

Plummer, Mark A. *Frontier Governor: Samuel J. Crawford of Kansas*. Lawrence, 1971.

———. "Governor Crawford's Appointment of Edmund G. Ross to the United States Senate." *Kansas Historical Quarterly*, XXVIII (Summer, 1962), 145–53.

Poll, Richard. "The Political Reconstruction of Utah Territory, 1866–1890." *Pacific Historical Review*, XXVII (May, 1958), 111–26.

Pomeroy, Earl S. *The Territories and the United States, 1861–1890: Studies in Colonial Administration*. Seattle, 1969.

Porter, Kenneth Wiggins. *The Negro on the American Frontier.* New York, 1971.

Randall, James G., and David Donald. *The Civil War and Reconstruction.* 2d ed. Boston, 1961.

Rhodes, James Ford. *History of the United States, from the Compromise of 1850, to the Restoration of Home Rule, 1877.* 7 vols. New York, 1893–1906.

Riddleberger, Patrick W. *1866: The Critical Year Revisited.* Carbondale, Ill., 1979.

Ridge, Martin. *Ignatius Donnelly: The Portrait of a Politician.* Chicago, 1962.

Roske, Ralph J. *Everyman's Eden: A History of California.* New York, 1968.

———. "The Seven Martyrs?" *American Historical Review,* LXIV (Jan., 1959), 323–30.

Royce, C. C. *John Bidwell, Pioneer, Statesman, Philanthropist: A Biographical Sketch.* Chico, Calif., 1906.

Rusco, Elmer R. *"Good Time Coming?" Black Nevadans in the Nineteenth Century.* Westport, Conn., 1975.

Ryland, William James. "Alexander Ramsey: A Study of a Frontier Politician and the Transition of Minnesota from a Territory to a State." Ph.D. dissertation, Yale University, 1930.

Sandburg, Carl. *Abraham Lincoln: The War Years.* 4 vols. New York, 1939.

Sanders, Helen F. *A History of Montana.* 3 vols. Chicago, 1913.

Savage, W. Sherman. "The Negro on the Mining Frontier." *Journal of Negro History,* XXX (Jan., 1945), 30–46.

Scott, Harvey W. *History of the Oregon Country.* 6 vols. Cambridge, Mass., 1924.

Shannon, Fred Albert. *The Organization and Administration of the Union Army, 1861–1865.* 2 vols. Cleveland, 1928.

Sharkey, Robert P. *Money, Class, and Party: An Economic Study of Civil War and Reconstruction.* Baltimore, 1959.

Sheldon, Addison Erwin. *Nebraska: The Land and the People.* 3 vols. Chicago, 1931.

Shelly, Walter Lumley. "The Colorado Republican Party: The Formative Years, 1861–1876." M.A. thesis, University of Colorado, 1963.

Smiley, Jerome C. *History of Denver.* Denver, 1901.

Snowden, Clinton. *History of Washington: Rise and Progress of an American State.* New York, 1909.

Spangler, Earl. *The Negro in Minnesota.* Minneapolis, 1961.

Speer, John. *The Life of General James H. Lane.* Garden City, Kans., 1896.

Spence, Clark C. *Territorial Politics and Government in Montana, 1864–89.* Urbana, Ill., 1975.

Stampp, Kenneth M. *The Era of Reconstruction, 1865–1877.* New York, 1965.

Stanley, Gerald. "The Republican Party in California, 1856–1868." Ph.D. dissertation, University of Arizona, 1973.

Stephenson, Wendell Holmes. *The Political Career of General James H. Lane.* Vol. III, *Publications of the Kansas State Historical Society.* Topeka, 1930.

Stryker, Lloyd Paul. *Andrew Johnson: Profile in Courage.* New York, 1929.

Thane, James L., Jr. "An Active Acting-Governor: Thomas Francis Meagher's Administration in Montana Territory." *Journal of the West,* IX (Oct., 1970), 537–51.

———. "Confederate Myth in Montana." *Montana, the Magazine of Western History,* XVII (Apr., 1967), 14–19.

Trefousse, Hans L. *Impeachment of a President: Andrew Johnson, the Blacks, and Reconstruction.* Knoxville, Tenn., 1975.

Unger, Irwin. *The Greenback Era: A Social and Political History of American Finance, 1865–1879.* Princeton, N.J., 1964.

Voegeli, V. Jacque. *Free but Not Equal: The Midwest and the Negro during the Civil War.* Chicago, 1967.

Wagoner, Jay J. *Arizona Territory, 1863–1912: A Political History.* Tucson, 1970.

Watkins, Albert. "How Nebraska Was Brought into the Union." *Publications of the Nebraska State Historical Society,* XVIII (1917), 375–434.

Webster, John Lee. "Controversy in the Senate over the Admission of Nebraska." *Publications of the Nebraska State Historical Society,* XVIII (1917), 345–74.

Wells, Merle W. "Clinton DeWitt Smith, Secretary, Idaho Territory, 1864–1865." *Oregon Historical Quarterly,* LII (Mar., 1951), 38–53.

———. "David W. Ballard, Governor of Idaho, 1866–1870." *Oregon Historical Quarterly,* LIV (Mar., 1953), 3–26.

Wharton, J. E. *History of the City of Denver from Its Earliest Settlement to the Present* [1866]. Denver, 1866.

White, Leonard D. *The Republican Era: A Study in Administration History, 1869–1901.* New York, 1958.

Wilson, Don W. *Governor Charles Robinson of Kansas.* Lawrence, 1975.

Wood, Forrest G. *Black Scare: The Racist Response to Emancipation.* Berkeley, Calif., 1968.

Woodward, Walter C. *The Rise and Early History of Political Parties in Oregon, 1843–1868.* Portland, 1913.

Wyllys, Rufus Kay. *Arizona: The History of a Frontier State.* Phoenix, 1950.

Zornow, William Frank. " 'Bluff Ben' Wade in Lawrence, Kansas: The Issue of Class Conflict." *Ohio Historical Quarterly,* LXV (Jan., 1956), 44–52.

———. *Kansas: A History of the Jayhawk State.* Norman, Okla., 1957.

Index

A NOTE ON THE AUTHOR

EUGENE H. BERWANGER is professor of history at Colorado State University. He is the author of two previous books, *The Frontier Against Slavery: Western Anti-Negro Prejudice and the Slavery Extension Controversy* and *As They Saw Slavery*, and has published numerous articles in journals such as *Civil War History* and *Pacific Historical Review*.